DESPERADO

Popular Music History
Series Editor: Alyn Shipton, Royal Academy of Music, London.

This series publishes books that extend the field of popular music studies, examine the lives and careers of key musicians, interrogate histories of genres, focus on previously neglected forms, or engage in the formative history of popular music styles.

Published

Desperado
An Autobiography

Tomasz Stańko
with Rafał Księżyk

Translated by Halina Maria Boniszewska

eǫuinox

SHEFFIELD UK   BRISTOL CT

Published by Equinox Publishing Ltd.

UK: Office 415, The Workstation, 15 Paternoster Row, Sheffield, South Yorkshire S1 2BX
USA: ISD, 70 Enterprise Drive, Bristol, CT 06010
www.equinoxpub.com

First published in Polish in 2010 as *Desperado: Autobiografia*, Tomasz Stańko with
Rafał Księżyk, by Wydawnictwo Literackie, Kraków. This first English edition published
by Equinox Publishing Ltd 2022.

BOOK INSTITUTE

©POLAND

ADAM
MICKIEWICZ
INSTITUTE

This publication has been supported by the ©POLAND Translation
Program.

This publication has been produced with the financial support of the Polish Ministry of Culture and National Heritage.

British Library Cataloguing-in-Publication Data
A catalogue record for this book is available from the British Library.
ISBN-13   978 1 80050 222 2 (hardback)
              978 1 80050 223 9 (ePDF)
              978 1 80050 244 4 (ePub)

Library of Congress Cataloging-in-Publication Data
Names: Stańko, Tomasz, 1942-2018, interviewee. | Księżyk, Rafał, 1970-
    interviewer. | Boniszewska, Halina Maria, translator.
Title: Desperado : an autobiography / Tomasz Stańko, with Rafał Księżyk
    ; translated by Halina Maria Boniszewska.
Other titles: Desperado. English
Description: First English edition. | Sheffield, South Yorkshire ; Bristol,
    CT : Equinox Publishing Ltd, 2022. | Series: Popular music history |
    First published in Polish in 2010 as Desperado : Autobiografia. |
    Summary: "Tomasz Stańko is arguably the greatest jazz musician Poland
    has ever produced. His career spanned almost 60 years until his death in
    2018. This book is a no-holds-barred extended interview with broadcaster
    Rafał Księżyk originally published in Polish by Wydawnictwo
    Literackie"-- Provided by publisher.
Identifiers: LCCN 2022005857 (print) | LCCN 2022005858 (ebook) | ISBN
    9781800502222 (hardback) | ISBN 9781800502239 (pdf) | ISBN 9781800502444
    (epub)
Subjects: LCSH: Stańko, Tomasz, 1942-2018. | Stańko, Tomasz,
    1942-2018--Interviews. | Trumpet players--Poland--Biography. | Jazz
    musicians--Poland--Biography. | Jazz--Poland--History and criticism.
Classification: LCC ML419.S73 A3 2022 (print) | LCC ML419.S73 (ebook) |
    DDC 781.65092 [B]--dc23
LC record available at https://lccn.loc.gov/2022005857
LC ebook record available at https://lccn.loc.gov/2022005858

Typeset by Witchwood Production House Ltd

Contents

List of Illustrations

Series Editor's Preface

Tomasz Stańko (1942–2018) was one of the major jazz trumpeters in the second half of the twentieth century, through into the first two decades of the twenty-first. This autobiography is not a conventional 'as told to' book, but a dynamic and evolving series of conversations with the journalist and music critic Rafał Księżyk between July 2008 and May 2009. Consequently, although it takes a roughly chronological route through Stańko's life and career, it strays into many of the highways and byways of a real conversation. From it, we learn more about Stańko's life and conditions and the background to his career than we might from a more conventional text.

I was privileged to work with Tomasz for BBC radio, including presenting a concert by his *Litania* sextet and co-producing his final 2017 London concert for broadcast, with his quartet including the pianist David Virelles. As a broadcaster and journalist, I interviewed him on various occasions, and I can verify that this book faithfully captures the nuances of his conversational style, but it also digs deep into the thoughts and experiences of a major figure not just of European jazz but of jazz, period.

Originally published in 2010, where the chronology of the Polish edition finished, this text does not cover the last eight years of Stańko's life, but it already places him in New York where much of the musical stimulation and music-making community of the final phase of his career had already been established. Reviewing many of his British concerts over the years for *The Times*, particularly with the trio led by pianist Marcin Wasilewski, I gave him the coveted 'five star' award more than once. I wrote, of his 2006 Bath Festival concert, that 'it ran through the whole range of human emotion, from joyous exultation to calm contemplation and from boiling anger to rueful regret'. Few artists in jazz have ever had such a powerful and convincing musical and emotional range, and it has been a privilege to hear him on top form so many times.

It is equally a privilege to be able to publish this memoir, and I am grateful both to his original publisher Wydawnictwo Literackie for making this possible, to his daughter, manager and guardian of his legacy, Anna Stańko, for all her help, and to the Book Institute Poland Translation Program and the Adam Mickiewicz Institute for their support. Finally, my gratitude goes to the book's translator Halina Maria Boniszewska for the sensitive rendering of his distinctive voice into English and to Dean Bargh for editing and typesetting this English edition, which catches the original accurately and faithfully.

Alyn Shipton
Royal Academy of Music, London
Series Editor, *Popular Music History*, for Equinox

1 Born Twice

When did you first hear a trumpet?
It's hard to say. I remember the first time I played one. That was at the end of the 1950s, when I was in the scouts. As the only boy in my scout troop who'd had any contact with music, I was picked to play the bugle. That was my first contact with the instrument. I'd been learning piano and violin at music school. But I was already listening to jazz on Willis Conover's American radio programmes. And when, on finishing school, I decided to go back to music, I knew it would be trumpet. Because of jazz.

What attracted you to jazz?
Many things. I realize now that I have a penchant for the unstable, the anarchic. If I'd been born later, I'd have been a rock musician or a hip-hop artist. This is all non-conformist music. Jazz was in opposition to school, to the stability and the bourgeois mentality that the family home had given me. I instinctively felt that jazz would be the best thing to help me in overcoming my weaknesses and changing my personality.

Let's start at the very beginning: in other words, with your family home. I've noticed that you use the term 'home town' in relation to two different places: Rzeszów and Kraków.
I don't remember much about Rzeszów. I left there at the age of six or seven. You have a fondness for your birthplace, a kind of geographical fondness. And that's why I've always said that I feel like I'm a Rzeszowian. I once visited the village where my mother was born. It used to be near Rzeszów; it's now part of Rzeszów. I got in a taxi after a concert and drove out there. I even had the impression that I recognized some of it. But anything to do with Rzeszów has more of a symbolic meaning to me.

Basically, I'm from Kraków. That's where I spent my entire youth. I remember being in a street gang. I think we were probably all members of that kind of gang . . . Well, anyway, I belonged to one – to the Sienkiewicza Street gang.

Tomasz Stańko, aged three.
Courtesy Anna Stańko

It's hardly surprising that you don't remember Rzeszów, because the Rzeszów where you were born ceased to exist when war broke out. Galicia. The melting pot of the Borderlands.

Quite. My grandfather was a sergeant in the Austrian army.

Your grandfather on your father's side?

Yes. My other grandfather was a farmer. My mother's family were country people. My father's family were very small-town bourgeoisie. But my father was talented. I don't know where he got it from. He'd always wanted to go to the conservatoire, but nerves got in the way. Professional musicians are predatory beasts, strong people. But my father had stage fright; maybe he was too sensitive. He took the entrance exam to the conservatoire, but he suddenly fell apart. So he went to law school.

Was that in Lwów or in Kraków?

Kraków. My father completed his law studies there before the war. He returned to Rzeszów during the war. He was initially an associate judge. Then, after the war, he took his judicial exam and became a judge. My mother was a teacher.

Did all your family come from Rzeszów?
My mother came from just outside Rzeszów, from Zwięczyca. My father was from Rzeszów itself. But their parents came from somewhere in Przeworsk, somewhere in Przemyśl. From the East. My grandmother on my father's side was of Ukrainian origin. And there were some Jewish roots somewhere. There was some convert in the family. I'm very much a mongrel, of mixed origin, as people are in those regions.

Have you taken any interest in tracing your roots?
Not particularly. I know about my Ukrainian and Jewish roots, mixed in with Polish roots. But I haven't traced my ancestry, as people do these days. But I'd be happy to have my DNA tested, so I could find out where my genes come from. They answer the question: where do I come from? Maybe I'm a descendant of Genghis Khan? Apparently, a large proportion of the Asian population is descended from Genghis Khan.

Have you ever had your horoscope done?
I don't like horoscopes. I don't even know what time I was born. And I'll never know now, because I don't have anyone I can ask.

Was your family much affected by the war?
Actually no. Of course, there were all kinds of situations. Apparently, an SS man patted me on the head. After some partisan action, some Germans burst into our house, but the piano diffused the situation. One of them played something. It seems that many of the SS men liked music, as you see in the films. Anyway, he played our piano, patted me on the head, and off they went. It was a stressful experience.

Are your parents still alive?
They're no longer alive. My mother died in the 1990s. My father died back in the 1970s.

What was their relationship like?
Like anybody, they argued a bit. My father wasn't an easy man. My mother was quite energetic, quite principled. She'd have her say. But their relationship was a respectful one, a traditional one.

Would you say that your mother was the head of the household?
Yes, I'd say that. On practical matters, it was my mother who made the decisions and pushed my father into getting things done. She cared about our prospects, about improving our situation.

Do you know why your parents moved from Rzeszów to Kraków?
Yes. My mother was pushy. She had this inner strength that kept her moving forward all the time; she wanted to expand her territory. I think she found

At the age of four.
Courtesy Anna Stańko

Rzeszów suffocating; she didn't want to wither away there. My father was rather inert, but she was the driving force. She had ambition. She ran the home and saw to it that my sister and I went to music school. She was also involved in music. She worked in the library at the music school that my sister and I attended. It was one of the first schools to have a primary school attached to a music school. I went there from my second year because it simply didn't exist before then. My mother went to teacher training college before the war. Then she didn't work for a while. Evidently, we must have needed the money, because she took an exam so she could get back into the profession, but she didn't want to teach; she preferred working in the library.

How do you recall your childhood?
I had a reflective childhood – all kinds of strange states of mind.

What do you mean by 'states of mind'?
I was peculiar. I was quite solitary.

You were a sensitive, somewhat introverted child?
That's right. That kind of thing. Yet, on the other hand, I was in a street gang. I didn't get into fights, like other boys did. To be honest, I've never been in

a fight in my whole life. I had to prove myself to the gang, and the first thing that came into my head was to throw a brick at a car. After that, I was the gang leader's buddy. That got me sorted somehow. I didn't have to do anything after that: I was under his protection.

Did you smash the windscreen?
Oh I smashed the windscreen all right . . . If the guy who chased after me had caught me, I think he'd have killed me. Cars were a luxury in those days.

Was that when you were at primary school?
In the first couple of years of primary school. I'd have been seven or eight years old.

What became of the gang?
It's a bit of a blur after that. I moved to a different street. And I didn't have any friends there. That was quite a dark period of my life, a depressive one. I was lost and all over the place. I was going to music school, yet unsure whether I wanted to carry on with music. My shyness made it difficult for me to socialize. It was like that for quite a few years – seven or eight – until I began playing jazz. Drugs helped me relate to people. I think that's very common.

That's why drugs are popular.
Of course. I think that's basically it. Drugs are nothing other than medication. For all kinds of things. They can stabilize hyperactivity or shyness. They stimulate the system.

Before jazz came along, was there anything that you were particularly involved in?
The scouts. I was a committed scout, one hundred per cent. My father signed me up. My first trip abroad was with my scout group. And it was through the scouts that I first came into contact with the trumpet. That's why I took trumpet lessons with Professor Lutak, who later taught me at the academy. He was a friend of my father.

What about the trip abroad?
During high school, we went to Yugoslavia, to a scout jamboree. I remember being disgusted at my older scout mates smoking cigarettes, thinking it was such an unscoutlike thing to do. I was like a puritan at that time. I was really into the scouts for a while.

You were also an altar boy.
Yes, I was. During that rather dark time. In the last years of primary school, before I'd got into music. I was very religious at that time. I remember breaking down on a pilgrimage to Częstochowa when all around me I saw sin. You know, the bottle. People are not saints. It put me off being an altar boy as well. I

thought it was going to be all holy, but what the altar boys mainly did in church was guzzle the communion wine and smoke cigarettes. So I gave up on that.

My life comes from idealism, but that was when I moved away from that, because ideals don't exist. But I was always inclined towards mysticism.

Did religion have an important role to play in your home?
Not particularly. My father was quite religious. My mother – she was a typical Polish Catholic. They did pray. But the idea of becoming an altar boy – that came from me.

Were you not drawn towards religion later on?
No. Quite naturally, I became interested in philosophy, and that helped form my world-view. I think I'm a person with pious tendencies. My mystical tendencies have found expression in evolutionism. I believe in evolution. What to some might seem like the harsh laws of nature isn't like that to me at all. I think it's rich and magnificent. Over the course of millions of years, life has been developing from one single atom, expanding, becoming more complex. Thought is a life form; the sound that I make on my trumpet: products of a living, carbon brain.

Do you have any stories, any anecdotes from your childhood that have stayed in the family?
I don't recall any, apart from that one about the SS man. We didn't talk that much at home.

What about members of your family? Any stories about them that might have lodged themselves in a child's brain?
There aren't any. We lived quite apart from one another. The whole family went in for this separate living. Maybe that's where my penchant for Witkacy's* philosophy of monism comes from. I like to describe myself as an IB: an Individual Being.

Did you not have much contact with your extended family?
For a few years, before I started school, I'd go on holiday to both my grandmothers. I still have some scraps of memories from that time. I remember my grandma's garden on my father's side. Maybe that's where my fondness for Rzeszów comes from. They had a beautiful garden, right in the middle of town. It's not there any more.

I went to Zwięczyca a few times. I remember one occasion: I was standing with a group of boys and feeling a kind of revulsion because they were throwing stones at tadpoles. When they hit the target, the tadpoles splattered.

---

* *Translator's note:* Witkacy (Stanisław Ignacy Witkiewicz) (1885–1939) was a Polish painter, photographer, playwright, novelist and philosopher who had a profound influence on post-World War II Polish culture. He is regarded as one of the leaders of the European modernist movement.

First Communion, with sister, Jadwiga.
Courtesy Anna Stańko

I stood at the back, behind them, and felt disgusted. Maybe that made me pull back from boys' games.

I remember different trips and holiday camps. I was always a bit on the sidelines, although I didn't have a problem relating to people; I just preferred being on the sidelines. I'd look at the situation as a whole. When necessary, I always managed to sort out whatever I needed to with my peers. That gang leader was my best friend, after all. He was really rough; I think he even ended up in prison. I remember his father: he was a tailor and used to make *ściborki*, these kind of Polish jeans.

You said that in your family you all lived isolated from one another.
We all lived separately. My father liked peace and quiet. My mother spent a lot of time at home. We each had our own room. We had three rooms and a beautiful, big kitchen. My mother either slept in the kitchen or with my father: it varied; but my sister and I had our own rooms.

Were there no emotional scenes?
No. My father didn't go in for that sort of thing. He didn't drink or smoke. He'd occasionally have a drink to be sociable. He hated name days. When we had vodka in the house, my friends and I used to suck out some of the vodka with a syringe and replace it with water. At one point during a name day celebration, my father took a sip of this diluted vodka. Our guests didn't say anything, but my mother did: 'But this is just water . . . Tomek!' We were a quiet, undemonstrative bourgeois family. Except that my father did love music, knew a lot about it and was very tolerant. When I began playing jazz, he never got in the way; on the contrary: he was supportive. He was completely immersed in music, and, being an unfulfilled musician, he felt ill all the time.

Was your father similarly inclined to introversion/depression, like you?
He was a similar kind of person, most definitely.

At that time, the working conditions for judges were not great in terms of the political climate. Your father did, after all, start working as a civil servant during the Stalinist era.
He definitely had to do some dodging. But it wasn't so bad. I remember later asking him whether he hadn't found it a strain. He said that he had, but he did add that they'd found a neat solution to the problem of pressure on judges. The President of the Court simply allocated the cases as he saw fit, and there was always a full spectrum of judges: some were more career-minded, others not so much. My father dealt with the criminal cases.

Was he a communist?
No. He was a socialist and he was automatically required to join the PZPR (Polish United Workers' Party). He'd joined the PPS (Polish Socialist Party) before the war, progressive student that he was. My father was not a communist,

but neither was he a person who made his views known. My uncle spent three years in prison for making a joke about Stalin. Ours was a run-of-the-mill household; like most ordinary people in those days, they kept their heads down.

Was there a lot of music at home?
Yes, there was. Definitely. My father always had his violin at hand, in plain sight.

Did he have any favourite style of music, any favourite composers?
No. He played the violin, and he simply knew an awful lot about music.

Did he listen to music on records?
We didn't have any records then. We did have a radio. I didn't buy my first tape recorder until after my first trip with Komeda.

You didn't buy a record player?
No. There weren't many records. A tape recorder was more use; we'd record a lot onto tape and had large collections.

Did your father play the piano as well?
My sister practised the piano. A great deal. Because of my sister's practising, I have extensive knowledge of the piano repertoire – not the names of the pieces or the composers, but a memory from long ago of motifs, like Chopin nocturnes.

Did you learn to play piano when you were at primary school?
I started with that. A classical education. Then my father persuaded me to take up the violin. I took my diploma in violin at primary school, but I wasn't particularly keen on it.

Right from the beginning, my sister and I were oriented towards music. After all, my father loved music and played all the time. Even while he was working as a judge, he had professional engagements. He played at the opera, with Kord conducting. Kord thought highly of him: my father had a very good reputation among the Kraków musicians.

Did he go to orchestral rehearsals?
He had two full-time posts. He went from the court to the opera. And my sister, Jadwiga, three years my junior, was a prodigy. While still at primary school, she took lessons with Professor Zbigniew Drzewiecki at the Warsaw Academy of Music. She graduated from the Academy and took master classes. She performed with Maksymiuk in Białystok when she took her diploma: he conducted, she played. She was highly regarded as a pianist, but she didn't want to perform on stage. Her nerves were the stumbling block.

She took after your father with her anxiety?

Yes, she took after my father. She opted for a normal life. She got married in Sweden. She taught music in a school. What a tragedy. She's unfulfilled and she's not well. We're not made to live like this. We need to find our thing in life.

I did find my thing. Although not straight away. It was only at high school when, along with Jacek Ostaszewski, I got interested in art that I began to flourish. Because, before that, I had no point of reference. I didn't particularly like anything. I didn't play like other boys did; I didn't use physical force. I'm slight; maybe that's why I wasn't drawn to sport. I naturally, instinctively, felt that I wouldn't achieve anything in that area. My shyness didn't help, and I didn't do well at school. On the other hand, when I began playing jazz, that's when my life began, like a new birth. I'd found my inner passion, the thing I had a natural capacity for.

2 First Cigarette, First Bottle

When you first started playing, did the family anxiety trait affect you?
Jazz made it easier for me to overcome that. Jazz. My first bottle. Because it was my first time playing at a party. Wacek, a friend from primary school, was playing with his friends, and he asked me to come along. I remember, yes . . . My first cigarette; I smoked nearly a whole packet of 'Sport' then. It was the first time I'd drunk wine. I drank a bottle of wine. And we played jazz. There was a chap with them. I can't remember his name. I know his nickname was 'Snake'. He was playing the trumpet. I picked up his trumpet. My lips were already well practised on the trumpet, and I managed to cough up a few sounds at that party. That would have been October-, November-time. I'd been play-ing trumpet at home for about six months, after my father had got hold of a trumpet for me. To get into intermediate music school, I had to play studies. So I played them on the trumpet. That would have been in Year 10, at high school – 1958. I was seventeen years old.

Things moved quickly, because, soon after, it was the Brubeck concert. I heard him live in Kraków, at the Rotunda. It was a big deal. I was listening to a lot of jazz at that time – Willis Conover's broadcasts on *Voice of America*. I listened to Chet Baker, Miles, of course, and the Modern Jazz Quartet. It was the era of cool jazz. I even remember my breakthrough moment. I was standing there, not knowing what to do, suffering from terrible stage fright and struggling to get out on stage and jam. That would have been around 1960, 1961. But something in me broke through; I pushed myself and went out on stage, and played. To get into music, I began playing at jam sessions.

Who was this Wacek?
Wacek Kisielewski. That immediately brings to mind this very interesting pair at primary school: Wacek and Kowal. Roman Kowal, a future professor at the music academy, and a journalist.

Is that the same Kowal who wrote a book on the history of Polish jazz?
The very same. As for Wacek Kisielewski, he later moved to Warsaw, studied there, and played in the duo Marek & Wacek. Kowal and Kisielewski went to a specialist music high school. But I gave up music. I didn't want to play classical music, neither on violin nor on piano. But then the scouts' bugle appeared in

In Kraków, early 1960s.
Courtesy Anna Stańko

my life. I had a brief stint playing some quasi-jazz on it at a May Day parade, on a float with a schoolfriend who was playing the drums. Even back then, I was inclined to dress eccentrically. I remember my mother customizing various second-hand jeans and jumpers for me. I persuaded my father to buy me a proper trumpet. I went back to music school to study the instrument. An uncle on my mother's side brought me a trumpet back from London, a second-hand one, with a certificate of origin. It had belonged to Humphrey Lyttelton, an English trad trumpeter. I still have it.

Getting yourself into intermediate music school, was that a serious statement you were making?
That was when I began to consider music as a future profession. I was two or three years behind Kowal and Kisielewski, but I soon caught up, and then I went on to music college. I suddenly changed when I started playing jazz. I had to re-sit Year 10 at high school, and I changed schools: I left Kochanowski and moved to Sobieski. And then there was music school. Not only was I attending two schools, I was also beginning to do well at school. I think I'd loosened up mentally.

In your archives I found a certificate from your time at Kochanowski High School, which states that you failed to go up to Year 11.
Were all the grades unsatisfactory?

It wasn't as bad as that. Your unsatisfactory grades were mainly in the humanities. But what was surprising was: 'exemplary behaviour'. That really is quite unusual for a student who hasn't made the grade.
Well, yes. I was a quiet chap; I just didn't do any studying. It was only once I'd changed high schools and, at the same time, got into intermediate music school . . . I met Kisielewski in the November, and there was that party where I started playing jazz. And I was attending two schools at the same time. That made it harder and I began living on the edge. I remember drinking a lot and leaving my school books behind at the Dworek restaurant. I very quickly began having a nightlife. Kisielewski and Kowal and I used to go to the Piwnica pod Baranami (a jazz cellar). My father dragged me out of there before my 'matura' leaving exam. They weren't letting any more people into the place; there were whole crowds of people standing outside. My father pushed his way through to the doorman – the one who wouldn't even let government ministers in: 'I've come for my son!' He went in and dragged me out. He could be a strong man.

That was a time when tastes were formed and new friendships forged. Besides Kowal and Kisielewski, Jacek Ostaszewski also popped up then.
That's when I got into art, philosophy. Kafka, existentialism. Jacek and I used to attend Professor Hodys's famous lectures on the history of art. He was a colourful character who used to visit van Gogh's grave. He gave lectures to the students at the Academy of Fine Arts, and we used to go and listen to them.

Jacek and I also used to go to poetry recital competitions. I got into art at high school. And, at the same time, I began to get all rebellious and anarchic. I didn't want to study. I didn't want to be sitting in school, slogging away. I preferred hanging out with my friends, even before drugs were really part of my life. I got into that quite late. It wasn't until that party where I met Kisielewski and Kowal that I started drinking wine.

What inspired you most at that time?
Dark things. Kafka. Kafka. Kafka. Existentialism. I've always been a dark person. Difference, alienation: that's what attracted me. I remember back then seeing a man on a train, crying. I thought: 'Shii . . . it. How can he cry like that?' And I felt a kind of revulsion, just as I had with the tadpoles, and the urge to move away, and contempt for the guy. Or, rather, not so much for him as for the fact that he was reacting to life in this way.

This 'outsidership', then, wasn't typical teenage maudlin alienation? Did you draw strength from this difference?
Strength from difference. Yes. I like being different. Which doesn't preclude the feeling that I'm a member of a herd; after all, a herd thins out, and someone gets left behind. There's nothing beyond him.

Your interest in the arts clearly inspired artistic endeavours of your own. When we looked through your private archive, you hurriedly covered up an old exercise book. Might that have been a novel?
I was a terrible scribbler. I used to write when I was in about Year 8 at high school, influenced by Kafka. Total rubbish. I realized that after a year. I also painted for a short while. Then I declared that I was more interested in art history.

Was the cultural climate of 1950s Kraków also dark?
That's how the world was then. The young people who were creating culture were the war generation. Although Teddy boys also made an appearance with their bright-coloured socks. I remember at night-time curling my hair around a pencil and tying something around my head. I used to perform all sorts of complicated operations to get that Teddy boy curl, that wave. I put a lot of effort into that. The Teddy boys had their own style, just as the hippies and hip-hoppers had later on.

A defiant element.
Jazz. Jazz. The Teddy boys and jazz: that was an obvious combination. Leopold Tyrmand wrote about it.

During the Stalinist period, jazz was branded a product of the rotten West, an enemy of the spirit of Socialism, and was officially banned until the political thaw in 1956. Did that have any influence on you?

I don't remember that period very well. But the fact that jazz was forbidden fruit was significant. I did, after all, listen to jazz on *Voice of America. This is Jazz Hour* and Conover's voice, introducing the music. I remember sitting by the radio at night. Quietly, because my parents would already be asleep, I'd turn the radio on in the kitchen and sit there with my ear against the speaker. And then: Jazz Messengers, Chet Baker, Jimmy Giuffre. Modern jazz from the word go. Conover was a true jazz fan. He'd play everything. We often heard new things. He was very quick to play Ornette Coleman, so quick that we knew about him immediately. Ostaszewski and I used to ask a friend who had family in the States to get hold of records for us. We had Coleman's 1958 recordings in 1962, maybe even 1961. And we also heard about this music from an American with Polish roots who'd come to Kraków. There was also Jacek Borowiec, a music fan from Jan Byrczek's time and the first jazz clubs. Jacek and I used to go over to his place and he'd play us all his records. He had tons of records. I occasionally bought tapes, as I recall, from off the radio. We had masses of music on tape: Ornette, Miles, Trane.

Did you ever try to transcribe by ear any of the music that Conover played?

Yes, I used to write down the music, but that was a commonplace thing. I still have some of the Coltrane music that I jotted down somewhere. The very act of writing it down is getting to know it. When you hear fragments played, and you're wondering where it's all going, you begin to understand the improvisor's logic.

It's difficult to capture improvised jazz in notation.

Of course. You pin it down. But, in doing so, you might well decide that, during improvisation, certain things occur unintentionally, that a musician wanted to play one thing, but it didn't come out right, and he suddenly started using his mistake, going with the sound. That's why the sound is so interesting in jazz. The sound springs from mistakes.

The jazz scene in Kraków was dominated at that time by the fathers of modern Polish jazz: Krzysztof Komeda, Andrzej Trzaskowski, Andrzej Kurylewicz.

Komeda, Trzaskowski. 'Gucio' Dyląg had already gone to Warsaw. Kurylewicz was still living in Kraków. My era was Stanisław 'Drążek' Kalwiński, Wojciech Karolak, Andrzej Dąbrowski. Musicians from Kraków. There was this trumpeter called Stanczew, a Bulgarian, who studied in Kraków and got married there. I think he went back later.

You once referred to Karolak as an 'arbiter of elegance'.

I remember once as a young lad walking behind Karolak in Kraków and having a good look at how really well dressed he was. I liked the elegance of the jazz musicians. I later bought suits off him. Regularly! We also used to go looking for clothes in the flea markets and bazaars, where you could find old stuff alongside clothes that people had had sent over to them in parcels from the States. The whole of Polish film and theatre used to hang out there: artistes who saw themselves as the social elite.

There was a big trad-jazz-inspired music scene in Kraków at that time.
In my opinion, these were mainly the klezmorim – session musicians, in the best sense of the term. We were practically the same age, but we belonged to different artistic generations. We did actually like one another, but they were traditionalists and we were modernists. Jazz freshened up when Byrczek revamped the jazz club. The Piwnica lot started going there. Wiesław Dymny hung out there all the time; in fact, he did some artwork on the walls.

That was Helikon at 15 St Mark's Street. Was it the first important club that you went to?
Yes, that was my first main club. The first time I went, I was with Kisielewski and we heard Komeda playing the piano. That was his last day in Kraków, just before he left for Warsaw. Jan Byrczek was back from France, where he'd been with Komeda; he didn't want to play double bass: he had some problem with his hand. He'd found the place and converted it. I hung out there all the time. Boy, did we hang out there! There was the Dworek restaurant nearby, and, on the other side of the market square, the Piwnica pod Baranami.

Everywhere was walking distance, it being Kraków?
I walked everywhere. To my friends', to music college, to the club. I lived on Pawlikowskiego Street. From Grabowskiego Street I could get to Karmelicka Street. And on the way, a few metres further along, lived Kisielewski, near the Dom Literatów (in other words, the Writers' House). Kowal lived on a different side of town, but also nearby.

Was it the music or the social group that attracted you to Helikon?
The social group . . . well, the 'feeling'. People who hung out there were edgy. The Piwnica lot were artists: bohemians.

How did Helikon compare at that time with Piwnica pod Baranami?
Piwnica was a cabaret place. Helikon was a music club. A jazz club, though not that much playing went on there. It was a very small place. You could get about twenty people in there, and right in the middle of it there was this huge post, a pillar, which broke up the sound and made it difficult to listen to the music. But people from Piwnica did use to go there. Piwnica was, at that time, the most exciting place in Kraków, a place where all the most interesting people used to meet: artists, university professors, dissidents. There was also

Krzysztofory where Kantor* operated. There were many interesting places. There was the Pod Jaszczurami club where Idrees Sulieman's New York Jazz Quartet played for a month: the first modern Black band in Kraków. And people jammed there as well.

Which people do you remember the most from those places?
Krzysztof Niemczyk – he's no longer alive – often hung out at the jazz club. A strange person: a bit a bit of writer, a bit of a painter. Even before the hippie era, he used to walk around with these little wings fastened onto his shoulders. A book about him has come out recently. I only knew him by sight. We all hung around Kraków. There was this George Tysz fellow, an American guy of Polish origin who arrived in Kraków with his girlfriend. We caught the free jazz bug off him; he got us into Ornette Coleman.

Were your first public performances at dances?
My first professional gig was on New Year's Eve at U Plastyków – the School of Fine Art – with Drążek Kalwiński. But I didn't play much at dances, only on a few occasions. It went something like this: 'Oh dear Lord – Stańko's arrived. That's the fun over.' Because I used to announce, for example: 'By special request: "Round Midnight"' – but no one had requested it; I just wanted to play jazz. Kisielewski, Kowal and I had tricks like that because we mainly used to play as a trio. I soon stopped playing at dances; in fact, I had a poor reputation. Musicians from the jazz club in Kraków used to say that I didn't swing. I later had a breakthrough jam at the Pod Jaszczurami club. Kuryl, Drążek and the bassist Piotr Lewicki were there, and I played with them, and then, suddenly, everything changed. Kuryl wanted to fix something on my trumpet and he said to the barmaid: 'You wouldn't happen to have any nail clippers, would you, because I want to fix something for my young friend here . . .' I felt as if I'd struck gold. Those words – 'my young friend' – were like sacred words to me. I started getting to know them. Then Dąbrowski thought really highly of me. I played with Karolak. I got myself established in the Kraków set. And I had my own bands. In my first band, there was Jacek Ostaszewski on bass, Wiktor Perelmuter on drums – he'd emigrated from Russia. No. It wasn't Jacek just yet. I can't remember that first bass player. Czarnecki? One of the local musicians who used to play at dances, and also played jazz.

---

* *Translator's note:* Tadeusz Kantor (1915–1990) was a Polish avant-garde painter, writer, stage designer and theatre director. In the 1960s he and his associated group of artists, theatre people, thinkers and philosophers put on art events at the Krzysztofory Palace in Kraków's main market square. The building is now home to the Historical Museum of Kraków.

Tavern musicians with ambition?
The ambition and the talent (that goes without saying) to cope with the more difficult jazz pieces. Only Ostaszewski, like me, wanted to play jazz right from the start. And he was excellent.

Those musicians hadn't yet released any records or done any concert tours. Did they live off what they earned in the taverns?
They lived off gigs. They played in the local taverns, at parties, at dances. Not Kurylewicz: he had concerts abroad. The best musicians composed film music. I too very soon started living off my earnings from film recordings. In Warsaw, I only played at parties at Dziekanka. We used to play jazz: Cannonball Adderley's 'Mercy, Mercy, Mercy', Blue Note stuff.

There weren't really very many strictly jazz concerts, were there?
There were very few concerts of any kind in those days. I remember 1968. I had the quintet then, and we played three concerts. With Komeda I played two or three concerts a year. We recorded a lot; we lived off our earnings from film music recordings. And I was already going abroad. Initially with Trzaskowski, for workshops in Germany. Then I used to go there with the quintet.

Your first serious band, Jazz Darings, was formed in 1962, when Ostaszewski and Adam Makowicz joined you.
Makowicz, who was then called Matyszkowicz, appeared early on. He came to the club with this bassist, Bogdan Wells. Ah, that's it! Perelmuter got them together and we formed a quartet. And then Jacek Ostaszewski joined us. He'd spent the previous year playing in a tavern in Zakopane, I think with Janusz Muniak, actually. Janusz came back and we started playing together.

How come Makowicz was there? He's originally from Cieszyn.
He quit school. He ran away from home. In Kraków he slept in a coal cellar; then he moved to the jazz club. He lived there during the most severe cold spell. Helikon was his home; he slept on the piano. It was only when he fell so ill that he was at death's door that he met a girl who took him in. He later married her.

He caught such a bad chill?
You know, it *was* the coldest winter of the century, and he did get tonsillitis, so he could easily have died. He was a very determined musician. He knew what he wanted right from the start. He knew he wanted to play with us then because Ostaszewski and I had a reputation for being uncompromising people. Only music mattered. Jazz.

Did your personalities clash in Jazz Darings?
We were joint leaders of the band, but our cooperation didn't last very long.

You mentioned that coming into contact with Ornette Coleman's music was crucial for you then. What was it about his music that you found so attractive?
The distinctive sound, the innovative approach. Lines without harmony. Until Ornette came along, jazz musicians had improvised on harmonic frameworks – I still do, because I find it a good way to build tension – but Ornette abandoned all that. He played pure rhythm, harmonically vague. Without a harmonic centre.

What about the trumpeter in Coleman's quartet – Don Cherry?
Cherry, with that dirty but very rhythmic sound of his, was really suited to this music. He was fundamental to my avant-garde education. I met him when I played with Komeda in Copenhagen. That would have been in about 1964. Cherry was living there, and he used to come to our concerts. He liked Komeda's music and loved playing 'Svantetic'. He was a fascinating character. His playing has its roots in traditional jazz. He had a particular, dirty technique, which comes from New Orleans, and a very hippie-like approach to life.

The most significant event for Jazz Darings was the festival that held its finale at the Kraków Philharmonic at the beginning of 1963. It was called the Great Contest of Amateur Performers from Southern Poland.
I won first prize as soloist. Makowicz came second. Our band won first prize. It was Jan Byrczek's festival. He ran Helikon and he knew what was played at the club. We were the young lions.

Did you often play at Helikon at that time?
Every day. We rehearsed there. It was our second home. I used to say I was going to do some studying but I'd go to the jazz club instead. It was handy for me to be attending two schools: high school and music school; I'd tell one of them that I had classes at the other, and the other way around. By being cunning like that, I was able to keep it all going. We played together until Trzaskowski took Jacek, Komeda took me and Kurylewicz took Makowicz. We were disassembled like that for Warsaw. Later, when I formed the new Jazz Darings in Kraków, which soon turned into my quintet, I had Muniak and younger musicians playing with me: the next wave – Janusz Stefański, Zbigniew Seifert. I was already inclined towards young musicians.

What is your most abiding memory of your high-school years in Kraków?
I remember the time I spent with Jacek Ostaszewski the best. Oh, and films: *Knife in the Water*, Italian neorealism. I used to like going to the cinema on my own. I saw *The Bicycle Thieves* on my own, films with Anna Magnani. I also used to go Piwnica, but I was less interested in the cabaret and more in the intense, edgy lifestyle.

3 Komeda

Where did Krzysztof Komeda first hear you?
It wasn't like that. Michał Urbaniak told him about me. I'd played with Urbaniak in the spring of 1963. The Southern Poland Jazz Contest had been in February. So it all happened quickly. Urbaniak was already famous on the jazz scene. He was in Zbigniew Namysłowski's band and he also played with Adam Jędrzejowski, the drummer from Trzaskowski's band. I was also becoming known. Jędrzejowski and Urbaniak wanted to form a band with me. It turned out to be a very interesting formation – a quintet with the bass player Tadeusz Wójcik and the guitarist Tomasz Krawczyk. We did a tour of Silesia – four or five concerts. That was my first tour.

What do you remember of that tour?
I remember Rybnik; we played there. We played in cultural centres. I remember Urbaniak trying to screw in a light bulb but his fingers were trembling so badly that he couldn't do it. We were living on the edge. Michał played brilliantly back then. I remember the music better than the places. We were playing difficult, modern, post-Coltrane-type music. Weird compositions. But there was just that one tour. We didn't manage it again. Jędrzejowski had his contracts. Krawczyk somehow later disappeared. He was a friend of Michał's from Łódź, a shy cat. Wójcik didn't make it beyond one bad review from Jan Borkowski, and he went off to play in a restaurant. And you have to be hard in this game.

So Komeda took an interest in you after Urbaniak had told him about you?
Word got out that I was a modern trumpeter who played mad music. And those older leaders – Komeda, Trzaskowski, Kurylewicz – were now mentally prepared for it; they wanted to keep up and be modern.

And they wanted to have young, creative musicians in their band, didn't they? The same procedure that Miles Davis had.
Exactly the same procedure. A very straightforward recipe for moving forward.

Were you familiar with Komeda's music at the time?
I'd heard him play a solo at Helikon. I'd been at his All Souls' Day concert in Kraków, where his sextet was playing. I was familiar with *Knife in the Water*. I'd

seen the film many times; it was fascinating to hear the music along with the film. The interplay of music and picture was brilliant: together they produced a purely artistic effect. And there was also a little record with music from the film: 'Ballad for Bernt'; 'Cherry'; 'Crazy Girl'. Komeda then became the most important person for me in Polish jazz.

You met him when he'd already got all that to his name?
I stood in front of Komeda, and I said, 'Hello, my name is Tomasz Stańko.' He'd been looking for me during Jazz Jamboree, and I'd simply come up for the festival. Someone said to me, some musician, 'Mate, Komeda's looking for you,' and I said, 'What are you on about?' but then someone else said the same thing. And then I saw Komeda. I went up to him. 'Hello, my name is Tomasz Stańko.'
'Oh, right. I've been looking for you. Your mother said you were in Warsaw. We have a concert the day after tomorrow. Well, I'd like you to join us. My band's let me down. We're rehearsing tomorrow.' And it worked out. I was staying with Wacek Kisielewski at the time. I borrowed a pair of trousers off him because I didn't have a suit. Kisielewski was taller, so I had to tie some string around them. During the concert, they started falling down.

Your first meeting with Komeda took place in the lobby of the Congress Hall in Warsaw, didn't it, during the same 1963 Jazz Jamboree at which you debuted on stage with the band?
Yes. We had two days to rehearse. There were meant to be some Danes playing with him, but they never made it.

Did you not know his music?
I didn't know anything. Apart from 'Crazy Girl'. They were difficult to play, those pieces, physically demanding. Long, complicated parts. But I played them. Urbaniak played, of course, with Maciej Suzin on bass and the sensational young drummer Czesław 'Mały' Bartkowski. He was in Namysłowski's band, which was doing brilliantly well then. They had some success in England with their record 'Lola'. Namysłowski was playing 'Piątawka' in 5/4 time, 'Siódmawka' in 7/4 time – time signatures that McLaughlin hadn't even dreamt of yet. Namysłowski's quartet was brilliant. Włodzimierz Gulgowski, Wójcik and Mały. Back then, no one played like they did.

Did Komeda have a new programme?
It was completely different music then. Modern.

Do you remember that concert?
I don't remember it. I can remember us getting a good reception. I remember the rehearsals more. On the corner of Krucza Street and Hoża Street there used to be an organization, SPAM (the Association for Polish Music Artists). There was a piano there, and that's where we used to practise. By the Grand Hotel, on the same side as the Grand, towards Mokotów, over by that Stalinist

construction. It was run by Tadeusz Górny, a chap who used to play the flute, but who now writes about books. Makowicz later slept there, when he came up to Warsaw.

After that concert, was it immediately clear that you were going to continue playing together? Did you get any sign from Komeda?
We knew straight away. We connected straight away. I became Komeda's court trumpeter; he took me everywhere. I recorded his films; we went to festivals. In those days, people who were interested in jazz had creative personalities. They came out of traditional jazz, but they were soon drawn into seeking out new ways. That was the drift. In 1963, I also started playing with Trzaskowski. We went to Antwerp. Zośka* started resenting the fact that I was playing with both of them.

What sort of relationship did you have with those older leaders – Komeda and Trzaskowski?
Respect. It was an honour for me to have been invited by Komeda and Trzaskowski. And new possibilities. I began going abroad with them. In 1964 I attended festivals in Bled, Kongsberg and Prague with Komeda. I remember a trip to Hamburg with Trzaskowski, to an international workshop, with a changeover in Berlin. The flower of European musicians used to come over to Hamburg. That's where I first met Tony Oxley. And from Hamburg I travelled on to Copenhagen to play with Komeda at the Montmartre. That was in the spring of 1965. In February we had an engagement at the Gyllene Cirkeln (the Golden Circle club) in Stockholm.

What's your recollection of those first trips abroad?
Fantastic. The first was a big festival in Antwerp. 1964. I don't remember who else played there. I went there with Jacek Ostaszewski and Trzaskowski's band, as a quintet. Janusz Muniak and Nahorny were with us. Włodzimierz Nahorny was from the Tri-City, but he played in Warsaw. He had his own trio; he played alto sax brilliantly. That was modern music; he got more romantic on piano. In Antwerp I smoked a joint for the first time in my life. And I said to myself, 'Well, bugger me; that's my thing. I'm going to be smoking this stuff for the rest of my life.' Later on, when I was touring with Komeda, the first thing I'd do was go straight over to our drummer, Rune Carlsson, to ask him if he had anything to smoke. And Komeda would try and get me to play; he was curious to know what effect it would have on my playing . . .

So, Komeda wanted to turn you into a guinea pig?
He wanted me to play. He wanted to know what it would be like, playing after a joint. But I didn't want to play, because at the time I only smoked after I'd played. We'd finished playing at the Montmartre and I'd lit up. Don Cherry,

---

* *Translator's note:* Zośka was Krzysztof Komeda's wife, Zofia Komedowa.

or maybe some Danes, went up on stage after us, and Komeda says to me, 'Go and play! Go and play!' 'I can't. I'm not in a fit state to move. Back off.'

He didn't try it himself, did he?
No. He didn't want to. Same with Trzaskowski. At that time, the widespread belief was that drug addicts all just died straight away. People made no distinction between hashish and heroin. Roman Kowal used to say that, when Bernt Rosengren came to play with Komeda, he'd be smoking something, taking something, fumbling around, getting stuff out, but no one knew exactly what it was. Komeda didn't know anything; now John Surman . . . Oh, Surman, now he did know . . . a lot!

We met him in Germany at the beginning of the 1970s. I was playing with my quintet then. Surman had his famous trio at the time. He had Stu Martin, an American, on drums. He was the guru for our quintet. There was also the bassist, Barre Phillips. They all smoked stuff. We wanted to live like that as well, and that *is* how we lived. We were known for not messing about, for doing the good shit, like all jazz musicians. Like they've always done and still do.

I remember workshops in Hamburg before that. There were two factions: the Polish musicians sitting with Trzaskowski in a downstairs room, drinking, and the others sitting upstairs and smoking hash. I was the only one of the Poles who smoked. I'd go down to the Polish room, and everyone would stop talking . . . 'God, you look so pale; you're going to pass out.' They were frightened. This was something different. These were drugs, after all. They preferred our traditional, tried-and-tested, Polish stupefying agent. But I was totally stereo. Alcohol and hashish. Just fine by me. I soon discovered the charms of combining the two. Stereo charms.

Was alcohol ubiquitous at that time within the jazz community?
The vodka flowed like a river. It was with us right from the start. In Kraków we used to say that good musicians didn't play during rehearsals, they just drank; the bad musicians just played. So I drank. Jazz and alcohol; it was fundamental. The whole community drank heavily. We did play, obviously, but propped up with booze. People don't drink like that now. Life passed by more slowly then; people were less responsible. During Communism people used to drink because what else was there to do? Komeda and Trzaskowski were heavy drinkers, but they could control it; you can't work otherwise. The same with me: all my life I've had control over the drugs, to a lesser or greater extent – to a greater extent when I had things to do. Why did the Red Hot Chili Peppers manage to overcome their heroin addictions? Because they had something to do.

Your foreign trips at the time were arranged through the state concert agency PAGART, weren't they?

We always travelled through PAGART. There was no other way. We got our passports through PAGART. I had no trouble with that. A path well worn by Komeda and Trzaskowski. I was playing mainly with Komeda then. I did like playing with Trzaskowski because I really liked the music, but I felt more involved with Komeda.

You also played with Trzaskowski's quintet at Jazz Jamboree. In 1964 the quintet played your composition 'Kwinty'.

'Kwinty'. It's coming back to me, now that you've mentioned it, but I don't remember the actual composition. That must have been Trzaskowski's initiative.

You didn't play your own pieces with Komeda, did you?

No, I didn't. Trzaskowski was more open.

You also had your first recording session with Trzaskowski, in January 1965. That's when his first album was released: *The Andrzej Trzaskowski Quintet*, nearly a year before the famous *Astigmatic*. The concepts behind these albums were similar – tone poems for jazz quintet.

Of course, the concepts were similar, except that Komeda had his own coherent music. Trzaskowski's compositions were good – kind of poetic constructions, really lovely. I enjoyed playing them, but Komeda's pieces were solid.

Those two bands weren't in competition with each other at the time, were they?

There was tension, but Komeda and Trzaskowski were high-class people. Kuryl as well. Three first-class leaders who competed with one another. But there was no dirty work as far as this competition was concerned; it was their women who gave them the grief. Zośka used to say to me: 'You're playing with Trzaskowski. How dare you!' But there weren't any big grudges; now, in a similar situation, there would be. Because, after all, at that time I was the only available trumpeter on the market who played modern music – and far-out modern at that.

How would you compare those three leaders?

Kurylewicz was the most mainstream. Trzaskowski was very intellectual. The most creative was Komeda. He had the most solid music, the best compositions. His music has stayed with us. It has totally stood the test of time. Komeda was the one with the strongest personality. He knew right from the start what he wanted to do with his music. He'd barely say a word during rehearsals, but his music was so strong that it was easy to play.

In those days, jazz was surrounded by an intellectual halo, wasn't it?
Of course. Jazz and existentialism. Jean-Paul Sartre and Miles Davis. It all went together and dovetailed. Jazz had status the world over. Rock and roll came later. In Poland, Leopold Tyrmand, Stefan Kisielewski and Marian Eile took an interest in jazz. Jazz musicians had the sort of status that my generation was ceasing to have. We were *just* musicians then. But Komeda, Trzaskowski, Kurylewicz – those were artists. All the film people respected them. Later, when Czerwono-Czarni came on the scene, jazz became niche. On the other hand, we were able to really get stuck into music proper.

Komeda remains a mythologized figure. How do you remember him as a person?
Even though he was barely ten years older than me, I felt a huge difference between him and myself. It wouldn't have occurred to me to have questioned him. He was like a guru. I felt a distance.

Was it Komeda who created that distance?
No. He didn't create any distance. We used the familiar 'you' form with each other. It was I who felt the distance.

You often stayed with Komeda; was there a kind of family atmosphere?
Definitely, definitely. When I came up to Warsaw, I often stayed over at his place on Wojska Polskiego Avenue, near Inwalidów Square. I was a bit like his son: a kind of child, you might say. I don't know why; after all, there wasn't that big an age difference. And Urbaniak was just the same age as me, but he was an old-timer: he'd been playing with Namysłowski for a long time; he was well known within the community and people said that, aged twelve, he was drinking vodka with the coal merchants. I was immature alongside them.

According to the Komeda legend, he had a child-like sensitivity.
He wasn't child-like, just quiet, calm. A gentle chap. Zośka was more predatory.

Did he have any quirks, any particular habits?
Quirks – no. He did have a distinct posture, a slightly stooping one, as if he were lost in thought.

Did he live in his own world?
You could say that. That's why we felt comfortable with each other, because I had a similar nature. If we did ever talk, it was about music. I can remember, as if it were today, how, before his departure for the States, we walked around the park in Żoliborz and talked about music.

You did say 'If we did ever talk' – does that mean that Komeda wasn't very talkative?
I'll tell you something: such was his talent that he'd not have to say anything, yet everything would be clear. He conveyed a depth of emotion. Maybe it's a question of charisma. I don't actually know what charisma is. It seems to me that charisma is a kind of experiencing of things at a deep emotional level, a sensitivity, an experiencing of things in such a way that they're communicated to other people. That's how it was with Komeda. He transmitted a particular kind of intense experience and it took hold in others. I think it's mainly because of this that I benefited so much from being with him because, musically, I was marching to a slightly different beat.

How did Komeda behave in his role as the group's leader?
He was very quiet. Zośka kept the band together. She was number one. She was in charge. She liked controversy. But the social set-up was very friendly. Lots of vodka, of course. Although, by then I was already into other things.

Your first real breakthrough as a band came during your stay in Denmark and Sweden, where at the start of 1965 you had a series of bookings in famous clubs: Montmartre and Gyllene Cirkeln.
We spent a month in Copenhagen. We stayed in private accommodation, not a hotel. I stayed with the Polish painter Krzysztof Leśniak. We also met up with Polański in Copenhagen. We watched *Repulsion* before its premiere. I only met Polański on that one occasion; there was no opportunity after that.

At the Montmartre we played with Urbaniak, but he already had one foot in a different camp. When he went over to play in a restaurant, he ended up staying in Sweden for a few years. Urbaniak had recently got married to Urszula Dudziak and was hanging out with a group of Polish musicians, because lots of jazz musicians had gone over to play in the restaurants. That was our only connection with the West. Urszula's brother was also playing over there: Lech, an excellent drummer. He played brilliantly with Komeda on the *Knife in the Water* album, with great subtlety and lots of swing. And then he left. He had a good contract; he was complying with his contract. Like Zbigniew Namysłowski's pianist, Włodzimierz Gulgowski. The same with the Markiewicz brothers. Dymitr Markiewicz was a very good trombonist. They lived in Malmö.

We often hung out with that group. It was the Warsaw network from way back. Zośka and Krzysztof knew them very well. We stuck together like people from the provinces; we didn't have international contacts right away. The reasons were prosaic but, on the other hand, those were very agreeable times.

How did you like Scandinavia?
It was wonderful. Just wonderful. We had those complexes that Poles have in the West. Compared to poor Poland, the wealth that we saw in Sweden

and Denmark seemed glamorous. I dressed myself with the money I earned doing gigs. I bought myself flowery shirts, Beatle boots, Chelsea boots. In Copenhagen I bought an excellent Tandberg tape deck. Komeda also had one of those. We didn't have records in Poland, but we could always get hold of recordings. We brought tapes over from the West. I had a whole library of them. I had that tape deck for a long time.

During the 1960s, there were many creative, Black jazz musicians from the States and from Africa living in Europe. They were particularly active in Copenhagen.

Copenhagen was a city full of jazz. Like Paris. Dope was cheap. Kenny Drew lived there. Don Cherry. Dollar Brand had a room upstairs at the Montmartre. Musicians there were two-a-penny; they were offered good gigs. And, when there's something worth listening to, people want to listen.

You got to know Don Cherry then.

Cherry liked my trumpet. Because I was supposedly playing free, but not quite. There used to be a divide: normal trumpeters and free trumpeters, like Cherry, Donald Ayler, Bill Dixon. They only played free, without a classical technique, but I combined the two things: I had a bit of a classical technique but I also played free. Cherry liked that. Our friendship grew from our time in Copenhagen.

Did you also meet up with any of the African jazz musicians who lived in Copenhagen at that time?

They were our models! Johnny Dyani used to singe his fingertips so he could play the double bass better. He and Dollar Brand came from South Africa. Dyani sounded different from everyone else. We can talk more about African music later.

Ornette Coleman was your greatest inspiration then. What was Komeda's view of him?

He didn't listen to him as much as I did, but everyone thought highly of Ornette because his music was original and cohesive. Komeda was more interested in Miles, in Trane. He also liked pop. He wrote songs for film and, being Komeda, he didn't treat it as hack work; he took a serious approach. He took a very serious approach to everything. Komeda drew my attention to the Beatles and to Hendrix, particularly, whom he saw play live in Malmö. He was fascinated by him.

How did Komeda's quintet function? Because you and he were the backbone, while the rest of the line-up used to change.

There wasn't a band. There was Komeda and me. Urbaniak already had his own life, joining us on occasion. Namysłowski sometimes played with us. We had either Rune Carlsson or Czesław Bartkowski on drums, Bo Stief on bass. Polish double-bassists would play with us: Suzin, Kozłowski. The best one was Gucio Dyląg. During our last phase, from 1963, Komeda and I formed the backbone. In fact, he used to say to me: 'Our band at the moment is us, the two of us.' I had a good rapport with Komeda. Musically, we understood each other very well indeed. I sensed his every thought and did what he had in mind. And what he was after was a certain type of imagination.

Earlier on, he'd had Jan 'Ptaszyn' Wróblewski in his quartet, and I remember they used to play a beautiful composition, 'Alea', and for a long time I wanted to play it. Later on he played in a quartet with Urbaniak. And then the quintet was formed. When Komeda found me, he'd got the person he'd been looking for. In the quintet, I used to do the things that I've carried on doing to this day: I played simple, very melodic motifs with a dirty tone and a coarse technique, which gave the music depth and took the edge off the sweetness of the melody, which might otherwise have come across as rather traditional. I think my role in the quintet lay in making it sound less traditional. That really suited me. That's why I didn't form a band at that time, even though I liked being a leader right from the start.

I was entirely fulfilled working with Komeda, as if I was playing my own music. I still play Komeda's compositions because they suit me. Komeda had an exceptional facility for writing musical hits. I don't feel the need for such neat motifs; depth and moodiness do it for me. But Komeda had a Mozartian lightness: no matter what he composed, it was wonderful to listen to and wonderful to play. It was beautiful, joyous, and so human. But it was probably also down to the fact that we complemented each other so well.

Apparently, Komeda looked to you when he forgot the notes during concerts?
That might have been the case. I don't remember.

A lasting strong point in many of the quintet's concerts and recordings was the rhythm section, which was made up of Gucio Dyląg and the Swede, Rune Carlsson. He is the only musician from outside Poland to appear on all the recordings made by the quintet.
Rune always recorded with Komeda. The Rune and Gucio rhythm section was famous. They played with Eje Thelin, whose quintet was then number one in Europe. Thelin's no longer with us. He was a brilliant trombonist. A Swede. When he toured Poland with the Swiss pianist George Gruntz, everyone went crazy about them, the whole Polish jazz community. That's when they met Gucio and immediately brought him into their band. Gucio was a great bassist. He and Rune made up a rhythm section that was number one in Europe. Thelin's band was a modern quintet: tenor, trombone and rhythm section with piano.

To this day, Manfred Eicher recalls how charismatic they were as a band. Manfred wanted to record Komeda for ECM. Why? Because the whole of Europe knew that no one could play the drums like Rune. When Rune began playing with Komeda, it was like when, in America, Miles took on Tony Williams. In Poland, instead of Rune we had Bartkowski playing with us; he played very well. Rune was often booked up. In Stockholm we played together for two weeks at the Gyllene Cirkeln. I remember Gucio saying to me there: 'Eh, mate – Rune wants to talk to you.' 'Are you mad?' I said, 'I don't speak English.' 'Go, just go,' he said, 'You'll understand each other.' You see, Rune knew, because Gucio had told him as much, that I had certain inclinations, that I enjoyed a smoke. We left the club and walked down the street, up the hill. He got a joint out. That's how I got to know Rune. We played together a few more times after that, not that many. The quintet didn't actually play many concerts. But it was actually with Komeda that Rune really flourished, because Komeda gave him the space. Thelin's music was more traditional, whereas with Komeda he could let fly like he wanted to; he had the space to be creative. I think 'Requiem' was Rune's best moment. A master!

What later became of Rune?
He still plays well, but something has changed. He's stopped being wild. Something's clicked in his head. He's started singing. He's diminished artistically. He doesn't feel like it. Well, it's changed. He's got married, and he's singing standards. I have the impression that, when he let fly in the 1960s, music drove him crazy. He went all the way, and then he began to lose his mind. He gave it up; he got scared of that kind of lifestyle and so he stopped living like that.

How about Gucio Dyląg?
Gucio was also a master; he played everything. He used to play Komeda's compositions absolutely brilliantly, but he also really liked playing pure, swinging jazz. The Phil Woods rhythm section with Daniel Humair and Gucio Dyląg was famous. Phil Woods & The European Rhythm Machine. Gucio played with the best people. He had a very good reputation. He played in the big bands. He used to live in Sweden, but then he moved to Switzerland where he still lives now. He's still playing brilliantly.

Dyląg's real name was 'Roman', and 'Gucio' was a nickname, which suggests a good-natured person.
That's how he looked. And that's how he actually was. He didn't lead a jazzy lifestyle; he took care of himself. Among all those jazz musician-drunkards who populated the country at the time, he really was a decent fellow. He did like his cake, mind you.

What sort of contact did you have with Michał Urbaniak at that time?
Urbaniak hired me first, and then we met up constantly. After he'd played with Komeda, he stayed in Scandinavia for quite some time, and I formed the quintet. He later told me that he'd been jealous of my quintet. We encouraged

each other. He came back to Poland, and, being an energetic person, he formed his own quintet, a very interesting one, with Karolak and Makowicz. He won a prize in a competition in Switzerland, at Montreux, and then he went over to the States. He settled over there, but we had the same agents in Switzerland, and later in Germany. And, when I was in the States, we met up every day. In fact, we meet up all the time.

Did you not want to play together anymore after that period with Komeda?
After Komeda's death, we had a joint project for Joachim-Ernst Berendt, but I had my own band and he had his.

We've talked about Komeda's concerts in the West. But you also had trips to the former socialist countries. Festivals in Yugoslavia and Prague. Tours of the GDR and Bulgaria.
I don't remember Bulgaria. There might have been something like that. That's possible. In Germany we played in Leipzig and Berlin. There was also a festival in Norway, in Kongsberg: 1964. I was in Kongsberg recently; they still remember the gig.

After the festival in Prague, in 1965, there was a record released: *Jazz Greetings from the East*, a compilation of bands from Czechoslovakia, Hungary, Yugoslavia and Poland.
I don't remember that record. I do remember the concert being good. The recordings took place shortly before the concert. Later on, they made them into a compilation album of bands from the festival.

Do you remember the musicians from that festival? For example, Karel Velebný, the Czech free jazz musician, who, in fact, soon after became famous for the album he released with the legendary New York underground label ESP-Disk, which also released Albert Ayler and Sun Ra.
That's possible. I don't remember those musicians. Velebný is a well-known name: a vibraphonist. I do remember Jacek Ostaszewski playing some brilliant bass at that festival. I have a better memory of the lightly opiumed Indian cigarettes that you could buy in Prague.

Did you notice any difference in the way that your music was received by the former socialist countries, compared to those in the West?
We got a brilliant reception everywhere. Please remember that, when Cecil Taylor played at Jazz Jamboree in 1965, he got a standing ovation. Don Ellis played. Modern music was very well received. Wherever we played with Komeda, we always got an excellent reception because we were playing music that was modern, but also melodic.

There was one thing that Komeda was a genius at: control over form. Jazz falls flat when we all cling on to our improvisations. Improvisation is a beautiful characteristic of ours, a very jazzy one, which we find tremendously satisfying to play, but because of it we don't have control over form, and everything falls apart. The playing can be brilliant, but it can also be terrible. But Komeda, goddammit, he knew that right from the start, instinctively.

It turns out, after all (and I'm proof of this), that it's always brilliant playing his music. Its form in no way restricts how we play it: our solos might be like this on one occasion, like that on another; I see how differently each saxophonist plays his music. Billy Harper played it completely differently; Bernt Rosengren, Joakim Milder and Adam Pierończyk – all completely different. Everyone plays Komeda differently. And it's not about talent. The composition lives on because it has a written-down dramatic structure, a closed form in which there is room for soloists. Masses of room: it can be played in all sorts of different ways. I have to work really hard at it as well. Control over form. I apparently do have it, though not entirely. Only a few people have it . . . Ornette! He only plays his own pieces, and they all have a specific form. Komeda had that too. Partly by chance, partly through film. He was a film composer and he wanted to transfer that knowledge of his (which he found hugely rewarding) and his way of composing to concert music.

Are you saying that Komeda's work in film music formed his compositional conceptions?
Definitely. If only the irregularity of his time signatures, which you hear in his film music. Jazz was very symmetrical, but Komeda sometimes extended a phrase by one bar, to synchronize the music with the image, which then changed the whole internal dramatic structure of the melody. He used this same technique when he composed music for stage later on. Lots of little things like that influenced Komeda. All the more so because he approached film so seriously. The majority of composers who write music for film treat film like a forgotten stepchild; not Komeda, though: never. He engaged with it spiritually, and by doing so he was able to analyse his ideas creatively. People liked Komeda's music and still do, because it's tight; it has a particular dramatic structure and beautiful melodies.

4 Poetry and Jazz

When, exactly, did Komeda's most famous album, *Astigmatic*, get recorded?
One of the most authoritative of the various historians of Polish jazz – your
schoolfriend, Roman Kowal – lamented the fact that one of the greatest Polish
jazz sessions is surrounded by confusion. The album cover says the date of
the recording is December 1965, whereas Komeda told Kowal that he nicked
Albert Mangelsdorff's rhythm section – Günter Lenz and Rune Carlsson – at
Jazz Jamboree, and was in a hurry to get that album recorded with them as
soon as the concerts were over. That would imply that you recorded *Astigmatic*
during Jazz Jamboree: in other words, in October.
We recorded it during Jamboree. Obviously, that's how it was. Namysłowski
played with us.

Why do we have December on the album cover?
Maybe that's when the music was mixed.*

When did Komeda come up with the idea of having Carlsson and Lenz as the
rhythm section?
Gucio wasn't there: he was on another job, probably in Sweden, and Komeda
wanted to record the album.

Did Komeda already know the German bassist on this recording, Günter Lenz?
I don't think so. There was a problem with bassists. Komeda wanted to have
the best musician available to him.

In other words – as was the case with your first engagement – the band's
eventual line-up was assembled ad hoc backstage at Jazz Jamboree. The
session took place in the National Philharmonic concert hall. Did you record
straight after the festival concerts?
Yes. We recorded by night. Jamboree was held at the Philharmonic then. The
recordings took place in the same large concert hall. We stayed behind after

---

* *Series Editor's note:* This is somewhat complicated. Komeda actually made two albums
called *Astigmatic*. *Astigmatic Live* was recorded half at the Jamboree and half at the
Jazzhus Montmartre in Copenhagen, whereas the studio album was made in December
1965. There were three bassists involved in all: Janusz Kozłowski (Jamboree), Bo Stief
(Montmartre) and Günter Lenz (Warsaw studio).

the concerts. People left, everything went quiet, and then we came back. The recording took all night.

At that same Jazz Jamboree, Komeda played a concert featuring material from *Astigmatic*. With a different line-up. Because he had a quartet without a saxophone. Komeda, you, and a rhythm section with Rune and, on bass, Janusz Kozłowski from Namysłowski's band. I was struck by the fact that the quartet didn't have a saxophone.

Urbaniak wasn't there; he wasn't able to come over from Sweden. Zbigniew had his own concert. We played as a quartet. We recorded the album with Namysłowski. Kozłowski didn't play at the recording session. Komeda really cared about getting hold of the best available musicians, and so he got Lenz.

On *Astigmatic*, you played flugelhorn, not trumpet.
I actually played flugelhorn for quite mundane reasons. Komeda's music required you to be phenomenally fit. I found playing the flugelhorn less strenuous. That said, I did use a trumpet mouthpiece. The mouthpiece made the sound more trumpet-like; there wasn't that thin, soft sound. I could achieve a harsher sound, which was tempered by the specific characteristics of the instrument itself. I managed to produce a timbre that worked brilliantly for Komeda's music. I also recorded 'Requiem' in 1967 using flugelhorn. Apart from that, I played the trumpet all the time. I don't particularly like the flugelhorn.

Do you remember the *Astigmatic* recording session well?
I remember the atmosphere. That large, empty concert hall, when we went back to the Philharmonic. I remember the feeling of calm that came out of that session. And Günter Lenz smiling.

In the cover notes for *Astigmatic*, Adam Sławiński wrote that Komeda's music has 'lyricism and pathos, the power of an ecstatically mystical experience'. Was that your experience, playing these pieces?
Yes and no. At the same time. As musicians, we experience things completely differently. Even if we're playing something quite sublime, we are constantly exerting control over it. In order to play, I had to have a very routine approach, yet at the same time I could feel that the music was exhilarating. I knew that right from the start, when Komeda first brought the composition in. I enjoyed playing it, thinking: it's so artfully written! That cunning logic in 'Astigmatic' with the strange constant rippling of the motif. The rhythmic drive of the melody. The motif is as simple as can be – everything depends on the rhythmic movement of the melody, which rises and falls. That's classic Komeda. He basically constructed the entire composition around those two elements – a rhythmic rising and falling. And I think the reason why Komeda thought highly of me was because I immediately, instinctively, picked up the flow of his compositions.

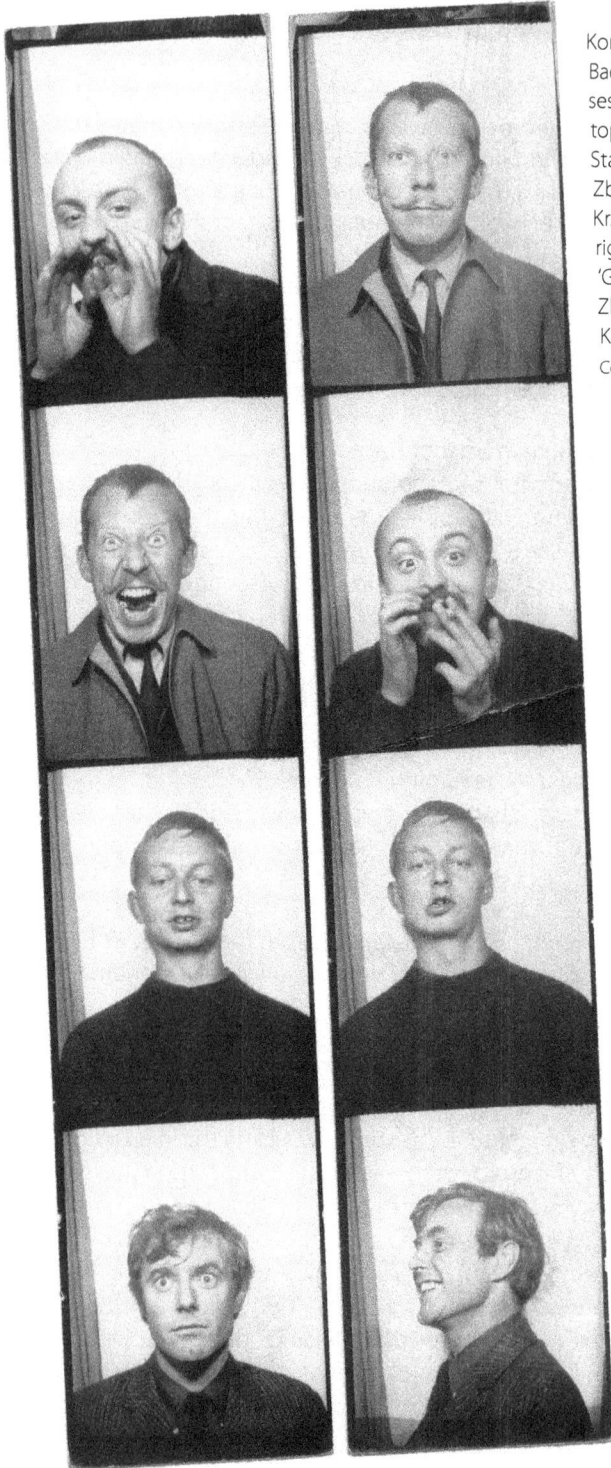

Komeda's band en route for Baden-Baden. Recording session: *Poetry and Jazz*. From top left, downwards: Tomasz Stańko, Roman 'Gucio' Dyląg, Zbigniew Namysłowski, Krzysztof Komeda. From top right, downwards: Roman 'Gucio' Dyląg, Tomasz Stańko, Zbigniew Namysłowski, Krzysztof Komeda.

Courtesy Anna Stańko

When I play with my musicians, I always have to point out these kinds of things to them, and they don't generally take too well to it. With Komeda, I immediately felt it: 'High'! When I recognized the logic of the composition in 'Svantetic', and particularly in 'Astigmatic', I got an incredible kick out of it. I was able to fall into a performer's trance – a 'mystical' one, as Sławiński would call it.

Such interpretations of Komeda's music align him with the Romantic tradition.
I think that's to do with the tunefulness of his music. I don't know whether that's Romanticism. 'Astigmatic': he thought that title through very carefully – astigmatism is a sight defect, an error in the way we see things. A Romantic motif. I don't know whether that's Romantic. I think it's more of a schizoid thing. I associate it with Komeda's limp, which he was left with after he'd had polio, with a sort of defect, a fault. An error in the way we see things is a twist, a mutation, a difference. That's what I'd say. But where does this solemnity come from? 'Astigmatic', 'Svantetic' – all the time this pathetic fallacy. I don't know. Solemnity is associated with pomp, with affectation, but there's no such thing with Komeda. Quite the opposite.

When you'd finished recording Astigmatic, did you feel that it was a groundbreaking record?
No, we didn't feel that. Now I do know that it's a masterpiece of a record.

At one time, Komeda's jazz would be discussed within the context of 'third stream'. Today, no one remembers third stream (supposedly a fusion of jazz and classical music) yet everyone's still talking about Komeda.
That's how composed forms were referred to at the time. The third stream, who drew on jazz, swinging melodies, forms for improvisation, created compositions within a classical framework, as closed forms. Jazz's strength lay in its open, unspecified form; you could play ten choruses, or five. A simple form of variations, because at that time – before Ornette opened up the way – you had to play choruses, apply a cycle: theme, improvisation, theme. Everything was open. Komeda closed the form. He saw himself as a composer; he thought in a traditional way. But it worked.

It's taken me till now to see this clearly and appreciate it, now that I know how difficult it is for me to control my own band when I give them complete freedom. Sometimes they go on for too long, sometimes not long enough. Whereas Komeda would have the form established right at the start. And that's the way to do it. The danger of doing it this way for jazz musicians is that their music may become uniform, closed, and wither and die. And, yet, it turns out that this music can live if it's written in a jazzy way, if it's jazz that comes from the soul. The closed form gives control over the dramatic structure, which is jazz's weak point.

Within Komeda's form, we can either lengthen or shorten improvisational extracts. The form has its own life on the inside. 'Requiem', in particular, is written like that. The music is written in a very specific, artful way: it's pure art. An abstract thing, which has no points of reference. It has to be pure to be refined. Twelve-tone music – Stravinsky turned music upside down, and it became the product of a very sophisticated way of composing. Sometimes, in Komeda's music, everything is constructed out of conventional ballad-like licks, but these building blocks are arranged differently, weirdly twisted. And then we get a unique form – Krzysztof Komeda. Whenever I hear *Rosemary's Baby*, I'm always surprised that there are two extra bars in there.

Third stream's fusion of classical and jazz soon turned out to be a dead end.
A dead end. Why force jazz and classical together? It'd be better if they filtered through to each other in a different way. I fill my inner being with classical music, classical aesthetics. The way that subsequently finds an outlet in my music: I let go with the flow. Mahler's *Adagio* and Bartók's *Four Orchestral Pieces*, for example, have undoubtedly got into me so deeply that they influence my compositions. It's like mixing colours on a palette: if you want to find a shade, a tone, you mix the colours, but their proportions depend on your intuition. When I'm being transported for a while by some music or other, my brain is full of its beauty. The more this beauty affects me, the more permanently the music lodges itself in my brain. It's changed me! In fact, I can control it. I can listen to whatever I like and power myself up with it. In this way, we can control what we do, if we believe in our own inner strength – that we too have something to say.

That's like downloading programmes into the brain.
Programmes that mutate within me.

You and Komeda didn't play much live. Was it the case that the quintet had more studio work than concerts?
Yes. I mainly worked with him in the studio. We did do lots of film recordings, after all.

Do you remember the film sessions?
Not much. What it mainly entailed was me and my friends sitting in a box room nattering to each other while we waited to record. We'd play through an extract, and then we'd record. 'Number 5!' We play number 5. We only listened back to the music when it was being mixed. Then I'd always be amazed and delighted by the way Komeda worked his motifs. The way he wrote his leitmotifs and adapted them; he'd change the key or add a beat. Playing those things and watching how he did it, I learned a great deal.

Did you record in film studios?
No. In Warsaw. At the very beginning, I'd travel up to Łódź. But the studios there were crummy. The best studios in Warsaw were the radio ones. We mainly recorded on Malczewskiego Street, occasionally on Myśliwiecka Street. Komeda had the time and the money. The studio was always hired out for two or three days, with the best engineer. The work was well organized. Later on, he'd travel to London, to Paris for recordings and had local musicians. The trade unions were strong over there.

Did work on experimental animated films differ much from work on feature films? I'm thinking of Komeda's recordings for *Klatki* ['Cages'], *Wiklinowy kosz* ['Wicker Basket'] and *Laterna magica* ['Magic Lantern'].
Mirosław Kijowicz's films. Shorts. I don't remember those films. I do remember Jerzy Skolimowski's *Ręce do góry* ['Hands Up!']. Andrzej Kondratiuk's *Klub profesora Tutki* ['Professor Tutka's Club'].

You also recorded his stage music for *Breakfast at Tiffany's* with Komeda.
It didn't feel any different recording music for the theatre. I can't remember those recording sessions.

After *Astigmatic* came the famous soundtracks to Polański's *Cul-de-sac* and Skolimowski's *Le départ*, and the Quintet's next album was *Meine süsse Europäische Heimat: Dichtung und Jazz aus Polen*, recorded in 1967.
That was a famous recording. Not long before Komeda left for the States. It was a brilliant line-up with Gucio, Rune and Namysłowski. The recording session was in Baden-Baden.

On that album, Komeda composed music that interacted with the poetry readings. Was it record producer Joachim-Ernst Berendt's idea to combine jazz and poetry?
They jointly selected the poetry. And Komeda wrote some phenomenal music. I remember the composition 'Dirge for Europe'. I've included it in my new quintet's repertoire. I also like playing 'The Witch'.

Did you record the material at the same time – the poetry readings and the band?
The poetry readings were added later.

Were you familiar with the poems? There's an interesting overview of Polish poetry in there: Szymborska, Miłosz, Czechowicz, Wierzyński, Gałczyński, Grochowiak, Bieńkowski, Herbert.
No. I didn't need to. Komeda knew the poems.

The opening track on the record is 'The Trumpet Player is Innocent'. Does the title encapsulate your role within Komeda's band?

I don't think so. I think that probably referred to the poem.

You recorded two of the tracks on *Dichtung und Jazz aus Polen*: 'The Witch' and 'Sketches for Don Quixote' again during that famous, final Polish radio session, when 'Requiem' was recorded.

Yes. That was a very good recording session, in M1, that large studio on Myśliwiecka Street. Zbigniew, Gucio and Rune played.

'Nighttime, Daytime Requiem' was a formidable composition; its first release was edited down from twenty-eight to twenty-four minutes. The full version was eventually released by Power Bros.

That's how long the piece took to play. Three parts. They all need to be heard. We also did a recording at Jamboree. The radio session came first. That's why we played it so well at the festival.

'Requiem' was Komeda's tribute to Coltrane; he composed the piece just after Coltrane died. Was Komeda fascinated by Coltrane?

Coltrane was a genius, after all. Komeda was familiar with his music. Miles and Coltrane were number one then. And Komeda, with his form and melody, entered the jazz mainstream.

The 'Requiem' for Coltrane turned out to be a 'Requiem' for Komeda himself. You recorded the piece in the autumn of 1967; then, a year later, the accident took place that led to his death.

We talked about me going over to join him in the States. It all happened so quickly. I tell you – such was his fate; such was his life; such was his karma. There's no fairness in life; there's just luck. He was unlucky. Zośka got lucky. Every so often these days, I dream that Komeda's alive, that I've seen him.

And is Komeda then the same as he was when you played together?

No. A completely different person. He's doing something else. Supposedly making music, but kind of ordinary stuff. Like it was with Rimbaud; as if he's stopped being Komeda. I have these dreams every once in a while – very realistic ones, like waking dreams. I know it's a dream; I say, 'But Komeda's dead'; not here he's not: 'Look, he's alive, after all.'

Did you have plans to join him in the States?

The plan was that, once he got settled there, he'd get me over and we'd play together with the American musicians. Komeda wanted to get established. Get a name for himself. And, knowing him, I've no doubt he'd have carried on with jazz.

Had it not been for that tragic death, how would Komeda's career have progressed?

I think he'd have become a film composer. I don't think he'd have given concerts; he'd have got more satisfaction from his films. Within the Hollywood production system, he'd have been in his element. He would have had the best performers.

For you, one of the consequences of playing in Komeda's quintet was a permanent move to Warsaw.

I was staying over in Warsaw from 1965 onwards. I think I moved there permanently in 1968. In fact, all the top musicians, apart from Karolak, moved out of Kraków then. Jan Byrczek had set up the Polish Jazz Association in Warsaw.

What were the Warsaw jazz musicians like?

More savvy. Many of them played in restaurants abroad; they had money. Same difference as now. They moved around more.

Before he left for the States, Komeda started work on the music to Kondratiuk's serial *Klub profesora Tutki* and he left you to finish it off. Is that how your film composing started?

It began with *Klub profesora Tutki*, but, it turns out, I'm not a film composer. I'm happy to write for film if someone wants my 'mood', my atmosphere. Even though I was very familiar with and admired Komeda's compositional technique, I don't copy what he did. I don't get drawn in as much as he did. To write a composition, a pretext will do for me; but he'd go in deep.

During your work with Komeda, did you make your own contacts in the film world?

I didn't have much to do with it. I was a jazz musician. I think I was the first pedigree Polish jazz musician. The kind that lives a jazz life, has his own position as a jazz musician and doesn't get involved in general social life, like jazz musicians used to back in the days of Komeda and Trzaskowski. We in the quintet were the first Polish jazz musicians to make a living entirely out of our own music. We didn't need to record film music or play in restaurants. After Komeda left, I recorded for film all the time; Nahorny and Trzaskowski and Kuryl too, I think, used to hire me, but I basically lived off the European market. I began playing everywhere then, to make a living out of my niche music.

In the late 1960s and the early 1970s, you also took part in a few pop music sessions.

I played with the Novi Singers. But they were jazz musicians. With Dżamble, because a friend of mine wrote lyrics for them. The rest was just session work.

How did your collaboration with the band Nurt go? They were, at that time, one of the most exciting Polish rock groups.

I played with them once or twice. As far as rock bands were concerned, I played with SBB the most, but that was in the mid-1970s.

On the other hand, your collaboration with Polish Radio's Jazz Studio was very productive.

That was Jan 'Ptaszyn' Wróblewski's band. He had a unique role, always something of an outsider's. He was younger than Komeda and Trzaskowski, and his jazz tendencies were such that he took an interest in new trends and new musicians. At one point he gathered Poland's best jazz musicians together into one formation: Studio Jazzowe PR (the Polish Radio Jazz Studio). He mainly wrote the music himself, but he also commissioned lots of compositions – much to his credit – from all different kinds of artists. And so this was an unusual band. I'm surprised by the fact that Polish Radio Jazz Studio doesn't have the place in our jazz history that it deserves. That was a very important period: 1971, 1972, 1973. Excellent sessions, interesting meetings. I sometimes listen to those recordings now: they're milestones. That band brought together the best improvisors and the best big-band radio musicians. The band operated based on two young line-ups: my quintet and Namysłowski's quartet, plus the radio musicians – first trumpet, Stanisław Mizeracki, and the radio trombonists. The rhythm section came either from the quintet or from Namysłowski.

How did this band work? Was it a studio formation? A big-band line-up that changed with every session?

Yes. That was the idea. A kind of workshop. The music was written down, but with space for improvisation. The sessions used to take place in the radio studio, in M1. That's where we used to meet. And Ptaszyn would commission the pieces beforehand. The sessions ran like film recording sessions. Totally professional: we'd play the pieces through quickly during the actual session, and then we'd record.

You once actually said in an interview that it was like having a permanent job at Polish Radio.

Because it was like having a permanent job – a very good thing for musicians. The pay from Polish Radio was very good and the sessions were fairly regular. A nice group of people, satisfaction from playing, and good music.

You wrote quite a few compositions for Polish Radio Jazz Studio.

I wrote a few. They were commissioned, for specific line-ups and specific rhythm sections.

Did you play those compositions later with your own bands?

No; I only wrote for large ensembles. Those compositions wouldn't really have suited a quintet.

How did you like those compositions of Ptaszyn's?

Ptaszyn was a creative artist; he liked tradition, but, at the same time, he was able to write in a very modern way. I can remember one particular piece – I can even remember the tune – that we played as a quartet, without piano. Like Ornette's music. Maybe more like Sonny Rollins with Don Cherry – there was a line-up like that.

When was the first time that you played with Ptaszyn?

It was in Warsaw. Even before I'd formed the quintet. Oh yes! It was at Jazz Jamboree, 1968. There was an unwritten rule on the jazz scene that, if someone wasn't playing at Jazz Jamboree, then that was bad. Every significant artist had to play there. Later, I used to deliberately flout that rule; I'd give myself time off. But I do remember the first time I wasn't going to be playing at the festival, following my last session playing with Komeda. I thought I'd go mad. I thought the stress of it would kill me. I can remember it. I can remember that moment, when I'm not playing and I don't have a band. 'Oh my God! What am I going to do?' In the end I played with Ptaszyn, in a quartet. I was lucky because it was a very interesting project. That band got noticed. Ptaszyn is highly regarded, but for something else. He's done as much for jazz as any of the greatest: Trzaskowski, Kurylewicz, Namysłowski, Urbaniak. There weren't many of them. Not to mention Komeda. That quartet didn't last long. We went our different ways. Everyone wanted to do their own thing. Jacek Bednarek and Grzegorz Gierłowski played in the rhythm section. A very good rhythm section. I was going to play with them later, and with Stanisław Cieślak too on trombone. We were going to form a band, before the quintet. We did rehearse, but the whole thing faded away. When I think back, we did play some fabulous stuff, our own music. Likewise, the music in Urbaniak's quintet was excellent, even before Komeda. That band faded away as well. What I later played with Ptaszyn was mainly radio sessions.

In your archives, I found some official correspondence from the film studios and Polish Radio. Typical of the socialist era. Certified proof that you'd attached to letters to do with registering in Warsaw and applying for an apartment. These institutions had certified in the official correspondence that you were an important colleague of theirs, and that your presence in Warsaw was therefore required.

I did try to get an apartment, but I didn't get one. Never. I didn't have a registered address either, and without being registered I couldn't even put my name down for a housing association. Communism could have finished me off. I'm not complaining about the system, but I certainly got nothing out of it. People were allocated apartments. It makes me feel good when I can manage on my own, with my talent. But at that time, everyone was on the same wage: genius or jerk, they all got the same. A jerk actually had a better time of it because he'd find it easier to lick the bureaucrats' arses. I didn't like doing that.

I've rented all my life. I rented off Danuta Kwiecińska on Skrzetuskiego Street, on Krucza Street; then off Jerzy Bartz in Żoliborz – three or four places. Bartz was a percussionist, from way back; he used to play the cruise ships and he bought a house in Żoliborz. There was a fabulous little flat down there in the basement. I moved out of that little flat to live with my wife on Górnośląska Street. When I moved out from my wife's, I lived in hotels, in tiny rooms, and at my mother's in Kraków. After my father died, my mother left Kraków and moved to Warsaw. We pooled resources and bought an apartment on Rozbrat Street. I hadn't been in a position to buy on my own before then. I didn't play in restaurants, and those were the only places where jazz musicians could earn that kind of money. I didn't make much playing jazz. I could afford a nice lifestyle – I never had any financial problems – but I couldn't afford an apartment. For a while, my mother and I lived together on Rozbrat Street. Then, later, when I was in a better financial position, I bought her a flat in Kraków.

5 Stańkomania

Your very first musical engagement at the New Year's Eve party at the School of Fine Art in 1959 saw your picture in the local paper, although, as yet, unaccompanied by your name. You had good press reviews right from the start.

That's true. That's what you need. That's why I always ask musicians how they started out and how well known they are. You have to go for it right from the off. Like Marcin Wasilewski and the musicians from the quartet; they were barely eighteen and already playing with me. I had a moment, early on, of being the worst. I was the scourge of the jam sessions. There was word going round that I was a bad jazz musician because I didn't know how to swing. But I soon had that breakthrough jam session with Kuryl and some great musicians. Maybe I needed to have the better musicians around me? I couldn't bounce off the less good ones, but the better ones gave me impetus. As soon as I began playing with Kuryl, I immediately felt appreciated. Since then, the only way's been up.

And then, within five years of that, the reviews of your performance at the jazz festival in Antwerp were sensational. That was your first performance abroad with Trzaskowski's quintet. Roman Waschko wrote in *Sztandar Młodych* ['The Banner of Youth'] that not only had the audience given your band a standing ovation, but that the folk tune 'Oj, tam u boru', ['Oh, There in the Forest!'] in the version arranged by Trzaskowski, had become a hit, and was being sung in the streets of Antwerp. Do you recall that? Was that just a typically enthusiastic coverage in the style of the organ of the ZSMP [Union of Polish Socialist Youth]?

Maybe that's how it was. I don't remember such details. I remember us always getting a good reception and fabulous reviews. When I began playing outside Poland, I was immediately in the top rank of European musicians, a guy still in my early twenties. It all started with Rolf Kühn's word. The Kühn brothers were in Germany then: Joachim, a pianist, and Rolf, who played the clarinet. They'd played at Jazz Jamboree. Rolf spread the word on the German scene that I was a very interesting trumpeter. That's what Berendt wrote about me as well.

In Poland – in fact, straight after you'd won the prize at the Southern Poland Amateur Festival – people started writing about you as the 'first trumpet'.

That is, in fact, what happened. Because who else was there playing trumpet in Poland at the time? There was only Alojzy Musiał. And then no one for ages, really. When I started playing with Komeda, I shot to number one.

Did it go to your head? After all, you were only twenty at the time.

Did it go to my head? You must be joking, with me on the Western market straight away and having to fight. Anyway – somehow it didn't. While I did have a high opinion of myself, my musical aspirations meant that I was also an unusually harsh self-critic. I never liked listening to my own recordings, because I didn't like the way I sounded. I still don't.

Did you keep setting yourself ever higher standards?

Yes. Definitely, yes. Frankly, that's an inherited trait of mine.

And maybe that ties in with the fact that, after you'd collaborated with Komeda, you went on to study music at college. And, yet, as a result of the Jazz Jamboree 1963 concert, you'd got your professional 'wings' and pocketed the title of first trumpet. Many musicians wouldn't have bothered studying after that.

Why music college? I got a piece of paper. College is college. It's better to have it than not have it. Anyway, I'll be honest with you: we had this club . . . International Lesser Club – a skivers' club. Its president was a guy who came into college every day, was officially in his fifth year there, and hadn't got any credits. I was vice-president, because I was never in class, but I passed everything. I went there mainly for the club. Jazz had kudos back then. The college professors were beginning to rate me. That's why things went well for me at college. It was quite funny in English class because my teacher used to say: 'I have to give you a "good" because you obviously know the language, being a jazz musician, travelling all over the world; so I don't even need to test you.' Playing with Komeda gave me status and I used to take advantage of it. Early on, when I had to ask for leave to perform, I did have trouble. I did have to re-sit a year. But by the time it got to my diploma exam, I was playing jazz pieces Partly classical and partly jazz.

What did you play?

I played Panufnik's *Gothic Concerto*.

Contemporary music.

The trumpet repertoire isn't a very large one. In classical, people mainly play Haydn's concerto.

Jazz musicians sometimes complain that music school is a bit blinkered.

I didn't think that. No one bothered me at music school.

Did music school have a big influence on your compositional thinking? I mean, you had composed music beforehand.
It didn't have any influence because I was writing jazz. I'd written for Jazz Darings. But even earlier, together with Jacek Ostaszewski. I was always composing. We started off playing Ornette, but then I began composing my own music.

Going back to your good press reviews: your international fame in the early days was due in large part to the support of the hugely influential German critic, producer and jazz activist Joachim-Ernst Berendt.
Berendt held an influential position, and he wrote that Jazz Darings was one of the first bands to play free jazz in Europe.

He also wrote that you were the first European trumpeter to play free.
That's what he wrote. Although that is odd, because there was Manfred Schoof in Germany, of course. I think Schoof was playing like that before I was. Maybe there was just a few months' difference. Or maybe I played in a more modern way? It's difficult to say. Actually, I did play modern very early on. That's why Komeda took me on.

Did you meet Berendt in Germany?
Berendt turned up in Poland. He'd had contact with Poland beforehand. I think he may have attended the first jazz festival in Sopot. And he definitely used to come over for Jazz Jamboree during the 1960s. In 1970 he invited me and the quintet to play at a festival that he was organizing in West Berlin.

'Berliner Jazztage' – that was a landmark concert for your career.
It was a bit of a fluke. We were first to play after the interval. The heavyweight bands were there: Charles Mingus's sextet, Oliver Nelson's big band, George Russell with his octet, I think. Fuck me! What bands! And we got a standing ovation. We didn't play for very long. It was a compact, short concert, not much over half an hour, well structured. We took our bow. I got off stage. Kisielewski had got hold of some stuff for me. I remember being in a great hurry to light up that hashish . . .

What was Kisielewski doing there?
Wacek Kisielewski was living in Berlin at the time. In a commune, with the hippies. With beautiful hippies. I was waiting for the dealer, who was meant to be coming over from his place. So off I go to the cloakroom. After a while I come back. After a long while. I can hear the applause. They hadn't been able to find me: 'People are clapping; you'll have to go out and play some more.' People had been clapping for around twenty minutes. They didn't want to let Nelson up on stage. There was a lot of commotion among the journalists. Maybe what helped was that we were a band from the East, but also the fact that it had been

the public that had singled us out in such company. It was simply a sensational reception. And that was essentially when my career really took off.

Among those first press reviews that you got, one stands out for its perverse maliciousness. It was written by Jerzy Radliński.
He was malicious.

Radliński ridicules people who 'love jazz more than music, and modernity more than jazz'. Paradoxically, however, while making these malicious comments, what he's in fact describing is Poland in the grip of a kind of 'Stańkomania'. That's an extract from the periodical *Dookoła Świata* ['Around the World'] from 1972, which ends with him sending 'Stańko to the Moon'.
Because the quintet was then at the height of its career. We returned from Germany like royalty. The hippie era had started in Poland. And we were very modern. Not just musically. We were the first jazz musicians to no longer wear suits but to dress like hippies. Word had got round that I wasn't afraid of experimenting with drugs. I smoked hashish. We had the aura of a cult band. Well, we'd had real success abroad. In the 1970s, I played with the quintet more than I ever played with Komeda and Trzaskowski. At the biggest festivals, we enjoyed equal treatment with world-class bands. We were the top Europeans.

But Radliński's comments relay what we'd today refer to as the 'pop cultural' aspect of this Stańkomania. He mentions how one fashionable young lady rings her friend and says: 'Did you see Stańko? Gorgeous! I've already told my old man that I just have to have one of those short sheepskin jackets.'
Well, yes: I did have this little sheepskin jacket. Hippie style. We were definitely flamboyant. I think it was mainly our look, our style that made our music so appealing. I was already harnessing pop culture. Only yesterday, I saw Kuba Wojewódzki, who lives nearby. He once wrote (something I found very touching) that jazz is a form of pop culture. I'm very happy with that statement. That's what it is.

The fact that I play niche music is another matter altogether. My albums don't sell more than forty-odd thousand copies. We do sometimes have bestsellers in jazz – such as *Kind of Blue*, eight million – but the record sales are determined mainly by the degree of difficulty of the music. But I am a part of pop culture. Pop culture forms a certain whole, in which there is room for everything, including very sophisticated music. People within pop culture have a particular operating strategy, which is a consequence of the fact that they are known. They might not listen to my music – and, to be perfectly honest, few people do – but they do know me. And the fact that people know and respect me, helps me play my niche music. Cultivating your image and existing in the media are aspects of pop culture and a kind of respect for the public. Those who turn their noses up at it and say, 'These are silly; these are smart', are displaying an old-fashioned attitude: the divide between the 'educated' and the 'country bumpkin'. The world's no longer like that!

Image helped me from the start; maybe I used it instinctively, but in a way that was me being true to my nature. Vitold Rek told me that, when the quintet came to play in Kraków, he was standing outside the Krzysztofory Palace and he had a hard time getting through the crowd that was trying to get into the club. There weren't any bands like that later on.

Regarding Wojewódzki and clothing – he's been trying to persuade you to release T-shirts with your image on them.
He's always going on about those T-shirts. I don't know why. He has his own T-shirts, of course. You want to be famous? Deal with it yourself. How? That's your business. You have to exist. You have to work at it. None of this 'I'm above all that'.

There are already some pirated T-shirts with you on them, based on the cover of *Music 81*.
No . . . ? Where?

I once saw some for sale in the lobby of the Congress Hall. Next to ones of Parker and Coltrane: you could get them in a few different colours.
I must tell my daughter to look into that!

At concerts with Komeda, you were still playing in a suit. When did your new style of dress first appear?
I bought my first flowery tie and flowery shirt in Vienna. I dressed to the nines when I played with Komeda. After a concert with the quintet in Malmö, I bought some Chelsea boots, with elastic bits in the uppers. I really liked the hippie style. At that time, Miles also dressed like that. I remember that little sheepskin jacket – one of those sleeveless ones. In the quintet we used to wear maxi coats, which reached right down to our feet; I brought them over from Hamburg. And along with those we wore broad-rimmed, floppy fedora hats and flowers in our hair. We were fashionable artists. The rock and roll in Poland was lousy at that time. Though Breakout were already playing,* and Włodzimierz Nahorny occasionally played with them. But jazz continued to have an elevated position.

Your flamboyance must also have irritated people.
That definitely irritated people. In that communist greyness, it wasn't like it is now when people in the street look different from one other. Everyone used to wear berets and nylon raincoats. If you saw a guy walking along next to you in a maxi coat and fedora hat, he definitely stuck out. We caused a sensation on the streets.

---

* *Series Editor's note:* Breakout played a brand of blues and rock.

Were there any fights?

Well, yes. I remember once walking along with my girlfriend, who was wearing a miniskirt, and this woman rushed up to her and ripped her skirt off. 'The devils!' she kept yelling.

Did you make a big impression on the girls?

Definitely. We had a few faithful groupies. None of the other Polish jazzers lived as rock-and-roll a lifestyle as we did.

When Chet Baker got famous in Gerry Mulligan's quartet, when they played in Los Angeles in the 1950s, he smoked joints non-stop, and during the breaks between sets he'd have sex with girls in a car parked outside the club. Did that sometimes happen here as well?

That did sometimes happen. We had groupies hanging around us at every festival. Sex, drugs and jazz. Rock and roll came later, but the jazz musicians were the first. Even before the hippie era, the rock musicians used to base their outfits on the jazz musicians'. The jazz musicians were always flamboyantly dressed. It was be-bop, after all, that started off all those style trends, which rock later picked up on. The name alone points to be-bop being like hip-hop. No one back then was as elegant as Dizzy Gillespie in his Parisian berets, were they? I remember a taxi ride in New York with Cecil Taylor. The taxi driver took one look at us and smiled: 'Jazz musicians!' he said.

The jazz musicians of the 1940s and 1950s were wilder than the desperado rock musicians who came later.

Wilder. Definitely wilder.

There was a compilation album that came out recently of recordings by Joe Maini – a forgotten saxophonist from the 1950s. He was seen as the successor to Charlie Parker, but he died at the age of thirty-four. He was a heroin user, but the cause of his death was something else. He apparently shot himself during a game of Russian roulette.*

That's how they lived. That's the life of a desperado. On the edge. Dicing with death. You have a different trip then. You think differently.

You like to refer to yourself as a desperado, and yet during your scout movement years you lived like a puritan. Did your contact with jazz and drugs drag you over to the other side somehow?

It took me a split second to switch over. I turned the family shyness, the stage fright and the lack of confidence inside out. The contrast! I tell you – in one day. That one party where I played with Kisielewski and Kowal. Cigarettes, wine and jazz. In one fell swoop. I started coming home late at night. As Witkacy

---

* *Series Editor's note:* This is contested. See, for example, M. Myers, "The Truth About Joe Maini". JazzWax blog, 16 June 2010. https://www.jazzwax.com/2010/06/the-truth-about-joe-mainis-death.html

said: you have the 'schizoid' type and you have the 'pyknic' type. I was more of a schizoid – the schizoid type with a certain kind of split personality. I'm still like that. That's why I chose the life of a desperado. There were many people like that. Modigliani, for instance. A delicate, sensitive young man, sick with tuberculosis. He was supposedly dying, but he went to Paris and changed completely – 180 degrees – and he managed to live a fair bit longer. It's easy to change track. To switch from puritan to desperado. I harness extremes. There's a professor who specializes in bipolar disorder (something she has herself) who's written that she wouldn't swap with anyone else. I understand that. I have it too and I wouldn't swap either. Those manic states are so pleasurable.

My father looked after himself and was a hypochondriac. But I'm the opposite. I went all the way – totally, completely, utterly – so much so that . . . well, actually, one might say it's a miracle I survived.

What sort of situations are you thinking about?
There was one rough patch when I was hanging around with the heroin addicts on Krakowskie Przedmieście Street. I collapsed in the street there. End of the 1980s, beginning of the 1990s. There was a little bench opposite the Bristol Hotel where the most desperate cases used to sit. And I'd go there sometimes. To self-destruct. I used to have moments like that, following on from alcoholic benders that lasted several weeks. I was never a regular heroin user. More of a sporadic one. Just like Russian roulette. AIDS had already appeared.

You've often stressed that you used drugs as a form of pain relief.
That's definitely how I see it. Not as a consciousness-expanding substance but as an anaesthetic. A particular kind of anaesthetic. You get a greater high, but also a greater low. It's about the contrast.

So were psychedelic drugs, such as hashish and marijuana, a source of inspiration for you?
Absolutely not. My art goes its own way. The idea that if I light up a joint my art's going to be amazing has always struck me as absurd. Maybe that's what put me off the hippies later on, that they were making a philosophy out of this state of stupor. I didn't turn hashish into a psychedelic phenomenon. I was closer to the philosophy of the Black musicians, who simply saw it as 'party time'. For me, it was an intoxicating substance that gave me a certain pleasure. I used it in the same way as I did fine clothes. I remember once thinking: 'Why, five minutes ago, I was feeling like a god, so I'm a god?' No. That's impossible. I'd make an adjustment. I'd immediately try to adjust my playing, so I'd have musical control. I'd try to level out the subjectivity of this state through my intellect and technique. Many people believe that dope stimulates talent, but sobriety gives greater precision. People like Parker were addicts. Only once he was under the influence was he normal. The complete opposite of what people think.

It's like with the leading rock desperado Lou Reed: when asked about drugs, he declared that, living in the era of technology in a huge city, he takes them not for kicks but to feel normal.

We now have a very unnatural situation. Civilization has leapt forward. We don't have the sort of threats we used to have – thugs with cudgels attacking the village. Life's becoming easier, yet surviving the everyday is a stressful nightmare. You need to tune into yourself – how to live. And when people can't manage, they turn to dope, to anaesthetize themselves. These days, anaesthesiology is a very important branch of medicine, because the success of an operation is dependent on the dose given by the anaesthetist.

There's also a huge market in prescription antidepressants.

That's the same thing. But much worse. Because narcotics are substances that people have had experience of since Sumerian times, maybe even before then. Even heroin comes from opium. Antidepressants are new products from the chemical industry.

Miles Davis even used the term 'Dark Magus' as the title of one of his albums. Neither white magic nor black magic, but dark magic. There were also those who did actually use it: Fela Kuti or Serge Gainsbourg – the first Frenchman to assimilate Black music to such a great degree. They were all desperadoes. They all strayed into risky areas, so they could harness the energy from the dark, chaotic borders of their consciousness and then turn it into art. That's what their artistry was based on. That's what dark magic is.

That's the lifestyle of a desperado. Then a person is close to so-called 'enlightenment'. A serious threat to our life changes everything. We have an epiphany. A condensed form of knowledge, of thought, of impressions. Of everything.

So, I guess expanding consciousness does come into play, then?

These are biological mechanisms, which we humans, as a species, crank up constantly. We are effectively automatons, after all. Our whole system of thought is 'yes' and 'no', 'plus' and 'minus'. It's written in the brain. What we are only just starting to do with computers has long existed within nature. Each one of us has everything written in the brain; we just need the programmes. I think that in our brains we have the programmes of the very first bacteria. There's this primal experience: when an organism is threatened by death, it feels the urge to live. It's a very primitive mechanism, which is evolving: for example, it turns into epiphanies. A heightened, exquisite state (which evolved out of the clarity of thought that served to protect us); it's associated with pleasure. We can hardly expect artists not to exploit it. Art makes use of madness. You know, people do all kinds of things . . . Those who like extreme sex strangle each other to make the orgasm more intense. And then they top it up with heroin, to get a full-blown orgasm. People get up to these sorts of things. Bam! Ramp it up!

Jazz musicians had speedballs. They mixed heroin with cocaine. I definitely used dope in my own particular way – alcohol, hashish and amphetamine. Lots of people do that. At one time it was said that some addicts take this, others take that . . . Well, maybe that's how it used to be. A hundred years ago. Nowadays, everything's taken together. Combined, cocktailed.

6 A Proust-Reading Boxer

You've just taken up residence in New York, in Manhattan, near Central Park. A few blocks away from Miles's house, on the way to Harlem.

Is that a dream come true?
People ask me what my dream is. Whether I dream of playing with anyone in particular. I don't have that kind of dream. To be perfectly honest, I play with whomever I want. Musically, I do what I want to. I have to take realities into account, but so does everyone. Even if you're Miles, you need to take realities into account. I don't usually have dreams but, if anything, then something like wanting to be a New Yorker for a while. I've always liked reading historical books: monographs about civilizations, eras and peoples. Just as Rome used to be the world's number one city – its centre; just as I used to imagine ancient Ur teeming with life, that's how I see the city of New York nowadays. With its streets – 53rd, 125th – where the history of jazz was written. That's where the clubs are. The Village Vanguard; Birdland. Places I loved as a jazz fan. And those I used to see in American films. That's what I wanted. And here it is. That's exactly where I live. Mine's 86th Street. Alongside the middle of Central Park, between Harlem and Lower Manhattan. When I first came to New York, thirty years ago, I stayed near 63rd, just where Central Park begins. I'd gone to see New York. Jan Byrczek was there. Adam Makowicz, Michał Urbaniak. I played a few gigs. There was a concert at Randy and Michael Brecker's club in memory of Zbigniew Seifert. I stayed for a month at the YMCA. After that, Edward Vesala and I stayed in Columbus Circle, in a hotel used by the hookers and dope dealers who worked 42nd Street. We stayed there right among those gangsters. When you stay in a hotel and hear the rumble of Manhattan, it's infectious. Everyone misses it down the line. They want to come back. I used to constantly think about settling down there. My wife used to live in New York. She has American nationality. Urbaniak's always going back there. He's back in New York again.

But you try living there. In that cruel devil of a place; and, beautiful as it is, it can strangle you with its bare hands. Depression will grind you down. Those crowds of people. And among them the insane: those who couldn't stand the pressure. There's a really hard-fought battle for survival going on there.

Do you intend to move to New York?
I'll not be living there much. I can already see that I'll barely be able to set aside more than a few months a year for New York. I have to travel all over the world to earn a living. Everyone travels. There's only Paul Motian who doesn't leave New York. That's a scoop, for a jazz musician to be able to do that, because the Village Vanguard and other places give him lots of gigs. Motian is seventy-six years old and only plays in New York. Everyone's jealous of him because he doesn't have to leave town. Everyone travels, to a lesser or greater extent. A lot of musicians teach. Reggie Workman, Billy Harper, Joe Lovano.

What sort of expectations do you have as a New Yorker?
I don't have any expectations. Well, I do have ECM here, and my agents. I'm mainly interested in meeting musicians and having one foot in the biggest and most important jazz scene in the world. I've already met many of the New York musicians at concerts, and I know who to pay attention to. That's how it was with Craig Taborn. I've offered him a gig and, as he lives in Brooklyn, I'll be asking him about the New York musicians. In America, there's still a split between the Black and White musicians. But I'll be hanging out with both; only musical concerns will determine what will suit me. Well, I don't know what to expect. I just want to live in a big city. How many times a year do I play in Warsaw? Once, twice. Three at most. Do I need to play more often in New York? No. I'm a free man. I've been alone and free all my life. And, that being the case, why shouldn't I make the most of my freedom?

The world today is one place. That's always interested me. Cosmopolitanism, the mixing of species, the fact that we're all alike. I could hardly not come to this city, when I get such a massive turn-on seeing such a mix of people in the street and in the subway. Other kinds of beauty, other ways of dressing. Different cultures. I'm also going there to brush up on the language. The laziest way of doing it. So I can read Faulkner in the original. I love him. Faulkner's narrative is so beautiful, so jazzy, as if it's rocking gently. We jazz musicians also have a narrative; as improvisors, we actually move in a linear way. I transform my narrative into music, in a different way, not rationally, but irrationally, more intuitively.

Life in a city which is the cradle of modern jazz, of the avant-garde, gives the impression of being the ultimate challenge for a jazz musician from Europe.
I don't see it as a challenge, but as a result of the path I've trodden, which I'm increasingly pleased with, even though it's been hard-going. It might seem that things have been easy for me. No; it's been hard. I've had to battle constantly with adversity. But, basically – I keep going. I keep going. I don't give up. Surely, steadily, I keep on going. I first made it to the world stage through ECM. I've been very successful. And, right now, I'm someone. I have a global position. This is the fifth or sixth time in a row that I've been placed between fifth and eighth as best trumpeter in the *DownBeat* rankings. I've also been placed as a

composer, which I'm very pleased about. Those are the critics' rankings – in other words, by people who know.

And what eminent company I've found myself in! Ahead of me: Roy Hargrove, Terence Blanchard, Wynton Marsalis, Dave Douglas. Enrico Rava's there too, along with me, the only one from Europe, but he lived in the States for fifteen years and he's very well known there. Definitely one of the best trumpeters around today. That's why I'm in no hurry. I'd like to record an album with the quintet now, and after that I'll check out the New York people. I think it'll take me about a year to get acclimatized over there before I really get going – shit, for the last time in my life. I'll take my time. I want to live comfortably, without any stress. Go to museums, art galleries, the opera, concerts, and live the life of a really big city.

Does this move also mark a new stage in your career? You've now finished working with the quartet that you played with for over ten years.
Definitely. I came out of the avant-garde, but I'm moving towards simplicity. When I started working with Manfred Eicher again in the 1990s, when I recorded *Litania*, I remember most enjoying 'Ballada' and the theme tune from *Rosemary's Baby*. Because they were simple. I didn't have things like that on my albums. But I've always leaned towards simplicity. When I met the quartet, I was delighted to have some musicians who'd come out of the more communicative, musical mainstream, and that I'd be teaching them free, so we'd be able to play everything, all kinds of things. I had a long period with them. I wouldn't want to play music that is wholly communicative, as in 'commercial'. But I am trying to become increasingly communicative. I don't know why. For my own pleasure. And also because I sometimes like listening to that kind of music too. At home I have fado alongside Caetano Veloso. I don't have any Prince or Sting anymore, but I did for a little while. I enjoy watching MTV. I thought Madonna's most recent productions were quite good. I really like the New Black pop culture, its image. I like watching it. I have quite a range. And I think that very modern music, free, is best listened to live, at concerts, because it's a certain kind of mystery.

I prefer seeing Cecil Taylor at concerts because listening to a record of his is like watching theatre on video. But when Cecil goes up on stage, he creates a depth, a mystical, esoteric depth. His artistry has different qualities. To experience these, you have to participate in the project. Because this is very serious stuff. It's improvisations, certain incredibly complicated structures – complicated, yet at the same time beautiful and deep, like you can sometimes get in the theatre.

I've had some contact with Krzysztof Warlikowski's theatre. I worked with him for a while, and I have a great deal of respect for him. I also have respect for the way he operates: for his energy, for his excellent artistic strategy. He knows what to take on, what to do. Nowadays, an artist should have all that. He should, because the world is increasingly complex and we all have to be increasingly excellent in different fields. I think that it'll eventually get to the point where, if we have two boxers, each as good as Tyson, and one of them has read Proust and the other hasn't, then the winner will be the one who has read Proust.

The whole world's going in that direction. We expect more and more of artists. That's why I'm going with duality. Alongside my tendency to take off in directions far removed from the cultural middle, I also have a tendency towards playing simply. It's quite an extreme approach, but it's one I like. I like simple melodies. That artistic duality of mine often clashes with the views of artistic purists, but I'm uncompromising, and so these same purists respect me as well. Tony Oxley has told me straight that he doesn't like the way I combine things in my playing; he doesn't like playing timed music and he doesn't play like that with anybody. He has with me. Because he liked playing with me. He was the first to say about my compositions, about 'Maldoror's War Song', that 'It's not such a rhythmically simple number. Everything inside it is bent.' It *was* bent.

I'm now working on new compositions and I've started with simplicity. But simplicity soon loses its value, and I have to add something, twist it, complicate it. I often start off composing with very simple structures, which I later complicate. That might seem a somewhat unnatural way of doing things. Yes, it is an unnatural way, but it does allow me certain possibilities ... When I have something complicated, for example a certain chord within a simple composition, it allows me to play expressively at that particular moment. With screams and timbre, rather than a nice tune or functional harmony. If I write a simple bossa nova, I can play: *Ooh-ooh-wuh-wuh-wuh-ooh – ooh-wuh-wuh-wuh-ooh – ooh-wuh-wuh-ah-ah-ah! Ah-ah-ah-ah-ah! – Ah-ah-ah-ah-ach!* As if I were screaming. An abstract thing. The kind of thing you didn't get in music, because pure sound was obligatory. Music came out of that; screaming was in nature.

In modern avant-garde music, the scream, rather than pure sound, was the focus of attention. I'd like to ask you about modernity. You've mentioned that in Kraków, in the early 1960s, there was conflict in the jazz world between the traditionalists and the modernists. And you, right from the start, clearly championed modern jazz.

Yes. I did that intentionally. I knew that, if I wanted to have my own style, I had to have my own sound. At first, my sound was similar to Don Ellis's. I didn't like Ellis, but he did have his own sound. I also paid attention to my own sound. Not that I practised it, because it's not something that you can get through practice. I simply wanted to have my own sound. I didn't know exactly what kind. Just my own. In tune with my soul, my inner being. I knew that the more modern the music I played, the easier I would find it to create my own style. I wouldn't have to copy. It would be easier for me with new material that hadn't yet been fully formed. It was all a conscious choice.

In that choice, was there a desire to surpass, to kill off, your masters?
No. No, not to kill them. Not to compete with them. To go beyond, further, to pick up just a thread.

To escape their influence?
That's what Makowicz did. I just didn't want to lose any time. I wanted a shortcut. As a music lover, I did listen to older music. Makowicz, on the other hand, ostentatiously, did not listen to the standards. To me that's a bit of a mechanical way of doing it – not listening to the masters.

It was precisely your modernity that fired Berendt's enthusiasm. He was fascinated by modern music, the essence of which, in those days, he regarded as free jazz with sounds that were dirty and deformed, which moved from form to abstraction and spasms of energy. What does modernity mean to you?
I am drawn to things that are unusual. There are always misfits within the population. I've always been drawn to these 'painted birds.'* I'm probably one of those too. I'd never played traditional jazz. I wasn't interested in its joyfulness and cheeriness. I preferred things that were dirtier, less academic. I associated classical music with purity, precision and permanence. Dirty, Black jazz – like Thelonious Monk's music – I always associated more with truth, a certain human truth. I still think that.

Attempts have been made to define modernity as an awareness of the discontinuous nature of time. The old time of religious communities and the cosmic sense of time give way to the jagged experiences of the industrial era, the shock of big-city life, which, of course, also gave birth to jazz. This ties in with what Berendt wrote about jazz, perceiving the chaos within modernity.
Interesting. There are lots of views on the matter. And we're constantly adding new ones. Of course, modernity is our inherent tendency to achieve what doesn't exist in nature. There is no such order in nature like that which Picasso painted in 'The Young Ladies of Avignon'. Paintings are not a reflection of a natural view. We display what we want to.

How does Rembrandt look at a surgical operation? In reality, that's not how light falls. But it's a certain viewpoint, which has a psychological basis. This is how the doctor who's carrying out the operation sees it – brightness in this patch of human body, but blackness all around.

Art is constantly bringing us fresh perspectives. It expands certain phenomena, just like life is simply an extension of a particular compound of amino acids. Before that, it didn't exist. Hence our pursuit of the modern, our respect for it, despite its being incompatible with our habits. Everything moves on. On and on.

---

* *Translator's note: Painted Bird* is the title of a controversial bestselling novel by Jerzy Kosiński (1933–1991). The term is now taken to mean someone who is an outcast and/or victim of persecution.

Is this also about going beyond ourselves?
Forever going beyond ourselves. We don't realize how rich and vast time is. It's a downright mystical phenomenon. Considering how now, as we're talking, we can tell each other so much over the course of three-quarters of an hour, so how many things might have occurred if we'd have been able to talk for a million years? And we've existed for several billion.

Your mystical leanings are coming out.
Mystical, because I feel the vastness and depth of this process of evolution. But, on the other hand, it has this prosaic and primitive mechanism; except that it's multiplied by infinity. Its mysticism is unleashed by number and time.

Do you have a sense of the supernatural without a sacred body involved, in the factual evidence of life itself?
Yes. Without the sacred. It comes from the very evidence of the mathematical fact of quantity and time.

That perspective of millions of years and the laws of evolution: is it not unsettling?
It is. It often gets to me. Well, it does and it doesn't – because it feels right to me. I think that our richness and the richness of life in general springs from genetic variations. Our modern times have allowed us to ponder over this. Billions of genes and two different ones within a certain group – well, that's a difference; it has to be, though it can be invisible. If a dog has a single grey hair, that's insignificant. Man's capacity for abstract thought might have begun on the same principle as that grey hair, which was a certain kind of defect, a genetic fault. We didn't need a skill of that kind. It was a random mutation, which turned out to be extremely useful. Abstract thought – in other words, numbers, mathematics – has created our entire civilization. Those who were able to count to ten rather than two – those who thought – survived. We are the children of evolution. This accounts for everything.

William S. Burroughs, whose early books you like, made this the main message of his later books: 'Man is an artefact designed for space travel'. When asked to explain, he'd say that dreams prepare us for space travel, because there's neither gravity nor time in them. This reads like faith in the power of imagination.
Expressed in a very literary way.

Do you attach any importance to dreams?
For many years, I didn't dream at all, because, when you smoke hashish, you stop having dreams. Now I do have dreams. I do attach importance to them in the sense that they do affect me; but I'm not a great believer in them. I think that they're disjointed; they're a product of the state we're in, but they don't essentially influence our life so much as have a relaxing effect on us. They

enable us to unwind and regulate that strange creation that is our personality. It's a natural way of maintaining our own equilibrium. I've actually noticed that there are certain uncomfortable things that I've forgotten. I ought to have remembered such important things, but they've been forgotten.

That's why some people go in for psychoanalysis, rebirthing and hypnosis, so they can recall those things.
I don't have any particular desire to do that. It's good that my mind's forgotten such things.

Your evolutionism is optimistic.
It's definitely optimistic. Though I supposedly have a melancholy nature, I think that everything we do, every occurrence, even the worst, is basically optimistic, because that's just how it has to be: that's the way. Evil also has a part to play in this. Gnosticism doesn't appeal to me. This is how things are meant to be. Fires are a blessing for forests. Maybe catastrophes are the foundation of our existence as a species.

To what degree has music proven to be a life coach for you, shown you the art of living?
Music is a certain order that we've arranged within sound, which doesn't exist in nature. Such an arrangement of waves doesn't exist. We had to make the instruments first, to create it. It's that abstraction that most appeals to me about music. My philosophical thoughts can be very private and very trivial. And it matters that they're trivial. For me, those big existential questions, those questions that remain unanswered, are not relevant. I am a part of some machinery that's living and moving forward. I feel instinctively that those existential questions that are somewhere within me, and powerful, could damage me. The great power of the ordinary and the average is that we do not dwell on it. We just live and enjoy the moment; we have babies. That's why music is so very dear to me. By its very nature, it's far removed from the ordinary, and, because it's what's most important to me, it also deflects my thoughts from those fundamental questions. In this way, it brings balance to my life.

Does music help you provide non-verbal answers to those fundamental, unanswerable questions?
Music does not provide answers. It deals with the same order of things in its own different, natural way. It doesn't need any questions, or any words, or any conclusions.

Is music important to you as an escape from reality, or is it more a means of creating new worlds?
Creating new worlds and beauty. A certain order, which manifests in this beauty and gets me into a specific state. A state that is both mystical and deep, and which we celebrate without posing those big, unanswerable questions.

The thing that gives jazz its particular expression, primarily against the background of the European tradition of classical music, is its rhythm and improvisation.
Rhythm and pulse send us into a trance, which is very old and still powerful. That trance is essential.

That's rhythm, but does the art of improvisation translate to the way you live your life?
Entirely. That's an important question. Because, I actually use the technique of improvisation everywhere. I don't like fighting, but I have to fight. I've spent a long time thinking about this. Everyone's fighting; rivalry is a fundamental part of humanity. I'm not making a value judgement. One might assume that this battle is the most important thing to do with life. We exist because it selects us; it's because of this that we're getting faster, getting better. When I need to, I do pick up a fuckin' axe and swing it around, but I don't like doing that. I withdraw from competition. Maybe that's why I don't like competing in races. I don't do sport. I do cultivate this aversion because it's a trait of mine: that's me. I reach my goals in a different way – thanks to improvisation. I don't attack; I go around. I use a chance event which takes me here and there. If something stands in my way – like this, in the middle – thanks to improvisation, I can think up a way to avoid it. I'd never have come up with the idea had I been fighting. In this way, I look for different solutions. And I usually find them. For example, capitalizing on a mistake.

The way improvisation works is that, when you make a mistake, you don't try to correct it, because there isn't time. If you were composing, then you would correct the mistake, but it's already here in real time. That being the case, you have to justify it.

I'm reminded of what Herbie Hancock said about playing with Miles. He recalled how Miles played a wrong note, a completely wrong one. He held the mistake. He reinforced it. And the music caught up with the note. Turbulence built up around that strange note. And the whole thing leapt forward! Something happened to the expression and the tension! The surge was incredible. That's what improvisation's discoveries are about. What Miles played was mistakes, but they were mistakes he allowed. His strength of character and his self-belief meant that Miles reacted this way instinctively. He didn't reject it or try to correct it. He held it! And life caught up with his mistake! And justified it. Something appeared that without the mistake would never have come into being. There are recordings like that. The expression increases. The whole thing changes in a magical way; it's not flat and accurate. After all, it's due to mistakes in the copying of our DNA that we exist, as people.

How can art not approve of this? Creativity arises out of mistakes. In the case of improvisation, for a piece to have power, you also need to know when not to play anything, like Miles did. You know, when you play alongside Coltrane, who does brilliant solos, you need to be Miles, so you can lead the band and have room for yourself. You have to rise above it, to not play anything. Following one big solo, you can't have another. Why? You have to have silence. Miles had a superhuman approach to the matter. Because it's a natural human reflex to want to show off too. Especially when it's your own band.

Zośka (Komeda's wife) once said to me: 'Why are you like that? It's so high-minded of you, that on *Litania*, on "Ballad for Bernt",* you didn't play a solo.' Well, of course I didn't. It was a 'Ballad for Bernt'. That relates to my faith in Miles: his philosophy rather than his music. I sometimes wonder why I'm so highly regarded, despite all my faults and failings. Maybe that's why. People place a very high value on technique – you see how highly regarded people like Chick Corea (or our very own Leszek Możdżer) are. We value artistic skill, but also the fact that people are beyond these things. Artistic skill is a beautiful thing, but we also value Monk, who had no pianistic technique. With defects, there is also power and greatness. Because defects are also fundamental to our humanity. Evolution doesn't do what's best, but what comes out. Something gets chaotically cobbled together, and from improvisational activity certain things emerge entirely by accident. Not what's best. No.

Are improvisation and mistakes inseparable to you?
It's about the freshness that comes from blindsiding with a mistake. It's a very refined technique. Anything that's valuable comes out of improvisation. Mozart. Chopin. They improvised as well. Or Lautréamont, in literature. *The Songs of Maldoror* – he improvised. *And*, on top of that, he banged out note clusters on the piano. Not chords. Note clusters! And that inspired his crazy writing.

And can improvisation also be applied to those big, unanswered existential questions?
It does help. For a long time now, we haven't had 'yes' and 'no'. Everything is in between. 'Yes' and 'no' would be too easy. And it's never easy.

In *The Revolution of Everyday Life*, a cult publication at the time of the Paris Spring in 1968, Raoul Vaneigem juxtaposes jazz improvisation and the art of living. With rebellious passion, he declares that improvisation allows us to live in the present, to escape all the rigours of civilization. He writes: 'The way we improvise our daily lives, in its best moments, can be compared to jazz

---

* *Series Editor's note:* The ballad – as its name suggests – was written for Bernt Rosengren, who was in the sextet that recorded 'Litania'.

improvisation.' And then Vaneigem goes on to mention the African sense of rhythm, which depends on 'introducing discontinuity into the static balance determined by rhythm and metre'.

There's a simple reason for that discontinuity: that much African music is three over two. There's never any continuity there; after all, this rhythm is a combining of even and odd. It's never equal. There's always a certain unknown. There's always something left that hasn't been added up mathematically. That's where the state of unease comes from. All of jazz, all of swing comes from that. Uncertainty. We can't divide two by three because it can't be divided. And yet it can be. As can their unaccented syncopation. Hence its fluidity, leading us into a trance, into a certain state of magic.

Trance as an answer to this unease?

Exactly. I think that's what it is. That indivisibility leads us into a permanent trance. It's a complicated philosophical phenomenon: the combining of even and odd. Mathematics, philosophy, the advanced sciences have tried to explain it. Yet here everything resolves itself artistically. When we play, we move into a state of unease and, so, into a higher state.

7 'I Was Marlene Dietrich'

Nowadays we only have a hazy recollection of your quintet from the late 1960s and early 1970s. The album *Music for K*, the one it's mainly remembered for, doesn't give much indication of the band's improvisatory nature. But isn't it actually this quintet that was your most important group?

It's difficult to say whether it was the most important one. No doubt your first group is like your first woman, your first lover. You remember her the best. And the quintet was effectively my first band. The preceding ones were supposedly mine, but this one was more like a real one. I formed it when I was already living in Warsaw. I can't remember what year it was. I was meant to be playing with Stanisław Cieślak on trombone, Jacek Bednarek on bass and Grzegorz Gierłowski on percussion. I was waiting for rehearsals, which were meant to be taking place in Krynica Morska, but they never went ahead. Somehow it all just faded away. So, I did some arm-twisting in Kraków and I found some musicians there. For the rhythm section I got drummer Janusz Stefański and bassist Jan Gonciarczyk – guys a few years younger than me, from Zbigniew Seifert's quartet. At that time, Zbigniew was only playing alto sax. A new line-up emerged (Stefański, Gonciarczyk, Seifert, Janusz Muniak) and turned into the quintet. Then Seifert began playing violin, only playing alto sax occasionally. He had a very interesting way of playing the violin – Coltrane-style. Muniak played tenor sax and percussion. All in all, we became a band with a very interesting sound. Gonciarczyk was soon replaced by Bronisław Suchanek, who was new blood and, for those times, had a very different way of playing. He had artistic inclinations, wide horizons. He was interested in art. We were a team.

Apparently, the quintet's beginnings came out of a few trial months with just Stefański: drums plus trumpet.

We duetted a lot in the jazz club in Kraków, to get used to playing with each other. I liked trying out drummers. I did the same with Edward Vesala. Duetting, to just get the timing, the rhythm and the trumpet.

In his famous *Jazzbuch*, on which a few generations of jazz fans have been brought up, Joachim-Ernst Berendt refers to the quintet on one occasion within a very specific context. He writes about bands (this is so spicy, I'm going to quote it), saying that they 'compensated for the isolation of the individual expressing himself without restraint (which is where a music that knows no harmonic or formal ordering factor may easily lead) with much stronger and more intensely personal collective relationships'. And, as examples of such bands, he mentions, among others, groups such as Albert Ayler's, Archie Shepp's, Peter Brötzmann's, John Stevens's and your own. Did you really live like that?

We lived as one organism. It was the hippie era. I was mainly friends with Bronisław Suchanek. But with Seifert as well, and Janusz Stefański. We spent time together. Stefański bought a car and we toured together. We were reluctant to bring women, wives or girlfriends, with us. On tour, a band's always together, and we got on very well. When you're on tour, you mainly listen to music. And, in the car after concerts, you talk all the time about the last gig. You talk non-stop about music. You could call it a never-ending education, especially in free music. When you don't talk, you're still saying something, because silence is also a kind of commentary. I remember moments of extraordinary elation playing with the quintet.

Do you recall any particular events or have any anecdotes that might convey the closeness that you had at the time?

We had nicknames in the band. Muniak was 'Marlene'. As in Marlene Dietrich. Maybe because of his long hair. Why? I don't know. Those were just random abstract associations. A kind of English humour linked to being high, to who knows what. The logic was fleeting. Seifert was 'Golda Meir'. She was the Israeli prime minister at the time. Maybe the association was to do with his looks? She had similar glasses. Suchanek was 'Sofia Loren'. I don't think Stefański had a nickname. And I was . . . Hang on! Sorry. I was 'Marlene'. Muniak was 'Greta Garbo'. At one point we called him 'Greta'. Muniak was a bit different. He was already married when he joined the band. His wife was really nice; she didn't interfere with the music. We were still at school when he, at the age of seventeen or eighteen, was playing in restaurants and earning money. He had to support the family. He played with some very good bands in the restaurant.

What about Seifert?

Above all, he was passionate about music. Music meant the world to him.

He had a classical training.

Classical. My father heard him play somewhere and formed my opinion of him: 'a fantastic violinist'. Seifert was one of the best violinists at music school. His professor couldn't get over the fact that he wasn't performing as a soloist. It's the average violinists who go into orchestras, but it was clear from the start that Seifert, with his flair, was centre-stage material. But he got drawn into jazz. Mainly Coltrane.

(here and opposite)
Promotional brochure for
the Tomasz Stańko Quintet,
prepared by PAGART (Polish
Artists' Agency), 1972.
Courtesy Anna Stańko

TOMASZ STAŃKO QUINTET

"...the greatest surprise among the non-big-band events at this year's Berliner Jazztage was Polish trumpeter Tomasz Stańko with his Quintet. This 28-year old music academy graduate presented some unusually live jazz of high calibre, with a specific style reminiscent of a truly international character."

Marianne Eichholz,
SAARBRUCKER ZEITUNG

"This album has just been voted one of the five best jazz records of 1970 by the European Jazz Federation. I'll go along with the EJF, but I would also add that the personnel represent five of the leading jazz instrumentalists in Europe today. The fact that they all come from Poland says a lot for the Polish jazz scene.

Together, they represent a very closely knit jazz group – and in this age of the free jazz movement it is often hard to find a closely knit group (...)

Suchanek, who was 20 when this was recorded, is a remarkable bass player. For his age, is outstanding – almost in the Davis, Garrison and Mingus – yes Mingus – echelon. Then there is Stełoński whose tasteful drumming must make him the best European drummer.

The two horn players, Seifert and Muniak, are good technicians on their instruments, and improvise well. They are, however, slightly overshadowed by the sheer brilliance of Tomasz Stańko – and he is Miles ahead of any trumpet in Europe – and the pun is intentional!

The jazz here is modern. Some might call it avantgarde which, to a certain extent, it is. But it can be enjoyed by those who are not turned in to the "way-out".

Some enterprising British record company should release this album".

Ed Mann,
GLOUCESTER WEEKLY NEWS, 1971

BRONISLAW SUCHANEK

Bass

Graduate of the Katowice Higher School of Music. Considered to be the best jazz bass player in Poland. Very much in love with classical music. Treats his instrument with great breadth; adapts and adds all new achievements in music.

Has accompanied many Polish and foreign musicians. Performances in Czechoslovakia, GDR, Denmark, West Berlin and GFR. Participated in Jazz Week '71 in Hungary and the Bilzen Jazz Festival in Belgium.

JANUSZ STEFANSKI

Drums

Acknowledged as the best drummer in Poland in the last "Jazz" monthly magazine poll. Graduate at the Kraków State Higher School of Music. Plays with the Polish Radio Jazz Studio and with leading Polish jazz groups. Also plays contemporary music. Has performed in Czechoslovakia, GDR, Bulgaria, GFR, Norway, West Berlin, Denmark. Participated in the Bilzen Jazz Festival in Belgium.

ZBIGNIEW SEIFERT

Plays: alto saxophone and violin. Composer. Graduate of the Cracow State Higher School of Music. Worked several years with his own quintet. One of the few violinists in Europe who play free jazz.

Currently collaborating with the international Bosko Petrovic group.

Has performed in West Germany, Hungary, West Berlin, Denmark, GDR.

Participated in the Ljubljana '71 International Jazz Festival.

JANUSZ MUNIAK

Soprano and tenor saxophones, flute.

Took first place in the "Jazz" monthly magazine's poll in the soprano and tenor saxophone categories.

Has worked with all leading Polish jazz groups. One of the first to play free jazz.

Has performed in Yugoslavia, West Berlin, West Germany, Denmark, Czechoslovakia, GDR, the USSR.

Was there any aesthetic friction between you, given that earlier you'd gone through an Ornette Coleman stage?

I listened to a lot of Coltrane. He was the best of the avant-garde. A modern musician. Because he didn't just make those famous quartet recordings, but formidable improvisations in a duo as well.

Did you listen to those great Coltrane demonstrations of free jazz: *Ascension*; *Om*; *Meditations*?

Yes, yes, yes. That was just coming in.

What was Seifert like in person?

He was a really lovely person. So calm. He was always fragile, delicate.

Was he aware of his health problems right from the start?

You could sense it right from the start. But he could also be a tough cat. I can't remember exactly how he managed to keep his quartet going with Stefański and Gonciarczyk.

Then in 1976, in Germany, Seifert recorded his famous album *Man of the Light* with Joachim Kühn, Cecil McBee and Billy Hart.

That was much later, because we parted company in 1973. I only remember him as a musician in my quintet. When the quintet disbanded, we left Darmstadt and returned to Poland, but Seifert stayed in Germany, permanently.

How free was the quintet's music?

There was a whole period, around 1967–1968, when in Hybrydy in Warsaw, we played totally improvised music. Some of the gigs were amazing. I remember one where we played together as one. It didn't get recorded, unfortunately. We played brilliantly at the workshops in Berlin, and in Chodzież. The thing with improvised music is that, at a certain point, for some unknown reason, it spirals out of control. It becomes more difficult to remember the old things; the music goes its own way. If you don't have any tenets, like Cecil Taylor (where there's no dramatic tension, but there is energy, a fast-running stream of energy), it's awfully difficult to control your playing. Besides, my penchant for lyricism made me compose certain things that were interludes within total improvisations.

At the same time, during your quintet era, did you also crystallize your own ideas as a composer?

I was always writing. Always. Because I'd read some interview with Coltrane in which he'd said that composing very much moulds your personality. When you play your own music, it's easier to create your own style. That is, in fact, the case. Writing creates the person, creates the sound. Not always, but it does help.

You immediately got an award for your composition at Jazz Jamboree 1969.
Maybe. I don't remember. There probably was some competition or other.

Did your album *Music for K*, which was released in the 'Polish Jazz' series (your debut in the role of leader) follow on from that award?
Definitely. Although that album came as a result of earlier developments. In 1967, in Kraków, I wrote *Msza jazzowa* ('Jazz Mass'). There must be a TV recording of it somewhere. The concert was recorded by Dutch television. That commission had a big effect on me. It made me into a composer. On *Music for K*, there are compositions that actually come from my *Jazz Mass*. It had been commissioned by the Dominican Fathers in Kraków. The concert took place in their church. I can't remember how that commission came about. They were progressive. They wanted to have young people in their churches and this project came up. I formed a kind of choir out of students at the music academy, who sang the *Kyrie* and other bits. The line-up was based on the quintet. Seifert, Gonciarczyk, Muniak.

I read in some review that later, at one concert, the quintet played a fragment from the *Mass* (the 'Kyrie') alongside the piece 'Psychodelia'.
Well, yes. Psychodelia. The hippies' lifestyle and the clothes they wore really appealed to us.

Did you get to know the hippie community well?
They were younger than us. To me they were like children who just say that that's how they live. I was most interested in life on the edge. What I enjoyed was frequently being in different states of consciousness. I'll tell you what interested me in those days. Ah, yes! I've just remembered. At one time I rented a fabulous little place on Krucza Street. I met this mathematician, Adam Obtułowicz. He's a well-known figure. He was also interested in music. He was a fan of free jazz, though not exclusively. The quintet used to go round to his place to listen to music by Tibetan monks. We were blown away by that music. The Tibetan monks were a great inspiration, and I mean a really great inspiration, for our improvisations and our sound. These were recordings with trumpets and cymbals. That's where Muniak got the idea for percussion instruments. It really did have an extraordinary effect on us. I was smoking really strong stuff at that time.

There was this one guy, an Austrian. One day, at Krucza, the doorbell rings. I open the door, and there's a bloke standing there, a young guy, ordinary-looking. 'I've been sent here by Leszek from Vienna. I'm in Poland now, working in computers. I'm a programmer. I know you're a smoker. I'm a smoker too. I've brought a joint.' He'd brought his gear with him. He wanted to get to know the musicians and artists in the city where he was working. He had incredibly strong hashish. He said that he used to do a bit of dealing, but that now he was a programmer. A strange guy. He worked for some economic planning commission. He programmed their computers. A very important role.

Did he work for the government?
Yes. He was an expert. He was very sure of himself. And he smoked a lot.

I'm reminded of the evocative title of part of one of the chapters in Alvin Toffler's *The Third Wave*: 'Computers and marijuana'.
Well, because they go together. The whole of Silicon Valley smoked. It was perfectly natural as far as that Austrian was concerned. It's just that his appearance was so ordinary. Well, he did work at the ministry. He used to hang out there all night. He'd often go to work straight from a party at my place.

Let's get back to the Tibetan monks. The power of pure sound in their music must have simply enchanted you.
To us it was pure improvisation. Though it was actually religious music, not improvised. But its sound was most unusual. The shock it gave me stayed with me for many years. In those days, the early 1970s, we listened to music together. But to different music from the kind we played. At that time we played free, but we listened to conventional music. Mainly early ECM records. Keith Jarrett, *Facing You*; Chick Corea, *Return to Forever*; early Jan Garbarek. We always had tonal music within us, but it had a modern form of expression. Obviously, Ornette mattered; George Russell, Coltrane and Miles. Miles was always there. Plus that strange music of the Buddhist monks. That inspired us. And, in those days, I also liked listening to Gilbert Bécaud. That more popular music was always hanging around me, somewhere.

Did you have views on Miles's various periods? Because, by the 1970s, he was already playing quite differently: electric and funky.
Everything was good. All the Mileses. I've learned that, if at some point I don't like something of Miles's, then after a while I'll definitely grow to like it. That's how it was with *On the Corner*. I didn't like it for quite some time. But lately – ah! Fabulous music.

They've just released a box set of the *On the Corner* sessions. All the recordings.
I like listening to those versions. Some of them are so gauche that you can hear how painful it was for them, giving birth to their music. It doesn't come easily.

And how do you recall the recording of *Music for K*? Because you recorded it in the National Philharmonic's huge concert hall, didn't you. That space must have made an impression on you.
The atmosphere was very good. I can't remember who recorded us. The Philharmonic crew. We recorded it quickly, within two days. Maximum. I liked playing ballads even then. I liked 'Cry'. I've actually recently been thinking about playing that piece. I have a better recollection of the *TWET* sessions.

Music for K escapes my memory somewhat. I recorded *TWET* in the Higher School of Music. And *Music 81* and *Lady Go* on Długa Street.

Music for K still surprises us with its great build-up of fury. People didn't use to play in that way at that time in Poland, except for maybe Włodzimierz Nahorny. His trio with Ostaszewski recorded the album *Heart* for Polish Jazz. That doesn't lack fire either. Your quintet's next studio album, *Purple Sun*, is completely different. Even though they're barely three years apart, there's a chasm between them.
There is a chasm. *Music for K*; we began with that.

This is how I feel it: fury combined with claustrophobia. The tension makes the music more vertical; the playing is stretching towards hymn-like tones. *Purple Sun*, on the other hand, is horizontal music. There's fury there, too, but the music is more open; it motors, tears ahead, and in this way it breaks the tension.
That's to do with us starting out. On *Music for K*, I'm kind of tense. The compositions kind of contained us. But, on *Purple Sun*, the music expands and spills over.

What did it do to the quintet's sound when Seifert moved over to violin?
He fixed a wah-wah to his violin, and it sounded like a guitar, and like a kind of keyboard as well.

We could compare *Purple Sun* to Miles Davis's recordings of the early 1970s. You're playing free, but funkily and with a jazz-rock kick to it.
Our music evolved. Obviously. Miles was a genius. All his funky albums were improvised music. That energy! There's a groove to it – it's continuous music. I'd very much like to have the opportunity to do some of my music with those kinds of grooves. But I don't have those kind of people.

Hence your sensitivity to percussionists?
Well, yes. There are not many people who play groove well. I really like playing with Joey Baron. He plays in lots of different ways, on and off. Brian Blade, who plays with Wayne Shorter, is a genius. His is the best approach for me. Blade plays gaps. He doesn't accompany. He reacts to the sounds; he plays figures; sometimes he pauses. He plays by means of melody, a rhythmic melody. He doesn't play that much trance, which has held sway in jazz up until now.

Why didn't Suchanek play on *Purple Sun*?
There were difficult rhythmic things there, so I took on a different bassist, so we could handle the session. A Swiss bassist, just for that one session. As it turned out, he didn't play very accurately, but he did play something or other. I regret that decision.

Poster from a concert in
Germany. Early 1970s.
Courtesy Anna Stańko

Did rock have an influence on the quintet?
I didn't listen to much rock then. I started listening to rock much later on, when I got married. My wife used to listen to a lot of good rock. She was a young hippie. We had Frank Zappa at home, and, more importantly, Bob Marley.

After that breakthrough concert at Berliner Jazztage in 1970, you and the quintet played more in Germany than you did in Poland.
Definitely more. There's no comparison whatsoever. We played a great deal; we toured constantly. At the beginning of the 1970s, we'd take out year-long visas. In breaks between jobs, we'd stay in Germany. I remember us living together for a while in a hippie commune in Würzburg. They took us in, so we could stay in Germany while we waited for jobs to come up. They gave us one or two rooms. There was a small cellar there with wine in it, which we made use of – booty from a resourceful German commune. They all came from rich families. We later lived in Darmstadt. Muniak with his wife, and the rest of us

in a kind of hovel. Those were wonderful times. Hashish and wine. Just like Baudelaire, you might say.

We occasionally played in Poland. There was no market there. We played individual concerts. In Olsztyn, in Kraków at Krzysztofory; at Hybrydy in Warsaw. At festivals. Jazz Jamboree; Jazz on the Oder. The Polish concerts were magical. The quintet used to go to music workshops in Chodzież. Two or three early editions. Laboratorium's musicians were there, workshopping at the time. We did activities with the musicians, and we played the weirdest concerts. There was one concert on the shop floor of a factory, during the breaks, when the machines got switched off. Totally free music. The workers sort of half-listened. We played in some club in Poznań . . . I remember us staying for a week in the Bazar Hotel. What was that club called? I can remember the hotel. Not so much the club. You see – that's how we spent time as a quintet. Stefański met his future wife then in Poznań. We did do quite a few concerts.

But we definitely played more in Germany. In Denmark we played a joint concert with Diana Black. We later played with her ballet company at Jazz Jamboree.

That was Jazz Jamboree '71. The quintet performed in front of Ornette Coleman then. Do you remember that concert? Performing in front of one of the masters.
You know, I don't remember Ornette's concert; I must have been preoccupied with my own. I think he was playing with Ed Blackwell then. With Dewey Redman. I'd always wanted to meet him. I think that was probably the first time I spoke to him. I always made it clear to him that he was the father of my music. Later, Vesala and I paid him a visit in New York. Ornette's going to be playing at my festival in Bielsko-Biała.

How did that particular programme at Jazz Jamboree '71 come about – a concert and ballet?
We'd played earlier at a big arts festival in Aarhus, which still takes places in Denmark to this day. We met a dancer there who wanted to dance to improvised music. She asked whether she could improvise something with us. Diana Black. An American from a young ballet company, Diana Black Dance Theatre.

Was she Black?
White. I invited her later to the festival, and she improvised with the band during our concert on stage at the Congress Hall. I dedicated my composition 'Piece for Diana' to her. When we played with her that first time in Denmark, it went brilliantly. It was hard-going in Warsaw. Because it's improvisation. We have no control over improvisation. It's particularly difficult with dance. I was later in touch with the dancer Liliana Alvarado. We performed together in Leipzig and Berlin. I played solo; she danced. She could in fact have danced

2. internationales new jazz meeting auf burg altena 26. juni 71

Programm

Beginn: 15.oo Uhr
im Innenhof der Burg Altena

Ansage: Heinz Werner Wunderlich

ASSOCIATION

Pierre Courbois	– Schlagzeug
Jasper van't Hof	– Elektr. Piano
Toto Blanke	– Gitarre
Siggi Busch	– Baß

PETER BRÖTZMANN TRIO

Peter Brötzmann	– Tenorsaxophon
Fred van Hove	– Piano
Han Bennink	– Percussion

ALAN SKIDMORE QUINTETT & GUEST

Alan Skidmore	– Tenorsaxophon
Malcolm Griffith	– Posaune
John Taylor	– Piano
Chris Lawrence	– Baß
Tony Levin	– Schlagzeug
Mike Osborne	– Altsaxophon

NEW JAZZ ENSEMBLE '71

a)	Wolfgang Dauner	– Synthesizer VSC3
b)	Wolfgang Dauner	– Klavinett, Elektr. Melodica
	Karin Krog	– Vocal
c)	Manfred Schoof	– Flügelhorn
	Gerd Dudek	– Tenorsaxophon
	Peter Trunk	– Baß
	Cees See	– Schlagzeug
	Karin Krog	– Vocal

THOMASZ STANKO QUINTETT

Thomasz Stanko	– Trompete
Janusz Muniak	– Tenorsaxophon
Zbigniew Seifert	– Altsaxophon
Bronislaw Suchanek	– Baß
Janusz Stefanski	– Schlagzeug

ALBERT MANGELSDORFF QUARTETT & THE TRIO

Albert Mangelsdorff	– Posaune
John Surman	– Saxophone
Heinz Sauer	– Saxophone
Barre Phillips	– Baß
Günter Lenz	– Baß
Ralf Hübner	– Schlagzeug
Stu Martin	– Schlagzeug

DAVE PIKE SET

Dave Pike	– Vibraphon
Volker Kriegel	– Gitarre
Hans Rettenbacher	– Baß
Peter Baumeister	– Schlagzeug

Ende: gegen 22.oo Uhr

(here and opposite)
The festival programme from Altena, where Tomasz Stańko performed with his quintet, 1971.
Courtesy Anna Stańko

JG·RECORDS
018 ST

LIVE
IN ALTENA

the
John Surman
trio

Zu beziehen durch
JG RECORDS, 586 Iserlohn, Sundernallee 41

without the music; I added in the music because I could see her movements and I could do the synchronization. Sometimes it came out brilliantly, but it was very difficult. Physically tough. Both for her and for me.

The composition 'Piece for Diana' appeared on the quintet's first German album: *Jazzmessage from Poland*.
It was that time. We also played it in Altena, at the old castle.

I've seen the photographs from that festival. A hippie audience.
Those were open-air festivals that young people used to go to.

John Surman and band also played at Altena. Is that where you met them?
I'd met them earlier. They'd been to Poland. And then we played together at festivals.

You've mentioned that this was an important connection.
Definitely an important connection. Surman's trio had a big influence on the quintet's music. They played very free. There was also another band – four basses: Dave Holland, Barre Phillips, Barry Guy and J.-F. Jenny-Clark. They recorded an album together. I don't think the material got released. We got a tape off Surman. We listened to that music non-stop.

With the trio's percussionist, Stu Martin, in 1973 you recorded an album for the record club PSJ.
Yes. *Fish Face*. I got him to come to Poland and we duetted at concerts. And he also had a synthesizer. Stu had also been at the workshops in Chodzież. I also went to see him in Brussels. I spent a week or so over there. It was a wonderful time. This is what our breakfasts were like: we'd pick fruit straight off the tree. And with that we'd have champagne and hashish. Stu lived a hippie life. I didn't even know that he was already into cooking heroin.

He caused a sensation in Poland. He liked to be provocative. I remember we'd been to the cinema in Poznań. Stu had come out all pumped up after the film – I can't remember what it was anymore – he stopped in front of the militia headquarters, and, with all his might, he started kicking some metal bin. When the militia saw this diminutive, long-haired chap, they rushed over to him, batons in hand. With smiles on their faces, because he'd so obviously provoked them. And, just as they began to beat him up, he started yelling, 'American composer!' He knew what he was doing. They took him to ER. The doctor said to them, 'Gentlemen, he's not drunk.' They didn't do anything to him. They were furious; they had to release him. They registered him at his New York address.

What about that *Fish Face* record? Stefański also played on it.
I also took on a second drummer. And added trumpet and synthesizer. Free music. Totally improvised. Later on, still in the 1970s, I got Stu over for the

festival at the new Hybrydy. We played as a duet. We also saw each other in New York when I recorded the *Heavy Life* album with Vesala. I saw him and Peter Warren, because they were in the same social group. It was from Martin that we rented the loft space for our band rehearsals.

In the second half of the 1970s, you summed up the quintet quite harshly. In one interview you said: 'We played superbly on two occasions, but they didn't get recorded.'
In those days I was very self-critical. That's slowly beginning to wear off. When I go back to those recordings, I say, 'God, that was very good music.' And then I'm delighted. Especially with *Purple Sun*. There was a time when I really disliked that album. I think that's connected to the fact that I associated those recordings with the music that was around at that time. I've now, to some extent, justified those things artistically through my life and creativity. They've taken on a different meaning for me. There's a recording by the quintet from Hamburg. A radio recording of a concert. It never got released, but it has been pirated, because it is in circulation. A fan in the States gave me that recording. There's a superb dialogue there between Seifert and me – incredible. The quintet's best playing.

Seifert's dead. Muniak runs a club in Kraków. What's the rest of the quintet up to?
Suchanek lives in the States, in Boston, and he's still playing. Non-stop. He's a sought-after bassist; he makes a living out of music. Same with Stefański. He lives in Germany. He has a very good reputation. He's a very distinctive drummer with his own language. He often plays with American musicians. He's played with Woody Shaw and Miroslav Vitous, among others.

In Germany you also played with the band Jazzpol, where, alongside Stefański, you had the keyboardist Władysław Sendecki.
That was much later, after the quintet. That was a touring project; we played a few concerts – not many. Sendecki was then one of the best Polish keyboard players. He played in the band Sun Ship. Now he plays on Hamburg radio. From time to time I play interesting duets with him. We'll be playing together again soon. We're occasionally joined by Leszek Żądło, a saxophonist from Kraków, who left Poland a long time ago and made a career for himself in Germany. We have Vitold Rek playing bass, or Paweł Jarzębski, Namysłowski's old bassist, who now lives in Switzerland. An excellent bassist.

Were you not tempted to stay permanently in Germany then?
I didn't really want to. I was quite lazy. I didn't really have any prospects there. There were more opportunities for me in Poland. I was more drawn to Brussels at that time. I was thinking of playing with Stu Martin. I had a wonderful time there with him. I remember how much I liked the fact his synthesizer was always pulsating away in his flat. He had this English machine, one of

(left) Festival programme from the jazz club Montmartre in Copenhagen.
Courtesy Anna Stańko

(below) 'Little Seiferts', in other words, leaflets promoting the quintet's concerts, designed by Zbigniew Seifert.
Courtesy Anna Stańko

TOMASZ STAŃKO QUINTET

TOMASZ STAŃKO	tp
ZBIGNIEW SEIFERT	as, viol
JANUSZ MUNIAK	ts, fl, ss
BRONISŁAW SUCHANEK	b
JANUSZ STEFAŃSKI	dr

concert management promotion

Beat Burri
Vonwilstrasse 51
CH-9000 St. Gallen
Agencja Koncertowo-Artystyczna „PAGART"
Warszawa, pl. Zwycięstwa 9, tel. 26-09-95
Telegram: PAGART   Telex: 81-36-39

the first to have knobs instead of a keyboard: a Synthi AKS. I think it's a real pity that that machine has fallen out of use and has been forgotten about. In Poland, Czesław Niemen had one, and Tadeusz Sudnik in particular used it in Freelectronic. I keep thinking of buying myself something of the kind. Stu had the synthesizer going non-stop, and, from time to time he'd lock into its pulse on his drums. You could say that he constantly had a composition on the go. Terrific! I also always have my trumpet at hand, and the piano open. In my home, everything is driven by music. I intend to do the same in New York. That's the kind of life I lead.

8 Ruhr Valley Jazz

As well as with the quintet, in the first half of the 1970s you played a lot in Germany with other international bands. Most famous is your performance with Krzysztof Penderecki at the Donaueschingen Festival in 1971.

I can remember *that* festival distinctly. I can even remember that Professor Penderecki bought himself a denim outfit so he wouldn't stand out, as the orchestra was rather colourful. The Pendereckis asked me out to dinner, as I was the only Polish performer. Soft Machine played after us. And then there was the party at the castle. Guests in tailcoats, society ladies, and alongside were the jazz musicians and Soft Machine. Our band was a free-jazz orchestra full of serious people: Kenny Wheeler, Manfred Schoof, Peter Brötzmann, Han Bennink. A large ensemble.

That evening began with you playing with Don Cherry.

He rolled out a little rug on the stage. There was a dog running around there, or maybe two; there was Baba Ji, his guru from Denmark, up there in his Tibetan robe, with his droopy eye. His wife. Neneh Cherry, his daughter. His little son, Eagle-Eye Cherry, was running around. A whole group of hippies. They were all up on stage. There was some beautiful young woman singing. And Don, in an oriental robe, playing trumpet and piano. We stood around him and repeated his phrases. He'd written us some simple tunes.

They were deeply rooted in ethnic music, as we can hear on the album *Actions*, which came out of that concert.

Ethnic, yes, but it was all his own compositions,* everything filtered through his personality.

Did he write down the compositions for the orchestra?

He usually had sheet music, unlike Cecil. They were kind of little motifs out of which Don built his entire composition during the concert.

---

* *Series Editor's note:* The title track 'Actions for Free Jazz Orchestra' is by Penderecki; Cherry's compositions from that concert and album are 'Humus' and 'Sita Rama Encores'.

And straight after that, the European Free Jazz Orchestra, as your band was called, shared the stage with Penderecki.
There the music was written out in full. Penderecki conducted.

But what about room for improvisation? After all, the piece 'Actions' was subtitled 'For Free Jazz Orchestra'.
There was practically no room for improvisation. Only, unfortunately, we weren't all so good at reading music. And, that being the case, improvisation took over, quite naturally. I don't think Penderecki was too pleased with that concert. He didn't have the kind of control that he was expecting. He's a composer who likes to have complete control of his own music, but everything here just got out of hand. A number of the musicians there had a particular sound and a fairly informal approach to notation. I'm not a master at reading music either. None of us was an expert at reading music, with exceptions, like Kenny Wheeler. We were more used to graphic notation. But this was difficult music. And, on top of that, we were unruly musical anarchists. I remember there was one point when Han Bennink was supposed to do a short drum solo. During the rehearsal, Bennink had listened and dutifully responded when Penderecki let him solo for a dozen or so seconds, but during the concert, he brazenly turned away and he *played*! The anarchy of the free jazz musician took the upper hand. But we did make an interesting sound. We got a very enthusiastic response from the audience.

Penderecki doesn't boast too much these days about *Actions*, and yet this was his debut as a conductor.
I don't think he likes it. Now you know why.

Anyway, where did this bold idea come from, to get the European Free Jazz Orchestra to play with artists as different as Cherry and Penderecki?
Joachim-Ernst Berendt commissioned it. He curated one of the days at Donaueschingen. Berendt formed the European Free Jazz Orchestra. He commissioned Penderecki to write a piece for the orchestra. That day there was also some Indian music, some performers from southern India. It was a very open and diverse festival.

I read in some BBC review that Penderecki's 'Actions' composition was inspired by a 1967 Globe Unity Orchestra piece with the same title.
I don't think so. I only began playing with Schlippenbach in 1970.

Globe Unity, Alexander von Schlippenbach's band, was then the biggest and most important free-jazz big band in Europe. Did he invite you to join the band after Berliner Jazztage?
Yes. I think Berendt was an inspiration to him. I played with Globe Unity at the Baden Baden Jazz Meeting, yet another series devised by Berendt. There

were bigger bands playing there. I played there with Bennink and Albert Mangelsdorff.

Globe Unity was such a big band, it didn't lend itself well to touring; I think those were just one-off concerts, weren't they?
Of course. Just one-off concerts. I'd go and join them for one job. I think, in total, I played a dozen or so concerts with them.

How did the work with Schlippenbach differ from the work with Penderecki?
It was quite similar, as I remember it. Because we couldn't read Penderecki as well as we should have done, while with Schlippenbach we mainly had graphic notation, though the music was improvised.

At that time, graphic notation for improvisation was also done by Cornelius Cardew, who brought together professional and amateur musicians. It was from his inner circle that the masters of British improvisation emerged, people like Eddie Prévost and Keith Rowe, who were involved with AMM.
I didn't have much to do with them.

In bands like Globe Unity or the European Free Jazz Orchestra, the musicians who came and went were the truly international free-jazzers. You got to meet Europe's top musicians then.
Many people came and went. I'd met them before at the Free Music Workshop in Berlin, where we'd played with the quintet. Jost Gebers is still running that series. He also runs the record label Free Music Production. I met Dutch and English musicians there. The English were in the majority.

Globe Unity also had giants like Anthony Braxton and Steve Lacy playing with them.
I know. I was less interested in Braxton. He was more intellectual. I was more inclined towards Ornette and the Art Ensemble. That certain kind of folksiness they had suited me more than Braxton's intellectual theories. Lacy and I knew each other. We often played together. We had a lot of respect for each other.

Did you form a closer bond with any of these musicians?
It varied. Friendships are always formed on the basis of instinct and intuition, or by chance. I remember one particular workshop organized by ECM in the 1970s. It was called Trumpet Plus. Eddie Gomez, Lester Bowie, Kenny Wheeler, Jan Garbarek and Jack DeJohnette were all there. I made friends with Eddie Gomez then. I always seemed to make friends with the rhythm sections.

Were you not tempted to duet with Han Bennink? At that time he was doing an entirely solo show on drums.
No. When he played solo, there wasn't much room left. His gigs were a cross between shamanism and performance.

At the time there was a powerful Dutch contingent on the European scene: Bennink, Willem Breuker, Fred Van Hove.* Was there anything in particular that set musicians from different nations apart from one another?

The Dutch used to stick together. I had less contact with them. More contact with the English. Tony Oxley, Paul Rutherford. He was a die-hard communist.

Rutherford's band Iskra 1912 was actually named in honour of Lenin's newspaper! An excellent band, by the way. Yet you came to them from a country where there was real socialism. What used to happen with regard to that?

We used to argue. I'd say that it was all crap. I was living through communism and I knew. And they'd say, 'Because you're not doing it properly!' They weren't interested in the facts. They didn't want to believe it.

Was Tony Oxley also a leftie at the time?

Absolutely. He lived for a while in the GDR. He couldn't stand it there very long, but he doesn't want to admit it. An idealist. Evolution has produced something whereby a proportion of people have some kind of romantic, anarchic tendencies. When the idealists come with a large dose of sadism, what comes to the fore is sheer cruelty. Lenin, Stalin, Che Guevara, Mao were cruel people. But the free-jazz musicians were romantics and artists who were playing with the idea of revolution and didn't really want to know what was bad about it. It's all fine and dandy, being a communist in England and having a band called Iskra 1912. I remember Charlie Haden recording 'Song for Che'. For them, Che was synonymous with an idea, no matter that he was a sadist, like the henchmen who used to finish off wounded knights with a misericorde.

One particular figure among the free-jazz leftie musicians in those days was the German saxophonist Peter Brötzmann.

Brötzmann . . . He'd studied painting. Free-jazz musicians were mostly visual artists who had much in common with performance. I saw a lot of Brötzmann. We played together in Globe Unity and with Penderecki. But Brötzmann didn't want to talk about communism: 'What do you people know about it? You've already got a different lot in power over there.' He was right, because by then Poland was being run by bureaucrats, the kind who just looked to their own advancement.

Did he talk about his sympathy for the far-left Red Army Faction? At that time, Brötzmann was recording albums dedicated to them, wasn't he?

He recorded those because he had a sense of the extraordinary nature of the situation, that they were fighting for a just cause against the bourgeoisie, whom he couldn't stand. The cynicism and hypocrisy of ordinary people is something

---

* *Series Editor's note:* Fred Van Hove (1937–2022) worked often with Dutch musicians, notably Bennink, but he was Belgian, born in Antwerp.

that all young people find disgusting. They have to exist, these idealists and these mad men, the sadists. Revolutions have to occur. Every now and then, a conflagration of societies. It's terrible, but that's how it is, and that's how it's going to be. That's how we've evolved, and that's better for us, as a whole species. That's why there are people like Brötzmann. Artists, whom those newly in power subsequently slaughter. Like Vladimir Mayakovsky. They'd be the first to go to the stake – Brötzmann, Rutherford, Evan Parker . . . He was the biggest communist of them all. Parker had strong ties with the Italian communist party.

Rutherford died in 2007.
I feel for him. During his lifetime, everything that he believed in has become devalued.

During your encounters with Brötzmann, Rutherford or Parker, did you have the impression that they were canvassing or campaigning at all?
No, no, no. I observed the colourful aspect of this thing from the sidelines. We were essentially professional musicians. Each of us had our own sound. Brötzmann played brilliantly. His Brötzmann–van Hove–Bennink trio was a *fabulous* band! While their aesthetic didn't appeal to me, they themselves made for an exceptionally colourful line-up. They were great to listen to. Because it was pure form.

Since, as you say, you weren't too keen on the powerful sound of German free jazz – as Berendt puts it, 'the Ruhr Valley sound' – how did you feel playing with Globe Unity, for example, which was one of the more radical bands on this scene?
I felt a bit strange. My romantic melodiousness made me a bit of an alien on the free-jazz scene. But I was highly thought of because of the quality, my own sound.

It must also have been strange for you when, driving from Poland to Germany, you crossed what was then the magic borderline with the West and immediately came into contact with people who were fiercely critical of life in the West.
It quickly became apparent to me. Contradictions and paradoxes. The most interesting people in the West were those who had leftist inclinations. They were always my best friends and the finest people: intelligent and open, tolerant and very modern artistically. They were lefties. It's still like that. The right, especially in the artistic field, is, to me, inextricably linked to failure, to compromise and, above all, to lack of talent. It's as if they're the least talented people in our business. Maybe that'll change one day. But it's still like that to this day. Do you know any talented right-wing artists? I can't name a single one.

European musicians from the free-jazz scene of that period had a strong tendency to cut themselves off from traditional American jazz and demonstrate something completely new.

Yes. I did feel that, but it did surprise me a little. Because, after all, they did have their origins in American jazz. Without Ayler, we wouldn't have Brötzmann or the English musicians. Jazz was an American art form. And the greatest artists came from America. This is essentially about movement, about tradition, education, certain principles. In the States, it was the difficult conditions that created the great artists. On the other hand . . . Ayler started it, but in Europe they played completely differently. Their ideology was different. In the States, a band like Brötzmann's trio would never have emerged.

What is this difference?

In the States, jazz had its origin in Black music, in swing, and that's why it had a different form of expression, a different lyricism. In Europe, it was more of an intellectually refined art form that referred to different aesthetic concepts. A large part of it was performance, theatricality, the colourful nature of the phenomenon. It's difficult to describe in words, but I do feel a distinct difference. It was also a question of personality. That's just what Brötzmann, Van Hove and Bennink were like, and that's their style. The quality of their music was undoubtedly as high as that of the Americans.

In those days, Schlippenbach wrote a *Free Jazz Manifesto*, in which he referred to Georg Trakl's poetry and Paul Klee's painting as inspirations, and musically he invoked Webern and Schönberg. Could you feel this modernist ethos within that community?

Yes. It radiated out. This was definitely an artistic phenomenon. And a very powerful one. A large number of young Germans got involved with free jazz. It was a kind of underground. Like today's modern hip-hop productions. But 1970s jazz is, to me, primarily festival music. Many years later, I met a taxi driver who had gone to free jazz concerts in his youth. He recognized me. He was very nostalgic about those festivals. Like today's young people who go to alternative festivals, where there's rock and the better kind of pop. The way the musicians looked, and their musical expression, both mattered – a kind of performance. It's no coincidence that there were so many visual artists among the free jazz musicians, like Brötzmann. It's still like that. Mikołaj Trzaska is also an artist. Artists listen to free music. Marek Kijewski knew a great deal about Mangelsdorff, about free jazz.

Did free jazz get taken up in Germany as a form of generational protest?

Generational protest. Yes, because of its leftie ideology.

Was immersion in the chaos of free music a way of recovering from wartime trauma?

I don't know. I don't think so. I didn't sense anything of the kind.

The counterculture of the 1960s also had an influence on the total liberation of jazz. Free concerts broke with the orderliness of the industrial age, stirred up chaos within consumer culture.

That too. Now there are fewer people with that outlook. Consumerism reigns.

It might have been Wynton Marsalis who said that, in the 1940s and 1950s, the most talented Black artists went into jazz because that was a space where they could make their mark. But now, fewer of the best musicians are going into jazz.

That's definitely the case.

At that time in Germany, Karlheinz Stockhausen was also experimenting with improvised music. It's interesting that when he spoke about his flagship composition *Aus den Sieben Tagen* ('From the Seven Days'), he used the expression 'intuitive music'; and you used to say that what the quintet performed was 'intuitive music'.

It was. But what he called intuitive music was more sophisticated.

Aus den Sieben Tagen doesn't have notation, as such. It's basically instructions for the performers. Stockhausen conceived them over a few days of fasting and meditation. The performer had to prepare himself in the same way for performance, cleansing the mind and body over three days, and then he simply had to play individual sounds, without thinking about what was being played. Those were the guidelines. Stockhausen recorded and mixed it in his studio.

I had a sceptical view about those kinds of activities. To me those things were less to do with music and more to do with some kind of philosophical speculations, which might make sense or they might not. I preferred jazz with its folk character.

But that problem, which concerned Stockhausen, Schlippenbach and Penderecki, was one that you, in a sense, went through yourself. I'm talking about the relationship between composition and improvisation. How did these two dimensions relate to each other in practice for the quintet? And for you yourself?

When we played in the quintet, we switched off. We switched off completely. Everything worked on the basis of us intuitively listening to each other. We were sensitive to the delicate nuances that gave us some kind of form to latch on to. I remember as if it were today, a gig in Hybrydy, with some incredibly good duetting on strings between Seifert and Suchanek. Whole structures emerged; some sort of symphony began to take form. But there is a problem with improvisation. It's simply the best music – if it works. Only, unfortunately, improvisation is beyond our control and doesn't always work. Many times in my life, I've taken off playing high-quality, mind-blowing free-jazz.

I remember certain gigs with Adam Makowicz where we were improvising and had complete control over form, and I know from the audience's reaction that those were quality gigs. Only you can't maintain that control all the time. That's why we write it down, and that's why we agree on it. That's why, in the quintet, we began to lay down certain things more and more. We used to say, 'Let's play it like this now'; and that *Let's play it like this now* became a kind of composition.

In 'Fleur' on *Purple Sun*, certain things are laid down, yet they're meant to be completely improvised. But, once we'd played them through earlier, something had already begun to establish itself; and we'd remember certain things. Free jazz is a strange phenomenon. That's where I've come from, and it's this type of playing that gives me greatest satisfaction. It's not composition, but improvisation that's my form of expression. I've been reflecting on free jazz all my life, and I've begun to equate it to an idea.

An idea is a wonderful thing. Without idealism, humanity wouldn't exist, but, at the same time, it's idealism that has given the world fundamentalism and the Inquisition, Hitler and Stalin. Idealism can quickly degenerate completely and descend into the utmost cruelty, into the utmost dehumanization. Evidently something in idealism that stops us having control over it. Maybe that's why we respect and want it so much, because we can't manage it . . . We go back to our usual human way. In the case of music – to composing. The idea of free jazz is such that it's best not to play it at all. We need to know about it and have increasing respect for it as a concept. Bow down to Cecil Taylor, even if you haven't heard him, but simply because he plays like he does, that he dares to, because that's extraordinary and wonderful. But if we use free jazz too much, that's dangerous. Music without control can become boring and bad. Better to love or respect it more and play it less.

In that case, what should we do about idealism?
Everyone should know that for himself, intuitively, depending on the situation. And watch out! Because we have a tendency towards brutality. We can't not be idealists; dry pragmatism is impoverishment, but we have to be vigilant . . . That's why, as far as art is concerned, it's good to be checked out by the public – will they come to our concert? Will they buy our album? If we think we're a misunderstood genius, that's dangerous and might end in musical degeneration.

Each time you mention Cecil Taylor, you speak approvingly of his intransigence, and yet one could regard him as the kind of genius who, to this day, most people don't understand.
I still have huge respect for him. And I don't know where the boundary runs beyond which art becomes brilliant. That's its mystery. There are no rules. No knowledge will guarantee that we're understood. What's left? We need to be open all the time. Not get stuck in our own self-belief. I'm happy to have had moments of complete freedom, and I'm still trying to get there. Except

that experience tells me that the best moments playing free can't actually be repeated.

To a large extent, it's actually transience that gives improvisation its charm.
Its charm does depend on that. That's why I'm so glad to be on my current job with Marcin Masecki. I don't have a composition. I don't have anything; and I'm forced to set up this 'job' so that it goes of its own accord. I'm making the arrangements. I phone Masecki, tell him something, not tell him something. The boys – because Pink Freud's rhythm section's playing as well – will be a little bit anxious; Masecki and I will be giving ourselves some freedom, because he's a musically sophisticated artist. And these young guys have energy and freshness, and an interesting groove. I sort it out in my head. I try to focus so that during the concert (just as Stockhausen tried to do with his fasting) I can get myself into a particular state of excitement. It's the same thing; it's about getting the brain to suddenly move onto a different wavelength. And see if beauty will break through again – that remarkable something: a rarely repeated sequence. I think that's what it's about. As with scales: every so often certain sequences repeat themselves. Do you remember? Nicolas Slonimsky (a relative of our Antoni Słonimski) wrote a book about it.

In Poland, only his memoirs have been published: *Perfect Pitch*. Brilliant, as it happens.
I'm talking about his *Thesaurus*. A set of scales. I have it. Slonimsky develops the scales according to mathematical principles. And, every so often, an extraordinary scale emerges, mysterious and unearthly in its beauty. And these are purely mathematical repetitive structures. A sound going up; a sound going down. Mathematically, he worked out x number of possible combinations between the sounds of the octave. Some of them have harmonics that fairly knock you off your feet. Coltrane found out about them and practised them like exercises.

That book of Slonimsky's went unnoticed until jazz musicians discovered it and picked it up. Eric Dolphy also practised those scales.
Slonimsky used to laugh about it. But some of those things are incredible. It's a law of nature: every so often, amidst chaos, beauty appears. We all want to find this principle and repeat it. I dream about it constantly. But it can't be done. So we make repeated attempts.

During that German period at the start of the 1970s, you also took part in a rather curious recording session: *We'll Remember Komeda*.
It was organized by Berendt. We recorded it in Frankfurt. In 1972. I can still see that studio. I can still visualize some things, but very selectively. I guess it depends on what I was smoking. The less I was smoking, the more I remembered. That particular session I remember exactly. We had this little Georgian guy playing on percussion: Armen Halburian. He'd come over from

the States. There was Gucio there, of course. I can see him as if it were today, with Peter Giger, who was playing on that enormous drum kit of his. There was Michał Urbaniak, Seifert, Attila Zoller on guitar. Me. Urszula Dudziak singing. A few days of production. Komeda's music. After all, Berendt had recorded *Jazz and Poetry* and had the rights to this stuff. And those were beautiful compositions, and that's what we mainly played.

The music on this album gives the impression of being a hippyish-psychedelic interpretation of Komeda. 'Crazy Girl', for instance, with its electric vibes.
Komeda is presented somewhat in the spirit of Urbaniak. I preferred the earlier recordings with Berendt. But everyone does their own thing with Komeda's music. We also played pieces from *Knife in the Water* – and that was Urbaniak's favourite music. Out of those pieces, it's just 'Ballad for Bernt' that's dear to me. I've tried, on a number of occasions, playing 'Cherry' and 'Crazy Girl', but, no . . . I prefer the later compositions.

During that session with Urbaniak, you're playing the piano. That must be the only time that happened during a recording session?
Nooo . . .

That's what it says in the album notes. On 'Dirge for Europe'. We can hear the piano there.
Maybe I played one note, when required.

During that German period, the band Unit also made an appearance.
That was a fantastic band. With Makowicz. Straight after the quintet, at the same time as I was playing with Vesala. There was even one joint concert with Vesala and Makowicz in Oslo. We played lots of standards. Coltrane. A few of my ballads. There was a bit of free music, but the core was standards. Adam came out of traditional music; I came out of modern. And that's how we met.

Ten years after Jazz Darings.
Yes. Unit was a great band. Makowicz played on a Fender Rhodes bass piano. He had two Fenders: one bass and one classical. He played that music in a strange way, a unique way. Mały (that's Czesław Bartkowski) was on drums. We didn't do any official recordings in that line-up. There's one, on a compilation from a festival in Hamburg. It's really excellent.

There was a Unit album for the Polish Jazz Association's record club in 1975. A quartet with Paweł Jarzębski on bass on two of the tracks.
But that wasn't how we played.

And earlier, too, on Polish Jazz, in 1973 the album *Unit* appeared, but in the form of a Makowicz–Bartkowski duo.

I don't know about that. That's possible. They started out as a duo and I joined them. We did big tours as a trio.

Mainly in Germany?

Only in Germany. The concerts were arranged by an agency in Göttingen, which I knew from back in my quintet days. We really did play a lot of gigs. We played together for about two years: 1974 and 1975.

In one of your interviews from the late 1970s, you mentioned that Makowicz was difficult to work with.

Oh no, no, no. He was already established then. That was after playing with Urbaniak. He was charismatic. Adam was very bourgeois at the time, and he had star quality, but it was brilliant playing together. He was already playing ragtime then, though not with me. We played very modern music together. A good band. A very good one.

It's astonishing that, having played free with the quintet, you then started playing standards.

It's not such an astonishing idea. In the olden days, standards is what Adam and I used to play together. In our first Jazz Darings. Afterwards, I was always playing around with standards in their modern guise.

Were the variations on themes far out?

Yes and no. We played over chord progressions. It's just that my sound and my way of playing is different: dirty. I played standards later in a trio with Vesala and Reggie Workman. Anders Jormin said that he first heard me play with that line-up in Gothenburg, which I can't remember any more. He remembered that the way we played 'Stella by Starlight' came as a shock to the Gothenburg musicians. Innovative.

What made it innovative?

I always played standards in the same unconventional language in which I played free jazz. I played over chord progressions with glissandi or dirty phrases, shrieks. But, at the same time, I was familiar with musical standards; I knew where I was; I felt the harmony. That's where it came from: from listening. I played with John Abercrombie recently, and it turns out that he doesn't know as many standards as I do. I was surprised. I do sometimes like to play a standard, when I have a good line-up. I get bored if the playing isn't creative, so I have to have good people. It was great playing with Adam. We never sank into that generic kind of walking where everything goes flat. That starts to inhibit me after a while. But when I had a rhythm section like Vesala and Workman – with Workman playing standards in an original way and Vesala flying free – I'd be inspired. I could retain the harmonic structure, but

I didn't have to. I could move away from the structure and just play certain scraps of the theme.

My free playing requires excellent musicians, but not ones like Brötzmann or those on the yass* scene, because those people play their own particular things and don't have so much of a universal imagination. The day before yesterday, I had a rehearsal with Masecki. That guy can play anything, because he's someone who has technique and an open mind. He takes things in such directions that it really is interesting playing with him.

So how did you get on playing with Bartkowski?
During Komeda's time, in 1963, Bartkowski was one of the best percussionists in Europe. The way he played 'Svantetic' – even Rune Carlsson didn't play it as well. Zbigniew Namysłowski discovered him, and when those two started playing together, Bartkowski turned out to be a genius. He had it all. Conception, sound, swing. The purebred bastard! Something happened to him later on. I don't know. He was in the army during the invasion of Czechoslovakia, and I think that deeply affected him. That must have been horrific for any ordinary person, let alone for such a sensitive artist.

What kind of person was he?
He was a lovely cat. I got on well with the musicians that I played with. Every one of them respected me as an artist. If, artistically, we're as one on stage, I don't care what anyone's like. At all. I can play with good people, with bad people; with religious people or agnostics. I don't care.

It probably did matter during your quintet period.
Well, it did matter, but it seems to me that in my case those kind of relationships don't affect my music. What I've always liked about jazz is that you can have an accountant standing alongside a madman, and the two of them feel great together, because they've played well together. That attracted me to jazz: its diversity and tolerance, and the craziness that comes of this juxtaposition. A contrast like that was very useful to me.

And what kind of reputation did you have among the musicians? Were you more the madman?
No. My reputation was . . . the very worst. Well, someone living on the edge. When the young musicians later used to tell me what they'd heard from their parents . . .

Which parents told their children stories about you?
Miśkiewicz. Michał heard about everything from his father Henryk.

---

* *Series Editor's note:* The term 'yass' was coined by guitarist and improviser Tymon Tymański to describe a variety of arrhythmic Polish avant-garde jazz current in the late 1980s and early 1990s. It mixes jazz, contemporary improvised music, punk and folk, and originated in the Tri-City and Bydgoszcz area of Poland.

Did his father warn him?

He did and he didn't. He was very pleased that I'd asked his son to play with me. Playing with me is a certain kind of honour. Jakob Bro and Jon Christensen tell me that they're proud that I've brought them into the band. Regardless of how I've lived my life, as an artist, I've always had a very good reputation. I don't remember anyone lambasting me. Even people who hated jazz respected me.

9 'The Full Catastrophe!'

In the early 1970s, you were always on the road. How was your private life at that time?
During *Jazz Mass*, I met my first love. Urszula: she's no longer with us. A very young woman with whom I had a really tempestuous time. That essentially lasted until my marriage. We'd argue, we'd fight, and then get back together again.

You'd fight?
Well, yes, because she couldn't stand me being involved with music. Urszula was very possessive. When I left for Warsaw, we argued about that too. It was also about hashish. Women don't like hashish, because it creates distance. A person becomes withdrawn and remote; you have no control over them. Unless you do it together, then that's a different story. That's how it was with Joaśka, my wife. But with Urszula, it was a tempestuous, adolescent love. It all began with *Jazz Mass*. I remember her coming along . . . I asked her in, kind of off the street. No. She came on her own. How *did* I meet her? She turned up somewhere.

She hit on me! It was usually the women who chatted me up.

Music initially pulled in the women, but then they became jealous of it?
Always. They'd always be angry. All of them. In fact, it was only my wife who was ever happy, but, right from the beginning, ours was a casual, artistic relationship.

What about your first love?
I can remember her as if it were today at that *Mass*. I can still picture her in my mind: such a beautiful, young girl. She was standing there in a short skirt. Urszula was friends with Jacek Ostaszewski's young wife, and he and I were very close friends at the time. Things got serious with Ulka (as I called Urszula), just at the point when I was supposed to be forming a new band with Jacek Bednarek and Stanisław Cieślak. I was waiting for them by the sea, in Krynica. They never came, but she did. So I gave up on the band idea. Then Ulka and I stayed over at Komeda's. He'd gone away, leaving us the keys to his apartment. We were there with Zośka's mother. Wonderful times. We became a

couple. By then I already had one foot in Warsaw, around 1967. I was playing in Dziekanka. My wife remembered Ulka from Dziekanka.

In Warsaw I lived at Danuta Kwiecińska's. There was this little house at the back of the former Dworzec Południowy (Warsaw South Station), on Skrzetuskiego Street. In those days that was on the edge of town. Danuta liked musicians a lot; her daughter worked for the Jazz Federation; maybe that's how I got to know her. Włodzimierz Nahorny rented a room off her first, then I did. I got on very well with Nahorny. For a while, he lived next door, and I used to hang out all day at his. Then, when he moved out, Janusz Stefański rented that room. I lived for a long time at Danusia's, with Ulka as well. Although she didn't allow women (she didn't like having strange females in the house), we somehow always managed to slip a girl in at night-time. She'd turn a blind eye. I did have trouble on a few occasions with the odd girl who didn't give a shit that she didn't like them. They'd deliberately go and ask her for something. She'd be foaming at the mouth on those occasions.

Ulka was very young. She was still at school. I got on very well with her parents. Her father was a professor of medicine, a well-known paediatrician, but she wasn't the best of students. And, because of that, there were problems all the time with travelling, even though her parents did let her go out with me. And we argued frequently. We couldn't stand each other. She was really possessive: a very possessive woman. We split up for good. I can remember that moment: saying to myself, 'I'm fuckin' free again!'

You said that it was the women who hit on you. Do you think that was precisely why they were possessive?
I think that could well be the case. Because, mainly, it was the women who hit on me, and I graciously went along with it. But Joaśka wasn't possessive. After Ulka, I was with Lechna. She was also a great love of mine. The early 1970s. A beautiful girl. I loved her very much. But I was a bastard, you know – hashish, vodka, and I didn't give a fuck about anything. I didn't listen to anyone, and I was difficult to put up with – I wouldn't compromise on anything. Everything was subordinated to the music. Any girlfriend I had could just stand at the back. Women don't like that. And these were usually hard bitches, because I don't like weak women. The women I was with were all strong personalities. They didn't want to be subservient, and if there was going to be a fight . . . I didn't want to fight. I didn't want to waste energy on those kinds of things.

Were you of the opinion that the world of male–female relationships was a separate matter, and that music came first?
Music is right there. It's a completely different thing. It's also a woman. It's even called *Muzyka*.* For me it's fulfilled the role of a life companion. I'm tied most closely to music; that's just how my life is. I like living on my own because no

---

* *Translator's note:* The Polish language has gendered nouns. The word *muzyka* ('music') is feminine.

one gets in the way of my playing whenever I want to. If, right at the beginning, I'd met the sort of girl, like some composers do, who, like a faithful dog at her master's feet, anticipates his every wish . . . But it wasn't like that for me. I'd jump from flower to flower. I'd have relationships that lasted a while, very intense ones.

I can remember, when I was still in Kraków, I used to drive my women out to Lanckorona, to the Lorenza guest house. I always started with that. Some of them used to work out that it wasn't the first time I'd been there. It was a picturesque place. You'd enter it through a tunnel of trees. The guest house was in an old wooden building. There was a portrait of Józef Piłsudski* hanging in the dining room. The owner was a pre-war chap. Good, home-made food. We didn't actually do anything there. There was nothing interesting in Lanckorona, apart from its beautiful marketplace, a two-minute walk from the guest house. A nice place to spend some time with your lover.

It seems you were a bit of a heart-throb.
I wouldn't put it like that. I wasn't a real womanizer, like some people I know. But I always had women hanging around me. Music pulls. Its colour, its energy.

You've mentioned a type of woman who, like a faithful dog, looks after her musician.
That wouldn't have worked with me. I'm quite overbearing.

Were there any women like that in jazz?
Trzaskower. Andrzej Trzaskowski's wife was like that. Michał Urbaniak and Ulka were a unit for a long time, because they performed together. Wojciech Karolak also had that sort of girl to begin with. There are some women who get it just right. Stu Martin's wife, the famous Lee. Enrico Rava's Lucia. Thelonious Monk's wife. Gato Barbieri had a famous wife. The most famous wife was Elvin Jones's: a little Japanese woman who used to set up his drums for him; and she was the only person who Elvin took any notice of.

Famous for what?
Famous for being alongside their musicians all the time. All the time, without being a hindrance.

What does 'without being a hindrance' mean here?
It means that they lived like the musicians and felt the hierarchy. You know, we jazz musicians have a hierarchy – how people play. It's a natural hierarchy. If someone (who as far as I'm concerned has no right to speak on the matter) says to me, 'Well, you didn't play your best today, did you?' then I start raging

---

* *Translator's note:* Józef Piłsudski (1867–1935) was a general and statesman who played a key role in the reestablishment of an independent Polish state in 1918. He is seen as a symbol of the Polish struggle for independence.

inside. You can't do that, like women sometimes do, making comments after a concert, just to say something.

What was Zofia Komedowa like? From what we can read about those days, it would appear that she was a kind of guard dog for Komeda.
Zośka was a dictator. She watched over Komeda like a lioness, like a tyrant. He was scared. He once had a girl with him, and Duduś Matuszkiewicz wanted to go in their room. Komeda got scared that he might tell Zośka. 'Duduś, I can't open the door because I'm in my pyjamas.' Do you see? It was a rare thing for Komeda to be unfaithful to Zośka. Once Zośka got into bed with me, right in front of Komeda. I was so embarrassed I didn't know what to do. 'Krzysztof! He's got a hard-on! He's got a hard-on!' Zośka was outrageous. Sex was important in her life. Komeda wasn't that bothered about it. He mainly got on with his music. And she helped him in an organizational way, so that he could write his music without any distractions. It was simply convenient for him to have Zośka. She arranged everything for him and lived her own life.

You mentioned that, during the quintet era, the women didn't go on tour with you.
We didn't take women on tour with us. The problems that Jan Garbarek's quartet had are well known. Bobo Stenson still talks about it today. Garbarek travelled separately with his wife, as did Zbigniew Seifert. Garbarek didn't smoke or drink. He went around sober – so it was difficult for him to put up with Palle Danielsson, Jon Christensen and Bobo. Women get in the way on tour. They mess things up; they pass judgement on concerts. Do you see? They voice their opinion on matters that to us jazz musicians are sacrosanct. An amateur, you might say, interfering with our music. You just want to tell them to fuck off. But you can't tell them to fuck off, because it's someone's wife.

A band on tour – is that like being in the army?
With the quintet, we lived together as a band, and we had our own different women at different times. Stories about sex were ubiquitous on tour. Crude stories, barrack-room stuff. You know – five single men. The girls didn't like it when we talked about them in that way, and they'd get angry. And we definitely made comments about how attractive the girls who hung around the band were. Our conquests. There were always beautiful girls around. Miles used to say that if there weren't any beautiful girls at the concert he'd better stop playing. And it's true. With art, there are always beautiful women hanging around. Always. Young and beautiful. All the time.

I'll tell you something. Some musicians ban their band members from travelling with girls. That's how things are these days. It seems that Adam Pierończyk won't tolerate any women coming on tour. There's a different atmosphere in the band when we travel alone: we spend more time together. We can talk about music. When we have women with us, everything falls apart. When the quartet went on tour, the women never came with us. Wives would occasionally travel up for one gig: Sławomir's wife, or Michał Urbaniak's wife, back when they were engaged. But, as it turned out, that was rare.

When you and the quintet arrived at the German commune, did you encounter the embodiment of the hippie idea of free love?
That's not what it looked like in practice. There were couples living there. But then, it wasn't a strictly hippie commune: it was a student commune. I've never lived in a hippie commune. That's as close as I got to knowing the hippies. Joaśka came from that community.

How did you meet your future wife, Joanna (Joaśka)? Did she hit on you as well?
No, it wasn't Joanna who made a play for me. In this case, it was a joint initiative. I'd known her for years. When I began playing in Warsaw, I met her in Dziekanka. There were these two sisters, the Renkes – well known in the clubs at the time. Her sister was a young lady who lived very much on the edge and hung around everywhere. How *did* I get together with Joaśka? We were always bumping into each other. We moved in small circles. And she *was* a beautiful woman. She was with that Austrian for a while – the one I told you about. Ah, I remember! We used to go out to clubs together, and one day he turned up with Joaśka. I was with Lechna then, but she couldn't cope with me anymore. It was horrendous. I don't want to talk about it. I feel terribly guilty thinking about her. I don't think she wants anything to do with me anymore. I don't know. I get on well with all the women I've been with, but I haven't spoken to her since we had our big break-up. I used to go around drunk all the time then. Soon after that, I ran into Joaśka and we got together.

You've mentioned your domineering attitude, music always being in the foreground. So, what was it about Joanna that seduced you into marrying her?
She impressed me. She knew how to be with a musician. She never got pissed off. She was an artist. She painted. She always listened to good music. That also endeared me to her. I remember the first time we listened to the Art Ensemble of Chicago, one of the ECM records . . . *Full Force*. Joaśka hadn't listened to jazz, but she had a feel for this music right away. Our early relationship was at the time of Edward Vesala's first visit to Poland. He came by boat. Joaśka and I both went up to meet him in Gdańsk. That's where we began our concerts. He brought over some terrific stuff with him. And then (I have to be honest), I was equally taken by the fact that she held her own smoking with us: always. And we were really serious, long-term users, unlike the hippies.

You mentioned Joanna's ties with the hippies.
She was one of the Polish hippies. Milo Kurtis, 'Prorok' (Józef Pyrz), Kora (Olga Jackowska). They were all younger than me. I had a bit of a condescending attitude towards them. I remember, one day, at my place on Krucza Street, we

were smoking a joint and one of them shrieks, 'Waaaaah!!! God!!! What's happening!!! Get a doctor!' I had some strong stuff. I said, 'Come to your senses, mate!' (I whacked him on the back.) 'Take it easy! Take a few breaths.' And he pulled himself together.

My Ulka was friends with Kora. I got to know Kora later on, at Jacek Ostaszewski's. Jacek was going through his hippie phase then. They were all part of the same clique. Ostaszewski was playing with Marek Jackowski in Anawa at Marek Grechuta's. Kora was hanging around. She was undermining Anawa then, and Osjan formed. She was the inspiration behind it, and they brought her into the band. At the time, she didn't have anything to do with music. She only really became big on the music scene with Manaam.

You recorded with Manaam on two occasions, the first one was at the start of the 1980s, on the album *O!*
I remember that! They asked me to. Though, at the time, I was really living on the edge. It was right at the beginning of martial law in Kraków. I was staying in the Europejski Hotel at the time, with a beautiful, young dancer: Bushka. It was a horror scene there. I remember the room being white because of all the matchsticks in it. Every time I smoked a joint, I threw the matchstick behind my back, like this, deliberately, so the room would fill up with matchsticks. The room turned as white as snow. And, at some point in the night, there was a *knock, knock* at the door. The helmet brigade came in. That militia lot with the helmets: probably the ZOMO.*

I remember being naked when they came in. I put my coat on over my bare body. Bushka was in bed, curled up into a ball with fright. She'd gone down earlier in the nude to buy some matchsticks. She really liked being provocative. And she took the lift down in the nude. A beautiful young ass. Can you imagine – in a lift, in the middle of the day, in the austere Poland of the time.

And they threw me out of the hotel. I was banned from the Europejski for a few years, although the people on reception really liked me. The militia man said to me then, 'If we started looking here, we'd find it.' I said, 'For sure.' They didn't know exactly what, but they had a good idea that I was on something. I think at the time they were more interested in finding underground leaflets.

And what about the recording session with Manaam?
I played for barely forty seconds. That's why that piece is so short. I didn't let it spoil the homogeneity of the music.

What made you decide you were ready for marriage?
There was a time when we felt good together. We simply wanted to settle down. Joaśka had had a turbulent life as well. She fell pregnant, literally on the day we got married. After everything that we'd got up to in our lives, as far

---

* *Translator's note:* The ZOMO (Motorized Reserves of the Citizens' Militia) was a paramilitary police unit during the communist era in Poland.

With daughter Anna and wife Joanna, Warsaw, 1978.
Photograph by Mirosław Makowski

With Anna at Piotr Młodożeniec's wedding, 1981.
Photograph by Mirosław Makowski

as our child was concerned, it was as the good Lord intended. We had a very unorthodox wedding. My father went searching all around Kraków because I hadn't told him where the wedding was going to be. I didn't want anybody there. I wouldn't have been able to stand all that ceremony. We were both like that. So, no one knew anything about it – just our closest friends, who were the witnesses. We took up residence in the Europejski, my favourite hotel, bought a crate of champagne, lit up a joint, and made our way on foot from the hotel to the registry office. There we said, 'Yes'. 'Yes'. Only then did I ring everyone: 'We've just got married! You're invited to the hotel for champagne.'

Were any of the musicians witnesses?
No – my friend Zdzisław, a jeweller and art historian, whom I've known for years.

You got married in Kraków, but you lived in Warsaw.
I moved in with Joaśka, on Górnośląska Street. Ania was born. Family life began very quickly. It didn't last very long: three years.

Could you not handle the challenge?
She couldn't handle it. Because I didn't change my lifestyle, and I was dangerous. I was inflexible. But I felt the separation very badly, because I was deeply attached to Ania. I was in a bad way. I remember it took me a long time to get myself together. Many, many months.

Did your wife throw you out?
No, she didn't throw me out, but she did let me know that she didn't want me in the house. We did get back together after that, but it didn't work. Nor did I want to be in the house either, because at that time I was going on benders. I felt that I was opening some kind of door and going into another dimension, into a completely different reality, into a totally different world.

Do you become a different person then?
I was wasted all the time. I could feel it coming on, and I'd start drinking. I'd go crazy. I remember shoving lumps of hashish (loose ones), into my pocket: fags, amphetamines, pills, all loose. A bottle. All my substances in my pocket. I'd put on a headscarf. I'd tie it under my chin, like a peasant woman. I'd put a hat over it, like the Peruvian women do. I was a Peruvian woman. I used to say, 'I'm a Peruvian woman!' Then I might have done anything. And I might go around like that for up to two weeks. Those benders started at Górnośląska Street, and then I'd end up booking into a hotel – the Solec for example – so I wouldn't have to go home. There was no knowing what might possess me. I had no restraint. I could feel distinctly that I was entering into a mad zone, where things were different, where different rules applied. I didn't know what those rules were, and I didn't particularly care.

What was it about this other world that attracted you?

The madness. The madness. Freaking out! The trip! In Remont, I used to like standing up against the amplifier, so close that the sound would push against me. I remember I used to have trouble on the door. The club managers would stand by me, so the bouncers couldn't do anything, and I used to provoke them. To create some danger! For the sake of the trip! The trip! I don't know everything I got up to. You don't remember it later. One drug dealer said that he saw me a few times in the Praga district with people who were so dangerous I could easily have got killed.

I can remember this one occasion in Bolesławiec. I woke up, as I recall, in a field somewhere . . . So, I'm walking through these fields. And there are these drunk bastards, these blokes. We're walking along together. I don't know where I am . . . Ah! I'm following them because they've got a bottle, and I want a drink. We sit down. One of them, with his great, big spade of a hand, takes hold of my hand. 'Ooh! Let's have a look at that!' I was wearing a gold ring. He took it and he put it in his pocket. I sensed the threat. I jumped to my feet and I was off. 'Fuck off, the lot of you!' They couldn't be bothered to run after me. I don't remember anything else. Maybe I did other things like that. My instinct used to save me. In some sly sort of way, I'd manage to avoid danger. That's how I navigated around that mad zone. I used to carry meat cleavers with me. I'd have a knife sticking out of my pocket. One time I went out carrying a spear . . .

What do you mean, a spear?

My mother was living with me at the time on Rozbrat Street, and she had a kind of bamboo cane. It was nice-looking. I'd take the bamboo and it would be my spear. With that scarf on my head. A hat on top of my scarf. I had a Borsalino then. I can remember going out with that spear and trying to get into Remont. I tried to get a taxi – you couldn't book one over the phone then. I walked out onto the Wisłostrada. I thought to myself, 'If I step out suddenly into this stream of traffic – suddenly, mind, so no one can get in my way – then they'll have to stop.' And that's what I fuckin' did. Of course, I nearly got killed. *And* there was a pile-up in the road. The militia arrives. And I'm standing there with a bottle in my hand, saying, 'The full catastrophe!' And one of the cars is a total write-off. The militia were actually quite nice to me. They recognized me. They took my name and let me go. 'We're not going to keep you, Mr Stańko. Just do us a favour, will you? Throw those knives away, get yourself home, and put yourself to bed. You can see what's happened.' They said it seriously. You see the sort of high jinks I got up to? You couldn't expect my wife to put up with a guy like that.

Was that the end of it?

There was a hearing. A lawyer friend got me off. I said to him, 'Maciek, I'll sign everything. I don't want to be there.' I didn't go to the hearing. He said it was a miracle that he managed to get me off, because I could have gone to prison. I'd caused a serious accident and endangered lives. Maciek still reproaches me for it. 'What did you get me into? The things I had to listen to on your account! Dear God!' But he did get me off. It was just the once that I got into that kind of situation.

When Chet Baker was imprisoned for drug trafficking, the famous Oriana Fallaci defended him in an impassioned article, in which she described him as a sensitive artist, suffering on behalf of millions of others. Do you think they used similar arguments in your defence?
And he was basically an ordinary drug addict! A demonic cat. Maciek probably had to say something along those lines. He told me it was a nightmare. Some guy's car was a write-off. And endangering life.

Were you already using stronger substances than marijuana or hashish?
I was taking speed. It pumped me up.

Was that the notorious Polish amphetamine?
No. A dopehead sold me some of the real stuff. He brought it over from Sweden, and he used to say, 'We'll soon be getting our own gear.' And, sure enough, Polish amphetamine appeared. Exceptionally good stuff. I used to buy it. With these kinds of performance-enhancing drugs, the body's tolerance increases. You're still sober but you're more high.

But, at the time of my marriage, I was mainly smoking, and a lot of it. That must have annoyed Joaśka. That Polish weed was too weak, and I used to distil the oil out of it. The whole flat would be full of little jars of milled weed, soaked in spirit. Expensive technology, too expensive, but that oil was much stronger to smoke. Once, I can remember not having had time to distil the oil off, so I took a jar with me on tour. I was doing solo concerts. Somewhere in Kielce, I drank a small glass of the stuff. As strong as a hundred joints! Concentrate. I was insatiable when I was high. It hit me in the middle of a concert. I got such a jolt! I had to stop playing. I couldn't play. So, you know, when you ask me about my marriage . . . It was tough.

Didn't the birth of your child give you a shake-up?
I loved Ania very much. But I didn't let it change my lifestyle. I was earning money, keeping my family. That's the kind of job it is.

Music gives a lot, takes away a lot.
That's right. I had more contact with Ania once she got to fifteen or sixteen. I was able to connect more deeply with her then, and, since that time, my relationship with her has continued to deepen.

1983.
Photograph by Andrzej Tyszko

After all those ordeals, didn't you simply feel lonely?

I don't feel lonely. I'm an Individual Being. IB. That term of Witkacy's really suits me. Not an alliance, or a group, or any patriot either: just an IB. I'm a Pole, I was born here; this is the language I speak. I'm deeply connected to this land, but, essentially, I basically mostly feel that I'm Tomasz Stańko. An Individual Being. I'm an unrepeatable collection of atoms. There isn't another one like me in the world, in the universe. I'm going along. Different people get stuck to me, different women, different situations, acquaintances. I'll be honest with you: I don't have that many friends. I have acquaintances. There was Roman Kowal. I'm good friends with Andrzej Tyszko and Tomasz Tłuczkiewicz. I feel closest to the people with whom I'm playing at any given moment. I feel connected to them through fellowship. Once the playing stops, that passes. I had an incredibly deep relationship with Vesala. The two of us were like brothers. We even look like we are in photos. I have tons of those photos. But, once we'd stopped playing, even though we did meet up, it wasn't like it used to be.

10 Green Face

In April 1974, you recorded *TWET*. In my opinion, that's your best album.

I like *TWET* a lot. It feels exceptionally good to me, that album: a really beautiful recording. I was a bit upset to begin with, because Professor Urbański, who recorded it, was known as someone who looked down on jazz. He was a professor at the higher school of music, in the sound recording department. A very traditional bloke, who couldn't even stand contemporary music, let alone jazz. He allegedly got students into trouble just for showing an interest in jazz. And then I find out that he's going to be doing the recording. And I'm thinking: 'Oh, shit!'

And you simply booked the recording studio at the higher school of music?

I didn't book the studio; Polish Recordings did. Urbański was assigned the task, as it were, because it was his studio. Disaster. What was I to do? Okay, so I ring him, and, with the utmost respect, I say to him, 'Sir! I'm going to be doing a recording with you. We have an international line-up, with a famous American double-bassist and a very well-known, modern Finnish percussionist. Would it be possible for us to meet and perhaps discuss the session and go through the details? As bandleader to session manager?' I made it clear that he was in charge of the whole thing, the fifth band member, co-creating our production: he was very happy about that. We met up and it was very agreeable. He totally got that this was a serious gig with an international line-up – not any old jazz, in some tavern or other, but modern music. He recorded us brilliantly!

During the session, Urbański sat at the back and listened. The atmosphere was superb; he ensured that we were able to focus and achieve a deeper, more mystical approach to our playing. It's always been like that with Manfred Eicher at ECM, but that was a rarity in Poland. In the radio studios, we used to just sit there, smoking, chatting – and then all of a sudden we'd be recording.

We've already talked about the gap that separates *Music for K* and *Purple Sun*, aesthetically: from fury to openness. There's a gap between *Purple Sun* and

TWET as well. *TWET* brings in spaciousness; in large part due to Edward Vesala, it carves out an entirely new dimension.

I write quite similar music, but I'm constantly widening the landscapes around me. That harmonic 'feeling' in 'Cry' – I'd already found my own language by then. On *Purple Sun*, it's fully developed in 'Fleur', a composition that I also used to play as 'Quintet's Time'. I like changing the titles of my compositions: this is all part of me as a person. My sound sphere is my beloved melodic lines, my dialogues and harmonic arrangements. The lines and dialogues lead to a harmonically complex code. I like referring to my compositions as codes or programmes; they allow me to improvise in different ways, depending on the line-up. So those albums are very diverse, although they do have a common root.

TWET sounds entirely different because the line-up is different: different times, a different style of improvisation. It leads to *Balladyna*, where the music's written down.

Did you just record improvisations on *TWET*?
That music was entirely improvised. So cool. That youngster, Tomasz Szukalski, who played phenomenally. And Peter Warren. The bass player I got to know at Stu Martin's – a Czech from America. He had *such* a sound!

You made the recording in the concert hall of the higher school of music.
We went up on stage, and we played sets, versions. We played for ourselves, as you do in a studio, because there was no audience. We were looking at one another – we'd been placed in a circle – I don't even think there were drums between us. We had more contact. The moment of concentration. The playing. Version approved. That's why I'd spoken with the Professor, so that we wouldn't have any of that 'Gentlemen! One more time please, because I didn't get the drums.' That's a nightmare, and that's what used to happen all the time with the Polish sound engineers. But, because of the authority the Professor had, his helpers were on such a tight leash that that way of doing things was disrupted. They'd worked hard to prepare themselves for the recording, so that nothing would go wrong. There wasn't any of that sloppiness that sound engineers always have, working on the assumption that you can always do it again. You can never do it again! You can't repeat music. And they learn to press the stop button, cut something out and move it. You can't cut anything out! This is improvised music! And, thanks to Professor Urbański, I acquired a way of doing things that I always used after that.

You recorded over one day, but I believe you ended up with extra material?
Yes, we recorded backup material. And then chose takes for the album.

The *TWET* quartet, 1974. From left: Peter Warren, Tomasz Szukalski, Tomasz Stańko, Edward Vesala. Courtesy Anna Stańko

What about the rest of the material? If the performances went so well, it would be interesting to hear what else was produced during that session.
You know – I don't know. I'm glad you've reminded me. Though I doubt they'll have kept it. It's thirty-five years ago now. Professor Urbański is long dead. They may well have wiped it; tapes were reused over and over.

What sort of reception did *TWET* have?
Excellent. I'd laid the ground with the quintet. Even the older musicians, like Wojciech Karolak, who didn't like free, respected my music. And then playing free became widespread. Nowadays, young musicians, whether they're capable of it or not, are keen to play free. The less capable they are, the keener they are. If I ask a guy whether he plays free, I'll hear straight away 'Sure, sure', and I can see from the glint in his eye that he's keen. Obviously, not everyone does it well.

After recording *Music for K*, wasn't the quintet offered another album with Polish Jazz?
No. We released two records in Germany.

Was releasing *TWET* your idea?
Yes. I wanted to have a new album out in Poland. I got the impression that Polskie Nagrania didn't want to be releasing much jazz anymore. It wasn't easy to get a record out. I managed it with *TWET* because we had an international

line-up; that was the selling point. I toured with that line-up first of all. I got Vesala and Warren over to Poland. I remember us playing in Wrocław at the Jazz on the Oder festival.

In Poland, you found Tomasz Szukalski for your new band.
Even as a young cat, he was regarded as a very good saxophonist. You know straight away if someone can play well; you only need to hear them once. When I met him, he was still a child. He was only about twenty and used to hang around Dziekanka. I can't even remember exactly when I brought him into the band, but I took him on because it was obvious that he could play brilliantly. He played well right from the start.

That's how it is with the best musicians. Janusz Skowron, Sławomir Kurkiewicz, Marcin Wasilewski, and the young Michał Miśkiewicz, were good right from the start; whenever I played with them, I was always surprised. Marcin Masecki's like that too.

At that time, in the mid-1970s, Szukalski was playing with both you and Zbigniew Namysłowski. Was there any competition between you?
I don't think so. I always had a lot of work. Playing with me was highly prestigious, because Komeda and the quintet had given me status. I had no difficulty hiring musicians; they'd drop everything to play with me. I didn't nick Szukalski off Namysłowski.

After Namysłowski released *Winobranie* in 1973, you two were the leading modern jazzmen on the Polish market.
Namysłowski was highly thought of right from the start, especially among journalists, who regarded him as a *wunderkind*. As a child, he could play brilliant trad jazz on the trombone, and then he set up his well-known band, Rockers, with Michał Urbaniak. And then there was his quartet, a really famous band. 'Lola'; 'Piątawka' – that's some tremendous playing. And *Winobranie* too. Might I have been jealous? When they drew comparisons between us, I could only be delighted. And, later, I carved out a strong position for myself in my own right. The quintet was, after all, the first Polish band to perform at major international festivals; we had agents in Germany. Maybe the journalists enjoyed stirring things up, but I don't think that there was any competition between us. Anyway, we used to play together; I played with Zbigniew's quartet in Geneva.

What did you think of *Winobranie*?
I liked it a lot. I always thought highly of Zbigniew. When I hear playing of that calibre, I can say: 'Beautiful music'.

A few years ago, there was a poll in *Jazz Forum*: 'The 10 best Polish jazz records'. The top three were *Astigmatic*, *Litania* and *Winobranie*. There are another

two of your albums in the top ten: *Music for K* and *Suspended Night*. I was astounded that neither *TWET* nor *Balladyna* were there.

People might not remember.

On *TWET* and *Balladyna*, which the quartet recorded, the second pillar there alongside you was the Finnish percussionist Edward Vesala. Did you meet him in Germany?

If we were recording *TWET* in the April, then I'd have met him a year earlier, also in the spring, in Germany. Vesala was playing with Jan Garbarek at the Jazzkeller. It was funny because, sitting right nearby in a booth was Trilok Gurtu, who was living in Germany at the time and trying to break through. I think that's where I met not only Vesala but Trilok as well. Garbarek asked me to play with the trio, Triptykon. We played with Arild Andersen and Edward. It was great playing with them. Garbarek was definitely playing free then.

The young Garbarek also played on a famous record by one of your favourites, George Russell, on *Electric Sonata for Souls Loved by Nature*.

It was for Russell that Garbarek learned to read music. He was an amateur and he didn't need sheet music to play jazz. But when he got the invitation from Russell, he learned to read music within a matter of months and he read Russell's difficult compositions with ease. Do you see? Garbarek's that kind of guy. He's talented and he has an innate facility for music.

That's an interesting recording. Russell, at the end of the 1960s, had a concept like Miles Davis did a few years later, because this is playing free fusion music with electronica and trance rhythms.

I don't know those recordings. I was interested in Russell's Lydian modes and the compositions he'd based on them. Brilliant. Now that you've reminded me of them, I think I'd like to play them again.

Was it in Garbarek's band that you connected with Vesala?

I liked the way he played, because his playing is unusual. Different. It has scope, colour. No one played on percussion like Edward did. He played melodically. He played a certain type of melody and provided an excellent counterpoint to my lyrical language. We just didn't have any bass players that we were particularly keen on, apart from Dave Holland, who played on *Balladyna*.

Your fascination with Vesala's playing turned into friendship.

It turned into a deep friendship. I asked Edward to tour with me in Poland. We played with Peter Warren. And that's when we bonded. Then he invited me to Finland, where we had an excellent line-up with the Finnish saxophonist Juhani Aaltonen and Arild Andersen, the Norwegian bass player from Garbarek's trio. We began scheming together. Later, Tomasz Szukalski had a permanent place in the band. He was very creative in that band; we particularly liked his sound, his expression. But we always had trouble with bass players. We'd occasionally

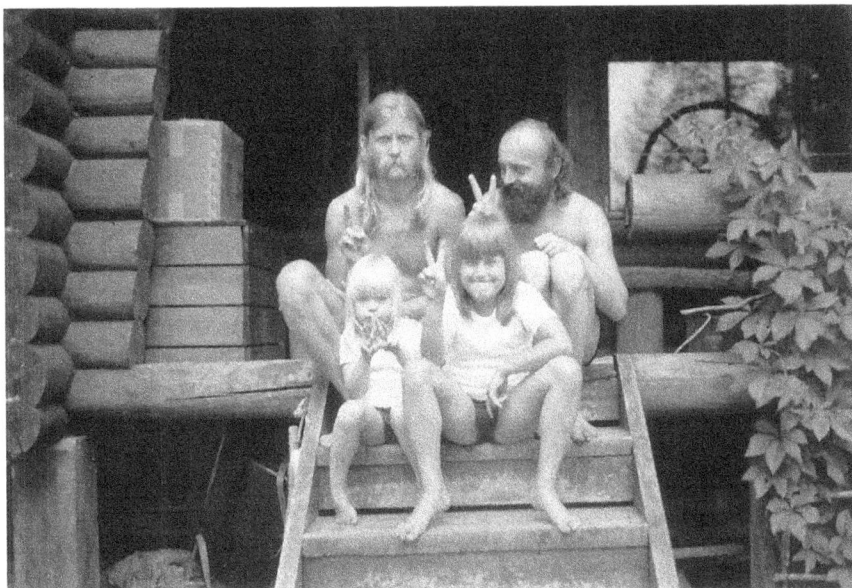

With Edward, Mintu (on the left) and Maria Vesala, on holiday in Finland, late 1970s.
Courtesy Anna Stańko

play with Paweł Jarzębski or with Zbigniew Wegehaupt; we'd also play with him in trios on occasion. We didn't do any concerts with Dave Holland – just the *Balladyna* recording. The Finnish bassist Antti Hytti played with us for a long time. He had an interesting sound, a sparse one. We did big tours with him in Germany and Italy. That's when we recorded a tape, *Live in Palermo*, which is still waiting to be released. We also played concerts in Finland and Poland.

Finland is quite an exotic place to be playing jazz.
It's a great place. Edward always arranged for us to have a sauna after a concert. There wasn't a lively jazz scene there; we'd have three random people coming to our concerts. In smaller towns, we performed in restaurants or cultural centres. In Poland, when the quintet played the small towns, the conditions were similar, except that in Finland we could also do gigs in taverns; they didn't put dances on then. Edward's situation there was similar to mine in Poland – an innovative musician in a country with a traditional mindset. He socialized with the most interesting film people, artists, creative people from all sorts of fields. Modern jazz had status in Finland at that time, like in Poland during the Komeda and Trzaskowski era. Although Edward used to get slapped down by those narrow-minded, mediocre musicians who used to say that he couldn't play, because he only played free. And yet he was a person with extraordinary imagination and huge charisma.

Edward and I hung around together all the time. We were friends. Totally. During his first marriage, Edward lived in Hakunila, a suburb of Helsinki. When I went over to Finland, his daughters would go to bed in their parents' room and I'd sleep in their nursery. We spent all our time together. And we smoked joints non-stop, from morning till night.

Did Vesala live a hippie lifestyle?
He definitely had a hippie lifestyle, a hippie look. He also kept company with hippies. Dealers, the underworld, you could say: desperados, actors . . . All kinds of people. I met the son of a famous Finnish composer, who was a dope dealer. We got on well with him; he was a nice cat; we often spent time with him. Vesala had a studio in Helsinki, a kind of box-room, where we used to practise. We'd play all day long, only going out to meet up with friends. And then we'd always go on tour. That went on for many years.

Then, in the 1980s, we had a trio with Reggie Workman. We went on a two-and-a-half-month tour. We played a lot as a duo. We also toured as a duo, mainly in Finland; Edward used to arrange that. It was a wonderful time. Wonderful, colourful music. Very high. There are some excellent tapes, which still haven't been released. We also had larger projects. There was one band: Edward and I, Charlie Mariano, Garbarek, J.-F. Jenny-Clark, orchestral musicians from Finland, Iro Haarla.

At that time, Edward got married for the second time, to a young pianist and harpist, Iro Haarla. Garbarek thought very highly of her. It was a brilliant line-up. Iro playing harp, Charlie Mariano on alto sax. And Jenny-Clark was the only bass player who loved playing with Edward. Bass players didn't like Edward because they found it hard-going playing with him; he used to slow the tempo down. Still, that virtuoso aspect of Jenny-Clark's playing fitted brilliantly with Edward's arched, ad-lib pulse. They felt great together, and they formed a sensational rhythm section. That session came after *Satu*, but before *Heavy Life*. The tape's lying around in the archives somewhere; it would be a pity if it never got released.

What about your collaborations as a duo? Were they not released, either? Are there any studio or concert recordings?
Edward hired the studio. There's a master tape, excellent quality. Edward had absolutely tons of tapes, many of them unreleased. Even those albums that were released haven't been re-released. Edward owned Leo Records,* and we don't know who has the rights to those records.

---

* *Series Editor's note:* This is not the same company as the UK-based Leo Records notable for the Russian free jazz in its catalogue.

On the cusp of the 1970s and 1980s, two of your own records and a few joint ones were released by Leo and by another Finnish record label: Love.
Love was a hippie label run by modern people with a non-commercial approach. But Leo was Edward's own label.

In 1978, on Leo, you recorded an album, *Almost Green*. With Vesala, Szukalski and Palle Danielsson on bass.
We recorded it in Sweden, in Stockholm. It's in the same vein as *Balladyna*, only it goes further.

Those green motifs, the theme *From the Green Hill*, returned more than twenty years later, on an album for ECM.
That melody returned.

Where does this greenness come from? Scandinavian nature?
A green face! Green from smoking. *Almost Green* – practically green; we were obviously smoking a lot. Vesala did get into trouble, after all; he was caught and spent time in prison.

They arrested him in Finland for smoking marijuana?
You know, he'd buy a kilo and save half of it for distribution so he'd have the other half at no cost . . . He still got away with it. He spent a few months in prison. They used to drive him to church, so that he could play the organ. He had a drum kit in his cell.

On another record that you made for Leo, your solo album *Taj Mahal*, the theme, this time, is 'Almost Black'.
That's how I used to group those titles together. But titles for me are abstract. In fact, they don't mean anything, and they're not supposed to mean anything. Just enough, so we know which one's which.

Among the compositions from that period, there's also one with the title 'Daada'.
It's nothing to do with Dadaism. That's what my daughter used to call me; it was her baby-babble at the time.

Yet Dadaism describes this music perfectly. It describes those sort of slightly bent melodic figures.
That's true. I can see that, when I look at it now.

I have to ask you about another particular title from that period. On *Rodina* from 1976, the first of a whole series of Vesala albums on which you appear,

In Finland, during a visit to Vesala's, late 1970s.
Courtesy Anna Stańko

there's a duet of yours with the title 'Dady and Komba'. That gives the impression that those were your nicknames.
Komba. Komba – Gąba. I used to laugh and say that Edward was like a sponge.* He smokes so much, he absorbs the smoke like a sponge. So he called himself Komba.

And I was 'Dady' because I was a daddy; that's when Ania was born.

There was also a 'Komba' theme. And that's repeated on a few recordings. Like, for example, on the Polish release *Live at Remont* from 1976, where you're playing with Szukalski and Antti Hytti.
I did 'Komba' for him. I arranged it because Vesala didn't write music. He used to whistle; he'd whistle certain things, and then I had to arrange them into a composition for him. I approved of this method because Edward was using his power and charisma.

Well, that's interesting, because on his albums from the mid-1970s onwards, Vesala took on ever-larger bands. Sound & Fury, his band from the 1980s, was a big band. And yet it turns out that he couldn't write this music down.
Edward always had a predilection for big bands. And he always had people who wrote his music down for him. I can't remember who it was who used to do it. Later, it was Iro who wrote down the big-band music. He used to whistle it

---

* *Translator's note: Gąbka* or 'sponge' in Polish sounds a bit like the made-up word 'Komba'.

to her. I tell you: it was astonishing. How *do* you write that down? But Vesala would insist on doing it his way, and that music was very strangely structured. A strange way, an altogether un-composer-like, untraditional way. A strange Finnish way. Those tubas, the combination of instruments, the line-ups: those were all his ideas. Iro had to write down that very unusual orchestration, to bring together Edward's amateurism and his 'high', and that power of his, that vitality. She wrote down the strange instrumentation and created a style that Manfred Eicher would be delighted to record, because it was something completely different.

You played on the first of Vesala's ECM records, *Satu*, from 1976. Szukalski's also playing there. You could say that it's an album in the same vein as *Balladyna*.
A little bit. But it was essentially Edward's music. Interesting music. I wrote one of the arrangements for him.

Maybe the melodic vibe of *Satu*, such a singing, hymn-like one, links it to *Balladyna*. The same with the whole series of records that you made together at the end of the 1970s: *Almost Green*, *Rodina*. Do you think that *Balladyna* had an influence on Vesala?
These were all our collaborations; we sat and worked on them together. Edward picked up on the melodiousness, definitely. Everything that we recorded later, all that began with *Balladyna*.

11 Bending the Note

Balladyna, recorded in 1975 for ECM, was your most important recording with Edward Vesala and Tomasz Szukalski.

It's strange. That record was treated very seriously by the American musicians. From what Jim Black and many Americans said to me, to them, it was shockingly innovative music. My international name was built on *Balladyna*.

On your travels, did you meet any *Balladyna* fans?

Absolutely loads. I can't remember names anymore, but I was told by a lot of musicians that *Balladyna* was the record that inspired them most in their youth. The way I talk about George Russell or Ornette Coleman, that's how people saw *Balladyna*. It was a different kind of playing from what they were familiar with – something that had begun in Europe, which they didn't have in the States. It was a joining-together of melodic playing with free.

Balladyna established a certain style, which I've essentially carried on with till now. A rather unconventional kind of scale and the particular application of two voices – because I relied mainly on two voices – defined my signature language. It's a language that isn't based so much on scales as on a certain melodic atonality. A simple-sounding, melodic music, but with a certain atonality, because there's an ongoing counterpoint from the second voice, which makes the whole thing abstract. Such is my concept. On the one hand, something incredibly simple and natural, maybe even crude in idea, and on the other hand an accentuated contrapuntal line. What I want, and what I take care to do, is to try to compose in a way that makes this line not so much strange, but as distant as possible from that simple beauty. Not ugly. Different: very atypical. It's about an otherness, where there are no rules, where no particular scale has a critical significance.

It's simply my aesthetic that imposes this otherness and accentuates it. I move into the realm of beauty, a beauty that has been acknowledged throughout the entire history of music, and, at the same time, I break it up completely, to find myself in an entirely different world, in which beauty is something else. And that's *all* my music.

All my compositions and ballads employ simple ideas, but sometimes a counterpoint will appear that knocks everything sideways. You don't hear it consciously, when you're focusing on the beauty, but it works underneath.

That second line allows me to play what I want; it gives me permission as a soloist to behave in a completely free way, to use a free language. I don't have to be in any particular key. I just need excellent musicians, who can interpret that second line and know how to bend it. Not everyone bends it. Vesala could master all kinds of bend. It was very close to his aesthetic.

Balladyna was your first album recorded for the German label ECM. What led to your making contact with the head of ECM, Manfred Eicher?
Edward had recorded for ECM with Jan Garbarek's group, and he knew Manfred. He initiated a conversation with Manfred, and Manfred immediately struck a deal. The recording session was set up very quickly, in Ludwigsburg, near Stuttgart. Dave Holland came over. We recorded the entire thing over two days.

How did Dave Holland come to be involved?
Eicher got him over. We said we didn't have a bass player. Manfred doesn't do that sort of thing anymore, but it's become the fashion among local musicians: they invite famous names and that makes it easier for them to secure recording deals. Manfred was the first person to have that idea; he'd always be putting some big name together with a group. In the case of *Balladyna*, it was a masterstroke, because Dave played everything, and at the same time he played free beautifully.

Holland was known at that time as Miles Davis's musician.
Yes. A great guy. That was the first time I'd played with a musician of that class. I remember him coming into the studio that first time, confident; he took the music; I'd given him the outline. He took the motif from 'First Song', played through the scale once and he'd found his bearings. He caught the movement of the melody, the most characteristic parts that would work for a walking bass. I saw him do it at lighting speed, and I heard straight away how he'd made the piece sound. He knew! He sensed the notes that were right for this music, the melodic bends, and put them through different configurations, different processes, intuitively. And it worked! I hadn't worked out a rhythm for 'First Song', and there was some discussion about what rhythm to start off with. Holland created it along with Edward; they co-created the arrangement.

What was your first meeting with Eicher like?
Good. Nice. He was known for being a demanding, difficult guy. But he turned out to be likeable. I never clashed with Eicher.

What role did Eicher play in the recording?
Eicher is always present; he becomes part of the band. He co-creates the sound. He makes suggestions; he intervenes. I think it was Eicher who suggested we change the rhythm in 'First Song'. What he wanted was for the free part to be anchored to a more traditional metre. And Dave started that ostinato riff;

Edward put something over the top and they fused together into a strange backing, which naturally gave the composition a rhythm.

Had Eicher seen the music beforehand?
No, that all happened as we were playing. Eicher doesn't change the notes. He can't change them because he's not a musician. He acts as a catalyst. He gives us an idea. He talks about changes and he has the authority to back it up. He can use his authority to make the musicians want to create something different. It's a practical technique and it always works. How does it work, though? No one really knows.

Asking that is like asking Ornette about his 'harmolodic' system. Trying to figure out what 'harmolodic' means: that's crazy. What actually is it? It doesn't matter, so there's no point asking. It's just harmolodic! I don't know if you know, but I know exactly what it is. It's the very essence of Ornette Coleman's music. But how does it work? What is it? Those are the wrong questions. There's no such thing as harmolodic! It's harmolodic when Ornette says it is.

Music is an abstract form. Supplementary information about music is something abstract as well. Not a definition, but a different notion. What kind of notion? Well, it's best expressed in a word like 'harmolodic' because it describes something that doesn't exist. And yet it does! It most definitely does!

The very sound of the word 'harmolodic' best conveys Ornette's music, conjures up his strange melodies.

Do you also associate 'harmolodic' with Eicher?
It's impossible to describe exactly how Manfred operates. The fact is, he has a stimulating effect. When you record with him, you find ways to express yourself that you wouldn't ordinarily find. Eicher works through his personality, his status and his charisma, just like Miles did.

All Miles had to do was stand on stage and the other musicians would behave differently from how they usually did. Miles would get his musicians and, with either a smile, or with contempt, or with indifference, he'd fuckin' line them up so that they'd play strong enough for him. I saw Miles do a gig where he just played with Keith Jarrett, with Gary Bartz just standing there not knowing what to do. Miles would let him in, just like that, for a moment's solo, but he and Keith played together: Keith did what he wanted. But we can't have everyone in a band doing whatever they want. On the contrary: if you have one person doing whatever he wants, then all the others have to sit there like fuckin' dogs and be afraid. If Bartz had pushed himself forward, he'd have changed the proportions, but it was Keith who determined the whole with his 'high' playing. That's why I really like working with Manfred; he does the same.

You mentioned that *Balladyna* was a written album. I think you just had the melodic motifs, didn't you?

Only the motifs were written down, but they were a big organizing factor.

If *TWET* opened up a new dimension in your music, then that's the dimension within which *Balladyna* establishes its melody. And that's what makes it extraordinary.

Yes, that's the natural way. I did come out of free, after all. To start off, free opens me up; via a quick process, I can independently create something new, which I then consolidate. *Purple Sun* and *TWET* still don't have any harmonic instruments on them. There aren't any on *Balladyna* either, but here I was able to determine a certain harmonic centre through melodic lines. Maybe it was more of a harmonic impression, which I made more focused later on in my quartets with piano.

On *Balladyna* it's the melodies that make the deepest impression. Where did they come from?

They're kind of lines. It's difficult to say where they come from. Just as it's difficult to say where Veronese got his green. That's me. Those melodies are the product of my brain, my IB, Individual Being. It's my melodic line and I like it. I like looking for simple elements, the kind that speak to the masses through their conventional beauty – even if this borders on kitsch, because I can always counterpoint it, and give it depth with some more refined idea, some second voice. It allows for an entirely new way of driving a melody, of winding it up, bending it, so that, totally unexpectedly, its simplicity and kitsch dissolve. Out of a combination like that, I'm able to create an astonishing line, which brings me closer to what I like best – to something that's between simplest and most difficult. Then I have those two things at once, alongside each other. I've thought this through deeply – that it's as important to touch the emotions of a simple woman as it is to write Beethoven's *da-da-da-daah*! Because this is what being human is. A very broad perspective on beauty and the role of the artist.

The melodies in *Balladyna* have a hymn-like ambience, even a sublime one.

Maybe so, but that's less important to me. What's important is my note, the one that comes in there. That *too too tee too taa daaaaa*! Completely different! Totally! That note is mine. It determines the counterpoint. And we're already in a different key. That *daaaaa* really helped me. I don't even know whether it comes out by chance. I start improvising, and then suddenly . . . I find it. It's like with modes: when you try to transpose them mathematically, every so often something emerges, something different. Most of the time, when you hit on it randomly, you don't find a mysterious note like that, but sometimes you do. And then I have a hook for a composition, and then I know how to continue composing. When I get down to composing, I know what I want.

When you're in a particular mode, you're using mathematical sequences of sound and there are usually standard combinations, like a scale; but, every so often, that structure becomes something exceptional, a kind of black hole, a junction. I'm always looking for those kinds of things, in all combinations. In harmonic music, I'm looking for that bend, that one note: *daaaaaa!* But the rest of the time we're usually moving around within known values or aesthetics.

That one note, that bend, gives the impression that its purpose is to give you some kind of way out, a way to . . .
To somewhere else. We have a bend. Maybe it's those knots that they call strings in physics. Suddenly we find ourselves in a universe billions of light years away. This is where there are some kind of knots in the fabric of the universe. Through these we reach other dimensions, a long way away, very deep – who knows where. Maybe I'm interpreting this in a literary way, but in mathematics there are strange combinations that appear every so often in numerical sequences. I react to this in an intuitive way. That's how I compose, while also using ordinary, very simple elements, bordering on kitsch, like that tapestry of a rutting deer.*

Do you think about features of folk music?
No. This isn't from folk music. I don't draw on folk music.

Maybe such elements appear intuitively, unconsciously.
Maybe. But it's not important. The important thing is to reach that point, that junction.

One might discern some eastern echoes in those melodies. Maybe that's the Galician element we're hearing?
Maybe it's to do with the minor third. Jewish and eastern melodies often use combinations of small intervals. But I wouldn't go reading too much into my Galician roots.

I remember a critic from *Tygodnik Powszechny* (the *Universal Weekly*) claiming to hear echoes of the old Polish hymn 'Bogurodzica' in *Balladyna*'s melodies. They seem to like discussing your music there: the trumpet part being like a prayer.
Well, no. It's not like that. I play in a very realistic way. I have to keep my feet on the ground to have control over the material. Even when I was smoking a lot of hashish, as soon as my lips touched the trumpet's mouthpiece, my clarity of thought returned within a split second. You have to have control over what

---

* *Series Editor's note:* This refers to one of the Flemish tapestries in the Royal Castle of Wawel in Kraków, which were evacuated from the country during World War II and eventually stored in Canada, before being returned to Poland in 1961. The images were well known after their restitution to their original location during the communist era.

you're playing, otherwise everything will fall apart. Sometimes I go into states where the playing's going great and I'm in some kind of euphoria. I have a sudden recall of distant impressions; one sound reminds me of another. So I play it; I keep that feeling going, like in a trance. But I doubt anyone notices. What gets me into a trance is the precision of my playing, the satisfaction of playing as well as I can. Of course, the listener might be experiencing my music very differently. And I definitely agree that my music is spiritual. But spirituality does not have to be religious. I'm not religious. Spirituality is a form of sophistication in life. It's a sign of richness, of complexity. God is a natural part of our consciousness, an expression of our complex brain development. The brain somehow produces God; at a certain level of complexity, a specific feature of the brain is faith.

How do you compose your melodic motifs? Do they come out of your playing, or do you sit down and write?
I sit down and write. I sit. Mostly behind the piano. I wrote *Balladyna* in a hotel, without a piano. I played on the trumpet. I can remember it as if it were today: it was in Germany and I was on tour with Adam Makowicz. I had two free days and I thought, 'Now I need to write some music.' I had no time, and we had a recording session booked. I shut myself away in this little hotel and did some writing. That's when the three main compositions emerged: 'First Song', 'Last Song' and 'Balladyna'.

When you're writing, are you influenced by what you remember from earlier improvisations?
No. I try to start afresh. I try to compose a certain programme, a code, which I'll subsequently improvise on. I also often write (as we do in traditional music) harmonic chords. That's how I did it for the quartet. I find it easiest to write when I have a concrete reason or a commission for a film or an album. I find it easier to work then. But I'm inclined to laziness, maybe because that gives me more time to be creative. I don't want to get down to it. It takes me a long time to write. My daughter urges me to get on with it. But I don't feel like it.

I find my new quintet, with guitar, extremely interesting, exceptionally interesting . . . I have a melodic piano and a guitar for the second voice. I might have three voices. I have two guitars – a low one (bass) and a standard one. I could play the melody in unison with them, like with saxophone. I don't want to play with saxophone now, to be honest, and I'm pleased with this new line-up.

All the same, you did recently play with a saxophonist. And that was the New Balladyna programme.
I played because Maciej Obara is a very good saxophonist. A very interesting young cat.

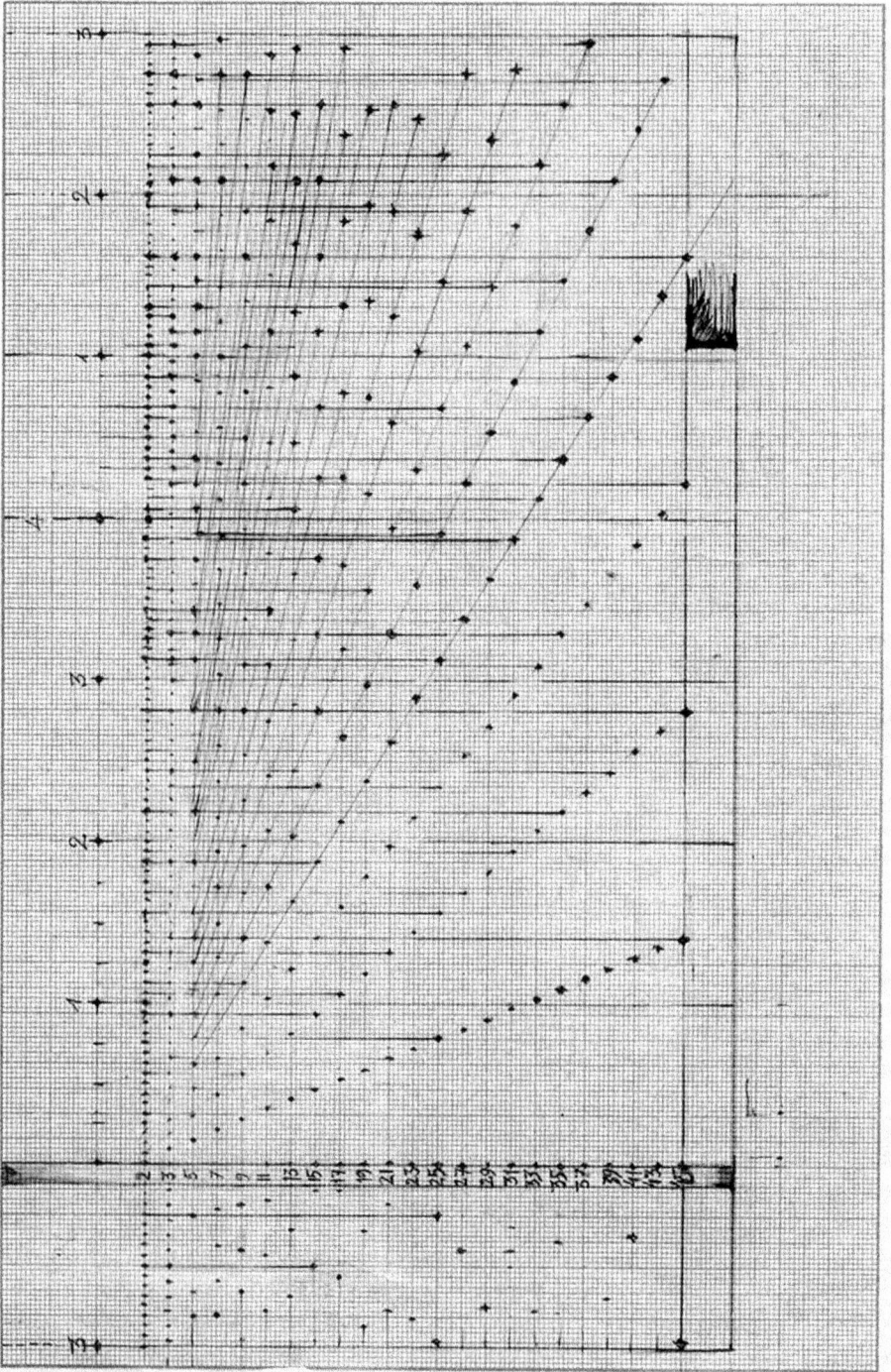

Rhythmic structures.
Courtesy Anna Stańko

Compositions from *Balladyna* have also appeared on the album *Lontano* and on *January*, the second ECM album from Marcin Wasilewski's trio.
Those are excellent, very intense compositions. I'm still pleased with them. And jazz compositions have a short life. People write new things all the time. I like playing old things. Like Komeda's music, which still sounds brilliant after all these years. I remember us playing *Kattorna* in Leipzig with John Abercrombie. Wynton Marsalis's drummer had remembered the motif from the States from Michał Urbaniak's performances, and he says, 'What's this? Is it some Polish tune?' In other words, it's distinctive music, immediately recognizable.

What exactly gave you the idea for the New Balladyna quartet?
These decisions often come about by chance. I got a commission from Copenhagen. I was already playing there with the quartet, and they wanted a different line-up. I had a Danish percussionist, Stefan Pasborg, and I was wondering what to do next. As Tim Berne was also in the area, I thought I might make up a quartet with saxophone, play pieces from *Balladyna*, add a few new ones. Anders Jormin played bass. We got a fantastic reception in Copenhagen. At a big festival in Tivoli, in the big concert hall. That was three years ago. Then, when I noticed that Obara had an interesting way of playing – he has a good sound – I thought to myself that if I'm going to be playing with him, then it should obviously be this programme because it is alto sax, after all. We played two concerts. We don't play often, but we do like playing together.

In the 1970s, you worked on a new album for ECM, but it never got recorded.
I worked on my second album for a long time. We'd even made some decisions; we'd met with Manfred at a recording session with Gary Peacock, just before martial law. Yet those difficulties we had communicating from Poland . . . Manfred thought well of me, but he didn't push it either. He had thousands of projects on the go. He was having a lot of success then with Keith Jarrett, Jan Garbarek, Pat Metheny. If an artist didn't look out for himself, it was left to chance.

I think ECM's development is all improvised. Eicher doesn't have any particular plans, and in any case he has various plans on the go at once and they can all change. He's interested in lots of things; that's his great strength, and that's the reason why, after all these years, ECM keeps moving forward.

At the recording with Peacock, we'd even decided on the line-up. I remember that Billy Hart was going to be on drums, but then I didn't manage to get in touch with Manfred. Maybe I was too slow. I was living a bit of a wild life at the time. The shutting-down of Poland through martial law had a serious effect on me. It caused me a lot of problems. There were no fax machines and it was very difficult to get through to anyone on the phone. And getting hold of Manfred by phone is a feat in itself. He's constantly busy because he's keeping tabs on everything. Tony Oxley's a famous case in point: he spent years trying to get through to Manfred on the phone. 'Manfred is in a meeting' is a famous catchphrase of Helga, his secretary. And I'd lose heart. And to talk to Munich, I used to have to book a call at the post office. With my usual bad luck, it might have taken me twenty years to get through to Manfred again.

Did you use the music off that album anywhere else?
None of it was written down. I didn't write until I had a recording booked.

Apparently, Werner X. Uehlinger, head of the Swiss label Hat Hut Records, has said that he'd wanted to produce Stańko in the 1970s, but he was afraid that Eicher would take offence. He was releasing a lot of what was premier-league free music at the time: David Murray with Andrew Cyrille, Oliver Lake, Joe McPhee.
That might be true, but I don't remember having had any contact with him. You see what we mean when we say chance? I'm looking for drummers at the moment. And now I'm reminded of Cyrille because he plays rhythmic music and he's free. I recently heard him in a line-up with Murray, here, in Warsaw. We'll have to meet up in New York. I'm also thinking about the pianist Craig Taborn. I'd like to perform my ballads – that delicate, neurotic, European music in a manly, rough way. I'd like to try it out with some New York musicians, have them play the harmonies not in a romantic but in a tough way. There's also this new bass player, Thomas Morgan. I've heard him play with Paul Motian. His playing was strange – interesting.

During your collaboration period with Vesala, you recorded an album in New York with the cream of the crop of New York musicians.
That was such a trip. Around 1980. A really interesting story. Vesala and I set off with a suitcase full of money. We moved in to a kind of junkie hotel, which Jan Byrczek had actually recommended. It was a transit point for drug traffickers on 42nd Street. When Cecil Taylor subsequently found out that I was staying there, he stood stock still and went pale; his skin actually went grey. 'My God!' he said, 'You wouldn't see me within twenty yards of that hotel. It's one of the most dangerous places in New York.' Because it was a hangout for mid-level drug traffickers, where bodies drop. We stayed there for a month; on top of that, we twice forgot to close the door and left it ajar. We had 15,000 bank notes in our suitcase, all our equipment, everything. And we had prostitutes wandering around in the corridors, the ones they had working on 42nd Street. And the mid-level drug traffickers: the worst kind, basically. But it was the cheapest hotel, and we weren't scared. We smoked dope, and they respected us for being artists. They absolutely wouldn't have harmed us. After all, no one does that sort of thing on their own doorstep. They'd finish someone off in the street, but not in their own home. They didn't even go in the room when the door was open. I have very fond memories of our time there.

What was the hotel called?

What was it called? Hang on . . . Let me think. There was a snack bar next door: *Śnieżynka*, a Czech bar, open 24/7 but serving breakfast all day. Nothing but breakfast. I used to see people turning up at five in the afternoon, sleepy-eyed, for their breakfast. It was near Broadway, and artists would come over. A fabulous location. It was on Columbus Circle, where the Lincoln Center is now. They knocked everything down, and now there's this gigantic office block with offices and shops and a concert hall, where Wynton Marsalis plays. Obviously, that hovel's not there anymore. Oh yes! It was the Apollo Hotel.

But we rehearsed at Stu Martin's place. Peter Warren and his girlfriend also hung out there. That was just before Stu died. He'd gone back to New York, split up with Lee, who'd stayed in Paris. He had a loft, and that's where we played. There were all sorts of girls hanging around there. I met a really nice one, who actually showed up at my recent concert in New York. This older lady came up to me, yet back then she was a beautiful young woman.

Musically speaking, what was happening then?

We were mainly looking for musicians. Putting a band together. We set everything up there. We picked people, rang them, walked around, smoked joints, went to the nightclubs. With New York there making this constant impression on us. Wonderful times.

You wanted to record an album in New York, but you hadn't got a band together. So Vesala's idea was: just go on the off-chance?

Just go! Take our money, our instruments. Find some people. Hire a studio. And record an album there. He already had his lines written down, his compositions. He had a few leads. We rang Reggie Workman, James Spaulding, Bob Stewart. The tuba player Bob Stewart helped us find Joe Daley for second tuba and Howard Johnson for baritone sax. Someone recommended we get Chico Freeman on tenor.

Each of those people is a different tradition. A great tradition. Workman played with both Art Blakey's Jazz Messengers and with Coltrane.

He plays everything. And with Woody Shaw he played free. And he wanted to play free.

What about James Spaulding? He started out with Sun Ra, and then he did a whole series of famous recordings for Blue Note.

Yes. Yet he's an ordinary, standard alto saxophonist. But, you know, we had a very cleverly-put-together line-up. These people were excellent. All professionals. It was brilliant playing with Spaulding. I'll have to meet up with him now in New York. A charming man!

Did Spaulding say anything about playing with Sun Ra? After all, he didn't half bend it and shake up the big-band tradition.

I don't remember. The only contact we had, in fact, was musical, while playing. We didn't have chance to talk. You could feel his power. I think it's all about professionalism, and their life-stories gave them more depth. If you've spent your entire life working with the best of them, then you're a conglomeration built out of noble materials.

Your longest collaboration turned out to be with Workman, with whom you later played concerts as a trio.

Workman is now a great friend of mine. At the time he badly wanted to play European, arrhythmical free jazz. That's what he valued most at the time; experimentation really suited him. He said he found it difficult playing with Edward, but, when big personalities meet, some of the difficulties can be very creative. Workman played beautifully. It's a great album. *Heavy Life.*

Was Vesala pleased with the outcome of this crazy expedition?

I don't know. When we later played with that band in Warsaw, at Jazz Jamboree, it went badly. They didn't like us. Spaulding bailed out at the last minute, or was that Chico Freeman? Rosengren was supposed to be there, but he didn't make it. We had Polish musicians: there was Henryk Miśkiewicz, Stanisław Cieślak on trombone, and Zdzisław Piernik on tuba, who was weak. Somehow the band didn't work. The Polish musicians didn't like Vesala. To conventionally educated musicians, Vesala was an ignoramus. It's the same principle as with the musicians from the music school circle in Katowice, who today fail to appreciate musicians like the Oleś Brothers or the yass musicians. It's a natural tendency. And that's why Vesala sometimes didn't go down well.

Your close collaboration with Vesala lasted from the mid-1970s to the beginning of the 1980s. Later, when you both had your own bands, what was your relationship like?

I was in contact with Edward, to a lesser or greater extent, right to the end, until he died. When I'd already started playing with Oxley, I met up with him in Sweden. We always kept in touch. In the 1980s I soloed with his bands on many occasions. I remember buying a flat for my mum and he helped me out; he lent me some money, which I was supposed to pay back through touring. We often toured together; we got on well together. I played in the band Sound & Fury and in the trio with J.-F. Jenny-Clark.

Vesala died in 1999.

He died of heart failure. He collapsed. He was at home on his own . . . He lived on the edge all his life, and, in his later years, he began drinking heavily. An absolute teetotaller who'd never touched a drop in his life, and suddenly he started drinking too much. He didn't know how to drink; he started drinking too much right from the word go. He once told me about his father, who drank heavily and died of a heart attack. He probably inherited his heart problems from his father. Edward was a depressive, and his depression led to aggression, and those aggressive tendencies turned into auto-aggression. Maybe he began drinking out of contrariness. Perhaps he was doomed.

12 Whistling in the Temple

The most unusual episode during your friendship with Vesala was your joint expedition to India, where in 1980 you recorded solo trumpet in the Taj Mahal temple and the Karla Caves. Where did that idea come from?

Vesala had some freaky friends who'd got into the Taj Mahal by night through some sort of hole in the wall, you know, and they'd played flute in there. They said it was no big deal. So we said, 'Let's go!' When we got there, it was just like the Vatican. Crowds of people, no time. The temple's open until eleven o'clock at night, and then, after midnight, the religion forbids noise of any kind. But we were already there. We had an Indian roadie, Kif Ganga, and a driver who'd got us there. We'd initially wanted to get permission to record in there. We'd gone to the Indian civil service, but when we saw the officials in their shirtsleeves and saw how the thing was going to go . . . we immediately gave up. It would have taken us two or three years to get it approved.

But Vesala was the kind of guy who liked doing things in all kinds of left-field ways. He was in his element when it came to making under-the-table deals, doing something on the side, buttering someone up. So he began scheming with the security. There were two lots of security guards: state security outside and religious, Muslim security inside. I can see him coming towards me, and he's saying, 'Mate, I had to give them a lot of money, but we're going in.' Edward had told them that I was a musician and that we were testing the acoustics of this famous place, but they wanted to check me out all the same. I had to show them that I could actually play. I was very nervous, because I didn't know what piece I could play for these security guards so that they'd know, within a few seconds of me putting the trumpet to my lips, that I could actually play. I tried to play with a nice tone, European-style, melodically, so that they'd conclude that I had mastery over my instrument. I managed to convince them. We arranged to meet up in two days' time.

We stayed in a beautiful old hotel in the English colonial style, on the road to Agra. Huge rooms with high ceilings. Birds peering through the windows. We'd take a rickshaw to pick up some hashish. There were state-run shops there where you could buy hashish legally. New stuff every day.

I spent the next two days going to the Taj Mahal without my trumpet to check out the acoustics. The acoustics were otherworldly. Especially when there were crowds of people going through. There was a huge amount of human noise in there, amplified by the echo. Because it was a big, fifteen-, sixteen-second-long echo. That's very big. I noticed that when I began whistling very softly, very quietly, I didn't initially hear anything through the din, but after a while, I'd start to hear my own sound, and it's such a selective sound that I can hear its every nuance. Through that din. An unimaginable selectivity. I tried to get a feel for the space.

Then, as soon as it got to 11 pm, we couldn't wait for the place to close because we only had until midnight. Muslim security took over. As soon as all the people left, we started playing. Unfortunately, Kif Ganga was a bit out of it. He felt at ease with us; he was our roadie and he held sway over our driver, because there's a rigid hierarchy over there. As it turned out, he was also a friend of Trilok Gurtu. He dressed in European style, spoke English, knew the local customs and was our translator. But, unfortunately, he was also our driver's boss, and he used to send him off to get some LSD. He got high just before we started recording. We could see he could barely stand up. He was mumbling, so we got him out the way, and Edward began setting out the equipment all by himself. And this was all by the torchlight of the Muslim security, because they were constantly keeping an eye on us.

It was a long recording session, until nearly half past midnight; we had an hour's worth of pure music. I remember getting back that night after the recording. I couldn't sleep. At four in the morning I was awoken by loud birdsong. Someone brought us a joint. To have achieved the near-impossible gave me a great feeling of relaxation. I felt wonderful. I even recorded the sounds of that morning. Insects, birds, the intensity of nature. I remember the fragrant air. And then there were further recordings. Edward hired an Indian band. He wanted to record an album of their marching music. Fabulous, local folk music.

Those were street bands, like in New Orleans. They got the brass sections from the English army bands.
That's right. And they added their own music. They played very strangely. I didn't play with them; that was meant to be Edward's album. Then we went back to Mumbai and recorded some more brilliant material in the Karla Caves. It's an old Buddhist site, carved into a hillside, famous for its acoustics. We had to take porters with us. There's a communal prayer hall there, surrounded by cells where the monks used to live. It's a heritage site now, empty: just visitors there. We were able to record as much as we wanted; the porters had no trouble arranging for us to stay on after dusk for the recording. We got the second part of my album done, and Edward and I recorded as a duo.

What were those famous acoustics like?
Very strange. Those little cells cut into the rockface acted like sounding boards. The walls were thick. The echo wasn't terribly long; it was actually quite short, but the sound was incredibly rich. Those sounding boards enhanced it; they didn't add echo, but harmonics. The sound was richer. A good recording.

Out of the Indian recordings, it was only your solo album, *Taj Mahal and Karla Caves*, that was released. Vesala released it on his own record label, Leo.
He didn't get around to releasing the rest. He left millions of tapes behind. He used to record everything. Now his children and wife are in dispute over it. Those recordings will never get released, because it's money they want, yet we know there'll be no profit in it. We know what's happening on the market.

It would be worth re-releasing *Taj Mahal* because it's like Stańko's trumpet under a microscope. The essence of your style, your melody and your bends. And besides, there are not many albums for solo trumpet. The best ones, Leo Smith's and Bill Dixon's are actually based on reprocessing the sound using special effects or, as with Hugh Ragin, on an academically phenomenal technique. But on *Taj Mahal* it's pure trumpet.
It's the acoustics that matter. I used the echo. I had three microphones. Two kinds of echo.

You didn't have all three microphones in the Taj Mahal.
No. There was a natural echo there. But I like using echoes. In the Taj Mahal I used a breathing system. With that beautiful natural echo, when you play softly, the echo is shorter; the harder you blow, the longer the echo. That's why the whole thing doesn't sound so mechanical. You have to get a feel for the space, the surrounding acoustics. And you can gain a lot from this, regulate the length of the echo. I'm pleased with that recording. That album did really well. It was in all the shops.

How was the whole trip to India?
We spent nearly a month in India. We went to a jazz festival. We didn't play there, but there was a Polish group going, and so we joined the party. That's how we managed to get out there in the first place. A very large jazz festival in Mumbai, Jazz Yatra, in which the Polish Jazz Association took part. They paid for our tickets; they somehow managed to get us the plane tickets for next to nothing. I think that festival's still going. Bobo Stenson and Palle Danielsson have told me about it. I can't remember which of our people played – probably Sławomir Kulpowicz, some traditional band. We arranged the Taj Mahal trip ourselves. We flew into Mumbai; from there we took the sleeper train to New Delhi; then we hired a car to get us to Agra. It takes nearly two days to get there. Half a continent. We sat in a carriage with the locals. We ate in the same places as they did. And then we returned to Poland on our joint ticket with the Polish contingent. Via Dubai.

Was it a sort of hippie journey to the East for you?
It was a kind of hippie trip, where hashish and the Eastern feeling did have an effect. But my aim was primarily musical.

Had you previously paid any attention to Eastern sounds in modern music?
There was a lot of Indian music around at the time – Ravi Shankar was popular
– and Coltrane and the Beatles drew on it, but it didn't have that much influence on me. I did listen to the Tibetan monks, but what I found fascinating
about them was how they sounded – their actual sound.

The mystical element through sound, but without the philosophy?
Yes, definitely.

The album *Taj Mahal and Karla Caves* turned out to be the crowning
achievement of your experimentation with solo trumpet. Such musical
adventures are rare among jazz trumpeters. In what circumstances did you
start playing solo trumpet? What actually gave you the idea?
That was quite a while ago . . .

My research tells me it was in 1978.
Probably. After the quintet disbanded, I played with Adam Makowicz, but that
was in Germany. I didn't have a band in Poland. I didn't have a rhythm section
here. If you live in Europe, you always have trouble getting hold of a rhythm
section. After Gucio Dyląg, I didn't have a bass player till I got Sławomir
Kurkiewicz. Merciful God! How long did I have to wait until another high-class
musician appeared! I'm talking about world-class. The first words I hear from
other musicians are: 'You have a good band. Bass player! Bass player!' Always!
Jim Black recently said that to me. Sławomir's playing is hellishly confident
and steady.

So, I didn't have a rhythm section. I initially thought I might try using some
sort of electronic pickups. I had an echo chamber so I could do repeats and
loops, but then at some point . . . I really like electronic gear, but I don't find it
easy using all that equipment and getting a line feed sorted at the same time;
and if I don't have a line, it's just too slow for me. So that's why I used to set
up three microphones. Two with different-length reverbs and one normal
one. I used the two reverb microphones a bit like sustain pedals on a piano,
to fill out the sound.

You didn't really get into experimentation with electronic equipment, then?
No. I gave up on it. I just ended up with the different reverbs, the sound aug-
mented using reverb. Oh, and my fitness . . . and, above all, the strength to
keep going mentally. To have enough material for an hour-long set, and to
play in an interesting way. I was writing music then. Throughout that entire
period. *Almost Black* dates from that period. I remember my father coming to
my solo concert at the Rotunda in Kraków. And yet he wasn't a jazz fan. And,
after the concert, he said to me, 'Hats off! That's a devilishly difficult thing you
did there. Many congratulations! I didn't realize you were such a great musician.' That was serious validation for me, one of the biggest compliments I've
ever had. The best review.

As a soloist, you played a lot of standards at your concerts: Monk, Coltrane, Silver.

Yes, I did. Of course. That was easy. It's a real luxury to get to play them on a single instrument. While it's meant to be difficult to play a one-line composition on the trumpet, at least it gave me freedom. I was able to play real free, yet very melodically at the same time. Different things; different timbres. I wasn't constrained by anything; I was able to fulfil my potential for playing in the jazz tradition. I played Miles's repertoire. Coltrane's blues from his *Blue Train*, *Giant Steps* era. I also used to play those pieces with Adam Makowicz.

Which pieces did you choose from Monk's repertoire?

I played Monk's 'Straight No Chaser' and mostly 'Well, You Needn't'.

Tricky themes!

Well, yes, but I was able to cut them up to suit myself, break off, linger on a theme and head off to some black holes. I liked giving standards this kind of treatment – I'd break up the structure of the chorus and, at some point, I'd leave the piece hanging and go my own way; then I'd go back to the piece, picking it up anywhere. A split-second decision, the skill of improvisation.

I asked about Monk because it was from reflecting on what Monk did that Steve Lacy's artistic individuality emerged. In the 1970s, practically at the same time as you did, Steve Lacy began playing solo in Europe, except that he did it on soprano saxophone. And he's now regarded as a symbol of the jazz adventures of that era.

Possibly. I never used to listen to any of that. Lacy played a great deal. He had it easier from the fitness point of view. Fitness is very important.

Evan Parker, another saxophonist, famous for his solo improvisations, whom you met in Globe Unity, worked on his circular breathing.

I did practise such things, but that's not what it's about. You can always manage your breathing. There's always a place where you can take a quick breath. That's not a problem. But what's different from the saxophone – with the trumpet, your mouth sticks out. The muscles of your mouth stick out, the whole top of it. You have to have a moment's rest. In big bands, the trumpeters always have breaks. After all, the trumpet isn't an instrument where you bite; you have to apply pressure. You have to have a break at some point. And, in solo playing, a minute is a very long time. I needed to have at least a bit of a break, and that's what the reverb gave me. I later saw Mike Brecker's solo concerts. He used to talk for quite a while between the pieces because that is, after all, a way of giving your mind a rest; you've finished your piece, your brain relaxes. But I don't like making speeches, so that's why I had to figure out another way. I played around with expression and timbre. My mouth had to be in good shape. I did sometimes manage up to one hour and fifteen minutes. That was the case that time my father came to hear me. You also need to have good acoustic conditions. The Rotunda had a kind of natural echo. That did help me. You know, you can have silence too, but it's a real art form to get the dramatic effect right, so the silence works. Your mind needs to be in good shape as well, and your pieces prepared. That's how my compositions got written, the ones I later recorded on *Taj Mahal*. 'Chromatica Song'. That was a strange composition! The chorus was based on the entire circle of fifths. It kept going down in semitones, so that there were effectively twelve choruses in the entire piece. I enjoyed playing a kind of mystical mathematics back then. I had a workspace in Remont. I used to sit there on my own, in this plain little room, cut off from the world.

Were you inspired by the constraints? Did you turn to your inner world?
Just to my inner world.

You've talked about elongating a sound using echoes and harmonics. In the New York avant-garde of the 1960s, an entire school called 'minimal music' emerged, which combined these techniques with aspects of Indian music. Its driving force, La Monte Young, had studied sacred Hindu chant, the breathing techniques and economy of which he transferred to the compositions which he based on drones and minimalistic changes in harmonic relations. That was also a mystical mathematics of sorts.
I haven't come across this music. But from what I've heard, there was solid theory behind it, not like with 'harmolodics'.

La Monte Young essentially composed using sound frequencies, and his music is psychoactive trance. The paradox is that the mathematical accuracy of his compositions affects the subconscious; the sensuous power of sound translates into a spiritual experience.
You could say that my mathematics was poetic. Poetry, rather than precise calculations. Some kind of figures, numerology. The excitement of number alone, as in the olden days, when number had a magical meaning. That kind of thing, although I had a tongue-in-cheek approach to magic. It helped me make decisions when I was organizing my compositions, but I didn't create any systems out of it. Nevertheless, I'm convinced that I had a very intense and interesting musical period as a result of playing solo. The solo playing really advanced on the recordings with Vesala; it developed me. To this day, I do like playing a bit of solo.

Did you record any of these compositions as a band of any kind?
I didn't really record them; there are just some scraps on *Taj Mahal*. A lot of those kinds of lines emerged. Melodic lines that included harmony. We could say that they were a form of self-improvement. 'Chromatica' never got recorded. 'Natka' . . .

Solo concert at Jazz Jamboree, 1979.
Photograph by Mirosław Makowski

You played 'Natka' in a quartet with Kulpowicz, and it featured on the album
Music 81.
Yes. I did play it, but not much. Because it's quite a difficult and uncommercial
composition in and of itself, to be honest. Later, when I recorded a duo album
with Janusz Skowron, there were also some solo trumpet pieces on it, but
different ones. My last phase of playing solo trumpet, after a break from it,
came just after the transformation, at the beginning of the 1990s.

In 1979 you played solo at Jazz Jamboree.
That was quite interesting. I had a good timbre, and my stamina held out.
I think Ornette played then as well. I have a better recollection of some of
my other solo concerts. There was this small venue in Kraków. That was an
excellent gig. I remember the one at the Rotunda. My concerts were packed
out. I also played solo in Finland; I was often the opening act for Edward's band.

You also played solo as the support act for the Art Ensemble of Chicago.
That was just after Jazz Jamboree at the All Souls' Jazz Festival in Kraków. I
got to know them well later on.

That must have been a challenge, because the Art Ensemble at that time was
one of the most vibrant bands on the concert scene.
Well, yes, but then again they couldn't have found a better support act. They
had someone playing free music, someone who was close to their aesthetic.
It was a beautiful concert. I saw Joseph Jarman later in Finland, where he
was playing with a band that Edward used to write music for. The UMO Jazz
Orchestra. They're still going. I used to play with them in the 1990s. They
had a project with Miles's music. I played 'Sketches of Spain' with them, and
Tim Hagans, an American trumpeter, played 'Porgy and Bess'. Hagans later
arranged my quartet music for big band. It was performed by a Swedish big
band, and I played the solos. We played a few concerts.

The Art Ensemble's concept of jazz in the 1970s was far more original than
the fusion that was fashionable at the time, and it was based on whole-band
improvisation, which had as its main parameters space and sound. *TWET*
maintains this spirit, doesn't it?
I didn't pay much attention to that. I was becoming less and less interested
in theoretical descriptions of art. What the Art Ensemble used to say was
like Ornette Coleman's harmolodics as far as I was concerned. Music is an
abstract form. I do have respect for those kinds of theories, but I don't really
test them out. What mattered was the Art Ensemble's sound and that magical
atmosphere, which came across most beautifully on their album *People in
Sorrow*. The atmosphere at their concerts came about through a combination
of magic and technique. A certain performance. Roscoe Mitchell came to my
festival at Bielsko-Biała, where he too created mystery, which permeated his
entire performance. At that kind of concert, people focus in a different way.

Were the Art Ensemble maniacs or super-professionals?
Professionals. All professionals, definitely. In fact, I'd go as far as to say that they cultivated the idea of being normal, professional musicians, open and tolerant people.

Did you play solo much in Europe?
There were some concerts. I can't really remember what. I don't think I did very many all told. Needless to say, Poland was closed off at the time. And though I was playing abroad regularly, it wasn't non-stop, just one-off concerts. I often played, regularly I suppose, at the Baden-Baden Free Jazz Meeting that Berendt organized. I played solo there. There was a strange line-up there on one occasion: musicians from John Surman's trio – in other words, Surman, Stu Martin and Barre Phillips – Albert Mangelsdorff, Johnny Griffin and me. A very strange line-up. We played concerts in Baden-Baden and Mainz, and we recorded before that.

None of those recordings was released.
Because they were radio recordings. Westdeutscher Rundfunk was involved in the festival in Baden-Baden. Those tapes are probably in the archives somewhere.

You also played a solo concert in Polish TV's Studio 2.
There was indeed such a concert. In a nest. They put me in a nest, and that's where I played a solo concert.

That used to be the number one light entertainment channel during the late Edward Gierek era, and you sneaked in there with some difficult music.
They invited me on . . . There have always been jazz fans around. In recent times, the status of jazz has gone up again. You can tell by how much respect rock musicians have for us. Not all of them, because Sting, for example, says he likes playing with jazz musicians, but he doesn't listen to jazz. They respect us, though they don't listen to us. Maybe that's how it works.

What do you think of recent trends at jazz festivals?
Patti Smith now plays at these festivals. There's not much jazz there, unless it's those 'jazz-lite' bands, like the now-deceased Esbjörn Svensson's band. People like it because they have fun. People want to have fun. People have fun in different ways nowadays. Maybe the other stuff will come back. Or maybe that modern jazz was linked to chaos, to war. Maybe we took to free jazz as we did because ours was a generation born during wartime.

You've often said that you were high, yet at the same time you were working a lot. You even mentioned a minute ago that those lines that you composed while playing solo were a kind of self-improvement. You strike me as someone who puts a lot of work into self-improvement.

Oh, definitely. I knew right from the very beginning that if I managed to break through, get up on stage and play, I'd be a hundred times stronger for it. I'm still doing that. Take this move to New York right now – it's the same thing because it's a kind of obstacle. Once again, I'm having to battle over certain minutiae, not music-related, admittedly, but of the kind that take me away from my music.

How important has self-improvement been to you?

I want to keep on developing. Although, I have to say, I'm becoming increasingly convinced that there's been no development. I've played well right from the beginning. It's not so much about development as about experiencing life through searching. It's not development; it's a kind of probing. A person reveals their natural strength very early on in their youth, and they don't develop so much after that. Like Rimbaud. What remains is the probing into different areas. The searching is very creative in and of itself.

In 1979, in a fascinating interview with Wiesław Królikowski, you said, 'If someone has talent, but doesn't know how to go about self-improvement, they're not going to become a jazz artist; they'll become a copyist, like in a pub band.'

Obviously. We educate ourselves. You have to know what you're looking for. You want to play solo? Simple. It's the sound. Once when I was in Munich with the quintet, Jeremy Steig was playing at the same concert, with Joachim Kühn, I think. And he was singing. I saw it and I thought, 'That's just wonderful!' I was fascinated by his singing. Flute players often do that, but the lines he played were different from the ones he sang. He made good use of his voice. At one of my concerts, with the quintet in the early 1970s, I also started singing.

Do you mean abstract vocals, like Urszula Dudziak, singing scat?

No, I mean singing while you're playing.

Straight into the mouthpiece?

Yes. Albert Mangelsdorff also used to sing. He played two notes simultaneously on the trombone.* This is actually a French horn technique, used by horn players in classical music. They play triads. Harmonics can be heard at a certain point, and they sound very beautiful. So I began doing that on the trumpet,

---

* *Series Editor's note:* Mangelsdorff was a proponent of multiphonics, in which – by playing and singing into the instrument simultaneously – two or more notes of the harmonic series can be produced, including triads, as mentioned by Tomasz Stańko.

though it's difficult to hear triads on a trumpet. On a trombone you can hear the harmonics; the sound is fuller. The trumpet is too weak.

Did you also sing while playing solo?
Of course. I sang and played triads. I've not done the singing in a long time, but I'm always using it subconsciously, adding a note. When I started trying out different approaches, after a while I noticed that I wasn't so much trying to sing as create two sounds. When you sing along with the trumpet, either in unison or at an interval, the sound is different, because it's been doubled. The sound becomes richer.

13 Mutant: A Hipster in Communist Poland

You were a downright decadent hedonist during the days of the Polish People's Republic.

To an extent, yes. We did like to start the day as we meant to go on. We led a dissolute life. In the European we'd have French wine and hashish for breakfast. Or at Stu Martin's – fruit off the tree for breakfast, but we mainly drank and smoked. We only ate when it got to dinner-time.

I remember going to Wacek Kisielewski's one time to borrow some money because I didn't have enough to buy bread. When Wacek split up from his wife, he lived in Warsaw for a while with a certain young lady. He was staying at the Victoria. So, I'm in reception and he says to me over the phone: 'Wait there, wait there. I'm just coming down for breakfast.' He came down to the dining room with his girlfriend. He'd barely sat down at the table when the waiter came up and, without saying a word, gave him a brandy. That's how he started his day.

Marek & Wacek were stars of the stage and screen. During the communist era in Poland, they were on TV more than Madonna is on MTV nowadays.

Pop music, pop. They were in the entertainment industry and they got wads of cash. They played concerts with Marlene Dietrich. Marlene had a crush on Wacek.

Marlene Dietrich?

Marlene Dietrich. She was still singing. When she was older, she lived in Paris and sometimes gave concerts. She also performed with them. Those kind of chicks always – while they still can – take an interest in young guys. And they usually manage to keep their looks for a long time.

Did the hotel environment suit you?

Very much so. Hotel life. Touring. For a while, after I split up with my wife, I kept my clothes in Kraków. And, when I came back to Warsaw, I'd stay at the Forum. I ate there. I'd got to know the people on reception, and even if I only rang a day in advance, they always had a room for me. In the Heweliusz Hotel in Gdańsk I had quite a strange incident with a beautiful young woman – Lady Go – to whom I later dedicated an album.

What's the story there?
She was a very young lady. Seventeen. She was still at school. I'd met her at some festival or other. She slept with me in my room, and one of my little tape recorders went missing. I thought it was her . . . It was an embarrassing situation. She left, mortified, but she knew that I'd be going back to Warsaw the next day. She was from Warsaw as well. She hitch-hiked her way back. It was an awkward situation, because I then found out that the hotel was notorious for having doors that didn't close properly, that you needed to turn the key in the lock. Thieves are well aware of this and they steal from rooms in the early hours because a lot of people forget about turning the key. I'd forgotten as well, and the tape recorder had been in plain sight. I'm a hundred per cent sure that someone must have come in, seen this valuable piece of kit and nicked it. 'Oh God!' I thought, 'She's such an innocent girl. I need to find her and tell her that it wasn't her fault, that everything's fine.'

And she was waiting for me at the airport in Warsaw. She was so shy; she didn't know what to say. We sorted it out. We were together for quite a while. As usual, I took her to Lanckorona. My mum liked her; she used to come round to our house. It was love. She used to write me such childish, charming letters.

Why 'Lady Go'?
She was called Gośka.

The opening piece on side 2 of *Music 81* is 'Bushka'. Is that dedicated to that girl that you messed about with in the hotel in Kraków?
Yes, she was my second big love of the 1980s. Just before Lady Go. We were together for a few years. I met her in Kraków at some party or other. And we jumped straight into bed. Her boyfriend caught us at it in the hotel. I answered the door wearing nothing but a coat. Bushka was in the bed, trembling. An awkward situation.

She was a dancer. She danced with a troupe in Kraków, at the University of Science and Technology. I tried to dissuade her from pursuing the arts and told her she'd do better to finish her studies. I had such moralizing tendencies: I lived like an animal myself, but I didn't want to drag others into it. I never gave my girlfriends anything to smoke. I lived like the devil himself, but I didn't advise anyone else to lead that kind of life. Unfortunately, however, I myself was an example of someone who was coping with it brilliantly. Bushka wanted to dance. I urged her to lead a safe life. It's a good thing she didn't listen to me. I was definitely wrong. She's still involved with dance. She went out to the States where she works as a choreographer. Contemporary dance. She married an American, also an artist, and she lives in Portland. I still meet up

Backstage at Jazz Jamboree 1980. (From left: Tomasz Stańko, Stu Martin and unidentified listeners.)
Photograph by Mirosław Makowski

with both Bushka and Lady Go. Gośka has a stable life. She married a journalist. They have children. She works as a journalist. As for 'Bushka', that's a
very fine composition.

**You mentioned that, when you played with Komeda, you only smoked hashish
after a performance. What about later on, with regard to smoking and playing?**
I always played after hashish. I never drank alcohol before playing, but I
don't remember ever playing without hashish. At the very beginning with
the quintet, I didn't have a joint before playing, because the hashish had too
strong an effect; but you know, later on, your tolerance threshold goes up and
the stuff has a weaker effect.

The quintet had a breakthrough concert at the Free Music Workshop in
Berlin. Wacek Kisielewski had got hold of some excellent stuff for us, which
one of the drummers had brought with him. He rolled a joint. I thought that
we'd already played two sets and that we'd finished for the night, but they
came up to us and said, 'You need to do another set.' We went back on stage.
I was completely *stoned*. 'Oh my God; we'll never be able to play . . .' But, at
that point, we seemed to acquire some sort of super-strength, because we
played a brilliant concert. People said it was an incredible concert. From that
point onwards, I smoked all the time. And then, all my life, I smoked before I
played. With Vesala – always.

Were you smoking when you recorded *TWET*?
Of course.

How come Professor Urbański didn't notice?
Of *course* . . . ! Edward, Peter and I were at it non-stop.

At Manfred Eicher's as well, when you recorded *Balladyna*?
I think I did a bit. Through dope I was in touch with all the best musicians, everywhere. The Americans always smoked, and they always knew who the smokers were. I remember Don Pullen coming up to me during a concert and saying, 'Come on, Tomasz.' And off we went to do some coke. And long before then, back in the 1960s, at a workshop, I was knocking around with Jean-Luc Ponty, but Ponty was clean. I also remember this concert, 'Trumpet Plus', in Hamburg, where I was messing around with coke. I never did much coke, but I did try everything.

That's reminded me of the famous story about Mezz Mezzrow.
That's right. A clarinetist.

He was White – the son of Russian Jews who'd emigrated to the States – and this guy had a complex, because, when he was starting out in the 1920s, jazz was only being played by African Americans, so he felt inferior. He called himself a 'Voluntary Negro', started smoking, married a Black woman and began selling marijuana in Harlem, which had come over from Mexico. He suddenly found himself being taken on by the best bands.
Well, yes; they loved him because he had good-quality stuff. That often happens, but he was a good clarinetist. Mezz Mezzrow. I know the name very well, though I never met him.

He eventually became a strong advocate of Louis Armstrong, and Armstrong, as we know, smoked marijuana every day and even wrote letters to the president about getting grass legalized.
I smoked all my life. But at one point I started cutting back. I was playing duos with Tomasz Szukalski at the time. We were working together on this project for a short time. The mid-1980s, after playing with Vesala. We played concerts in Berlin, in France, two jobs in Hungary, and we had a short tour in Poland. We initially had Milo Kurtis with us on percussion. But that line-up very quickly turned into a duo.

So Szukalski and I went to Hungary. And I didn't take any gear with me. 'I won't be able to buy any over there,' I thought. 'It'll be interesting to see what it's like playing without smoking.' I was in pieces after the first day, but I realized that without smoking it was still good. I was even furious about the fact that I'd actually played *very* well. Better even. I just couldn't sleep. Then I realized that this was to do with something else.

The thing is, after smoking we feel good, because it numbs our whole system. But then we become addicted, and the pleasure comes from satisfying that addiction. We know for a fact that this stimulates the release of dopamine, which governs our reward system. That's it. A simple process. Basic. At the same time, it has side effects, the primary one being that it numbs us. Well, you know, these days, now that we're increasingly complicated beings, it's just as important for us to have our mental states numbed as it is to have our physical pain numbed. The mental pain, the stress everywhere, it's huge.

What about the kind of side effects from smoking like disorientation or forgetfulness? Did you not have any problems due to that while on tour?
For a long time, every time we were about to begin, for a second, I didn't know how to start my own composition. Strangely, though, I'd then always have this *pow!* moment, and then I knew. Well, you do forget: there were many times when I'd forget while I was playing. You forget little things like the opening note. Or notes, full stop. But it all depends on your skill. I could read music. I'd played with Ptaszyn Wróblewski in the Jazz Studio at Polish Radio and I'd had good training. I had no problem smoking and reading music at the same time. But later on, after I'd not read any music in a while, I did have some concerts where I was stoned and I couldn't read anything. I was befuddled and I couldn't manage.

But people can get used to anything. You can even learn to play drunk. Except that when you're very drunk you just lie there and mumble because the nervous system is paralysed. Not after drugs. After drugs you can play normally, and, when you use drugs all the time, you get used to it. I never left anything behind in a hotel. There was just the one time in my life when I left my trumpet behind on a train, and that was after I'd stopped smoking. I was travelling to Kraków; I got off and I didn't take my trumpet with me. I went back and, by a miracle of God, the carriage was still standing in a siding because part of the train had gone on to Przemyśl. That would have been a disaster – and while I was sober as well.

Did nothing like that ever happen to you while you were 'under the influence'?
Never. You watch yourself more.

You give me the impression of watching yourself in general. You work at self-improvement. I'd just like to go back to that interview from the second half of the 1970s where you say, 'If someone has talent, but doesn't know how to go about self-improvement, they're not going to be an artist; they're going to be a copyist, like in a pub band.' You then add, 'Because that unexpected something will be missing from his playing. The fact that, at some point, he might play in a different way.'
Well, yes. That unexpected something . . . I'm always saying that art is an order that doesn't exist in nature. A Buddhist flute may imitate wind, but those kinds of compositions don't exist in nature. These are all different structures

1978.
Photograph by Mirosław Makowski

– invented by man. Like the fine arts: initially, it was about finding innovative ways of showing light, but then fine art became more and more abstract. It always goes along those lines.

Innovation is the key. I love it. I'm drawn towards things that don't exist yet. And I make it happen. It's good to have both things at the same time – technique and innovation.

And does this pursuit of the unexpected in music lead to self-knowledge?
Of course it does. We can get to know ourselves better, find out who we are. Probably some day people will tap into this by having their genotype tested. They'll be able to find out their predispositions and weak points. If I had known that I was predisposed to arteriosclerosis, to high blood pressure, I'd have lived differently. Dietetically.

But you do feel healthy, don't you?
I do feel healthy, but I have to be careful.

Have you made any unexpected discoveries about yourself through music?
I have had moments where I've had the impression that such things do actually happen – while improvising. Improvisation is a beautiful thing, but the way I operate is more the result of my reflections, of my world-view, which I carry through to my art, so to speak. Technical skills aren't my strength. I carry my intuition, my attention and my sensitivity through to my sound. I try to reflect my emotions. My compositions are kind of codes for the significant contradictions and reflections that I don't want to verbalize or even externalize. Those reflections are for me and nobody else; very often they're false theories.

There used to be a painter called Seurat, who painted tiny dots, and he was convinced that he'd come up with a brilliant theory. But he painted like that because he was Seurat. Not because he'd invented those tiny dots. The theory, the patent, in and of itself has no value. The value lies solely in the fact that he was Seurat. Beautiful canvases. I recently saw some of his original paintings. Fuck! It's insane, the way it works! Those tiny dots! But it's not the dots in themselves. What's at work here is the way Seurat saw the world, that he saw light in this way, and presented it like that.

You once said, ' "Artist" is a fancy word. I have my own personality and I'm able to translate it into the language of music.'
Maybe I did say that. But I actually like the word 'artist'. Personality is the most important thing.

Through jazz, you changed your personality.
It's difficult to change your actual personality. For me, it was the details that changed. Like I already said, it's easy to move from one extreme to the other. If someone used to be shy, he can easily become very self-assured. It's more difficult to stay in the middle and achieve mental stability.

In your case you were initially a well-behaved but low-achieving pupil. Then you turned into a mischievous but smart boy who did well at school.

That's exactly what happened. When I changed school. But it's not a change of personality; it's the opposite of that, a 180-degree turn. I moved from one extreme to the other, but I was the same person.

Did you turn into a sensitive tough guy?

Yes. I think so. I think that's quite a common thing.

Common for an artist?

I've always felt that in this day and age an artist needs to be both hard and capable at the same time. He can be shy as well. Have you heard the saying? They say that Hollywood actors need to be made out of feathers and steel: very delicate and very resistant to blows.

You often talk about contrasts.

I have contrasts within me.

The sensitive, shy guy and the hard-driving, tough one.

Exactly. That's where it comes from. There's that other side, the bad one. I think it's been like that since the beginning. That's who I am. Like I said before, at the age of four or five I stood watching some boys throwing stones at tadpoles. I remember my revulsion but also being rather fascinated by this evil, because to me this was evil. I don't remember whether I did any throwing. I don't think I did. I was always standing on the sidelines in situations like that. But they weren't; they actually stood and watched as the tadpoles got splattered. It's rare for me to feel the kind of emotion I did then: a kind of disgust, a fear, but a fascination at the same time. Evil does sometimes arouse my curiosity.

I sometimes wonder what sort of people the Gnostics were. I don't see the world in the negative terms that they did. Evil exists. It's in a minority, but, like everything, it tends to spread. Evolution relies on chance. There must have been some mutant fish that got beached on dry land and the bugger managed to survive. And it's because of this that life has evolved. Such a mutant had the right, so to speak, to be a son of a bitch, so it could survive. He was angry and evil. I accept that this is how it is, that this is a by-product of all this beautiful life. And now, what are we to do with this by-product? I can't accept evil, but it has to be, just the way it is. Evil can be beneficial because it helps us deal with certain selfish matters. But goodness is better. Evil is a form of atavism.

The fact is: misfortune hardens people. If we're cruel, we're harder, more resilient in the face of life's difficulties. Hence the satanic inclinations of certain rock musicians.

There's a famous essay by Norman Mailer from the 1950s: *White Negro*. He wrote about mutation through jazz. Through the character of the hipster, he described a generation of White boys who got into jazz after World War II. He starts with a vision of the collapse of civilization. He was a Jew and he fought in the Pacific. And in *White Negro*, he wrote about the hipster. He associated jazz with ecstasy – civilization has declined; we need to get away from history, jump into the present. That's what the hipster, the 'White Negro', does when he gets into jazz, marijuana and a state of heightened arousal. Mailer also writes that, in the urban jungle, paranoia is a natural form of adaptation. The hipster is a brilliant psychopath, a White man who changes his own nervous system, as in the phrase 'he absorbs the existential synapses of the Negro'. It's like the mutation of a White boy who gets into jazz.

That's how it works. It's always the same. I associated jazz with ecstasy, freedom and difference. I have pondered over it: where does this difference come from? Every one of us wants to be the leader of the pack but, when there are millions of people, it becomes increasingly difficult to be that leader. So that tendency turns into difference. Being different. Standing apart from other people, seeing as we can't lead them.

You were a buttoned-up little boy from bourgeois Kraków, but you later became a hipster. Would that be this restructuring of the nervous system? Mezz Mezzrow, who we've already mentioned, also went through such a change and referred to himself as a 'Voluntary Negro'.

Maybe. Maybe. But I do think that, somewhere deep down, I've stayed the same. Despite what you might think, everyone can live more easily if they want. Even if you're painfully shy, you can get along very well indeed, if you manage to turn your shyness to your advantage.

Once, when I was chatting with a friend, I said that I didn't have any self-confidence, that I didn't have any particular views about anything. And he replied, 'Mate, you've got it better than I have, because I just plough straight on, all sure of myself . . .' (that was true: he didn't have any doubts about any-thing) '. . . and when I come up against a brick wall, I smash up against it and end up in bits. But you'll run around that wall a hundred times, and eventu-ally find a hole in it, or you'll jump over it, or crawl under it.' That's true. And I'm aware of that.

The important thing is for us to get to know ourselves, to assess ourselves without any hang-ups. Because we have survived as a species up to now, this means that we are exceptionally strong. After all, we have billions of years of continuity, from bacteria and those tiny little mammals that used to hang around with the dinosaurs. Seeing as we're still alive, still multiplying, what's the problem? We are exceptional. A lack of self-belief impedes us more than anything else. It's just about good and bad luck. The important thing is to believe in yourself. That gave me heart.

But didn't you yourself become a mutant through jazz?

In some sort of way, yes. You know, when you live that kind of life, some of your blinkers fall off. Your thinking becomes flexible.

The French thinkers Félix Guattari and Gilles Deleuze, hugely influential on the intellectual youth of the technological era, wrote that it's better to be a wandering schizophrenic than a paranoiac sprawled out on an analyst's couch. The same idea appears in Mailer's *White Negro*.

Yes. A good analogy. It hardly needs saying but as a family we definitely had a nervous, stressed disposition. And I can remember, as if it were today, having a drink of wine, lighting up a cigarette, going up on stage and playing. And I'm still playing. My sister didn't go on stage. Nor did my father. These drugs make us believe that we can achieve more, and because we often have a low opinion of ourselves, because we underestimate ourselves . . . well, it might just turn out that we *can* actually do certain things.

Although there have been cases where people who've been going heavy on the crack have tried to stop a truck because they actually thought they were that strong. Like I did, on the Łazienkowska Highway, shouting 'The full catastrophe!'

Right at the start, when you were first getting into jazz, how significant was the fact that this was Black music?

Very. Really very significant. To me, being Black in music has pure value. Black artists have a particular approach to time. Their time is a swinging one. That was the most importance piece of information for me as far as jazz was concerned. Because what is this pulsating music? It's about a perception of time that's based on undulation, on regularity. The European way of thinking, the classical one, is different.

The French writer Boris Vian, who wanted to be a jazz trumpeter, stated that, at best, a White man might play like '37th-rate Black jazz musicians'. Did you share that complex?

There is some truth in that. I did have that feeling. But, in some strange way, you forget about it when you're playing. At least, I would. I didn't evaluate what I did. I didn't think about my place within jazz. Now I don't have any complexes. A few White people have succeeded in playing in their own style, and they've provided a counterpoint to the Black sound. Gerry Mulligan, Lee Konitz, Bill Evans, Scott LaFaro all made their contributions to jazz with their mellow sound. There is, after all, an aesthetic difference between African-American jazz musicians and European ones. Primarily a rhythmic one.

African-American jazz musicians also have their own masculine, rough lyricism, which emphasizes the rhythm that flows from their culture, an incredibly precise rhythmicity. All swing is nothing more than an unusually precise rhythmicity. Here, playing with a certain delay is precisely timed and explicitly put into words. And the way it's described is using slang terms, such as hitting it 'behind', 'right there', 'well after', 'near' and 'alongside' the beat. This slang makes explicit the distinctions between these different types of 'feel'. Very practical. A mathematical calculation couldn't describe it as precisely as this. But intuition does. African culture wasn't born out of counting but out of dance. Jack DeJohnette once told me that this swaying rhythm comes from a 'dancing feeling', the rhythm of a heavy, dancing body. And from this dance comes the rhythm of the drums. The weight of the body sets it in motion; and the rhythm is heavy as well, a different one from the tapping and stamping of the *kujawiak*.* It's like with a trumpet mouthpiece. A machine might have formed its shape very precisely but the lips can feel it a hundred times better. The body has unusually precise exploratory abilities. It's about the sensual, human element of discovery.

With Black music, then, the essential thing for you was this difference in rhythm.
That's right. As a free jazz musician, specifically a European free jazz musician, in the early years I started out with a rhythmic ad libitum, peculiar to Europe. The slowing-downs and speeding-ups of tempo, totally ad libitum. That was my quintet's preferred approach, especially when playing ballads. The same with Vesala. It was a particular kind of rhythm, not the kind played by African Americans: a hard, Black rhythm, played asymmetrically. My rhythm came from what you might call an arched, curved treatment of time.

But I've always been interested in *timing*. I've always thought that I'd find it easiest to play if I had two lines, two conveyor belts (which is how I imagined it), where, on one of these, time is measured in an arched, ad lib way, like with a stopwatch, while on the other it's measured against a pulse, running at equal, pulsating intervals. And I jump from one conveyor belt to the other, from one time to another.

Music is, after all, art within time. It has to count out the time during which it lasts. Pulsating time is counted using a method that hails from Africa. It pulsates in this way because the rhythm is indivisible, because it's a two/three rhythm. Its indivisibility is infinite. That's why in this pulsating, swaying rhythm, there's a certain magic. It can send us into a trance; it allows for communication with the listener in an intuitive, very biological and natural way. At one time, that was the most important thing for me. Now I understand that we also need to be familiar with other ways of using time. That enriches our music.

---

* *Translator's note:* The *kujawiak* is a Polish folk dance in triple time.

14 At Remont

Without clubs, there is no jazz community. In Kraków, the most important club for you was Helikon. What about in Warsaw?

To begin with we played at the old Hybrydy on Mokotowska Street. That's where the quintet played that gig that I mentioned, where Zbigniew Seifert and Bronisław Suchanek played some superb openings on violin and bass. There was one bit of the gig that was unbelievably creative. I used to go to Hybrydy. I used to meet up with Milo Kurtis there and also pick up something to smoke. And then, of course, there was Kuryl [Andrzej Kurylewicz]'s Piwnica. An iconic place. The whole of the Polish jazz world used to turn up there and hang out. It was in an excellent location, right in the Old Market Place. Right nearby, I think it was on Piwna Street, Włodzimierz Nahorny had a small rented ground-floor flat. Whenever you went past, you could always see whether Włodzimierz was in. *Knock, knock!* and then you'd either go inside or carry on to Kuryl's. Nahorny hung out all the time at Kuryl's. They played together in a quintet.

Was the atmosphere there similar to the one at Helikon?

Different. It was different. It was kind of Kuryl's private club. It was mainly Kuryl who played there. The city had given him the club. In the old days, his wife, Wanda Warska, used to sing there, and Kuryl played with his quintet. A club like that was a phenomenon in Poland back then. Wanda had fixed it. She had a talent for that kind of thing. She knew how to talk to people in power. She'd sung for somebody somewhere, and the army used to help her out. At any rate, she managed to pull off something that was impossible in those days. A private club.

Seeing as it was mainly Kurylewicz playing there, does that mean that the social side of the club was more important than the playing?

The social side, absolutely. It was a place where we all met up. Trzaskower (that's Andrzej Trzaskowski) and the film people, and Nahorny's trio. I went there whenever I was in Warsaw: 1965, 1966, 1967. I'd turn up in my new out-fits. But then I stopped going so much because I had concerts; I was on the road with the quintet. Maybe I could have made the time to go, but we used to get together as a quintet, so we didn't need so much of a social life. We'd go elsewhere. To jam sessions at Medyka, to Hybrydy. At Medyka there was a Dr Mosakowski who organized the gigs. Those were student clubs, but we had jam sessions there.

Who used to go to those jam sessions?
Everyone did. All the important people in Warsaw. The same with Hybrydy. That's where Namysłowski started out. When Michał Urbaniak came back from Sweden, he practically moved into Hybrydy. That was around 1968, 1969. We used to meet up with him as well. We'd go round to Władysław Jagiełło's. He had a trio at the time. We used to smoke at his place; he had a lot of gear. During my quintet period, I used to pop round to Władek's and light up a joint, and then we'd walk together to a jam session at Medyka. Jagiełło had previously played in a pub in Scandinavia with some Black organist chap. He began smoking weed and he brought back a lot of stuff.

What about the Riviera Remont club?
That was later. The second half of the 1970s. There were gigs there. Waldemar Dąbrowski, who later became Minister for Culture, started out at Remont as a student entertainment officer. The club was managed by Waldemar Deska, who put regular gigs on. As well as jazz, Remont also embraced punk.

There was a lot more going on there than in Hybrydy and Medyka, wasn't there?
The most. Totally. A great deal. Hybrydy moved to the city centre, where they supposedly still held gigs, but it wasn't the same. In fact, all the live jazz gigs moved over to the student clubs. There was also Stodoła, where we went as well, but they had trad jazz on there.

You had a practice room at Remont.
I was given a kind of box room to work in, because we normally rehearsed on stage in the room where we had the gig.

Did you come across Helmut Nadolski and Andrzej Przybielski around then? They were the most important figures among the new generation of free musicians at that time. And they also played at Remont on occasion.
Not much. I didn't come across them much. But I can tell you that I really like Przybielski. I thought highly of him because he could play brilliantly. He was uneven, but sometimes his playing was outstanding, exceptional. That's why I got him to play on *Peyotl*. Przybielski does have his hang-ups, and there are times when he won't play a thing, but he *can* play like nobody else. He started out in Piwnica in Warsaw, back with Kuryl. He always played free. And he was the only Polish free jazz musician to have an extensive, intuitive knowledge of old jazz, of everything, of jazziness. Przybielski was very jazzy. He just knew. He felt it, the son of a bitch. He knew about things that musicians talk about among themselves that are really high-level.

Przybielski's strange behaviour has become the stuff of legend.
Well, because he is, as Witkacy would put it, schizoid. Basically. But that didn't bother him in the least. Never. At least, that's my understanding. He's just that kind of person. That's how he behaved. OK. That's his business.

How about Nadolski?
He was a kind of guru, but it was Przybielski who for me had that strange, incredibly interesting knowledge.

Czesław Niemen took those two into his band when he moved into jazz.
Yes. They also played with Jagiełło. I had my quintet. I was interested in jazz music *sensu stricto*. But Niemen wanted to have his own band to go on tour with.

At Remont, Przybielski and Nadolski played in a band called Supergrupa Bez Fałszywej Skromności ['Supergroup Without Any False Modesty'].
There was something of the kind. Who was it played with them?

Janusz Trzciński and Andrzej Bieżan.
Bieżan. He's dead. A composer and pianist in the contemporary music field with a predisposition towards jazz musicians. Tadeusz Sudnik later hung around with him. Bieżan was very highly thought of – someone with wide artistic horizons. He used to get together with jazz musicians, with Nadolski, Przybielski, for improvisation. We had a lot of respect for each other, but we didn't play together. Trzciński, on the other hand, was a percussionist back from Andrzej Trzaskowski's day, from his sextet. 'Trzcinka'. He later ran a café on Krakowskie Przedmieście Street.

Wild guys?
Wild guys. Completely free music. They didn't all smoke. Some of them didn't smoke that much, just a little, with restraint. They lived in the clubs. They were a bohemian lot.

Andrzej Mitan was also very active on the Remont scene.
He was. He was a bit of a performer, a bit of a visual artist, a strange singer with a loud voice. Mitan's still playing. I met up with him recently when he was organizing a jazz festival in Radom. He works in all sorts of strange places. Cultural centres, the Ministry of Culture . . .

Were you not tempted to play with them?
No, I stayed out of it. I played more serious music, professional. I didn't improvise to that extent. They were too free for me. They played very modern music, but I wasn't particularly interested in it because I had my own thing. And I had a very specific taste. I had the pick of the musicians. When the quintet was breaking up, I had my sights on people like Edward Vesala, Adam

Makowicz, that direction. I needed people who had greater musical skills. I did sometimes take on Przybielski, but he was unreliable. His behaviour was notorious: he'd give the music stand a kick to make the sheet music fall off so he wouldn't have to read it. That was when I started playing more rhythmic music with Sławomir Kulpowicz.

You formed a new band with Kulpowicz.
That band actually came out of Remont. That's when I met a girl, Alicja, our band manager. I said, 'Shall we go on tour, then?' That's how that band came about, back when I was living in Remont.

You were living in Remont?
I stayed there when I broke up with my wife and moved out of Górnośląska Street. After I got back from India in 1979, 1980. And then I went back to Kraków. In Kraków I lived with my mother. My father had died. We moved to Warsaw. I lived with my mother for quite a while, here, once I'd bought a flat on Rozbrat Street. A few years. But before then, when I used to go up to Warsaw, I'd always stay at the Forum Hotel. As soon as I'd finished a concert, I'd go straight to the Forum. Andrzej Tyszko had his studio-workshop nearby. I became friends with him them. Marek Piekarczyk from the rock band TSA also used to go there. He was always careful, sensible.

Did you get into rock then?
I got into rock when I heard the records made by the masters of rock. But before that I liked it for its image. TSA looked fantastic. They had a good image, something that jazz musicians were already starting to lose. Jazz had become rather academic and there was no image to it anymore.

Young audiences had deserted it for rock.
Of course.

What do you mean by 'jazz had become academic'?
It was dominated by polite, well-rehearsed playing. Devoid of charisma, without any kind of dirty edge. That's what I liked least about it. Our quintet was the opposite of that. Including our outfits.

That whole era at the end of the 1970s and the beginning of the 1980s wasn't terribly interesting for jazz, anywhere in the world either, because that was the fusion period.
At that time jazz musicians were playing copies of funk – a kind of pub music. Everything was becoming more bourgeois. And now they call me a 'bourgeois'. That's what the yass musicians say.

You started listening to rock because of your wife?
That was incidental, because she had records at home. Then I also started buying records that were more pop-like: Sting, Prince, Red Hot Chili Peppers, Roni Size, Wu Tang Clan. But I mainly listened to that sort of thing at my friends' places. But at that time, thanks to Joanna, we had the Stones, Zappa and Marley. Marley! I began listening to a lot of reggae. I got to know people on the Polish reggae scene. I used to have my own little spot at Remont, by the stage, and they had their little spot in some back room. They were on the right-hand side of the building, with access from the hall of residence, and I was right in the middle, near the stage. We saw each other all the time. I knew them well because we smoked together.

Before Dariusz Malejonek had his conversion and became a central figure in Catholic rock, he had a festival hit with his band Kultura: 'Weed is good for pneumoconiosis, weed is good for tuberculosis, weed is the emancipation of the nation.'
Well, yes, a clear case. At that time, I was smoking more than they were. I heard it said that my brain had been completely addled by marijuana!

Later, under the name Izrael, they released the album *Nabij faję*, with plumes of marijuana smoke on the cover. They recorded it with the jazz pianist Wojciech Konikiewicz, who was also a regular at Remont.
But that was much later. I also remember the rock band Brygada Kryzys. Izrael came after that. Paweł Kelner used to appear there. Małgorzata Pyza. Robert Brylewski. Malejonek. There was a large group of people hanging around there. I don't know where most of them are these days. There was a drummer, a bit of a cult figure, who later died in Holland. What was his name?

Luter (that's to say, Jacek Lenartowicz).
Luter! Yes, yes. I had a great time with him. Because they were wild young guys.

That's when there was a punk/New Wave breakthrough in rock. And it was these very people who were responsible for it. Were you aware of that?
I definitely saw that happening. And I really liked it. They were creative. I respected all the musicians, but it was those punk and reggae musicians who were the most interesting back then. They were high. They carried on like I used to do in my youth. For me, the spirit of the thing was always more important than the technique. I had more of a spiritual connection with them. I liked their image. The way they lived their life.

So were you not tempted to play with Brylewski, Malejonek and the rest of them?
I've always had a lot of respect for them. Then and now. But, back then, when they played reggae, I'd think of Marley and I'd feel his greatness. With Marley I was most impressed by his musical perfection. His music was so beautiful

because of its unbelievable rhythmic perfection. That bass! The way it moved! I did give it a bit of thought: why the bassist played such strange lines. I used to ask people about it, but no one at the time seemed to have picked up on it. But he played lines like that because he went at the bass as if he were playing the drums. He used his fingers like you do on congas. It makes no difference which conga you hit. What's more important is the power of the rhythm. Hit it here and you have a better rhythmic bounce-off, because you'll get a certain kind of beat.

In your view, is that way of playing a question of technique or intuition?
It's a question of technique. It's a drumming technique. The pitch isn't important. The pitch of a drum isn't crucial; what matters is that I get this fuckin' *Bam!* sound here, but more of a *Baaam!* sound there. It's to do with the *way* I strike it, in other words: the accent not the pitch. What kind of sound – that's immaterial. It's the accent that matters. The accent! *Buh-don buh-daam dah tah buh-don dah dah tah.* The way they played those basses! I thought, 'Shit, why do they go for that sound?' But they'd arranged their fingers in a certain grip and didn't move them at all. They couldn't care less about the pitch. They just hit the strings. They go with the rhythm.

We still haven't talked about another important Warsaw jazz club. The Akwarium.
I was involved with the Akwarium. I was, and still am, a fan of Mariusz Adamiak. I like predatory characters who love music. I'm not a fan of Adamiak's aesthetic, but I do value his love of music. I have respect for such people. I often played at his club. He was always open to everything, and he gave me that opportunity.

When were you most active at Akwarium?
I don't remember exactly. In the 1980s, just after Adamiak took over the club. The Polish Jazz Association had discovered the place. Adamiak leased the building off them, so to speak, and then later got the city authorities to agree to it being his club. And they spent all their time fighting to get Akwarium back. They said that he'd stolen the club off them. Except that, earlier, they'd not done anything with it, whereas he'd been active. It's good to have an organization like the Polish Jazz Association because it helps out musicians who are really in need. I don't want to judge them. But it's the kind of organization that needs 'doers'.

Was it a good place to play?
Absolutely. It was also a place for meeting up. I spent a fair chunk of my life there. It was in Akwarium that my would-be wife and I decided to get married. Oh, and there were the gigs. There were lots of things going on there. After Jazz Jamboree we always met up at Akwarium. That's where our line-up on *Bluish*

At Jazz Jamboree 1981, with Sławomir Kulpowicz.
Photograph by Mirosław Makowski

made its debut, and our band with Tony Oxley, just before *Bosonossa and Other Ballads*. All the Polish jazz musicians played there. Adamiak's Akwarium was a kind of hotbed, much more important than Tygmont is nowadays. Despite appearances, Tygmont has a more commercial approach. They might say it doesn't, but it does. What sort of stage do they have there for the musicians? What kind of sound system? You have people talking, sitting around eating. People also ate in Akwarium, but it was all separated out better there: you sat downstairs; upstairs you listened to music.

When Akwarium disappeared, there were no decent jazz clubs left in Warsaw, right?
I don't think there's been one ever since. Akwarium was the only real jazz club, like the one in Kraków, a long time ago.

Do you think the jazz club scene changed a lot in the 1990s?
You know, I didn't play that much in those clubs. I mostly played large concerts. There's a different atmosphere in the clubs. I wasn't a big fan. The big ones

appealed to me, like Birdland in New York, New Morning in Paris, Club Seven in Oslo. You have a show there, a concert-like atmosphere.

Let's get back to Remont. You mentioned that it was there that you formed the quartet with Kulpowicz on piano and the Vitold Rek–Czesław Bartkowski rhythm section.
That was a Polish band between the quintet and the quartet. We played a lot.

Before then, in the late 1970s, for a while, you didn't have a band at all, and then it all started with Kulpowicz's band, 'In Formation'.
That's what Sławomir called it. He put that band together. He took on Mały and Vitold Rek. I knew them. Vitold played in Sun Ship. A very good bassist. I approved of them. I started writing music for the band and we'd play.

Witold Szczurek, who later changed his name to Vitold Rek, was a musician from the same generation as your fans.
Well, yes. Szczurek and Kulpowicz – that was my fanbase's generation. We recorded two albums together. We played a lot of concerts. Only in Poland. It was only later, during my Freelectronic period, that I played a lot with Vitold in Europe. Vitold held the rhythm well. A strong, stable bassist. We also used to meet up outside of music, although the contact was mainly musical. Music was ubiquitous in my life. All the contacts and relationships I had came mainly through music.

Those two albums, *Music 81* and *A i J* ['A and J'] appeared within the space of two months, between the summer and autumn of 1981.
I recorded those records practically at the same time, in the same studio on Długa Street. Slightly different compositions. I produced them and sold the tapes. One album to Polskie Nagrania and the other to Poljazz.

Overall, *Music 81* is the stronger of the two albums. *A i J* is rather wild -- heavy compositions. But *Music 81* has a groove to it, played with downright Latin verve at times.
Maybe. *81* is more orderly.

The melodies there are expressive, but twisted into a kind of grimace, possibly even something grotesque.
They're dirty. That's how I wanted to play them, to make those nice little melodies dirty. Like with Bushka: I told her to be a decent person, but I was a devil myself. Only Kulpowicz played in a traditional way. That band was too normal for me. That's why it didn't last long. We got on well together socially. That was after my wife and I had separated. We did big tours of Poland. We often played in Wrocław, in Rura. We used to stay in fine hotels. Fabulous! Good times. I was with Basia later (she had concerts as well) and, later still, with Viola. Two of the women that I was with back then were also my managers. I'm still in touch with Basia. We often phone each other. She's very dear to me.

Was it because of those women that you began playing in Poland more?

It was difficult to get out to the West at that time because you had to have visas. Before then, I used to have an annual visa for Germany, but later on it was really difficult to get that sort of thing arranged.

Did you also have an annual visa for Finland?

We didn't need visas for Austria, Finland and Sweden. We needed them for Norway but, once we were already playing in Scandinavia, we'd get in without any problem. Due to Poland being closed off, I was somewhat on the sidelines. And, anyway, I was living dangerously and wasn't in a fit state to do business.

15 Purple Liquor

When we were going through your archive, a leaflet fell out for a Cecil Taylor concert: 'Music from Two Continents'. When you saw it, you said, 'Those were difficult times. 1984.'
You know, I was *really* living on the edge at that time.

How was that period in terms of music?
A bit empty. I was playing less then. Poland was closed while martial law was in place.

Was it different in the 1970s?
We were like royalty. The planes were empty. People didn't travel much, and PAGART [Polish Artists' Agency] arranged everything for us. As part of that system, PAGART worked very well for us. We paid them ten per cent, and they arranged everything. I didn't need to sort out visas, or anything. I'd go along to PAGART after a little brandy at the Europejski. I'd smoke a joint on the way and enter their offices totally relaxed, and I knew all the people who worked there. First of all, there were the managers' rooms: Andrzej Marzec, Andrzej Kapkowski. Then there was that really nice Danka, who used to arrange all my flights. Every single one. Paid for in złotys. The passport rooms weren't so nice because they were staffed by army people, but people I knew all the same. And there were also runners who used to go and get the visas.

In an era when covert collaborators were being sniffed out, I have to ask: did those nice gentlemen in uniform make you any interesting propositions?
If any of the people there had connections to government departments, well then they treated me well enough. Jazz operated in the margins, and they just weren't that interested in it. No informer ever approached me for information.

Did PAGART change much in the 1980s?
No. It was the same people. The conditions changed. You had to wait longer for visas. I missed a few work trips because of visa problems: too long a delay.

You once referred to that era as a percussion-free time in your own work.
Freelectronic played without percussion. In C.O.C.X. we initially had José Antonio Torres on percussion, but later we had Lakis Apostolis Anthimos

playing drums. In those days I felt comfortable with Lakis. I knew him back from SBB days, and, when SBB disbanded, we started hanging out together. It was through Lakis that I got to know SBB. I met him during an exam. I was required to be on one of those jazz committees whose members were even more learned and academic than the schools that they'd never finished.

Are you referring to the accreditations? Those notorious exams that amateur musicians used to have to take in front of their elders?
Exactly. I had to fight on Lakis's behalf, and he only just passed. Yet he was an excellent musician. I didn't like having to sit on those committees. I hated it, because we'd been sitting where they were virtually the week before. I remember Janusz Muniak kicking off with these pub musicians who'd told him, 'You can't read music. You're useless!' And those same committees, they'd take it out on all the poor rock musicians who couldn't read music. They'd ask them these typical academic questions. It used to make me laugh. But it was actually very important for these musicians to get their accreditation because it was all about money. Without accreditation, you were an amateur musician and on the lowest rate of pay.

What was it like playing with SBB?
They knew how to improvise. Both Lakis and Józef Skrzek, in particular. Experienced musicians with a lot of charisma. Before that they'd played with Czesław Niemen. I played with them in the mid-1970s. I did a whole tour with SBB. That was the same year that Don Cherry took part in the workshops in Chodzież. We had our workshop activities, and then we all got onto a coach that took us to Jazz Jantar, where I played with SBB. Don was going through his hippie phase then. He went everywhere with Baba Ji, his guru, and with his family, his dogs, his rugs. He bought himself a scythe in Poland. On the way to Szczecin we stopped off at a village craft shop. Don stepped off the coach in his oriental robes, with Baba Ji behind him, and we went to buy this scythe. The whole village turned out. It was a really colourful scene.

Why would he want a scythe?
To cut the grass in his garden with. Not using a machine, but with a proper peasant's scythe. I had a strong spiritual connection with Don, always, from my time in Copenhagen. An incredible cat. The last time I saw him was in England at the Bracknell Festival. 1983. I was playing in an international big band, and he was playing with Neneh, in the band Rip Rig & Panic. And Don was already living on the edge then. I thought, 'Shit – if he can do that, then I can do whatever I want.' I saw him snort a line of cocaine, down half a litre of brandy and remain completely sober.

At the Bracknell Festival, you played with Hoarded Dreams, Graham Collier's big band. There was even an album released of that concert, which came out in 2007.
Yes. What, they've released it? I didn't know. Who played in that band? I remember it being a big line-up.

Collier had a strong trumpet section in that band: you, Manfred Schoof, Kenny Wheeler, Henry Lowther and Ted Curson.
Curson's a friend from way back. He recorded with Andrzej Trzaskowski. A nice cat. A really nice cat. We used to meet up in Finland as well – he was there a lot.

Collier is known as one of the top British bandleaders. Wheeler and John Surman were his disciples, so to speak: they came out of his band in the 1960s.
Maybe. That was good music. The formula was big band, but it was more like a kind of workshop. We did a tour of Germany first. And then we went on to England for that one concert at the festival. We were playing really well then. I can't remember much from that time. A little bit maybe, if someone reminds me. I was smoking a huge amount around then. After I split up with my wife, I was fucking around like an animal. I think, also, I was maybe carrying on like that because, at that time in Poland, you could live your life without taking any kind of responsibility. I didn't have to worry about working every day. When I brought 2,000 or 1,500 notes back from Bracknell, I had enough to live off for two months and not want for anything.

It had its attractions.
Fuck the attractions. It nearly killed me.

That's when you formed the band C.O.C.X. Was that just after your quartet with Sławomir Kulpowicz disbanded?
Straight after. I was hanging around with one of Lakis's friends, Wojtek. A film student. He was shooting a short film for film school, and this film was about me. A strange film, shot in Kraków, in an orangery. That's where I had the idea for the album *Lady Go*, which came out of C.O.C.X. Wojtek designed that strange *Lady Go* album cover. C.O.C.X. – he chose that name. 'Call it C.O.C.X.!' 'Koks' [coke], obviously, but written differently. Straight away, the symbols popped up, because it looks like 'S.O.S.' in Russian.

C.O.C.X. actually came out of a rock project. It was funny, the way it came about. It started with some concerts that Basia, my new manager, had arranged. Lakis, on guitar, was the key figure. Jerzy Piotrowski was our first drummer.

What about the film?
It was a film school short. A very abstract film, in which Marta, my then-girlfriend, had a part. It was made up of completely unconnected scenes,

scenes in an orangery. Flowers of some kind; snakes of some kind. Marta's standing there naked in the water. Surrealistic images.

A psychedelic vibe?
Definitely a psychedelic trip.

Did Wojtek make any more films after that one?
He went to Germany. I do see him occasionally. I think he works in German TV now.

The C.O.C.X. line-up – it was a bit like SBB but with trumpet instead of keyboard.
Musicians from SBB. We had a tour in Silesia arranged. And I just couldn't play those concerts. Piotrowski left because I'd played for five minutes and then given up. At the next gig, I played for fifteen minutes. I couldn't manage it. I cancelled the tour. I eventually put the brakes on in Wrocław, at Baśka's. Then in Warsaw we had a gig at the Akwarium. I played with Ryszka, with Andrzej Rusek on bass guitar, and there was Lakis and me. That was a rock line-up too. I wrote two or three compositions at the Akwarium. 'Fioletowy liquor' ['Purple Liquor']. And that turned into C.O.C.X.

But why couldn't you play?
I was drunk. Completely wasted. I hadn't prepared any music. I didn't really know what to play. And I wasn't even particularly bothered, either.

Is the title 'Purple Liquor' a reference to your knife-edge lifestyle?
Evidently a knife-edge lifestyle, because we're talking about methylated spirits here. That's when that purple liquor appeared. I drank a bottle of methylated spirit at Baśka's.

Apparently, people used to filter it through bread.
I didn't filter it through bread. I saw a bottle with a skull on it. I drank the lot, but out of a crystal glass.

The skull really appealed to you?
A lot! You know, I was on a desperate bender at the time. I didn't care about anything. I wrote 'Fioletowy liquor' and got going with C.O.C.X. I began writing music. And once I'd written a few things, I took José Torres on so that I wouldn't have to have a drum kit in the band.

Why no drum kit?
Because drums – rock drums – were too powerful for me, and uninteresting. Torres, with his Latin rhythm, nailed it better.

Where did José Torres come from as a percussionist?
He was hanging around. Well, someone discovered him.

He'd played with John Porter earlier.
With Porter. Maybe it was Vitold Rek who discovered him. He knew Porter.

Where did the idea come from for the Latin and Afro-Caribbean rhythms in C.O.C.X.'s music?
The idea was for it to be a kind of bossa nova.

What about reggae? C.O.C.X. even played a piece called 'Babylon Samba'.
Well, you do know that I used to listen to Marley. And I rehearsed in Remont, where Izrael were hanging around.

While we're on the subject of song titles, the C.O.C.X. album has a track dedicated to a woman, 'Mademoiselle K'.
There was such a girl.

And who's this 'Mister DD' – the name of another track?
Mister Degenerate. That refers specifically to me.

So, once again, you had a band of foreign musicians. Lakis, a Greek; Torres, a Cuban. Was that just by chance?
Just by chance. They were good musicians. At that time I was also starting to play with Janusz Skowron; even before Freelectronic I had a band with Torres and Skowron. We did a tour of Silesia.

With C.O.C.X. you moved away from jazz. Although this was just a specific project. Neither entirely jazz, nor pop, but essentially chart material with a Latin beat, electric guitar and catchy tunes. Were you accused of going commercial?
It was well received, despite being a controversial project. People said different things about it. Well, it was a kind of free pop. Or something? I had a different approach to it back then. Because this music was high. I was living high. I wasn't making an album that would sound like pop just so it would be easier to sell. It was a different idea, a very specific one, which was that, when I was with a woman, instead of putting on a Marley album, I'd put on one of my own. Light stuff. Into bed. Now I can see that this shows my natural tendency towards communicative music. That was how it found expression at that time.
    It was a strange period, the 1980s. I was spending less time with Vesala, although we were playing together all the time – trios and duets. I toured with his Sound & Fury and we met up in the band UMO. I spent a lot of time in Finland. I played in a duo with Tomasz Szukalski and in a duo with Janusz Skowron, with him playing on a Roland keyboard. There was also a TV programme recorded in the Wieliczka salt mine, with me playing solo. I

had a project with a band in the STU Theatre which developed into *Lady Go*. I played with Tomasz Hołuj, with Vitold Rek on bass, and we had Czesio too. I had this friend, Czesio. He was a bit of a trumpeter, a bit of a fine artist and performer, a bit of a dope user, an artist. He didn't have any one particular job to do at this concert. He had a very wide remit. He was supposed to play the part of a wizard, a juggler – just to do his thing.

You recorded the *C.O.C.X.* album in 1983 with Lakis, Torres and Vitold Rek. But there was also a different C.O.C.X. line-up, with Ryszard Styła on guitar, Rek and two conga players: Torres and Zbigniew Brysiak.
I did play with Brysiak. I think Stanisław Soyka recommended him.

That was your line-up at Róbrege.* One of the most important New Wave rock festivals in Poland during the 1980s. Despite its name, it wasn't all about reggae; there was punk as well.
I remember that gig. It was in Warsaw, in a tent. I think it was called 'Intersalto'. Brysiak and José were there. José's playing was a bit too Latin, in the narrow sense of the word, so I wanted to broaden it out, and Brysiak was perfect for that. Brysiak is a specialist in broadening things out, in unusual things.

You played in front of a totally non-jazz audience.
A totally non-jazz audience, but we went down really well.

Who played alongside C.O.C.X.?
The Lipińskis, the Brylewskis, the Malejoneks of this world, who hadn't yet achieved saint status, and in fact were damaged goods. I can't remember their names because I didn't listen to those kinds of bands. I hung around in the background. In those days, I felt more comfortable there than I did on a jazz stage, because my style, the way I lived my life, was similar to theirs. I was a bit like their dad!

In that C.O.C.X. line-up, you also jammed with the legends of Kraków's rock underground, the band Düpa.
Aah! We did meet up, yes. It was Vitold Rek who knew Piotr Marek. Marek later committed suicide. He was screwed up mentally. I played a festival at Hybrydy, where Marek performed just before he died. I was playing in a duo then with Stu Martin, and Marek was playing solo guitar. I was surprised to see him so stressed out. He had terrible stage fright. A strange guy. I liked his paintings. And his wife. His paintings were depressing, but realistic. His band was later called Püdelsi. That's that Kraków band that Maciej Maleńczuk appeared with. You see, I've always had a thing for desperados. I like them and I fit in with them.

---

* *Translator's note: Róbrege* literally means 'do reggae'.

Brysiak was part of the Częstochowa circle. Very strong at that time in terms of indie jazz. Brysiak sometimes played with the jazz standards band Tie Break, from Częstochowa.

Tie Break. I felt good with them too. We got on well, Ziut Gralak and I.

People used to call them 'punk jazz'. In any case, Gralak used to play trumpet with the punks and Rastas from Gliwice. There were some fabulous bands like Śmierć Kliniczna and RAP.

I met Tie Break at a concert. I was playing in Częstochowa with Sławomir Kulpowicz and Ziut came up to us.

Stanisław Soyka, who became a good mate of yours, also collaborated with Tie Break.

I was friends with Soyka, but that was much later on, at the start of the new era. The late 1980s and early 1990s. He was living a similar life to mine at the time. We took to each other. We got on great together and had a mutual understanding. We saw a lot of each other, although I didn't play with him that much. He invited me to his concerts a few times, and I played with him. I still think highly of Soyka – for his voice, his approach to art and life. He was a classy musician right from the start, crystal-clear in his focus: he knew straight away what he wanted to achieve.

There was one other colourful character from indie jazz who was also involved with Tie Break: Włodzimierz Kiniorski played with them.

That was later, although I'd met Kiniorski very early on. He used to go to the workshops in Chodzież. I got to know a lot of people through those workshops. Later, 'Kinior' and I recorded the music to an Agnieszka Holland film. It was her film school assignment.

Did Kiniorski always play free?

Definitely. Free right from the start.

Tie Break and Kiniorski are examples that prove that not all Polish jazz from that period was straight-ahead jazz. Young, modern musicians also appeared in Szczecin, Warsaw and Silesia. Later on, those musicians joined forces with Tie Break and then, under Wojciech Czajkowski's leadership, Free Cooperation came into being – a band that was the manifestation of this new scene.

I didn't know them so well. There was also another trend in Free Cooperation because they had Andrzej Przybielski playing with them. And, as you already know, I've always thought very highly of Przybielski.

Shortly after, a band emerged from that indie scene, which shook up the Polish mainstream and made a name for itself at European festivals. Young Power.

Oh yes. The late 1980s.

You played with them on their album *Man of Tra*. Did you do anything else together?

No. I liked that band. They were very good. I mean, they had Piotr Wojtasik playing with them. But I only met up with them from time to time.

On the Polish indie scene, you also collaborated with Osjan.

With Osjan, yes, because that was Jacek Ostaszewski's band. And Jacek was a friend of mine, the first musician I ever played with. You know, I'm not sure Jacek feels the same way as I do about our playing together and our friendship. I can still remember us playing our first compositions. I think highly of Jacek as an artist, a charismatic person. He never compromised. Oh, and I knew Milo Kurtis very well. I had a deep personal connection with Milo. I regard Osjan as a whole as a very interesting musical group. After all, they were precursors of what we call world music now. And I'd never turn them down.

In 1978 you played on an Osjan album. How did it feel amidst that Eastern vibe?

I went to their recording session. The music didn't feel too alien to me. Remember that I used to listen to Tibetan monks. I had a very wide range. I was interested in all sorts of things. Years later, I had the great pleasure of playing with Osjan on *Tribute to Don Cherry*.

Still on the subject of your former flirtation with rock. I've seen a photo on the internet, because otherwise I'd never have believed it. You on stage with the band Mech.

There was a band called Mech. Who was in it?

Bluffmania, Tasmania. Those were some of their albums. A group from Warsaw. A moustachioed bass player: the frontman, Maciej Januszko. And a keyboard player, Robert Milewski. He was working on an album of his own but it was never released. He went to the States, and I think he's still there.

Yes, yes, yes. I think I probably know why I played with them. I was hanging out in Remont, and they used to practise there. Where did you see the photo?

Pracownia 52. They have some brilliant photos from that era.

Makowski did that.

Mirosław Makowski. He was very friendly with the rock and blues band Krzak. The blues scene at that time in Poland was as strong as it's ever been.

Yes, yes. Lakis knew them. I met Jerzy Kawalec through him. I occasionally played with Krzak. Very sporadically.

From among the rock circle, were you closest to Lakis?

To Lakis and Krzak.

Talking about strictly jazz events from the first half of the 1980s, the most important of those must have been your collaboration with Cecil Taylor. Did you regard playing with Cecil as a kind of baptism? He was, after all, one of the founding fathers of free, a giant of modern jazz.

Yes, it was a baptism, an unbelievable one. A big deal. I was getting more and more popular. First there was the Orchestra of Two Continents, autumn 1984. I went to the rehearsal in Prague. That's where we started the concerts. An excellent line-up. Karen Borca on oboe, who at that time was Jimmy Lyons's wife. Lyons on alto sax, John Tchicai on alto sax, the now-deceased Frank Wright on tenor, Gunter Hampel on baritone, Enrico Rava and me on trumpets. Oh, and there was a large rhythm section: André Martinez and Rashid Bakr on drums, William Parker on bass.

Was that band put together for Taylor's European tour?

Yes, for the tour. It was quite a big tour. We played in Prague, in Warsaw at Jazz Jamboree, at a festival in Paris. Germany, Switzerland, Italy. There's an album that we recorded in Milan on the Soul Note label.

How did Taylor end up calling you up for this line-up?

I don't exactly know. I have no idea. But I was already well known. The quintet had already played with Herbie Hancock.

Had you not met him before then?

No. I got a phone call from his agent, Gabi Kleinschmidt, who was organizing the tour. We met up in Prague. Cecil later told me that he'd remembered our first meeting. He came in, full of energy; he liked my playing. Then he asked me to join him for his next gig, in Berlin. Free Music Production arranged a festival for him that ran over several days. Summer 1988. There's an album from that festival – a whole box set. I played in Cecil's big band: the European Orchestra. We had the young Louis Sclavis playing bass clarinet. We also had Enrico Rava and Han Bennink.

What was Taylor like in person?

Great. I felt great with him. His craziness, his attitude to business, really appealed to me. I like all sorts of genres. I like to broaden my artistic range, so as not to make the same mistake that Witkacy made with his contempt for jazz. That sort of contempt is a mistake. Art has no borders and it develops in different directions. That's why, unlike most people on the free jazz scene, I do like commercial stuff. They are pretty dismissive about it, but I can separate me as a musician from me as a consumer, a fan. I am also impressed by – and I have a really high regard for – people who are completely uncommercial.

Cecil's like that, and he impressed me massively. His compositions had an extraordinary beauty. 'Womb Water'! My God, I absolutely loved that piece! I lost what I'd written down, and I later asked Cecil about the composition. He couldn't remember it. He had a careless approach towards it, like he was just

OPER DER STADT KÖLN
Intendant Prof. Dr. Michael Hampe

– JAZZ IN DER OPER –

Montag, 15. Oktober 1984, 20.00 Uhr

CECIL TAYLOR SEGMENTS

MUSIC FROM TWO CONTINENTS
(Uraufführung)

CECIL TAYLOR, piano
JIMMY LYONS, sax
KAREN LYONS, bassoon
FRANK WRIGHT, reeds
BRENDA BAKAR, vocal
WILLIAM PARKER, bass
RASHID BAKAR, drums & perc
ANDRES MARTINEZ, drums & perc
ENRICO RAVA, trumpet
TOMASZ STANKO, trumpet
JOHN TCHICAI, sax
GUNTER HAMPEL, bass-clarinet

Technische Leitung: Peter Haenle – Tontechnische Anlagen und Mitarbeit bei der Einrichtung: Firma Musik-Sound Ingo Hersch (Oldenburg) / Willi Brauß – Tontechnische Einrichtung Wolfgang Bars – Beleuchtung: Magnus Rösch – Inspizientin: Jenny Brock

Konzertflügel: Bösendorfer

Cecil Taylor

Invitation to a Cecil Taylor concert, also featuring Tomasz Stańko, Cologne, 1984.
Courtesy Anna Stańko

firing off amazing ideas at random. He'd throw these compositions around and they'd disappear into thin air. That to me was very noble, that sort of artistic stance. Cecil lives like an artist; he's an improviser. His music lives in the moment, when he's actually playing it. Sometimes it comes out better, sometimes worse, but it makes no difference to him.

In a way, I do the same thing. I play all the time. I make recordings, but will any of it last? I don't think so, because life nowadays is too fast. For a short time, something or other will linger on, but I don't think it matters. The moment I'm in, when, as an improviser, I'm living in that moment and giving it my all, that affects my life.

What I also value in Cecil is his homogeneity, the complete homogeneity of his pianistic structure. I'd love to invite him to the festival in Bielsko-Biała. I'll invite him, pay him well, but I'll ask him to play a solo piano recital, like the one he did at Jazz Jamboree in 1965. That's my dream. A major figure, a giant of a figure. I think very highly of Miles, but he couldn't grasp this kind of music. An artist always has a boundary beyond which he will not venture, but art has no boundaries. And Miles wasn't keen on Cecil's music, or on Ornette's.

Actually, artistically, Cecil has remained consistent.
The same since 1965. He has fixed structures of a certain kind, where he plays energy. He plays that all the time.

In the big band, Orchestra of Two Continents, Taylor didn't just play, he composed as well.
Cecil wrote lines. He has his own linear structures, a certain kind of linear run, which he likes. I suspect that he slows down the improvisation in his brain and writes it down. The way he did it on tour was to dictate those lines to us, those kind of 'snake lines'. He'd say, 'C up to D; D down to C'. He'd indicate whether the line was going up or down; we'd have to write it down at lightning speed. He didn't write notes; he wrote symbols: C, D, E – it didn't matter about the octave. It was usually within the scope of a single octave. When he did this with his hand, that meant it was over an octave. He wasn't precise about everything. The rhythms would be determined during rehearsals. But after a rehearsal, he'd change it. In Warsaw he gave us the running order and then just before we went on stage he changed it, and once he was on stage, he'd start playing in different keys. Everything felt up in the air. And that's why we played so sparsely. You know, everyone wanted to appear alongside Cecil, and to play longer and longer solos. The chaos that ensued from that was difficult to get a handle on. Yet he somehow managed to control it.

Keeping a band at that level of uncertainty: does it not lead to conflict?
Tchicai liked to know what was happening. He got fed up at one point. There was always uncertainty in the band. I get the impression that Cecil did it on purpose. And it was this very uncertainty that ensured control over the dramatic structure. Otherwise there'd have been permanent chaos. This might just be my own interpretation, but it seems to me that when you have such a large number of good musicians, it brings a certain kind of economy into the structure. Who knows? This might just be my view on some of the technical matters. Maybe Cecil wasn't doing this quite as intentionally as I imagined.

Did Cecil somehow control the band on stage?
Cecil didn't control anything, but William Parker, who was his right-hand man, helped him to write down those 'snakes'. We played together and there wasn't much room for solos. You could call it collective improvisation. A kind of chaos that would mesh.

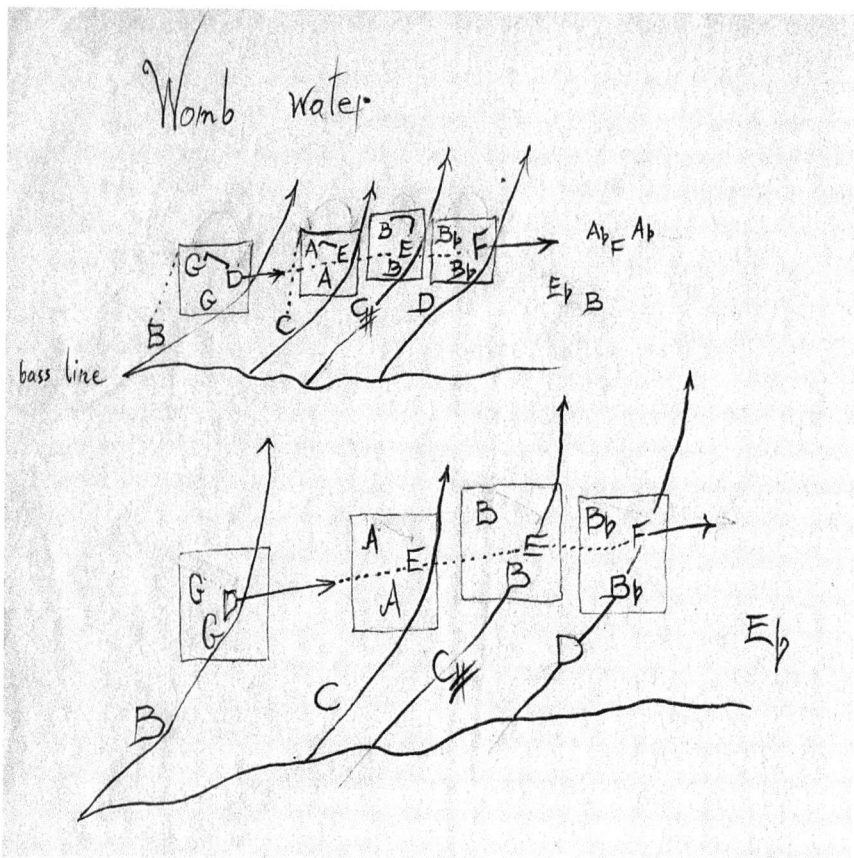

A surviving part of the score for Cecil Taylor's 'Womb Water'.
Courtesy Anna Stańko

William Parker has now grown to be one of the most active musicians on the New York improvisation scene. He records scores of albums, from covers of Curtis Mayfield songs to tantric chants.

A guru. But he didn't make such a big impression on me back then. I was surprised to see him as Taylor's right-hand man. Cecil had a particular approach to music. He played. He sat down and played. His personality, his expressiveness – it just worked. Even when he came out from under his piano when we did a joint concert with the Art Ensemble of Chicago. He came out from under his piano and started to dance. We were standing on one side of the stage, the Art Ensemble on the other. Cecil mingled between the two.

Two Continents and the Art Ensemble of Chicago on one stage?
Yes. It nearly ended in a fight.

Why?
Cecil was pissed off. He wasn't too keen on the Art Ensemble. He was jealous. But we had to be on stage together because that's how they'd set it up at the Paris festival. Martinez was in charge of the band then. We were a strong and close-knit unit, but we weren't playing, and Lester Bowie came over to ask what the matter was. Cecil didn't want to play with them, but he did dance during their concert.

Is Cecil in a state of constant excitement?
Constant excitement. He surrounds himself with art. When I paid him a visit in New York, his apartment was all cluttered up with books and paintings. He had Kosiński on his bookshelf. A classic New York intellectual. He knows everything about art. He's fascinated by literature, opera, ballet.

Taylor is gay. While pop musicians have, of late, been turning this to their advantage, in jazz there's no talk of gay people.
Well, what is there to talk about? Cecil never hid it.

Is being gay in jazz connected with being an outsider? That's what Taylor's radical music might suggest.
I don't know. Miles used to laugh about having given Bill Evans a fright when they first started playing together: 'You know what you have to do to be in this band? You got to fuck the band.' And Evans did get scared: 'I can do anything, but that – no can do.' But they were taking the mick. Cecil was uncompromising and upfront about being gay, right from the start. He loved men. And he was very manly with it. He was upset on tour because he'd been jilted by his lover. He used to pull Vesala's pigtails. He even once grabbed me by the ass in a taxi. I said, 'Cecil! Man! I'm an old cat. Watch yourself.' That's how he was. The thing is, it doesn't matter. If someone is different, they have a different way of operating, which is an asset to the whole of society. Gay people have within them the wisdom of two sexes simultaneously. That might sound far-fetched, but if we have among us an increasing number of people who in a natural, unostentatious way, show their orientation, then society will get used to the fact that a certain percentage among us is like that, and will become more tolerant. For me people are: a Frenchman, Zośka, a gay person, a blonde person, a Bavarian, a pirate, a doper . . . That's how I describe people.

Did you get to know any of the Two Continents musicians well?
I hung out with Frank Wright. I also liked André Martinez.

Was that the first time you'd met Enrico Rava?
I've known Rava for a long time. He played at the festival in Bled, where I went with Komeda. And then we saw each other at various festivals. We always got on well.

He's taken a similar path to yours. He started off in a European country that wasn't associated with jazz. He played free, and then he became an ECM star. Where did he play free?

With Steve Lacy, for instance, in the early 1970s.
I think Rava has been playing like he does right from the very beginning, but he liked different things and tried different things, with all kinds of people. He was like that. I mean, he did live in Argentina for a long time. He played with Gato Barbieri. He was in the States for a long time. He had a green card. Cecil knew him. Everyone knew him.

How was it that second time you played with Taylor, in Berlin?
There was a workshop in Berlin. Different line-ups, different combinations. Cecil also played solo. That was a difficult time for me. I was taking a lot of drugs back then. I was very high. But it was nice there in Berlin.

In Berlin you met up with the old German crew from the free festivals of the 1970s. Peter Brötzmann and Peter Kowald played there. Oh, and Evan Parker.
We used to see each other all the time on the road. Non-stop. I particularly liked Brötzmann. I always kept in touch with the German scene, playing with Albert Mangelsdorff and Joachim Kühn. I'm still in touch with Cecil. I see him a lot. That friendship also grew through Tony Oxley, who was always playing with him.

What turned out to be the most important thing about playing with Taylor?
Just associating with him was a very big deal. He's an exceptionally original being who lives in his own strange, imaginary world. Yes, he used intoxicating substances, but he always had self-control. In the mornings he used to do some kind of magic, shamanic exercises. He'd work on himself to emerge from his state of oblivion, but he liked to be constantly stimulated. He never got so high that you couldn't get through to him. Maybe towards the end of the evening, he'd switch off briefly, but then he'd suddenly get up, come up with something, and follow his own trip.

An artist who lives in his own world and emerges from it into reality?
He rarely emerges. He doesn't like to.

16 Peyotl

In the mid-1980s, you became interested in the sounds of electric jazz.
I always liked electric Miles, but I didn't like fusion. Fusion was very simple music. I didn't find anything of interest in it, apart from Weather Report, which had fantastic musicians.

Were you more into electronic music? For example, in the wake of Miles, who claimed to have been inspired by Stockhausen?
Maybe Miles had studied Stockhausen. I didn't listen to electronic music. I listened to electric Miles. When I met Tadeusz Sudnik, he was into classical electronica. I'd say that electronica spoke to me on an intuitive level, like a new paint palette.

When you had Sudnik, an electronics wizard, and Janusz Skowron, a jazz pianist who had an electric sound, Freelectronic emerged. A band with no drums but with two keyboard players.
Sudnik played without a keyboard, on potentiometers. I'd make fun of him for playing the radio. He was constantly twiddling the knobs.

What gave you the unusual idea of putting Sudnik and Skowron together?
We all ended up playing together just by chance, and they complemented each other's sound really well. Sudnik's contribution put an end to my percussion problems. After C.O.C.X., I didn't want to play Latin rhythms anymore. Vitold Rek played very rhythmically. Skowron is excellent rhythmically as well, and Sudnik gave it what drums normally give you – scope. Drums fill out the sound, while cymbals don't just provide rhythm, they fill the space with their own kind of mass. The momentum becomes trance-like. In Freelectronic, Sudnik's electronics gave me that kind of sound, very modern and arrhythmic. Vitold's trance effect, combined with the rest of the quasi-acoustic sound, created an interesting effect, because Skowron actually treated his electronic instruments in an acoustic way, while Vitold alternated between playing double bass and electric bass.

Vitold Rek turned out to be your most important musical partner in the 1980s. He turned up in all your bands from that era, from the quartet with Sławomir Kulpowicz to Freelectronic.

He and Skowron.

What did he have that meant you ended up playing together for so long?

Vitold was a very good bassist. He had a steady rhythm, a strong rhythm. He himself was also a composer, and a bandleader, which gave his playing more power.

What about Janusz Skowron?

He determined how well the band played, too. I needed to play with very good people, and there weren't too many of those in Poland. Tomasz Szukalski, Vitold Rek, Janusz Skowron. One-offs. I saw Skowron play with String Connection, and I liked him. I played with him a lot, and we're still playing together. We played quite a lot as a duo. He's one of the most interesting artists I've worked with. A mature, strong pianist. And a keyboard player. I like him most on keyboards. He has his own individual sound. He's played on all my most recent film productions. I really like the album that we did together: *Opowiadania dla 12-letniej dziewczynki* ('Short stories for a twelve-year-old girl').

The Freelectronic sound was also partly a result of Sudnik using his own home-made electronic gear.

Sudnik played best on an AKS synthesizer. He played sparsely and carefully. He gave me space and he stimulated Skowron's imagination. Maybe that was a band with two or three albums' worth: there wouldn't have been anything else interesting after that.

But it was with Freelectronic that you recorded what you referred to as your favourite work. The album *Peyotl* was made in 1984–86. You put it all together slowly and precisely.

Slowly, very slowly, I'd say. I wouldn't use the word 'precisely' because I worked quite chaotically, in all kinds of ways. *Peyotl* built up over a long time. I made a loop, and then we added the parts. For example, we came up with the idea of bringing Andrzej Przybielski in. Sudnik and I spent ages working on the tapes in the studio. It was crucial to get the text to fit: that's what required the precision. For the music, we started off with a loop, and then I added individual instruments and Marek Walczewski's voice. I put the trumpet on right at the end.

Was the rhythm loop created first?

That's right, the rhythm loop, which was actually based on three Messiaen modes.

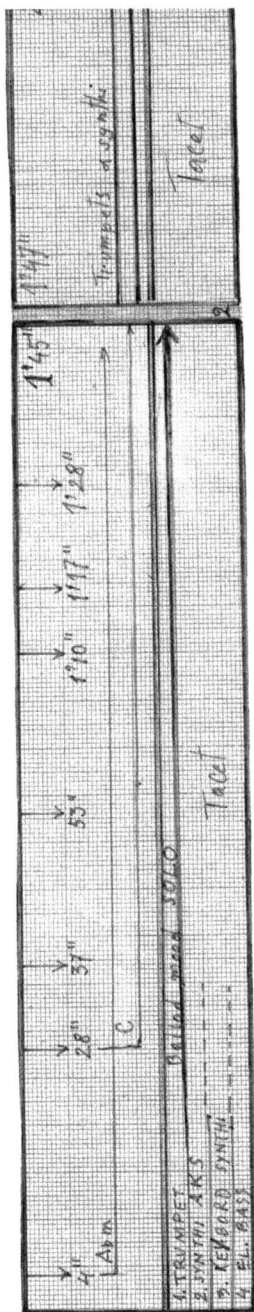

A Freelectronic score.
Courtesy Anna Stańko

How did the recording with Andrzej Przybielski go?
Like I said, I have a high opinion of Przybielski. I asked him to the *Peyotl* recording so I could at least put down something of his, and he came out of it phenomenally well. He hardly played a thing during the session: he just stood still. And then he'd suddenly take off just for a second: *Prrr rrrrrvvrr prr*. That was it. But it was what I wanted. I've recorded his aesthetic, his persona. A brilliant artist. Brilliant.

Out of all your albums, *Peyotl* is the one with the strongest funkiest groove.
Because it's funky material. That was the high point of my groove period.

Where did this funk come from?
I had an interest in that kind of funk. Well, it was Miles who inspired us to do things like that. I still think about playing that kind of music. A lot. Increasingly so. Only, I need some musicians, a good rhythm section. Maybe I'll find one in New York.

On *Peyotl*, Marek Walczewski's narration makes a huge impression. He's so expressive!
He's crazy. He took to it like a duck to water. He loved it. The sound he makes when he says *namulczyki* then *potworny negr*. The way he said it! *Potwor**rr**ny neg**rr***. He loved saying it. I'd met up with Janusz Zakrzeński earlier. He sat just here; he came to see me in Rozbrat Street. When he saw the text, he said, 'You know, it's a bit crazy'. He laughed about it for a bit, but the text frightened him off because it is actually pretty savage. Whereas, as soon as Walczewski took a look at it, I knew straight away from his expression that he loved it.

The text, as read by Walczewski, obviously comes from Witkacy's *Narkotyki* (*Narcotics*), but it was edited by you?
It was. But I didn't change anything. I just cut bits of text out. Once I'd made my choices, Walczewski read the whole thing, and then I cut and edited the tape with the voice recording.

Did Walczewski have the music playing while he was reading?
He could hear the loop. He was allowed to read however he wanted, but because of that he read rhythmically. I remember the recording session. I was sitting with Sudnik; we'd really got ourselves in the mood. Walczewski arrived. 'Please don't worry about it if you go wrong: just carry on reading.' I have very fond memories of it, and I often wonder if, seeing as I still have the tapes with Walczewski's spoken word, I shouldn't record *Peyotl* again. I have all those tapes with some very interesting mistakes by Walczewski. Just fantastic. Instead of **hamulczyki**, he sometimes said **namulczyki**. If he went wrong, he reinforced it. Three times he repeated **namulczyki, amulczyki**. A total improviser. It was a short session. He came into the studio, recorded it once, twice, a third time. That was it.

Where did the idea come from for an album with spoken word?
I was thinking about rap. Rap was starting to appear then. But people had tried it before. There was Jon Hendricks with *New York, N.Y.*

Are you talking about the narration on George Russell's record? Which was released on Impulse in 1958?
A fabulous record. That inspired me, that rhythmical speech of Hendricks's. He's rapping there, isn't he! Everything comes out of something. Rap came out of jazz.

But, in the end, you opted for a professional actor.
I was initially thinking of maybe having Kora (that's Olga Jackowska), or using some sort of mechanical voice, processed through a synthesizer. But then I realized that I needed an actor; I needed to record it then edit it. I'll give him rhythm! I'll group the words into the right phrases. Like that. And so I did in fact record Walczewski, and I cut up the tape. I spent a very long time working on that.

With regard to putting the rhythm into the words, the most brilliant bit is the finale of *Peyotl*: 'Mycie się, śniadanie' ('Getting washed, breakfast'). Walczewski creates an entire drama out of just those two words. I'm now wondering to what extent that's to do with the editing.
The editing. I edited it. We already had the loops and the tapes with his voice. We recorded everything first, then we edited it. I worked with Sudnik the whole time.

What was Sudnik's role?
He was primarily a sound engineer. He worked in the Experimental Studio at Polish Radio. He had his own little cubby hole there. That's where we worked, that's where we cut the tapes up.

There's no information on the album to say that it's Polish Radio's Experimental Studio.
We just did the editing there. I also did a composition for the Experimental Studio. They'll still have it in the studio archives.

An electronic composition?
Electronic. Concrete music composed of natural sounds, recordings of environmental noises. Storms, squeals – that kind of thing. Cicadas and sound effects.

How did you go about recording that?
Onto a tape. It was a composition for tape. Without trumpet. Though maybe I did add some improvisation? We worked as a pair: composer and producer. I made use of Sudnik's sound library. He'd come up with various options, and out of that material I built up a piece for tape. That's how you compose for tape: it's like you're using building blocks. The composition was commissioned by the Experimental Studio. They even sent it to a festival in Bourges.

When was that?
During the *Peyotl* period.

What was guiding you while you were using such an open formula? Was it the sound?
Just the sound. That form doesn't have any rules.

Nowadays in jazz we often hear electronic prepared trumpet sounds. What's your view on that? You never even used traditional prepared trumpet methods, did you?
Musicians are allowed to do whatever they like. But I personally don't use sound effects on the trumpet. I don't even play with a mute. I just play my own sound. That was an obvious decision for me. I don't want to lose the character of my own tone.

You've also collaborated with a few composers of electronic music who have come out of academic circles: Włodzimierz Kotoński, Krzysztof Knittel and Marek Chołoniewski.
I met Kotoński right at the beginning, back when I was playing with Komeda. There was this one composition for five improvising soloists. Kotoński wrote it for jazz musicians. I can't remember who played it. Urbaniak? Maybe Namysłowski.

Did it work?
The composition involved some paratheatrical activities. I think we played it during the Warsaw Autumn, but I'm not sure. I played lots of Knittel's compositions later on. I played *Sonata for Tape and Trumpet*. It was Knittel

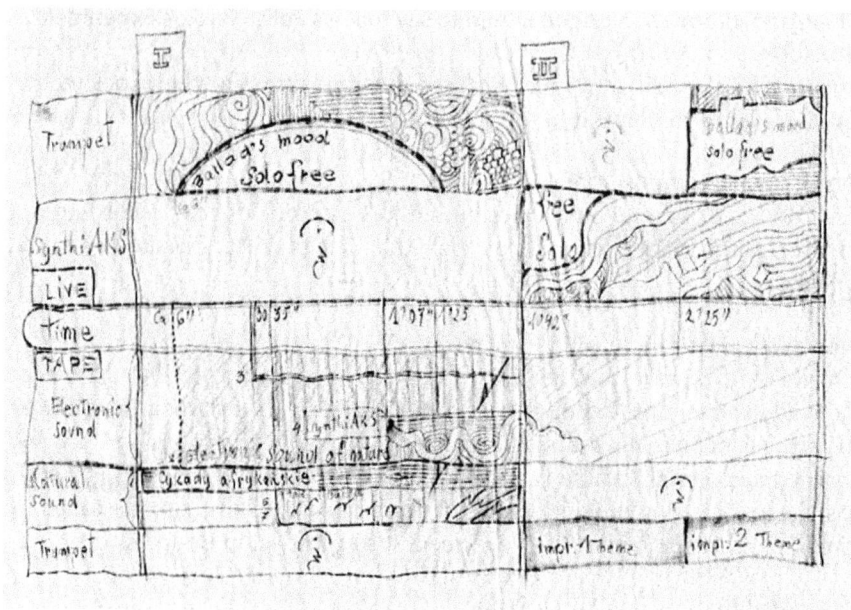

The score for a composition for Polish Radio's Experimental Studio.
Courtesy Anna Stańko

I worked with the most. At the end of the 1980s I often played with him in Freight Train Ensemble, and it was through Knittel that I met Chołoniewski. I played on live soundtracks for films with Chołoniewski and Włodzimierz Kiniorski. We played to Murnau's *Nosferatu*.

Kiniorski recorded a very interesting montage, *Nang Pa*, with Sudnik in the 1980s. Apparently, the Polish Jazz Association label bought the material, didn't release the record, and the master tape disappeared. On this recording, Sudnik went even more crazy than he did on the Freelectronic records.
Sudnik is a strange character. He was supposedly a sound engineer, but he's actually more of an artist.

A tinkerer, as is the case with composers of electronic music?
A tinkerer. Oh yes! That's just the best description. A classic tinkerer. He's got this tape somewhere, some overdrive somewhere, there's a recording going on here, something's spinning round over there. Everything scattered about. Libraries of sounds. He has a studio at home now. Nothing's finished. We spent a lot of time together. *Peyotl* was a long time in the making.

There was also a second *Peyotl* session. For the purposes of a TV programme.
That second session still hasn't been released. I have tracks from that recording. I had a different line-up then, a really good one. Jackson (Piotr Wolski)

1. Wszystko zaczęło się od małego, złotego pąączka bananowatego Belzebuba, małej rzeźby ze szczerego złota, tak wycyzelowanej, wyrobionej, że zdawało się być tak wycyzelowanej, wyrobionej, że zdawało się być dziełem jakiegoś naprawdę belzebubicznego, z miniaturzałego Donatella nie z tego świata, który całe życie swoje strawił na wykucie tej jednej, jedynej rzeczy. Cud stał się.
Belzebub ożył nie przestając być martwym, złotym Belzebubem, uśmiechał się, strzygł oczami i nawet kręcił głową. Mimo to dobrze wiedziałem, że to co widzę przed sobą jest tylko kawałem szczerego złota. *ca 40"*

15. Cudownej piękności morze, oświetlone jakimś hiper-słońcem. Z boku pasiaste potwory ocierające się o siebie, w rodzaju rekinów w kolorach białym, czarnym i pomarańczowym. Potem widzę ich przekroje, jakby ktoś w moich oczach porżnął olbrzymie rekino-węże salcesony niewyrażalnej piękności. *ca 20-25"*

13. ... brzeg jeziora pokryty tropikalną roślinnością. Wiem, że to jest Afryka. Jako też pokazują się na brzegu Murzynki i rozpoczyna się kąpiel. Wśród splątanej gęstwy wyrasta powoli posąg bóstwa w formie wieży spiczastej z obręczowym ornamentem. Posąg rusza oczami, Murzynki pluszczą się w błękitno-brudnej wodzie. *ca 25"*

Notes for *Peyotl*. A selection of Witkacy's text, used on the album.
Courtesy Anna Stańko

and Zbigniew Brysiak on percussion instruments; Janusz Iwański, Marcin Pospieszalski and my young quartet, because that was later, in the 1990s. The backing tracks were recorded separately, with space left for the trumpet and the text. I keep wondering about whether to do something with those backing tracks. I could overlay them with solos and Walczewski's spoken word from the first recording, because I was less keen on the TV recording.

In the TV version of *Peyotl*, there's also Wojciech Pszoniak alongside Walczewski.

I wanted to have the text in different languages, and Pszoniak, even if he didn't know the language very well, would have no inhibitions and totally go for it. He worked through the sounds.

Pszoniak actually makes up languages.

Yes, yes, he made up some bullshit, goodness knows what. His sound. He's a talented cat. When he heard Walczewski's natural and masterful rendition of the text, he decided to go in a different direction. In a very interesting way. He improvised. Nina Terentiew, who was the producer and who'd come up with the idea for the programme, helped me get hold of him. She wanted to have him.

Did Terentiew commission this project from you for TVP [Polish Television]?

Yes, Nina commissioned it, and then she was annoyed because it was difficult music. She'd embraced the spirit of commercialism by then, for which she has my respect, because that's her strength. A very clever woman. I must thank her again for *Peyotl* because it was a very interesting production. An expensive project, a large team and difficult music. Programmes like that don't get made anymore.

The TV performance is interspersed with commentary from academic experts on Witkacy: Professors Micińska and Jakimowicz, who try to make sense of this wild text. Was that your idea?

I can't remember. I think it was the producer's.

Peyotl has recently lived to see a third incarnation.

Andrzej Smolik did that. We were going to do something together, and he got all fired up about *Peyotl*. He said he was brought up on that record. It seems like a lot of young people back then took to that record. I gave him all the recordings so he could do whatever he wanted with them. He made his own arrangements. Brilliantly. He's a motherfucker, that Smolik! We have a band with his musicians and we play concerts with that material.

In the second half of the 1980s, Freelectronic was the first of your Polish bands with whom you started going to prestigious European festivals again.

Not many, but we did play.

It began in 1985, when Freelectronic performed in Italy at the Rumori Mediterranei festival.

We played with Enrico Rava.

He had Tony Oxley in his band then.

Yes.

Throughout that festival there were a lot of key musicians from the Italian scene, like Pino Minafra, Mario Schiano, Gianluigi Trovesi.

I remember Trovesi at other festivals too. A well-known cat. The same with Pino Minafra. Schiano's a free jazzer. I'd often meet the Italians on tour, at festivals. Theirs is a strong, distinct scene. I don't know much about it. Minafra in the south, Trovesi in the north and Enrico, who was always situated between them. It's very melodic music. But I can't remember much from that particular festival. I was completely out of it. Apparently, they drew comparisons about us, Rava and me – I was like the powers of the night and Enrico was the sun. It seems that the playing wasn't too bad, although it must have been a bit peculiar, because I was really stoned. Vitold had to tell me how we got there: I have no recollection whatsoever. We flew to Rome, and from Rome we took the train south. And during the transfer we lost Skowron. We get to the train station, we leave Skowron on a bench, the train's due to leave in three-quarters of an hour. Suddenly there's no Skowron! We flew into a panic. People told us that he'd been taken to hospital. We get in a taxi and intuitively pick out the nearest hospital. We fly through the main entrance, right past the doormen and go straight into the main area. And there we see a nurse trying to get Skowron to lie down on a bed and he's grabbing her by the boobs. With that characteristic smile of his. We said we had to take him to a concert. We somehow managed to wrench him away and get back in time to catch the train. What happened next Vitold only told me recently: 'It was night-time when we got there. When we meet for breakfast the following morning, you, with a smile on your face, are holding your hand out. You've got a great big block of hashish. How did you manage to get hold of that within the space of a few hours, in the middle of the night?' I managed it somehow. I don't know. I must have been really out of it.

But do you remember the concert in Bochum, where Freelectronic played with the guitarist Sonny Sharrock?

We played in Bochum, and somewhere else in Austria.

Bochum was a really interesting festival. 1987. There was Blurt, Toshinori Kondo and Tristan Honsinger, Material and Alfred 23 Harth. We could call it a full-on punk-jazz festival, and those artists remain the essence of that aesthetic to this day.

Maybe so, but I didn't listen to that stuff. We hit it off with Sharrock. The festival's producer arranged things in such a way that we ended up playing together. An excellent cat. He had his own glissando sound. Very free.

What sort of playing style was it? I mean, Sharrock is one of the great legends of Black free jazz.

We didn't have any rehearsals. There was a soundcheck and we played. He played what he wanted. I can remember a very friendly atmosphere. We were the same kind of freaks. I've never had any hang-ups about the people I've worked with. We played good gigs. I treated them as equals, and that's how they treated me too. I had a good reputation and my own fuckin' language. The Americans were most appreciative of it, because they know very well how difficult it is to have your own language. It still works well for me, this personal language of mine, being different.

You also went to France, to the Le Mans festival twice, in 1984 and 1988.
I did. I played with Michel Portal, and then as a duo with Szukalski and with Freelectronic.

What was the encounter with Portal like?
Very interesting. I have good memories of it. It was a quartet with Daniel Humair and J.-F. Jenny-Clark. Delicate music with French *esprit*. I also played in a trio in France with Humair and Henri Texier.

They must have held you in high regard at that festival, because I've seen a ten-year anniversary booklet commemorating Le Mans. They put photos of you on the cover.
Those were lovely festivals, but I can't remember much about them. That period was full of black holes.

Those mad photos capture it perfectly. And we can see your new image coming out here. Towards the end of the 1970s, you began changing the way you dressed. Your hippie clothes gave way to a nonchalant elegance in the spirit of *fin-de-siècle* bohemia. You can see it on the cover of *Music 81*.
I like to dress well, for my own pleasure. The hippie era was over, and clothes had changed, obviously, but it was mainly a question of imagination. Take Don Cherry, for example: in the 1970s he went for hippie robes and turbans, yet I once saw him at a concert in a Tyrolese hat and knickerbockers. Cecil Taylor used to wear a hunting hat with a hole cut out of the brim. He used to peer through this hole. He'd cut it out on purpose, you know, for the ride. For a while Paul Motian used to perform wearing a mountaineering outfit. Yet, all the while, there are some musicians among us who look like office workers. I've always liked how in jazz we have, standing side by side, exemplars like Don Cherry and then someone like Kenny Wheeler – dressed like an accountant in a sweater and long-sleeved blazer. But these people feel just great when they're together, and they understand each other artistically!

For ages I wore this sweater, which I'd bought in Prague in a folk art shop, a kind of loose jacket with buttons, white, comfortable, very original. Vesala and I used to wear ponchos: he discovered this Peruvian shop in Germany with some really sophisticated ones. Vesala used to wear a huge white one that reached down to the ground.

I like hats. I've always had good hats. Stetsons, big Spanish brims. I sometimes wore hats and flat caps made by the firm Kangol. I've just discovered this fabulous hat shop on Fifth Avenue. I've bought myself a little fedora, and I'm going to go back and look at their Stetsons. I've got this other shop I go to on Houston Street which has flamboyant hats. I found myself a little hat like the one that Clint Eastwood wore in the westerns – lower than a top hat but higher than a cowboy hat. Fabulous! Over in New York, I'm back to playing at hats.

The most famous of the Freelectronic concerts was not in fact Le Mans but their appearance in Montreux in 1987, which was recorded for the *Switzerland* album.
That was a big festival. A good concert. I think Terje Rypdal also played that evening.

Does the album only contain a part of your performance? It's barely forty minutes long.
I think that was the whole concert. We didn't play for very long.

Is it a good reflection of what Freelectronic sounded like live?
Yes.

Apparently Sudnik produced it, yet Freelectronic didn't do much studio work.
We also did two sessions on the radio. There are still some recordings somewhere that Rafał Paczkowski did, one of our first performances. We didn't actually play that much.

Was it you who made the decision to disband Freelectronic?
It disbanded of its own accord, sort of naturally. We'd played ourselves out. Vitold left for Germany.

Freelectronic started playing again in the twenty-first century. You even played in Częstochowa at Ziut Gralak's festival, Garaż, in 2004.
That was just a few concerts. Rek wasn't there anymore. We had Szabas (Adam Kowalewski) on bass. Then we had Sławomir Kurkiewicz. Sławomir is every bit as good as Vitold, but the fact is that Freelectronic was based on Vitold's strange rhythmic sound. I thought very highly of Vitold as a bass player: he played a major role in that band.

Let's stay in the 1980s because there are a few more interesting sessions of yours. First of all, there was the album you recorded, *Voice from the Past: Paradigm*, with Gary Peacock.
I met Peacock when I was in New York with Vesala. And then he invited me to a session in Oslo. We had one rehearsal and then we played. I spent a week there. That was in the summer just before martial law. I was staying with Milo Kurtis then.

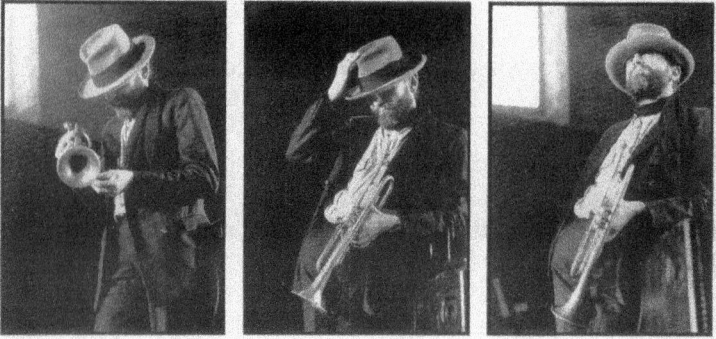

LE MANS
1979/1989

DIX ANS DE JAZZ EUROPÉEN

Tomasz Stańko on the front cover of the tenth-anniversary booklet from the French jazz festival at Le Mans.
Courtesy Anna Stańko

Peacock's group was an ECM supergroup with Jan Garbarek and Jack DeJohnette. You later had your own project with DeJohnette.
We played together at Jazz Jamboree in a trio with Rufus Reid. In the early 1980s, when Miles was still playing. Jack is a very sociable guy. An open cat. The first time I played with him was in Trumpet Plus. Eddie Gomez and Jack were in the rhythm section. Jack also played with Peter Warren.

How did the duo recordings with Andrzej Kurylewicz come about?
That was in 1982, 1983. I had the idea because Kuryl said that he wasn't playing jazz anymore. I bumped into him at the European after I'd come back off tour. 'Andrzej,' I said to him, 'what have you got to lose? . . . I'll arrange a session. Why don't we record some improvisations as a duo?' 'Sure. I'd love to.'

Kurylewicz, whom you essentially extricated from his jazz limbo, deals with it brilliantly.
That's exactly what I wanted to do – get him out of that limbo. Because he was one of the few musicians from the old days that I still thought very highly of. As for the records from those days, my favourite was Komeda's *Knife in the Water*, but also the quartet recordings with Kuryl, with him both on trumpet and on piano, particularly. He was an exceptionally good pianist. Oh, and we recorded *Korozje* ['Corrosion'] together. I produced it. I negotiated a figure with him and I hired a studio. Three, four hours of recording. Concentration – *bam!* – recording. Finished. No retakes. We went in and got out. It turned out exceptionally well. We'd achieved what we'd set out to do. Kuryl called it *Corrosion* – typical Kuryl terminology. It is corrosion.

Corrosion of what?
It sounds good. Corrosion. Corrosion is also a kind of interaction.

Did you play any concerts with Kurylewicz?
No, just studio work.

You also collaborated with Grzegorz Ciechowski when he was on the top of his form. You played on the album *Tak Tak!*
Ciechowski asked me to. He hired me. I just went to the studio and played. It was only the one session, no concerts. I accept invitations like that on the basis of whether I fancy doing them or not. I tend not to play as a sideman, but sometimes if I'm in a good mood I let myself be talked into it. On this occasion it was Ciechowski's wife, Małgosia Potocka, who persuaded me. They practically carried me into the studio. I was there for fifteen minutes. It was the same with Kora when I recorded 'Zwierzę' ('Animal'). I went straight in, played, and came out again. I also recorded with Maryla Rodowicz, but I can't remember what.

Then, more recently, you recorded with Anna Maria Jopek.
I mainly did concerts. There was just one recording. You could call it work, but it was very pleasant work. She sings beautifully. I really enjoyed playing her music.

And can you remember a colourful episode towards the end of the decade – the session in Athens?
I recorded *Chameleon*. Lakis found a producer in Greece. It was a kind of extension of C.O.C.X. Lakis recorded the drums and guitars. There were a lot of overdubs. Janusz Skowron played keyboards.

Was Lakis living in Greece then?
He lived in Greece for a long time: he was there during the C.O.C.X. era. He's only just recently moved to Poland.

Greece isn't typically associated with jazz.
Our producer (Vangelis Katsoulis), who was also our publisher, was a musician. He recorded with Arild Andersen, Markus Stockhausen. Maybe he'd heard Freelectronic.

The *Chameleon* album was originally only released in Greece. Did you go there with the studio and publisher already lined up?
Exactly. The producer had his own studio near Athens. It was springtime, beautiful weather, a massive garden, good grub. Fabulous!

Maybe those idyllic conditions are why this is your most pop-like material. Particularly on account of that light, electronic sound.
Pop-like – that was how I wanted it to be. I've always had leanings towards pop. That's why I'm playing with Smolik these days. Even back then I wanted to record something like that. We had the opportunity, we had the producer, lots of studio time.

How would you sum up how the 1980s went for you?
The 1970s ended in martial law. I had a quartet then with Sławomir Kulpowicz. I had a session with Gary Peacock and I recorded on *O!* with Maanam. Just before martial law came in, I also had this big radio production in Stockholm, where I spent a week with my wife and with Ania. The trumpeter Bosse Broberg, who also worked in radio, commissioned me to do some big-band music, which I recorded with the Swedish Radio Big Band. Martial law put restrictions on quite a few things.

Then I had all sorts of strange projects: C.O.C.X., the collaboration with Sudnik, a very wide range of exploratory projects. I felt trapped in Poland. It was a desperate and decadent time. After martial law ended, to be honest, I went downhill. It was the darkest, most destructive period of my life, the 1980s. Yet, at the same time, I did some interesting projects.

That period ended for me when the French projects came along; that's when I applied the brakes. I knew that something was happening, that something needed to change. I played with Christian Muthspiel, made *Bluish*. The new era begins with *Bluish*. New times, which are still ongoing.

17 Shortcut!

The figure of Witkacy has cropped up a lot in these conversations. What was it that first drew you to him: his writing, his philosophy or his painting?

I was primarily drawn to Witkacy the painter. For a time, I was fascinated by art and had my own favourite painters. To begin with, van Gogh was the most important one of them, then Modigliani, Cézanne, Klee – my favourite colourist – and the German Expressionists. I'd been to see the reproductions with Jacek Ostaszewski.

I liked Witkacy as a painter, but not entirely. I was less keen on his Pure Form, in other words things that were important as far as he was concerned. I preferred things that he attached less importance to, like the portraits he did just to earn some money. That tallies with my notion that art should be useful, yet artists don't usually value what comes to them easily, what they can casually dash off.

But art actually has this strange, mysterious perversity, with its preference for things that are created casually. And that's how we get these paradoxes, like when Mussorgsky's orchestration, which was once regarded as inept, and which Rimsky-Korsakov improved, is now recognized for its creativity. That's the essence of art. Because art relies on the unknown, on creating that which doesn't exist, and not on proceeding according to the rules. And that's why Witkacy's portraits caught my eye. I still maintain that they are the most beautiful, most peculiar to him, innovative and fresh, unlike anything else in the history of art.

I also thought highly of his books, although I didn't read them much, barely skimmed through them. I was less drawn to his philosophy. What I found most interesting was his monadism, but monadism is a more general thing. I was keen to read that little book: *Narcotics: Unwashed Souls*. And I was surprised to find out that Witkacy was never a drug addict. If you read him, it turns out he hardly took anything: he mainly just wrote about it. I had that confirmed to me by Professor Micińska. He was a hypochondriac. He only took cocaine a few times in his life.

What really interested me about all these studies of Witkacy was that they revealed his approach to discipline. Those razors, his exercise rituals, the Müller system. I have an Allegro shaver as well; my father used to use it. I was basically fascinated by the fact that Witkacy was so disciplined. I was drawn to the reverse side of all that craziness of his – to the fuckin' mathematical thing, everything all mixed up. He was a mass of contradictions! That's why I decided to get into the peyotl visions. It wasn't about the visions themselves, or the text, but about the artistic imagination that's reflected in there, that unbelievable brain. Witkacy had a psychedelic interior with an extraordinarily artistic imagination. Maybe that's where his warped images come from. His form of sensitivity was perhaps the result of the contradictions within his personality. That was what captivated me the most. And the melody of it, the sound of the text that Walczewski interpreted so masterfully: *Hamulczyki! Namulczyki!* That repetition unleashes the sound of the word inside you, as if it's ringing in your brain.

Did Witkacy's musings on 'The Mystery of Existence' make an impression on you as well?
Not at all. To me they were meaningless. You know, I used to go to philosophy lectures. My interest in such serious matters disappeared pretty quickly, that way of thinking. I now have more of a flippant attitude towards those kinds of things.

Flippant?
There are billions of IBs (Individual Beings), so we need to approach things with humility. Kant was wrong. It's his train of thought that's of value, not his pronouncements. A single person cannot nail down universal knowledge. What matters is the path he takes, his way of thinking. That's how it is with Witkacy.

According to Witkacy, an artist teeters on the edge of madness and perversion.
And then throw in the Allegro razor and the exercises. These are contradictions. We're getting more and more fucked up. We're retaining more and more genetic extremes within us. These extremes do help us, because life is complicated. To be a madman and a pedant at one and the same time – that could somehow brilliantly determine our survival in today's world. Madness is a kind of shortcut, knowledge via epiphanies.

Witkacy's Individual Being was about the individual in opposition to the world, an escape from the agony of the ordinary.
He couldn't conceive of the idea that, in addition to beings as complicated as his own, who think in terms as rich as his, there is also the ordinary. I battle with that concept and I've reconfigured it in my own mind. Because the fact is that our inner riches, our beautiful imagination, everything comes to nothing. There are billions and billions of Individual Beings, each with their own unique experiences. We see our own uniqueness as great, yet it's nothing. Just the same as a carbon atom, a little more complicated maybe, but still, it too breaks down into subatomic particles, which break down into quarks.

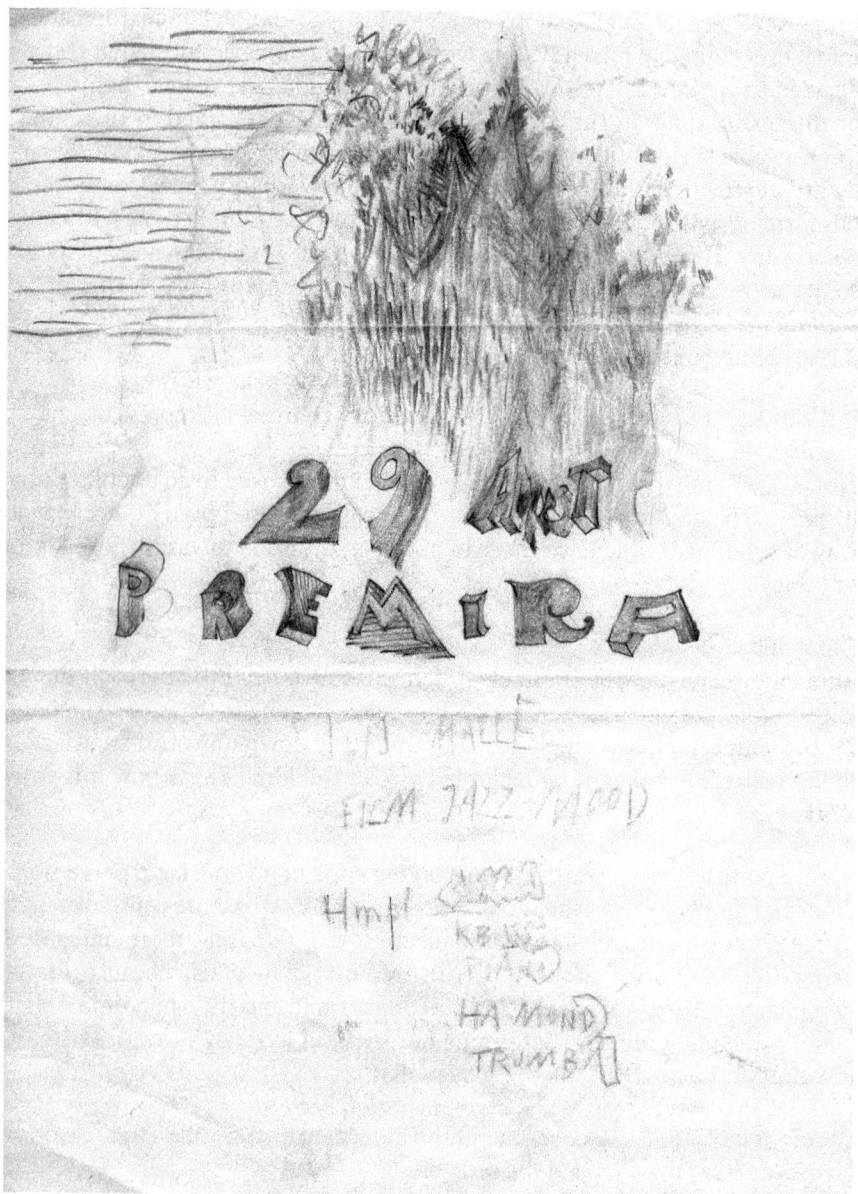

A sketch by Tomasz Stańko.
Courtesy Anna Stańko

Everything is one entity. Witkacy didn't want to know about that; he couldn't come to terms with it.

You try to come to terms with the fact that you're nothing, not even a speck of dust. How many IBs like that have there been throughout the whole of history? Every dog is an IB. The complete futility of life is totally at odds with conventional human values. But it's so cruel that it's almost metaphysical. Of course, it's just one point of view. My point of view. I find it easier to live with that.

Witkacy couldn't accept the fact that his moments of rapture, when he wrote, painted, gazed at the mountains, all amounted to nothing. I think the complete opposite. That very feeling of being nothing is there to be embraced. It's what drives me. For me, it's metaphysical and divine.

According to Witkacy, as our civilization developed, it brought about a metaphysical decline.
That is very much the case. Roman Kowal once told me about Walter J. Ong. Ong was an American scholar, a Jesuit, who, among other things, studied language, and Kowal drew on these studies for his own jazz research. Why was Homer's verse so beautiful and rhythmical, and why did nothing as rich ever come after that? It was killed off by writing, because rhythm hadn't been there for the purposes of beauty, but for recall. It's more difficult to remember a complicated phrase, though once remembered it's harder to forget. When writing appeared, we no longer had that need. And then print appeared. Things are becoming more banal, but they do have an increasingly wider reach. Excuse my language – but fuck verse; we're better off with writing. More gets done faster. That's how civilization works. Witkacy drew his own conclusions. Maybe his greatest contribution was just being Witkacy, just like Jagger's is being Jagger. Not the result of his activities, not his writing, but the kind of personality that he was. What matters most is that his IB was the way it was.

But does Homeric verse have anything to do with jazz?
Kowal put jazz and Homeric verse together on the basis that Homeric verse was passed down from memory, and jazz has its origins in music that hasn't been written down. The organizing principle of jazz was African: it was based on a rhythmical phrase. And then, suddenly, a civilizing innovation arrived, a shortcut, because that music began to appear on records. Music that hadn't been written down was made permanent on tape. A strange amalgamation came into being. That's what Kowal was researching.

The recording itself became a kind of notation.
That's the trick right there. As if jazz had skipped over the civilization of notated music.

Schedule for the day: mid-1980s.

Courtesy Anna Stańko

For many African Americans, it was records, not concerts, that meant they could listen to jazz, because they took to that medium straight away. After all, the first Black-owned record label, Black Swan, was founded in Harlem in the early 1920s!

And what's important is that the recordings captured the sound – something that notation can't convey.

You could learn to play jazz from the records.

Of course. The sound is the essential thing in jazz. When people recited Homeric verse, they also remembered about the sound. But the written word doesn't convey that. It has a depleting effect.

It has occurred to me that the famous cool, kind of muffled sound of Miles's trumpet might have had its origin in the jazz that he used to listen to on the radio during his childhood. What must the trumpets in Ellington's big band have sounded like coming through a 1930s radio speaker!?

You could explain it like that. But Miles didn't have a muffled sound. He had a different sound. I don't know how Miles got his sound. But it was different from the sound that other trumpeters had at that time. And he developed that sound.

And what's your view of art in general? You often cite examples from the world of fine art.

I like painting. I like looking at beautiful pictures, where people have created a new reality, one that doesn't exist in nature. Painters have their own way of looking at things; they see light differently. Stażewski* once said to me, 'You know, abstraction. Well, I just look and I see. I see! Shortcut.' The way I understood it is that, in the space of a moment, with one single impression, he captures the outline of a shape. As if he's pressed a flash button. People perceive the world in all sorts of different ways. They look through the prism of their own mind and their own IB. Contemporary conceptual art also creates scenarios that don't actually exist. Like the concentration camp that Zbigniew Libera made out of Lego bricks. The contrast! Nothing more than simple contrast. The child-like innocence of toy building bricks and a wicked, murderous system. The contrast, the incongruity, that has an effect on me. All of us have incongruities like that within us: we're both gentle and cruel. Why was I such an alcoholic? I loved the fact that, when I had a horrendous hangover and then had another load to drink, I suddenly went from hell to heaven.

---

* *Translator's note:* Henryk Stażewski (1894–1988) was a Polish artist, a pioneer of abstract painting prior to World War II, and subsequently a constructor of monochrome reliefs, many with moving parts.

And have you got into video and multimedia installations?
I'm into them when I'm looking at them. But there are just so many of them . . .
I liked Bill Viola. Purely by chance, I went tripping with him.

I like going along with chance encounters, because chance encounters have a strong effect on me. Once when we had a concert in London, I went to the Tate. Among this multitude of pictures, all very jumbled up, I spot this little picture from Provence. Cézanne. I'm immediately reminded of Kraków. I become all emotional. I'm in a different state of mind. I start going deep into this particular reality. The curator had organized it brilliantly. I understood at that moment the power of the curator: the son-of-a-bitch controls the situation. Next to Cézanne, there's Picasso, van Gogh. A host of giants. My whole adolescence passes by in front of those pictures.

And then suddenly there's a door. I go through it and I'm in an empty room. There are some screens showing Viola's films. It was such an incredible contrast that I came out practically reeling. I'd taken a shortcut into a completely different territory.

You were friends with artists in the fine art world.
I've always had artist friends. I met many of them through Joaśka. I was very friendly with Marek Kijewski, who's no longer with us. He was a great sculptor. I think it'd be a travesty if his name didn't go down in art history. But it will, even though his pieces are ephemeral. If you make sculptures out of sweets or non-material light installations, you can hardly expect them to survive. I was once going to buy an installation that he'd made out of fluorescent lights (it was one of his tributes to Cage), and I'm sorry now that I didn't, but it was already starting to fall apart. He didn't look after it. Fluorescent lights hanging from the ceiling, burned out. How could you repair that? It wouldn't be his anymore. I've kept the things that last. I have his *Kwadraty* ['Squares'] at home, dedicated to Malewicz, and his centipede: *Tom's Pet*. I've just loaned them out for an exhibition. The Centre for Contemporary Art in Warsaw has put on a Kijewski retrospective. He was also very knowledgeable about music. He loved music, especially European free jazz. We smoked together. We got on really well.

Kijewski had completely different points of reference in his life. He started off in an artistic group, along with Mirosław Bałka, with an interest in the grotesque and the absurd. He was fascinated by the mysticism of colour in Russian Orthodox religion. Then he flirted with pop culture, imitating Warhol.
That's true.

Were you familiar with his SSS creative system? Surfing, scanning, sampling? He explained that our mind surfs the world, and then, at a certain point, it scans what interests it, and samples it in our brain.

No, I wasn't familiar with that. But that is how it works. It's a good way of coping with the complications of today's world. We can't choose a path through logic. To make the most of the rich experiences that the world has to offer, to soak up its variety, we effectively have to surf and intuitively select. That's how your personality's formed. In fact, you can stand anywhere, but it's you who has to do the standing. You stand there and you create yourself. Just like the curator of an exhibition, you can create an exhibition of your own life, using your own shortcuts.

I ask about Kijewski because he was the one who got you into doing joint projects.

We did do a bit of collaborative work. I recorded a few things for him, which they played during his exhibitions. Recently, just before he died, I recorded *Trójdźwięki* ['Triads'], but he never got to hear it.

For the exhibition *Trzy tryptyki* ['Three Triptychs'] he actually composed the music for you to play.

I wrote what he commissioned, which was in fact *Trójdźwięki*. Each sound was played at random on three different sources, and then the three sounds overlapped and moved around over each other.

How did you manage, working on a commission like that?

Really well, because I knew the scope of what was required, and I had freedom. I was able to choose the three lines that were going to intertwine and overlap.

Did you go to the open-air exhibition at Orońsko, where the music was premiered?

I didn't take part in it. I sent the tape, but it didn't get used. That music's making its first appearance now, in Warsaw.

In Orońsko, there was also the *Bifurkacje* ['Bifurcations'] project, with its reference to chaos theory.

He did mention that. That was his last period; we weren't in touch so much then. We didn't talk much about art, just talked fucking nonsense, and something would find its way out between the words.

Did you get any similar commissions from any other artists?

No. Oh, wait . . . I did collaborate with Zbigniew Warpechowski, a performance artist. Back in the day we did a joint performance, and we did a repeat of that recently. We did a show without an audience. Zbigniew recorded it. The recording was supposed to provide evidence of the action for a gallery in

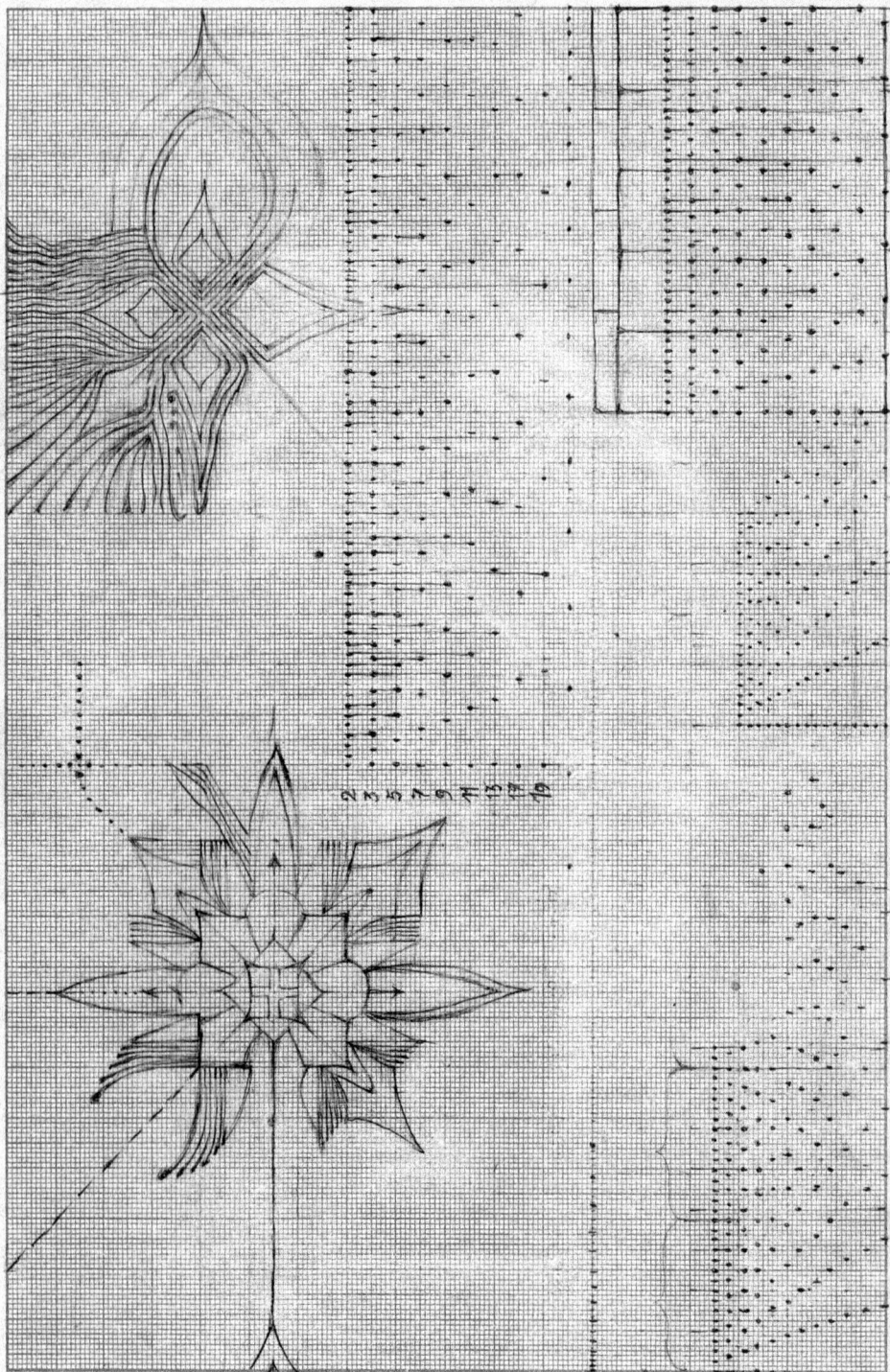

Rhythmic structures.
Courtesy Anna Stańko

Lublin. He read out his writings about art and finished it off by setting himself on fire. I set myself on fire as well.

There was also a project with Mirosław Bałka, *Walking-Waking Up*. An interesting film in which you wake up some penguin litter bins with the sound of your trumpet. Those litter bins they used to have, shaped like animals.
Bałka recorded that video for me. I wanted to include something of his for my festival at the Fabryka Trzciny.* He said, 'Okay' and he did it for me. The penguin idea was his: you could call it a video sculpture.

There was also Henryk Waniek, who did the album covers for Freelectronic's *Peyotl* and *Switzerland*.
I got to know Waniek through Stanisław Soyka. A very interesting character, a really engaging personality. Meetings with him were really refreshing – mind-expanding. He's a very mystical human being. He embraced a wide spectrum.

What sort of interests did you have in common?
Our conversations were general ones, on a very wide range of themes. It was the vague nature of it all that was the most interesting part: we'd go off in all sorts of different directions.

Waniek collaborated with the group Oneiron, led by Andrzej Urbanowicz.
In the 1970s, that Silesian artistic community apparently led as hippie-like a lifestyle as your quintet did at that time.
Yes. A psychedelic community. I wasn't in contact with them, just with Waniek, when he lived in Warsaw. During the *Peyotl* period, I used to go over to see him in Żoliborz. He designed a superb cover for that album. The *Switzerland* cover was brilliant, too.

Had you given him the music from these records beforehand?
He had listened to it. I think he had a business-like approach to these projects, but I think he also found them fulfilling. I'd give him a commission, and he could do whatever he wanted. I loved his pictures. They were a bit too expensive for me at the time. I was less keen on their symbolism, more on the colour. Lovely colours. They pulsated with a kind of calm beauty.

What about the paintings you have around you in the flat?
Those are Joaśka's pictures. I think they're brilliant. She's a colourist. It's colour, pure colour. I usually take anything down that starts to irritate me. These have been hanging up here for years, and they just get better. They increase in power. Joaśka ought to look after her affairs: the art market's brutal.

---

* *Translator's note:* A former arts and cultural centre in Warsaw.

How do you get on with your pictures at home?
They keep me calm, give me a kind of energy. It's about the effect that they have on my personality. A little time needs to elapse before I get used to a picture.

A moment ago, you mentioned a conversation with Henryk Stażewski.
There's a guy called 'Krokodyl' – Jacek Malicki. He's an old hippie, a very interesting character. He's an artist himself and he's been hanging out with artists for years. He promised he'd introduce me to Stażewski. I wanted to buy one of his works. There were still things to buy at the time, and those little things were cheap. Krokodyl arranged for me to visit his studio. I got the opportunity to meet the master and exchange a few words. Stażewski was one of the last surviving artists from that groundbreaking wave of modern artists, like Picasso.

I bought two small pictures. We had an excellent conversation; I asked him about abstraction: 'What does the abstract mean to you?' 'You know, the abstract – well, I just look and I see. I see! A shortcut. I look, and there's my shortcut!' He indicated with his eyes what he took in. A shortcut. If you close your eyes and then suddenly open them again, what you see first is a certain outline of a shape. That's how he looked at things.

And then he told me an important thing – Stażewski was then in his mathematical period of moving figures – and he told me, goddammit, that in his later years he'd added a dash of poetry . . . He showed me on the picture that I have here. Look, see the geometrical figures here; and coloured stripes here – 'a dash of poetry'. Goodness knows what. Not like him. Yet him all the same.

I understood that in life you need a direction, a consistent direction. You can't wander around. I began with free jazz, but I always fancied playing beautiful music, and I managed to do that through my melodies. If I have such a tendency, that's the direction I need to take. My consistency comes from my simplifying things. My music's becoming more melodic and communicative all the time. It doesn't matter what direction I take, as long as I'm consistent and keep trying out new things without looking behind me too much. That's how I understood Stażewski.

18 Empathy for the Devil

Do you like flirting with the female journalists who interview you?
I know what you're talking about here. There was this article once: 'My Life with Tomasz Stańko'. Were you thinking about that?

No.
I had a very weird thing happen to me once. There was this girl, a very strange girl: Iwona. I was completely wasted when I went to see her the first time. I was going through a difficult period, right at the start of the 1990s – that's when I was most out of control. On the street I saw a sign that said something like 'Poppy Emergency Room', and I thought, 'Oh, maybe I should go in there. Maybe they'll tell me something useful?' I was just following my instincts, not looking for anything in particular. So I went into this emergency room, dressed in my usual flamboyant clothes, because, basically, I was feeling good: I was drunk, full of amphetamines and hashish, lots of different substances, all thoroughly diluted with alcohol. Towards the end of a bender, as well as alcohol I used to like having some amphetamine together with barbiturates. And, of course, I smoked hashish constantly. Non-stop, like tobacco.

So in this emergency room, I met Iwona, a lovely, very young woman. She said to me, 'You might only live for another week, maybe two. There's no point me even talking to you because there's no hope left for you.' That shook me up. And that's how I met Iwona. I was with her for a while. I composed a piece about her: *Szurnięta szczeniara* ['Crazy Kid']. A ballad, composed to play as a duo with Janusz Skowron, and which I still play to this day. *Skaky Chica* is how Tomasz Tłuczkiewicz translated it for me: 'A shaking chicken'. A lovely title. And, would you believe it, she went and wrote an article for the magazine *Skandale:* 'Moje życie z Tomaszem Stańko' ('My Life with Tomasz Stańko'). She revealed everything – that my elderly mother was right next door in the apartment when we ... Yet my mother was taken with her. My mother usually hated other women, but she bowed down to her, or something ... She had this gift. I still see her occasionally. I thought you were asking about that.

No, I wasn't, but an interesting story's come out of it all the same. Were you offended by the article?

Offended by *her*? No. Dear God, no. Although it did create a bit of a scandal. That paper was a complete rag. I don't know how she ended up there. She was such a scandal-monger. She was a junkie herself, to begin with, then suddenly she quit the dope and became a fervent campaigner. She wrote these really lovely poems about opiates. They really affected me. We had a brief romance, which she wrote about. I wasn't even angry. That's not why we split up. It didn't last because there was quite a big age difference. Crazy kid. That's what she used to call herself.

I was going to ask about quite a low-key interview that took place in Poland somewhere, before a concert. I got the impression that you were trying to hit on this journalist through Miles Davis. Because you quoted a fragment virtually verbatim from his *Miles: The Autobiography*, where he's talking about his devil, sitting beside him, waiting to be fed again.

Oh, maybe, because in the band we used to say that everyone has their own Joseph devil. He's sitting there right next to you, looking out for himself all the time. He has to live, and his food is substances, metaphorically speaking. I'm telling you, I got away from dope using my own imagination. I did therapy on myself. I used metaphors and imagination. I personified my addictions because that made it easier for me to destroy them – through aggression, for instance. I used art, which is my own specialism. To reprogramme my brain in the right way, to get it to start working differently.

I think that addictions are a primitive thing. We have a very high opinion of our own consciousness, but I think that, in this case, the brain is working at a very simple level. It doesn't give a fuck about my health, despite being my own brain. It experienced some pleasure and euphoria on one occasion – and now that's what it fucking wants. And, because it's a complex thing, it invents all these kinds of temptations. These can be eliminated in just the same way. In other words, we can load the brain with new information, false information, which can change the way it works. Powerful hunger mechanisms can be suppressed by means of cunning and ingenuity, strange methods – poetic ones, not necessarily therapeutic.

In other words, the devil is a personification of an addiction?

A monstrosity. Like Maldoror. Miles, and other jazz musicians in the States, used to call it the 'monkey'. A monkey takes over a person, and the person, as stupid as a monkey, reaches for dope. They used to say 'monkey'. I used to say 'devil'. We sometimes said 'Józef'.

Why 'Józef'?

You know – 'Joe', commonly known as, just an ordinary person.

The devil and music: that motif keeps coming up in culture, especially in the world of jazz. It starts with blues musicians at the crossroads, who promise to sell their soul to the devil in exchange for musical ability.

They used to say that? It's the same with Faust. I'll tell you something, though: that devil – that's you and me. I am, in fact, the devil. The dark side of my personality, which needs to be suppressed or locked up. We do need it now and again, because it triggers aggression, and in certain situations in our lives it can help us survive. In primeval times, we wouldn't have got anywhere without it. If we hadn't been ruthless, we wouldn't have survived as a species. The devil is a synonym for our dark side, which we refer to all the time in stories – and in *Star Wars*. We're all purportedly aiming for the light, but we still use the dark side and act like assholes.

But is it not the case that artists in particular need to draw on this dark side?

I think – since we're going down that road – we can use everything, but we have to know how far we can go. That dark side of our power – in other words, the dark side of human nature – is an atavistic trait. It's what we very much needed at one time. We no longer do, but it's still within us. Is it not sheer cruelty when a male lion tears young cubs to pieces, and then the female lion comes on heat so that she can produce more young? But it's in his nature: that's how evolution has normalized things. We are all mammals, so that same thing is within us, but as an atavistic trait. What is more modern, if we want to be simplistic about it, is altruism, love – those things that religions advocate.

Devilry in an artist's life is also associated with something else. In his biography of Marcel Duchamp, Calvin Tomkins finds among Duchamp's recollections one that refers to his Lucifer-like coldness. In an artist's life, that Lucifer-like aspect is linked to egoism and emotional coldness, which come from the fact that life is subordinated to art.

Egoism is a simple form of self-care. Altruism is a higher one. Orzeł, the dog that Małgosia and I used to have, would simply headbutt a rival out of the way and eat what was in the bowl. In order to push a person away, people will simply blame that person for some imagined wrong. Since we do have that powerful dark side within us, we can hardly blame artists for being fascinated by it, because it is a mysterious and threatening thing within human beings.

You refer to a certain period in your life as a diabolical one.

Yes. That's a kind of shorthand. Dope was ubiquitous in my life at that time. Dope releases the dark within us, and the aggression. When I'd start on a bout of heavy drinking, I'd feel myself entering a different territory, where different laws apply – there's no help to be had, we're on our own, all that's left is egoism. A cruel super-egoism and the pursuit of pleasure. That's why I liked alcohol in combination with other things. In my most extreme period, I'd be doing cocktails – amphetamine, hashish, vodka, all together.

How long did that diabolical period last?

A long time. A dozen years or so. From the late 1970s onwards, I just got wilder and wilder. I liked going on benders. I liked going on a binge: just doing that, nothing else. I first got into amphetamine when I was playing with Vesala. Then at some point in Poland, amphetamine took over, very strong amphetamine. And ultimately that bench, where I used to sit with the heroin addicts. There was amphetamine-dealing going on there as well. It was very good stuff: incredibly strong, easy to get hold of. We used to take it with barbiturates. Barbiturates have a really bad reputation. It doesn't get talked about because they're legally available, on prescription; but they lead to a physical dependency, like heroin does. When someone comes off barbiturates, they need to spend days under medical supervision.

Did you ever use any under-the-counter prescription medicines?

Fairly common drugs, like Valium. The old drugs were particularly good. The older the drug, the better it was. Luminal was brilliant. Reladon, which they don't make anymore, was the best. The heroin addicts on the street used to take that because it made the effect of the heroin more powerful. You'd buy it under the counter, or doctor friends would write out prescriptions for you. You could lie and say you were taking it for a hangover. 'Would you prescribe a few?' And those few, which were meant to last months, would get used up in a couple of days. But I didn't take barbiturates regularly. I began to drink heavily. When I had the time, I'd start drinking first thing. Drinking's dangerous as well. If you drink half a litre of vodka on an empty stomach, it acts like heroin. I gave up alcohol before anything else because it was the most dangerous. No. I gave up amphetamine first, but that was easier because I wasn't so addicted to it. I never took much amphetamine. I took it now and again, if I was on a bender. I associated amphetamine with drinking, and I knew that once I'd started, I'd lose two, three weeks of my life . . . I tried to work out different ways . . . What happened with the amphetamine was that I simply stopped going over to Żoliborz to buy it. I gave up alcohol for good in 1992.

Had there been a lot of alcohol?

Drink was the basis. I'd been a drinker all my life. We always drank. Komeda drank. All the musicians drank. I drank with the quintet. Not with Vesala. I had a break from it then. He was a teetotaller. I went through a period of ostentatiously turning my wine glass upside down. But the idea is that, if you add hashish to alcohol, you get stereo. Alcohol revives you, makes you feel more sociable, like cocaine. I found that kind of stereo very pleasurable. I didn't have any hangovers at all for a few years. No trouble. I felt great. But the body's tolerance threshold increases. I began taking some strong stuff. I can remember, as if it were today, the first time I bought some amphetamine. There was this dealer down by Remont, a total wreck. And I thought, 'Why don't I buy myself some?' I bought some and I really liked it. It was good stuff, original, factory-made.

In Junkie, William S. Burroughs wrote that drugs are not so much a high as a way of life.
Well, because they are a way of life. Definitely. Of course they are.

When you talked about how you started out with hashish, smoking for you was a way of relaxing.
Hashish was the nicest.

But speed, amphetamines: that's the polar opposite state of arousal.
That was more powerful, because I was already drinking heavily then. And when I took amphetamines, I was able to drink more. I didn't have a hangover. A stronger drug inhibits weaker ones. It's well known that people in Hollywood used to take heroin for a hangover. In Chandler you can read how they used to prescribe opium and heroin for a comedown. Except that it all becomes mixed up later on, and a diabolical cycle kicks in.

What about psychedelics?
I took LSD a few times and had some generic kinds of trips. One time I even played after taking LSD, at Remont. I had a hard time of it, because my trumpet kept getting longer. I had no control over it: that's why I didn't particularly like it. The specific effects of psychedelics didn't work for me: hallucinations and spatial distortion.

I took some mushrooms in New York. I was on my way from the Apollo hotel to Urbaniak's, and I had a yellow trip. Everything was yellow and whirling around: the roads with cars going uphill and downhill. Some people like that kind of thing.

Was there a particular moment when you realized you were addicted?
You know, it was a difficult thing for me to notice. That's because I was always upfront about everything. I wasn't the sort of person who hid their dope or drinking. I didn't hide it from anyone. It didn't matter to me what people thought about me. I had money, and people usually hide behind their money, so no one forces them to become a dealer, or anything else. No one could ever force me to do anything. But nor could I explain it to myself. But, all the time, I felt it was a temporary state. I didn't know how it was going to happen, but I did know that, when I wanted to stop, I would. And, eventually, I didn't really have a problem doing it.

I can remember, as if it were today, the moment I realized that I was addicted to alcohol. It was during a tour with Vesala in Sicily. I just wasn't drinking at all then because he didn't drink. I had a long break from it then, and I didn't have any cravings, or any desire to drink at all. I remember the hall in Sicily: a beautiful, baroque interior with wonderful acoustics: we just played acoustically, without microphones. The bass was pulled upwards, the drums downwards: a sensational dynamic. It was a famous place.

Someone brought us some whisky and I said, 'No, thanks, I don't drink.' But, during the concert, I went down to the dressing room to have a cigarette and there stood the opened bottle of whisky. On an impulse, I just poured myself about half a glass, took a little sip . . . And something was triggered inside me. I finished off the glass. 'Well, fuck me! What's this? I've got the same as what alcoholics have! Well, well.' I didn't have any more to drink, but I did have a serious think about it. I'd only drunk a tiny bit, and yet a chemical process had been activated. It gave me a craving for alcohol. That was the late 1970s, but I had felt it before. I used to like buying myself a bottle of wine to drink on my own, while reading, and I started not being able to control myself. If I had one glass, I liked to carry on.

You've also referred to that period as 'life underground'.
Because it was a kind of underground life. I'd get manic; recklessness would take hold of me. We drink ourselves senseless because that takes us close to death, and death is our close companion. At the interface between life and death, we experience flashes of insight. We enter a psychological state which we can't access in any other way.

Life underground is also where the drug dealers and drug addicts are.
Yes. I liked it very much. The dealers, addicts, street drunks. I knew all the neighbourhood drunks. I never took any of them home with me, but I would go out onto the street and buy them a bottle. Now they're all dead.

What was it that attracted you to them?
The thing is, you feel good with these people. We're all the same. There aren't any big differences between us. The differences between a wretch and a genius are minimal. There's a kind of human camaraderie.

A camaraderie at rock bottom.
Yes. At rock bottom. We get drunk in the morning on an empty stomach. Fuck the fact that I'm a great trumpeter and they're nobodies. We're the same! We suffer in the same way, have hangovers in the same way. It's like when you read Burroughs's *Junkie*. He was a great writer but he treated the guys on the street as equals. There was one guy among them whose big life's ambition was to be given a job as a hitman. That was his dream, but he was rubbish at it, so no one gave him any wet work, because he'd have got caught and spilled the beans. Warhol made films about those kinds of people on the streets of New York. You should see what you get over there: rock bottom over there is total rock bottom. People become depraved; the so-called higher feelings disappear. Well, they do, but at the same time they don't . . .

I saw all that on Brzeska Street. I used to like going over to the Praga district for my first few sips of the day and drink under the arches with the locals, on a horrendous hangover. That was risky behaviour on my part, as they could have mugged me. There was a certain guy there who always fascinated me. He was a total and utter wreck. He could barely speak anymore but he did have this little dog, a Prague Rattler, which he must have loved ever so much – sometimes anyway, because he was certainly cruel to him on occasion. I suppose he did have to take out his aggression on something. But an animal doesn't understand that. It only remembers the love.

So, I think that feelings don't just disappear: they get scattered. Ecstatic, euphoric states emerge and, at the same time, the worst, most bestial instincts come to the fore. The greater the difference between those two extremes, the more you become aware of those states, and the experience becomes all the more powerful. The more you're at rock bottom, the more intensely you feel things. And, when you propel yourself upwards from that rock bottom to a state of euphoria, what a contrast! Hence this tendency to wallow in the gutter, so you can then go from hell to heaven.

What about the drug dealers that you had dealings with?
In Poland, to begin with, there weren't any real dealers. Of course, users like me always had connections. We'd buy from people who grew marijuana. I remember one guy who used to sell it in little milk pouches. At that time milk was packaged in small plastic bags. He used to trim them, and he had a price per pouch. With the Polish cannabis, you never knew whether it'd be stronger or weaker. Sometimes they had strong stuff. One musician friend had his own hectare of cannabis which he'd grown from seed. The first time round, the stuff wasn't very strong. He'd neglected it, but the cannabis self-seeded and so, the following year, he ended up with another hectare – really strong stuff. Everyone said that this stuff gave you a downer, that it was no good because it was fiendishly strong. I had bags of the stuff. It did vary, but in general there weren't any dealers. It was sometimes easier to get hold of amphetamines than marijuana, because the Poles had started producing amphetamines and going over to the West to deal. The heroin addicts also took amphetamines. When I was smoking every day, I had to have stuff all the time, which is why I also used to bring it over from abroad.

Were you not afraid of the smuggling process?
Well, I was afraid, but, you know, we still brought it over. There are different systems. On the train, you throw the stuff away in the toilet, wrapped up in paper, somewhere among the rubbish. If they seize it, well, it's not mine. But they never seized it, so I used to bring it over. Then the dealers came along. It was the Balcerowicz era then, convertible currency. It was worth it.

Krystian, whom they once wrote about in *Wprost* magazine, one of the first, began bringing the stuff over from Holland. It was reasonably priced. He told journalists that he was Soyka, Kora and Stańko's dealer. He complained that I'd ring him every day because I only wanted to buy small. 'Buy yourself some more!' 'I don't want any more. I just want one gram. Fuck off. If you're not interested, I'll go somewhere else.' So, he'd give me a gram at a time. In *Wprost* he said that he used to have to drive over to my place. He never had to – the dickhead. Unfortunately, it was always me who had to drive to the dealers. It was when they started bringing it over from Holland that it became a regular market.

What were those dealers like?

Different. There are some complete bastards among them, exceptionally cruel people, depraved. I came across that kind in the West. The ease with which they acquire money destroys their humanity. Hashish dealers are, in the main, very interesting. Colourful characters. There was one guy who had a boa constrictor. They dress elegantly – in a street kind of way, of course. They have their own particular taste in fashion, but they do have one. That kind don't do anything; they just smoke joints and earn money from the joints. Those kinds of dealers make enough to live on; they're not the big-time dealers – they're users themselves.

One guy lived with his grandma, who probably had Alzheimer's, because she didn't realize what was going on. She was just really happy that there were so many young people round their house. There were basically crowds of people just coming and going. I had a good position there because I was an old cat among these children who had run away from school. I smoked more than any of them. Only the dealers smoked as much.

After I'd had a joint, I'd be euphoric, and the world around me would look beautiful. That's why the dealer would look wonderful too, and his surroundings charming and interesting. I liked the dealers. I liked being involved in illegal business. The illegality itself really suited me, because you can always somehow get hold of dope. A certain shortcut also comes into play when you're using drugs like these. Dope highlights a person's nature. A miser would turn into a super-miser, a swine into a super-swine, but a good person would become very good. To me that was wonderful, because I like watching people, observing diversity. Many of those dealers and winos are dead now.

Oh yes! There was this guy, 'Czapa'. There are five of these winos standing there. One of them is quite fragile, and daft with it. He's begging for some vodka. And the strongest one of them says, 'I'll give you some if you want, Czapa, but only if you drink half a litre in one go'. And the fucker knows that if you drink half a litre in one go, you can die. The swine knows, but he gives it to him all the same. He doesn't give a shit. And this Czapa, he did die. He drank the bottle because he wanted if for free. He was small; maybe he was a bit hungry, maybe he drank it a bit too fast, because there are ways you can get round it. He was greedy and he died. Such is the law in that kind of place.

During that underground period, did you live on your own, just drugs and music for company?

I did have a social life with friends, but less so as time went on.

Did the realities of martial law have a big effect on you?

That was all going on in the background. I was too stoned back then. Although I did suffer the consequences: problems with visas, or a militia raid on a hotel in Kraków when I was recording *Zwierzę* for Kora.

During that diabolical period, did any new ways of doing things appear in your life, any new routines?

They were there all the time. I had a routine, a tried and tested one. I'd know that if I had a concert in four days' time and was going to the West, I'd have to go to PAGART to get my passport. I'd get everything sorted out through a fog in the days running up to it. You know, in the morning you're sober; you might stink of alcohol a little bit, so first you have a joint, then some amphetamine, and then you don't feel anything. That's when you're strong and you get everything sorted. But I'd have to put the brakes on after that, because I couldn't play when I was drunk. I couldn't manage it when I was drunk. I had no control, I couldn't feel. That's why I had to come off the alcohol and amphetamines completely, because my brain associated the two. I could only smoke.

Did you not play after taking amphetamines either?

I did play, but badly. I sometimes played when I was drunk as well, but that didn't go well either. But I got myself into a routine. I'd shut myself up in my apartment, here on Rozbrat Street. For a minimum of three days, but three days would be enough. The best way to do it was to start off really strictly: in other words, on day one, give up absolutely everything – alcohol, tobacco, amphetamine, hashish, stop eating, stop drinking.

So you did your own detoxes?

Yes, yes, very intensive ones. I wouldn't allow myself anything. I didn't sleep. I had to organize some physical activity for myself. I'd clean the apartment. The best thing is to keep moving, to not sleep. I wouldn't sleep at all for the first two days, but I could after two days. By then I'd been purged, I'd feel mentally clear. I had a kind of system then, to stop myself going back to drinking: I'd nibble on a bit of Anticol.

Is Anticol a drug like Esperal?

A bit like Esperal, but worse, because you take it orally. I never used much of it: I'd just nibble on a little bit. A friend, Milo, recommended it to me: he'd mastered the technique. Just a tiny bit, so as not to poison yourself, because it's terribly toxic, and after 48 hours I'd still have alcohol in my bloodstream. I'd have a quick nibble and then I'd feel protected. I'd feel more confident about not being sucked into it again, because I could have so fucking easily got sucked back in again.

After all that, I could light a small joint. A small one, a tiny one, barely anything, to be high, to get out of the two-day-long nightmare, so my brain could have a little rest in a pleasurable state. I'd often compose then. In that borderline state, a bit euphoric, a bit delirious, I produced some very good compositions. On day three I'd practise all day long. I'd very slowly exercise my mouth. By the time I got on the plane, I was feeling strong.

So that home-made detox was essentially getting ready for work.
Clearly. That's why it entered my brain so easily.

Did you go back to drinking when you were on tour?
Not to drinking. To smoking. Then later I played without smoking. I recorded my albums for ECM without smoking, because smoking had started to make me feel like shit. But when I got back from concerts, as soon as I got off the plane, instead of going home I'd go straight to my dealer. Right away. I'd be counting down the hours till I could buy myself a joint, a whole *load* of stuff. And I'd buy it. 'What are you having today?' . . . 'Ten grams!'

19 Peruvian and a Minor Sixth

I've noticed a relationship between your music and your alcohol/drug-fuelled binges. When we were talking about *Balladyna* and the specifics of your melodies, you talked about bending, about a note that bends the melody, taking it into different musical worlds, where different laws apply . . .
Yes, yes.

You also said about your binges that, when they started, madness would follow and you'd enter a different reality . . .
Through the door into another land.

So in both these instances, another world appears.
It is similar.

Is it the same world?
It is the same world. A different world. A different dimension. It's a dimension, not a world. Another dimension, like in your sleep, when you can fly, do all sorts of things.

It's a very unsettling situation when that different world that you're looking for in your music suddenly materializes in reality, but at the price of danger and madness.
You could put it like that, but I wasn't looking for it. I was living it. I always had those kinds of inclinations because I'm a mutant. I have an otherness within me, which sets me apart from the rest of the herd. That otherness has different manifestations. It's not a typically alcoholic thing, my entering some other dimension.

That's why, when I was high, I enjoyed dipping into books on popular science – like Lee Smolin's book on the theory of multiple universes. I didn't fully understand the cognitive aspect of it, but I had a brilliant time reading it when I was high. My imagination would have a field day. I could feel it. I think that physicists who are able to imagine distorted space in literary or poetic terms make more interesting observations. They have a kind of literary imagination, alongside a scientific mind. I don't have a scientific mind. I don't understand physics, but I can imagine these things in artistic, poetic terms, and I associate them with various musical things.

Like the minor sixth. A minor sixth is a minor sixth, but it has so many shades of melancholy that it leads me into a state where I can feel it with my whole body. A lovely, heavy state, which I associate with hangovers or being high. When I'm playing, I can imagine some kind of distorted, empty spaces, that conjure up the cosmos. Well, fuck me! That, I think, is the reason why I lived on the edge so much. That's my way of experiencing life.

When you're composing or playing, do you sometimes visualize images?
Sometimes. Very vividly. Although, by and large I don't do visuals. It's more a case of the intensity of the experience. I sometimes recall a particular state, and I don't know whether it's come from a dream or from reality. Like here, on Rozbrat Street, I'd be lying here all smacked out and feeling time slowing down. There'd be some strange symphony playing. I'd hear sounds completely differently. I'd try to remember, but I couldn't. It's just the intensity that you recall very strongly.

Sounds from the outside, or sounds from inside your head?
Sounds that came in from outside. But it's the brain that interprets them. Like the ticking of a clock: your brain slows down and, instead of ticking, you hear some strange *whirr – whirr*. Fuck me! A completely different dimension! You experience time completely differently. Everything gets distorted, mixed up. Time gets mixed up. I mean, we pick up what our brain interprets: our brain filters reality according to what's of use to us.

When I used to read popular science books, I'd take scraps of ideas from them. What I liked most was what from a knowledge point of view, was worthless. But I don't give a shit about knowledge. What I want is sensations, the intensity of experiences. So I interpret the world in all sorts of ways. I connect certain things on the basis of associations, of different kinds, sometimes ones that are not so obvious, the kind that you wouldn't formally associate with each other, but to me go together. I've had it happen to me many times on stage where I've played two notes, an excerpt of something or other (I couldn't even say what) which have triggered an association (it must have been stored in my brain) with some spiritual state that I'd been in at some point. Just playing that two-note excerpt, or some phrase, and, straight away, I'm in another dimension.

I live like that all the time. I remember when I first started listening to music outside the home. I used to listen to Miles a great deal. When Walk-mans appeared, I'd listen to *Tutu* and albums from that era. I absolutely loved walking around in those different states, listening to music and transferring my musical consciousness to what I could see: soaking in the beauty of my surroundings, of the trees, the landscape, the figures. Euphoria! I mean, when

1996.
Photograph by Andrzej Tyszko

we see a figure in one of van Gogh's paintings, it's not the figure we're looking at, but the beauty of the picture. I suspect that it's my inclination to experience reality in a solitary way that has given me so many of these revelations, which, needless to say, dope helps with.

Ultimately, your contact with that different world turned out to be self-destructive for you.
Because it is connected with self-destruction. Well, actually, I don't know whether it's connected, but I made that connection. I now think that, instinctively, I was heading for the bottom, just so that I could bloody well spring back up again, rise to the top again and return to reality. But these are things that we can't erase. I'll never forget those states. They will influence me. I'm different. Just as Burroughs was different.

At the end of the 1980s, you turned to dope.
To self-destruct.

Why self-destruct?
To reach total rock bottom, to join the worst of them, the dopeheads on the bench on Krakowskie Przedmieście Street.

Lots of rock musicians used to hang out there.
I'd got to know them at Remont. I was knocking back a huge amount then – alcohol with speed. I used to hang around with them, but I didn't come across any rock musicians on Krakowskie. Musicians were like a kind of aristocracy among the dopeheads. I used to meet up with the last bench. They had nothing.

I remember one of them. We were sitting together on this bench – he was a thief. I think he'd been to prison. Very different in appearance from the hippies – and, sitting next to him was his girlfriend – a skivvy-in-a-milk-bar type. We were sitting there, chatting, and he kept nudging her and saying that, if she fell asleep, she was dead. That kind of life.

I remember another one – the way he looked – when my mate saw him, he ran off. He says to me: 'Why bother buying the stuff? Come on. Let's go down to the allotments. Have you got any money? Let's get a taxi!' He knew where to find some good poppies. He was really nice, a really intelligent cat.

So I stood on lookout; he just nipped onto the allotments and returned with an armful of poppies. The taxi driver gave us a strange look. We went back to my place and he made an infusion out of the poppy heads. His technique was lightning-speed. He only stole my coffee. He had to steal something.

Heroin soon leads to a physical addiction.
It would take me a long time to get addicted. How many years did I have to drink before I felt addicted?

But it was after heroin that you collapsed.
I did, because I'd overdosed. The dealer said to me, 'Be careful, mate, because this stuff's really strong.' And I said, 'Yeah, okay, okay.' He jabbed it into me because I didn't like injecting it myself. And I'd barely come out of the stairwell and I was totally fucked. Is that what you call a collapse? I was aware of everything. I could feel things but I couldn't move. I was taken away in an ambulance. And those bastard paramedics, they wanted to rob me. They couldn't find anything, though, and they were furious. In hospital they recognized me: 'What have you taken, Mr Stańko?' 'Nothing,' I said. But they knew. They gave me something, some drug for heroin that reverses its effect, cancels out the drug.

Was that a warning sign?
I didn't take it as a warning sign. I'd just taken some strong stuff. It was something else that got me out of heroin – AIDS. I worked out the odds. I felt safe to begin with, because I used to buy fresh syringes, and I always went first. But I found out later that everyone uses the same syringes, and I realized that someone with AIDS might have used the syringe before me and could infect me. The procedure was that they had these large syringes out of which they filled the customers' syringes. Anyone could have inserted an infected needle into one of these syringes and it made no fucking difference if I had a syringe of my own. I said, 'Fuck this!'

Then I stopped taking amphetamines. I started putting the brakes on. That braking process took me a long time. I thought seriously about giving up alcohol. The periods without were becoming longer. I just wanted to smoke hashish. I was getting more and more out of control. It was that Peruvian stuff. I'd go crazy. I'd wake up somewhere in the Praga district in dangerous areas, where there was a lot of crime. I could have got killed. Reason told me that this kind of life was impossible. I was drinking too much. I was beginning to feel suicidal.

Depression?
No. I wanted to slit my wrists because I thought it would feel good. 'Why fuck around. I'll go the whole hog. I'll explode.' To not feel bad. The idea of cutting my wrists in the bath, like Petronius. Well, crazy ideas. A different way of thinking, bordering on death. Well, I don't fuckin' know where that came from. Later on I'd think, 'Oh my God! I'm going to have to be careful. I need to put the brakes on.'

People say that an addiction is an escape.
I didn't have anything to escape from. Everything was going well for me with my music.

Maybe some deep-seated trauma, then?
No. It was just the lifestyle. Quite simply. I always liked that kind of lifestyle. What about Modigliani? Didn't he live differently? What about Miles?

If it wasn't an escape, maybe it was a quest? A kind of hunger?
It's a quest for a certain type of enlightenment. Yes. It's obviously a quest. You're thinking in a different way then. You're feeling good, you're euphoric. You're thinking of all kinds of things, creating new combinations, linking your dreams to your music, your playing to your emotional experiences. In the old days, when I'd get high and listen to music by the Tibetan monks, that was just the most incredible experience. That music was totally unlike anything I'd ever heard. Its colour, enhanced by hashish, conjured up an entirely different world. It was a quest for otherness. For something that doesn't exist. That's why I'm an artist, because I'm drawn to what doesn't exist. I find this world boring. There's always something missing. I want to be in those different worlds. I want to transcend myself.

At that time, you turned your apartment into a kind of tropical environment and began collecting exotic birds.
I was high. Sky-high. I'd go out and buy these things, just because I felt like it. When you're high, you have different ideas. A joint, a little drink, a bit of amphetamine, with these beautiful birds here . . . And they just took over. I gave them their own room in my apartment. They looked lovely.

What kind of birds were they?
Different kinds. Parrots, Australian sparrow birds, Japanese quail, some kind of blackbird. Then one day I realize that I have over twenty birds.

Did they start to breed?
No. They sat there in their cages. I kept buying them. I'd get a taxi to all these different shops. The taxi would wait for me and I'd bring them home in their cages. The room was hung with cages. They were open, but the birds liked to sit inside them. They'd fly out if I came into the room, so that I couldn't catch them. I used to love doing things like leaving the door slightly ajar and sitting quietly in the bath. I knew that after a while they'd start coming out, on foot. The parrots in particular liked doing that, stepping out to see what was going on. It made me happy to see them getting to know the territory. If I peered round, they'd be off somewhere else. It was difficult to catch them later on. They'd sit on the flowers, high up.

And what did you do with those birds?
At some point, I started giving them away.

There's something else which reminds me of those exotic birds. In your archives, I saw a sheet of paper, carefully chosen coloured paper, covered with what looks like calligraphy. You'd neatly written out a rather surrealistic text, no doubt when you were high?
A kind of graphic art. I used to really like doing that, particularly when I was high.

That calligraphy was so intricately detailed that it must have been the result of a manic episode of some sort.
A kind of manic high. Yes. I used to do things like that. I smoked a lot while I was doing that. I'd sit down and doodle, let my hand go wherever it wanted to go.

The thing that I read was some kind of strange culinary recipe.
Yes, yes. All kinds of different things joined together, so the whole would have a nice shape, a very 'high' one.

Did that use to calm you down?
I wouldn't say it was a way of calming myself down. More a means of self-realization, of self-expression. I liked doing it. I also liked writing programmes. I still like writing out nice programmes for my concerts. I sit down in my armchair with a sheet of good-quality paper. I get my pencil out and I enjoy writing it out nicely. It's a kind of calligraphy. It makes it easier for me to arrange the music. It's the kind of thing that's very popular with people when they're bored, and at one point it was known as 'conference' or 'meeting' doodling. I used to do lots of that kind of thing while putting an album together. You have

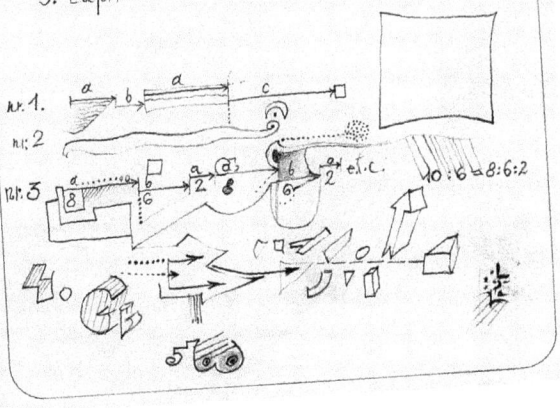

Freelectronic concert programme, Wrocław Philharmonic, 1985.

Courtesy Anna Stańko

lots of time then: you're listening to the music for the fifth or sixth time; you don't want to listen to it anymore.

What records did you most like to listen to when you were high?
Different ones. Lots of Miles. Mainly Miles. Coltrane. But what I also liked doing (although my neighbours didn't like it so much) was pairing two pieces together and alternating between them, like very loud James Brown and Bach's *Mass in B Minor*, or James Brown and Mahler's *Adagio*. I even made myself some tapes like that, which I still have. I also liked listening to Eric Satie when I was high.

Does Satie have a soothing effect?
Soothing? It's difficult to say. It's kind of square.

6 ty lipiec 91 szego około 9 rej rano :

1. Śniadanie :
7 kawałków banana ; 7 truskawek ; 3 paski czerwonego
jabłka ; 4 paski zie-
lonego jabłka ; 6 ka-
... zamrażanie, zamrażanie, wałków kiwi ; 2 plast-
-ki brzoskwini ; 12 cze-
-reśni ; 30 porzeczek ;
START ... -troche wiśni ; 38 borówek ;
13 kawałeczków i zias-
10⁴⁷ dwa płatki czer-wone)
11⁴⁵ dwa płatki białej hek czosnku.
11⁴² trzy zwiędłe płatki białej róży. 0 14⁰⁵. 21 orzechów laskowych

jem, ...jem, jem ——→ konstruuje, komponuje, jem
obserwuje,

Nr.2 Rozpoczynam 332 P.M.
3 czosnki / 30 pinirek / , 2 pietruszki , marchewka (młodziutkie)
2 selery , liście selera, koper , Mięso – WÓL : 21
13-7-1

Sałata :
Cebula
Pomidory

In the late 1980s, the drugs market in Poland expanded. There were more temptations, and yet that's when you decided to put the brakes on.

To tell you the truth, that really helped me. The fact that there were dealers meant that I could buy whenever I wanted, and however much I wanted. I didn't have to stock up. Before that I used to stock up, and that made me smoke more.

When I had the opportunity one time, I bought around a quarter of a kilo of strong hashish. I got through the whole lot in three weeks. But once I had daily access to a dealer, and I knew there was stuff available, I was able to gradually reduce the amount. I think that if hashish and marijuana were made legal everywhere, the whole thing would sort itself out. From what I've observed, there's a certain group of people who are drawn to dope, and they'll always take it. The weaker ones among them will fall victim to it, but if they weren't to topple over, their lives would be a nightmare, just tiptoeing around, with no enjoyment. But dope helps some people get through, just as pharmaceutical drugs help people get through an operation.

We wouldn't have modern medicine without anaesthetics: ninety per cent of operations wouldn't go ahead. It's the same with drugs – they simply take

Programme from a concert at the Montreux Festival, 1987.

Courtesy Anna Stańko

away the pain, including the pain of existence. Only it's terribly easy to over-dose. We know what a difficult branch of study anaesthesiology is, a whole branch of study about how to apply anaesthetics.

So how can an amateur cope with all this? A person who, on top of everything else, lies to himself because he derives pleasure from doing what he does and can find a million reasons to use those drugs as often as possible.

I think it's a new form of natural selection, which enables a person to enter a different dimension. I think that addictions have really strengthened us as a species. In Freud's time, cocaine addicts didn't overcome their addictions, yet now, you know, we keep hearing about rock bands that have given up dope and not had any particular problem doing so, not even with heroin.

I've read about people in Hollywood in the 1980s, when Asian 94, unbelievably strong stuff, became the in-thing – nearly pure heroin from the Thai Golden Triangle. It made its way down into Hollywood's lower ranks: hairdressers, make-up artists, people working in animation all took it to get high. It was cheaper than going to a bar in an expensive neighbourhood.

A whole system evolved so that people could take these drugs. People knew that this substance was addictive, and after two or three months they'd go on a three- or four-day detox. Those days could be monstrously hard – I should know. So hard that they had to have a system. The wealthier among them would go to a clinic. The poorer ones would book into a hotel, without telling anyone. They'd shut themselves away and, if they managed three days there, they'd be strong enough to stop taking the stuff. After all, what's three days? Nothing. I'm definitely a better person than I was before I took drugs. One hundred per cent. I'm stronger. I quite rightly cut off my unnecessary hypersensitivity, which had held me back in life. I levelled certain things out.

And how exactly did you level things out?
By using toxins.

Do you think they might have killed off certain things within you?
Yes. The poisoning itself matters less, in fact. It's about the actual giving up of these toxins, which is incredibly empowering. It's this new state that matters the most.

What's this cutting-off of your hypersensitivity all about?
Hypersensitivity is unnecessary, as it causes too much stage fright, anxiety. I told you, it runs in my family. But when I went to that jam session that time, drank some wine, I felt clearly as if a certain door had opened in front of me. That door stayed open. The key had been thrown away. I could go in and out whenever I wanted to.

What's your view on the theory that soft drugs lead to hard drugs?

I know tons of people who only smoke hashish. In fact, I'd say that it's not true because, take me for instance: I really liked hashish and that state that follows on from hashish, but I was never interested in cocaine. Cocaine has a short-term effect, and the high is an ordinary one, which is actually what cocaine users really want from it: they don't have any of the kinds of weirdness that you get after weed, where you have that very particular state of neither hallucination nor euphoria. With cocaine you get activity and clarity of thought, but with a deeper feeling, and it doesn't last very long.

But it could equally well be true that soft drugs do lead to hard drugs. I see a different type of dependency. It's an individual thing, and I certainly don't think that it can be used as an argument against the legalization of soft drugs. I'll be honest with you: I don't know whether they should be prohibited or not. Because, personally, I liked the illegal aspect of the business. It's difficult to say how things would have turned out if these substances had been in the pharmacies.

But I do think that this period of drug-taking that we currently have will just be an episode in human history. I can't give anyone any advice. I can say one thing for sure, though: I wouldn't want my daughter to smoke. I didn't want my daughter to smoke the stuff. And that too was one of the reasons why I gave up smoking. I don't know what strength that argument has. I am very happy that my daughter doesn't smoke. I'll not say any more, otherwise I might jinx it. That one thing I've just said is clear, and what's also clear is that what I've got most satisfaction out of lately is not my artistic achievements but being clean.

20 The View from the Tightrope

Did you find it difficult giving up the toxins that you'd been putting into yourself all those years?

It happened in a fairly matter-of-fact way. I never had the feeling that it was going to be a permanent state for me. I used to think, 'I'm young, so I don't give a fuck. But I'll have to grow up eventually.' And it all happened exactly like that in the end. I came to the conclusion that it was high time to settle down because there were hard times ahead. I was no longer going to be able to come back off tour and spend two months completely wasted like I used to during the communist era: completely out of it. Under that system, no one worked. We were all hippies.

And now that period's drawing to a close, and it's high time I take care of my own business, because no one else is going to do it for me. That was my main reason. And the sense of my own freedom, not wanting to be dependent on anything. The dealers were starting to bug me. Not all of them, but the vultures among them. But many of them are like that because it's the sort of business that makes people greedier. It's easy money, after all: there's a constant stream of clients, a little danger at most. Actually, there's no danger because they pay the police off.

I was horrified that the addicts were such slaves to their habit. A dealer once said to me, 'What? You're not going to buy anything if I put the price up? But you have to buy something.' When that bastard said that to me, I thought, 'Fuck you! I'm not buying anything!' I was absolutely appalled by the lack of freedom. I've always felt myself to be a free man. Yet here, it seemed, I couldn't do what I wanted to. So when that bastard said to me that I had to smoke, and I had to go to his place and put up with the stench of his apartment! To be honest with you, it's also because of that particular dealer in Żoliborz that I stopped taking drugs. He used to live on Czarnieckiego Street in a kind of hovel. Whenever I went round, he'd be cooking up heroin because he was on heroin and speed. He was dealing to pay for his addiction.

At one point he said to me, admiringly: 'You're taking a lot, mate. You're taking a lot.' And I thought to myself, 'If this wreck is telling me that I'm taking a lot, then things have got very bad indeed.' To me he was an example of a complete wreck. He died not long ago.

Did the fact that you were ruining your health not make any difference to you?
You know, it actually didn't. Not especially. Let's put it a different way: I don't like it when I *have* to do something. It took me a long time to give everything up. I weaned myself off things slowly, not in one fell swoop. I instinctively did what suited me, reducing the doses.

There was this one point with cigarettes. I'd nearly given up smoking cigarettes, and then I found out that I had high blood pressure and that I mustn't smoke. So, just to be contrary, I immediately took up smoking again. And then it took me another few years before I finally gave up.

Did you smoke a lot of cigarettes?
I smoked constantly. I gave up cigarettes after everything else. Cigarettes were the last toxic substance that I parted company with. I was always giving up smoking. Cigarettes were the hardest thing for me to give up. I didn't even smoke that much. A packet a day minimum, sometimes even three, but sporadically. Basically, a packet a day. Honestly? What I liked best was to have a smoke on an empty stomach. Later on, when I started putting the brakes on, for a long while I'd save two cigarettes, two filterless Camels, to have on an empty stomach. To me they tasted best on an empty stomach because, after a break, I'd get a really pleasurable hit. Nicotine also does that, like everything else.

When did you start thinking about giving it up?
The late 1980s, the early 1990s. That was my worst period, when I started taking heroin. Rock bottom. I thought, 'I need to stop.' It took me a while. I can remember precisely that my life changed dramatically in 1992. I began going on tour again. I started running. I was thinking of doing meditation but my therapist, Adam Kłodecki, put me in touch with some guy who did yoga, which was even better, because it's a physical thing. He was also a non-drinking alcoholic. He used to come to my place, and I'd do yoga with him. I got into yoga. I practised it every day. A friend got me into macrobiotics and also gave me shiatsu massage. And I was also running. I did that to change things, to do something completely new. And when I went on tour I stopped bringing hashish with me to work. That was the first thing: I stopped doing what all the dope people most want to do – smoke as they play. I did the opposite: I smoked after playing. I thought it'd be better if I wasn't high, as my playing itself is high. And, sure enough, I didn't feel any worse. For a while, I had trouble sleeping.

You mentioned a doctor, a therapist.
There's this doctor, Adam Kłodecki. I'm still in touch with him. I like him. He was recommended to me by Janga-Tomaszewski. This guitar-playing actor

used to come round to mine, and he somehow persuaded me to pop in to see him: 'What's the harm?'

Did you complain about the problem with alcohol?
Everyone, including me, knew that I was very heavily addicted. Well, it had me on the ground. I was on a downhill slide. By the time Ania was born, sometimes, instead of going to a bar, I'd find it quicker to go to the pharmacy. I used to buy Azulan. It was very good: it was the strongest stuff you could get. And it was nearer. I had so many of those Esperal implants. Shitloads. I still have a couple of packets left: I don't know whether they're fakes or the real thing. I used to go to clinics in Kraków and Warsaw. Except that I'd later relapse and not care that much about it. That's the kind of approach I have. I might get scared when a mouse runs past, or when the light suddenly goes out, but as for worrying about alcohol finishing me off – no.

Apparently, there were occasions when you'd shut yourself up in your apartment and people would pass you some alcohol through a spyhole in the door.
It was the same with Jan Himilsbach. Even I used to take alcohol round for him. If Himilsbach rang – 'Help, help!' – to ask for some alcohol to be brought round, my mother, who supposedly really disliked alcohol, would say straight away, 'Can you just take that beer round!' And I'd take some round.

Did you know each other well?
Not very well. Andrzej Kondratiuk had introduced us, but we rarely saw each other. He knew I lived nearby, and that's why he used to ring.

You didn't use to shut yourself away?
I didn't have to. I didn't drink every day, just periodically, but I did know that I'd have to give it up once and for all. I knew that if I didn't give it up, I'd just carry on drinking. I knew that I had to sort it out in my own mind and be very resolute about it: 'NO!'

I once had this silly idea: I went somewhere, a long way away, so as not to drink. I found it really tough, and the next day I hotfooted it back the whole fifteen kilometres. Maybe that works for other people, but it's different for me. I have to make my own resolutions. I have to want to do something myself, not because I *have* to: because, if I *have* to, then I won't have to. Then it definitely won't work. 'To want to' is the key term. There are very many variations on the theme of why people stop taking the stuff. Everyone has a different opinion. Because, on the one hand, it's an horrendously difficult issue, and yet, on the other hand, it's a ridiculously simple matter.

The most important thing for you is to rearrange everything in your head, isn't it?
Just that. That's how I set up my own therapy.

And you found the words 'I don't want to'?

I found the right kind of 'I don't want to'. An appropriately arranged, appropriately embedded 'I don't want to'. That's the most important thing. The giving up in itself isn't what's so difficult. The difficulty lies in maintaining discipline, in pulling back before saying 'no'. Because you have to say it in a certain way. Not in an 'Oh God, I can't!' way because that's a nightmare, agony. It's called a 'dry hangover'. Everyone will tell you there's no guarantee of success and you're bound to relapse. I didn't use the words 'Never again', because they're negative, in some way disabling. I simply said, 'NO!' Without debating whether it was good or bad. A simple 'NO!' No, because I can say no, because I want to say no, but also because saying no makes me happy. It makes me happy because I derive pure benefit from it. I can do whatever I want, but it just so happens that I no longer want to do this. The same pleasure I get from smoking a joint, I now want to get out of being clean. The same kind of pleasure, the same high.

Did that 'NO!' actually work effectively in practice, without any hiccups?

I remember exactly how it went with the alcohol. I had a gig of some sort with Stanisław Soyka and I slipped up then. Shit, I slipped up in a really big way. And I was back to square one. That's when I said, 'OK. Fuck this. This time I'm done with it'. And I stopped.

I did slip up once more after that, a few months later. I was at the Pod Jaszczurami club in Kraków and it got me in the classic way, with me thinking I'd got some aches or pains of some sort, and feeling nauseous, and maybe I'd got food poisoning and that a glass of vodka would do me good. But I knew that I couldn't drink, because I had a concert the following day. That's why I just had a glass, because I thought that my awareness would shield me from drinking the following morning. But it didn't shield me. I went and bought lots of beer. I was sober in the evening, but when I got up the following morning at 5 or 6 am, I went straight for the beer.

I was mad as hell with myself, but I still drank that beer, trying to drink as little as possible because of the concert. My anger at having broken my resolution built up within me throughout the course of that day, and then I played that gig and I said, 'F-U-C-K T-H-I-S!' I stopped drinking before I started playing, and then I threw out all the beer and I rang my doctor.

I didn't have any Anticol, otherwise I'd have been nibbling at it, like I used to. 'Doctor, I have a favour to ask you: I'll be in Warsaw after 11 pm. Will you still be up? Could you possibly drop off just one tablet of Anticol for me? I've slipped up, and I don't know how to get going again'. He came round. He gave me the tablet, which I took. And that was the end of that. I haven't drunk alcohol since then.

When was that exactly?
1992. I remember it precisely because, do you know when I felt sure that I'd made it? When I lost all my teeth. In 1992 I had a nightmare with my teeth. What a fucking disaster! And then something happened that brought me some tragic cheer, so to speak. There was a terrifically strong, optimistic aspect to this tragedy, although at the time I still didn't know how it would all turn out. What was certain was that my teeth had fallen out, that it was over with the playing. I knew that, but I was still lying to myself.

I went to play a concert in Poznań. Just before I was due to play, I started practising. Well, I see it's not working. 'No fucking way. I can't do it. I can't play.' I had to call it off. It was meant to be a *Bluish* concert with Vitold Rek and Jon Christensen. I was standing there in the club and thinking, 'Holy shit! So I'm not going to be able play for the rest of my life. What a disaster!' I went back to my room. And, about an hour later, I'm thinking, 'Good God! Oh my God! I haven't felt like having a drink!' That was unbelievably important to me. You know, every alcoholic turns to drink in that kind of misfortune. The most dangerous thing for an alcoholic is when his life starts falling apart.

My life was up shit creek, yet I hadn't had a drink. And this was only six months after I'd given up. I said, 'Very good. If that's how it is, then I'm going to strengthen my muscles and I'm going to play. Fuck it! I'm air pilot Maresyev!' That's when I was reminded of this book . . .

The Story of a Real Man?
I read it in my youth. Of course, it was all untrue. But that's not the point. The point is the power of belief. You don't know how something's going to come about, but you believe that it will.

Was it at that point that you said goodbye to drugs?
I started smoking again because I hadn't smoked hashish for quite some time. I started smoking because I was at home, stuck in this fucking place, practising twelve hours a day. I'd smoke to have some sort of pleasure. Not very often, because I wasn't drinking. I carried on smoking for a few more years after that, until *Litania*.

Running helped me a lot. I found out later that running releases endorphins. It's a well-known thing now, but back then I didn't know about it. The fact is that, after running, I'd be on such a high that it was then that one of my best compositions got written: 'Morning Heavy Song'. It really is a good composition. Bobo loves playing it. It goes through all the modes. It's theoretically interesting and kind of dark, heavy – very me.

Giya Kancheli, a composer who records with ECM, told Manfred Eicher that it's an interesting composition. I wrote it when I was sober. I was high after running. And I thought, 'If I can compose like that, what's the fucking point of smoking? It's ridiculous.' But, you know, you do have to say it to yourself. At the right moment, you have to really want to say it and get it embedded in your brain. None of the addicts do that, because, subconsciously, they still want to get wasted.

The breakthrough for me was when, in the middle of this tragedy, I realized that I didn't need to drink anymore. That gave me enormous strength. The first thing I did was decide to start playing again. And that happened pretty quickly. The concert in Poznań that I'd cancelled had been in June. By September I was recording for Louis Malle's *Damage*. And then I played a concert at Jazz Baltica with David Murray. When Zbigniew Preisner rang me at the start of July, I thought, 'What am I going to say to him?' And he fuckin' says to me: 'Davis used to record for Malle, so now you'll have to play.' And I said, 'Well, I don't know. I'll let you know.' That proposal helped me with my determination.

In August, I played a concert at Akwarium with Skowron and some of the young musicians. I was getting desperately wound up about going up on stage, and I remember not being able to play anything. I wasn't even fit, and I kept bleeding. Well, I've finished, and everyone's applauding, the same as ever. So then I thought, 'Well, then: I *can* do it', so I agreed to do *Damage*. I had to get myself ready in a particular way. I was playing for whole days at a time, slowly getting my mouth used to it, pacing myself very sensibly. They sent me the piece and I played through it a few times. And it went okay. When I listen to that recording now, I don't notice any difference.

Was that Preisner's composition for the Louis Malle film?
Yes. A very good melody. All of the music was excellent. Preisner is an excellent film composer.

Was losing your teeth related to your addictions?
No. I take after my mother with that. My mother had periodontal disease. And then we realized that she'd lost her teeth at the same age as I'd lost mine, almost to the month. That's how strong an effect genes can have! My teeth weren't as healthy as they could have been, but I didn't think they were that bad. I had gold teeth for a while. I had all my fucking front teeth in gold. A kind of drunken fantasy. I remember how delighted Don Cherry's daughter was when she saw me: 'What beautiful gold teeth!' I'd had an ounce of gold put inside my mouth. It had all started to weaken, and I had to get rid of it.

When a trumpeter loses his teeth, is that like when a pianist breaks a finger?
It's worse. Although it's difficult to say, as once a broken finger's set, sometimes it can't play at all. That said, Bill Evans managed a whole gig with just one hand. He took heroin. A lot.

Gary Peacock told me that heroin had caused paralysis in the whole of his right hand, and they had a really good gig lined up. He couldn't turn it down because otherwise he'd have got fired. And he did the whole thing with just his left hand. No one noticed. Everyone was delighted.

The problem with the trumpet is that the mouthpiece rests on the bottom lip. You don't squeeze from the bottom, you squeeze from the top, but the lower lip is the support. The lip sits against the teeth and becomes a sort of cushion which precisely regulates the flow of air. And I had trouble with the bottom lip. It's OK now, but, shit, what I had to go through to begin with! Honestly, it was horrific. I mean, even when you just change mouthpieces on a trumpet, it's difficult to find a new position: it takes years for your mouth to get used to it.

It was only by the time I was halfway through playing with the Polish quartet that it felt natural again, and I'd got the old form back. I just had to get through it. It was the early 1990s and my career was starting to take off. That was when ECM approached me. I think that if I hadn't been a drug addict in the past, and was sober now, then I don't think I'd have been able to carry on with it, because you need to have had practice in a certain kind of resilience, that masochistic type of resilience to blows that addicted people have. And now I'm changing my mouthpiece yet again. I feel as if I'm losing control again. But then, the sound that this new mouthpiece makes is so beautiful that it would be a pity not to use it. I'm going to have to be hard again. It seems like that's my fate. That's karma.

What is it with these changes of mouthpiece?
It's to do with condition; it's not easy. Coordination is difficult. Playing trumpet is a very complicated business because of the technique. You have to have a tiny hole set up in your mouth, incredibly precisely. It's through this that the stream of air passes that determines the sound, and that has to be coordinated with your fingers. It's so precise that even with the slightest disruption, like changing your mouthpiece, you lose control.

I'd like to go back to those words of Miles's that you quoted, about the devil sitting next to you, waiting to be fed. Is there any other way of feeding the devil, apart from with drugs?
There's no other method. You either have to give him the stuff or he sits next to you, pissed off, waiting patiently. The poor thing believes it's going to work.

In the end, then, successfully overcoming your addictions means living with this sad devil.
That's all there's left. He'll only die when I do. He's always there within me, but getting smaller all the time. But that doesn't mean he's any weaker. On the contrary. I have the impression that the longer you stop for, the more dangerous it is. That's how it works. The longer you stop for, the more careful you have to be. That's probably the way the metabolic system works in the body. I can feel it distinctly. I'm under an increasing amount of threat while being increasingly sober, but in this permanent state of increasing threat, I have greater clarity of mind.

Is clarity of mind the body's reaction to threat?
That's a good way of putting it in theoretical terms. I can't actually allow myself to be aggressive, immoral, sinful, or do any of the different kinds of things that would previously have taken hold of me and rendered me helpless. I can't be helpless now: that's too dangerous. I'm walking that fucking narrow tightrope, and I'm going to be walking it for the rest of my life. It's not like I'll get anywhere. I won't get anywhere. That's the only way. But what I can see around me is an incredibly beautiful landscape – so beautiful that it takes your breath away. All I have to do is learn how to walk that tightrope and pay attention: then it's pleasure and profit all the way.

What sort of tightrope is this?
I'm using metaphors. People walk a tightrope, high up, even though it's dangerous. But that tightrope always has a beginning and an end. In my case, there is no end, but the miracle that surrounds me can only be seen from this very tightrope. I have to keep walking it, all the while being very careful.

Does intoxication equate to falling off the tightrope?
Intoxication is the classic falling off the tightrope, so that we can immerse ourselves in that surrounding beauty. We could carry on with these metaphors forever more. But drugs are just trivial matters. There's so much talk about them nowadays because the subject itself is a lurid one. But it's like with your dirty linen – you don't show it, you don't talk about it because it's an irrelevant matter.

When you think that people were imprisoned in concentration camps, in labour camps, and they got out and they lived. What's heroin compared to that? Nothing. Life can be very hard indeed. People do encounter serious threats. Anyway, drugs are a private matter, concerning a person's innermost being.

I talk about it because I treat the matter as a therapeutic one. I get certain things off my chest, and I realize that I'm strong. It helps me toughen up. And what can I say: I'm an addict. Talking about it reminds me of the fact, and of those states that I've had permanently stored in my brain as pleasant ones. But the state that I'm in now – of 'pure high' – I wouldn't change that for anything.

21 The Feminist

What's your reaction to the label 'cool jazz'? You once called it the music of your youth.

That's what it was. I used to listen to cool jazz, though I preferred Black music. I'd listen to Jimmy Giuffre, Lee Konitz, Gerry Mulligan and, of course Miles's *Birth of the Cool*. Most often I listened to Mulligan's famous quartet with Chet Baker. Mulligan's baritone with Chet's trumpet made a very interesting sound. It was a modern, intriguing sound at that time.

What about the aura surrounding that particular music? That famous cool style. Did that also make an impression on you?

It was supposedly cool jazz, but I didn't feel the cool. For me it was simply White playing, a different sound, more delicate, more gentle. It wasn't as rough and virile as the Black bebop or hard bebop phrasing. You could call it 'cool jazz'. I preferred listening to Art Blakey's Messengers, to Bobby Timmons and the whole pool of Blue Note musicians, or to Charles Mingus. The Miles I preferred was late Miles – but I liked his quintet with Coltrane the best.

And what do you think of Chet Baker? Some call him a White dude who stole Miles's sound.

That's bullshit. Chet played real music. That was his style. They were just jealous of him because he was like a Hollywood star.

While the rebelliousness of bebop was aggressive, in cool that manifested as indifference. Researchers have established that the jazz term 'cool' has its origin in the courtly culture of fifteenth- and sixteenth-century Africa. It meant reining in one's effusiveness, and referred to women. That brings to mind Miles, who used to say that he got his style from his mother. Within that macho personality of Miles's, there's also a feminine side, specifically to do with his style. Have you ever given any thought to feminine traits within your own personality?

I haven't given it any thought, but I'm sure I have many.

Do you owe much to women?
It's difficult to say whether I owe much to them, but they've certainly played a part in my life, definitely. If only in terms of the feminine titles that I used to give many of my compositions.

Did the most important ones make it to the titles?
I don't know whether it was the most important ones. Sometimes the deciding factor was chance or emotions. There's a composition called 'Sunia'. I used to have a little dog, and I really loved her.

You've already talked about Bushka and Lady Go. But the list of feminine words is a long one. I had to write them down. On the _A i J_ album, for example, there's 'Natka'.
That's not a name. It doesn't mean anything. It's a word from Ania's childish vocabulary. A very interesting composition, which I didn't play very much, though I do like it. The _A_ and _J_ in the album title are Ania and Joaśka, my daughter and my wife.

With C.O.C.X. you recorded 'Mademoiselle K'.
There was a young lass with that name somewhere along the way – just a platonic love.

Not as important as Bushka and Lady Go?
It's difficult to say what's more important – a fleeting affair or a longer relationship.

Then you released the album _Matka Joanna_.
Joaśka thought it was for her, but it's actually to do with Jerzy Kawalerowicz's _Matka Joanna od Aniołów_ (_Mother Joan of the Angels_).

Is 'Celina' on this album also a character from the film?
Yes, from the film.

'Leosia' made it to the title of your next album.
My mother. That was recorded after my mother died. I dedicated the album to her.

'Sarah' appears on _Suspended Night_.
'Song for Sarah' is for Sarah Humphries from ECM. She still works there. She was Manfred's right hand in Munich, and she now runs the New York part of ECM. Sarah brought _Litania_ to market. She loves music. She's Tim Berne's wife.

On _Lontano_ there's 'Piosenka dla Ani' ['Song for Ania'].
For my daughter.

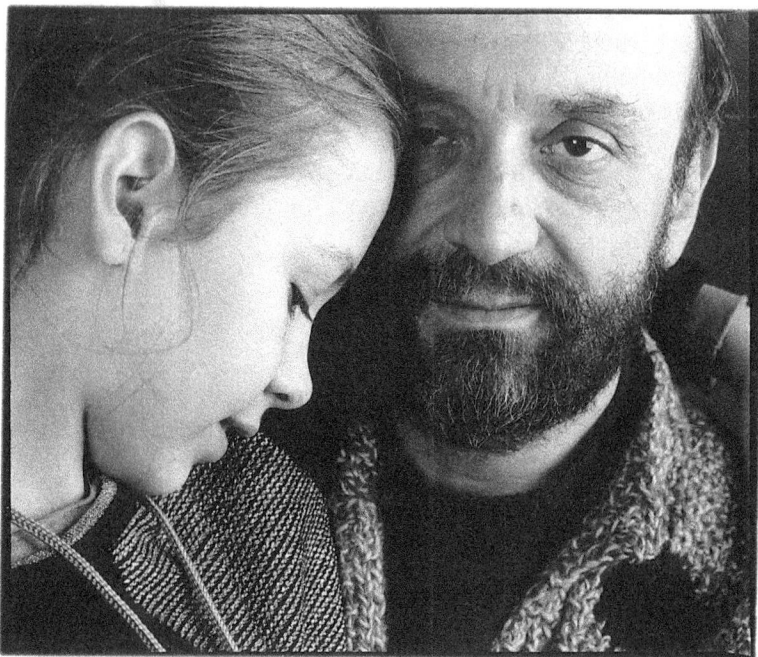

With daughter Anna in the 1990s.
Photograph by Andrzej Tyszko

What was your relationship like with your daughter?
My only child. We have a strong relationship. At one point, she moved to Kraków and, for a few months, she lived with me and her grandparents. Then later, when Joaśka went over to the States, we were meant to be living together. Ania was seventeen at the time. We nearly killed each other. Ania's a strong personality and isn't terribly flexible, and I'm a bossy person and impose my will rather as a matter of course. As neither of us wanted to give way, we both came to the conclusion that it would be better for us to live separately. I wanted to buy an apartment near her, which I did. As I'm not your typical good father, I wanted to have her nearby. We lived separately, but I cooked dinner for her every day; I took care of her. We've become closer over the years. Particularly since we've been working together; we're in constant contact, of the kind that parents no longer have with children that age. Ania's thirty.

The separateness that you got from your family home has shown up in your relationship, hasn't it?
That's true.

Were there any stormy moments with Ania during the difficult period of adolescence, when you had to assert your authority as a father?
I didn't have to be a father in that sense. I had no behavioural problems with Ania. She did well at school. She was calm, and I was tolerant. I was lucky to not have to worry, lucky that things worked out well of their own accord. I think it was because her parents were crazy that she went for the contrast, and Joaśka and I were keen to cultivate this. We let off steam on her behalf.

How did it come about that Ania became your manager?
It came about quite naturally. Ania had done a degree in sociology, but the job offers she was getting were uninspiring. I can't remember now when and in what circumstances I first wanted her to represent me. And that's how it stayed. Ania was interested in doing it, and she did it really well. Normally it's not the best set-up, having your daughter doing it, but it works for us. Ania is quite simply a really good negotiator. And she also has a certain – a kind of indescribable, creative way of thinking, which is invaluable and exceptionally rare in this line of work. There's an increasing number of women in the music business, because they're capable on the one hand of being hard, often harder than men, yet, at the same time, they're flexible and considerate. That duality makes it easier for them to operate.

At one time you had managers that you were in a relationship with.
There were two that I was in a relationship with – for a short time, but nevertheless. Viola, and Basia, particularly.

Were they your managers to begin with, before a relationship developed, or was it the other way around?
It was their idea really. You know, women like to have a kind of stable – four or five single men in a band: their property. It's a very feminine thing. Women like crazy men. That's how it worked, with them putting in most of the effort because, with my desperate kind of lifestyle, it was difficult at times.

Did they make better managers than those with whom you had a strictly business relationship?
I don't think so. But it was convenient, you know, because we were together. It didn't last very long – a year, eighteen months.

You then had a serious, long-term relationship.
I was with Małgosia for well over fifteen years. A long time. We were very close. I lived with my mother for a while, for a second time, because in the intervening period she'd been living with my sister in Sweden. It's difficult in that kind of situation because it's not natural. That's why I bought my mum an apartment in Kraków pretty quickly, near to where she'd lived previously, and then I started a different life here on Rozbrat Street.

It was back then, in the late 1980s, that I got together with Małgosia. I'd known her from way back: I'd met her when she was eighteen. Then she'd got married. We met up again when she was a mature woman; she was splitting up with her husband, and we got together.

As mature people, getting together after lots of experiences, was this relationship different from the previous ones?
I'd been with a few women, but music had always had the upper hand. It had governed everything. Music requires us to practise in solitude: that's why musicians are a bit different – at least I am . . . Gośka and I were very close. We spent a lot of time together, but I needed my own space and we lived separately. I've never lived with anyone for very long. We used to have a dog, a Rottweiler, who was a bit like our child. He was called Orzeł. I bought him for Gośka. And, to be honest, it was after Orzeł died that we broke up. We'd both come to the conclusion that our relationship had been going downhill, and when he died we were no longer tied down so much, just as if a child of ours had died. It really affected us.

I haven't had a long-term relationship since then, and I'm very much cultivating this solitude. I have a few homes. I travel a lot. I have to work a lot these days – the older I am, the more I work. To maintain the good level of fitness that I've had throughout my whole life, I have to work increasingly hard at the physical side of my profession. I have to practise more, practise harder, totally devote myself to my music, because age take its toll. I'm weaker. I can maintain my fitness, but I do have to put the work in. Solitude is a consequence of my life and a very natural state for me.

Here, on Rozbrat Street, you have a little practice room. You could say that, in there, you're cutting yourself off from the outside world even more.
Exactly. We're back to the Individual Being again. I think that the more evolved we are as people, the greater our tolerance of solitude. It's not a coincidence that we have single people in large cities: it's a consequence of humanity's development. We're not talking here about ordinary loneliness, which might be the result of an inability to find oneself a partner, or of shyness. This is a different kind of solitude, which is a consequence of life choices, and isn't really loneliness as such.

I have friends. I'm on the road. What kind of loneliness is that? The fact is that I like spending time with bands. I feel good with the musicians with whom I play.

In front of his apartment in Warsaw. Early 1980s.
Courtesy Anna Stańko

Have you noticed that you've become a favourite with high-end women's magazines? I've recently seen articles about you and interviews in *Pani* ['The Lady'], *Zwierciadło* ['The Looking Glass'] and *Viva*.
Indeed. It's come as a bit of a surprise. I had an interview not long ago with Mrs Domagalik for *Pani*. Really fascinating. She's a very interesting woman. We spoke about all sorts of things, even women's magazine kind of things.

Did Domagalik try to approach you from a feminist angle?
A little bit, but I am actually a feminist.

A feminist?

I think in evolutionary terms, and I know that it's not possible for evolution at its highest level to have invented a species where one sex might be inferior to the other. Women are definitely different from us, but it's a different kind of intelligence. This whole scheme of nature depends on the sexes in these higher evolutionary forms complementing each other, and only together constituting their species as a whole. On occasion, it's been males who have been the stronger, on other occasions it's been females, but everything has been carefully weighed out to ensure that the species prospers. We need both male and female intelligence, so that we do have differences, because differences drive things forward.

In cultures where the role of women is restricted, civilization loses out.

And yet, during our sessions you do say things about having upset women, stressing your overbearing nature, for example.

I *am* overbearing, but I have a keen sense of tolerance, and I feel strongly about equality of the sexes. That's one reason, among others, for my isolation. I prefer being single, because where you have a relationship, you have to have a boss. Being together is difficult. Someone has to roar and assume control. But I don't want to waste time on battle and domination. I'd have to be scrapping constantly, because usually I like strong women, who don't want to give way either. I don't like fighting, and I'm not ashamed of that. I'm convinced that the era of women is coming because, in our present circumstances, it's they who are the stronger. Male physical strength is no longer required for survival, and women are more resilient mentally. There are no primeval forests anymore. There are huge cities offering an easy life, where women can raise children on their own, and men are becoming increasingly weaker. Matriarchies did use to exist. Now, once again, women have strength and power. You think they don't know that they're more resilient in this new era? They absolutely do know they are.

Women are strong, while the templates for masculinity have fallen into decline.

That's true. They've become devalued, and it's increasingly difficult to create them, especially in wealthy societies.

Strong women are at the forefront of mainstream pop culture, while men are represented by the baby-faced boys from the soaps, and the proverbial gay stylists. Even famous musicians dress like that. And maybe that's why women's media take an interest in you, because you represent a more traditional template of manhood.

Do you think so?

And while on the one hand you talk about respecting women, on the other hand you go on to say: zero compromise.

Well yes; I don't know why I've become so popular with women's media. Women's magazines take an interest in interesting people. When they run out of celebrities, they sometimes use other people. And if you live for a long time and stay active, the power of your name increases. They know my name, although they don't necessarily know who I am. I appreciate pop culture, and I realize that if I'm well known, it makes it easier for me to conduct my artistic business.

We've talked about your dedications to women. But your composition titles can be literary dedications on occasion as well. We've already talked about Witkacy. You've told us about Lautréamont (aka Isidore Ducasse),* but I'd like to return, if I may, to the subject of *Die Weisheit von Isidore Ducasse* ['The Wisdom of Isidore Ducasse']. What kind of insight did the author of *Les Chants de Maldoror* have?

I thought this title through very carefully. I had the book at hand. Back then when I was high, I was taken aback by the beautiful, lyrical *Poésies* and the cruel text of Maldoror, published as one volume. For me, the motto of *Poésies* – 'I replace melancholy with courage . . .' – sums up this madman's insight. Lautréamont's wisdom is encapsulated in this motto's handful of words. I gave the composition a German title because I liked how it sounded. *Weisheit* sounds hard: a certain contrast appears. It's about contradictions, which are at the very core of both me and everyone else. We can benefit from an understanding of contradictions. Evil, destructive traits can easily be turned into their opposites. When you've swung really high to one side, it's easier to swing across to the other side than it is to find yourself in the middle. And what I like most is the contrast between extremes.

Your next literary dedication is *Under the Volcano*. Did you identify with the main character in Malcolm Lowry's novel?

The alcoholic Lowry's famous novel: it's very dear to me, because I'm also an alcoholic. He wrote about things that I experienced, those manic states, half-delirious, who knows what they are.

What about your piece 'My W.S.B. Friend'? Is that about William S. Burroughs?

No, it's something entirely different: *white small ball*, my 'little white friend'. It's about pills. I had lots of those pills – 'speed'. I didn't dedicate anything to Burroughs, but I'd have been happy to do so. I find his writing beautiful. *Junkie* and *Queer* are particularly lovely with their strangely rough lyricism. I'm

---

* *Series Editor's note:* Isidore Ducasse (1846–1870) wrote under the pen name of the Comte de Lautréamont and in his short life produced two books: the *Poésies* (published under his real name) is a series of maxims comparable to the one singled out here by Stańko, whereas *Les Chants de Maldoror* concerns Maldoror, an evil figure at the heart of an often violent and surreal narrative.

Score for the composition 'My W.S.B. Friend'.
Courtesy Anna Stańko

less keen on *Naked Lunch*: it's contrived. I like Burroughs's language: simple, while describing complicated situations. He wrote about deep, *really* difficult experiences in a dry language, you might say, and he succeeded in drawing out the contrast in all of it. Can you imagine what he must have gone through after all that heroin? He was like Baudelaire, a refined cat, but he hung around with the junkies at the very bottom of society. Being on the streets of New York is one thing, but in Tangiers that's just total rock bottom. He was a tough bastard.

Burroughs wrote from the position of someone who has been through a heroin addiction, but he had a particular approach to it, because he was fascinated by the way addiction causes changes in metabolism, changes in the way we experience time, and also mutations of the body.

That's what happens. It's deeper than it might appear. I think I'd be a different person if I hadn't taken dope.

Are books a form of relaxation for you, or inspiration?

Inspiration. More often than not, I read books in little scraps: a few pages at a time. Faulkner's narrative, for example, helps me with my narrative. While improvising, I fly off at a tangent, like he flies off with his sentences and his meanings. The same with Joyce. I associate those swaying phrases with playing, with jazz, with my thing. I really like distant associations. Completely different aesthetics suddenly side by side: I loved it when my perception skipped over like that. Contrasts again! I do like them. They explain humanity to me, and that's why I want to be tolerant about everything. Even when I'm not, I still want to force myself to be so, because that enriches me. Even if I were biologically averse to homosexuals, I'd remember Burroughs's description of his love of young boys: how sublime and beautiful it was. Difference means more, and I'd like to be weightier, broader. It's not about understanding, about getting my head around things, but about becoming broader. I'm deliberately using that word, because this isn't about improving myself, but about broadening my spectrum of sensitivity, making it wider.

'A rough lyricism' – how you describe Burroughs's prose translates brilliantly to your sound.

Maybe it translates less directly to my playing and more to my artistic ideals. The Black sound has that virile, rough lyricism. The ballads of Coleman Hawkins, Ben Webster, or Coltrane, or Monk's chords. There's Burroughs-like lyricism there. We don't have that in European music. Our lyricism is more exalted: all oohs and aahs. I do have that European shit within me, that melodiousness, but I have massive respect for the other music. My dream is to record my melodic compositions with some Black dudes, who experience things differently. I don't know if I'll ever do it, but now that I'm in New York, that's the direction I want to take.

Craig Taborn's told me that James Carter doesn't go to the clubs down-town: he goes to Harlem. I'll have to pop in there and see the musicians. I might invite them to Bielsko-Biała, to introduce the audiences to that scene, to the Real Deal, homogenous music as expressed by the African-American contingent. They play ballads differently, but the depth of emotion created is the same. The method is different: more virile. They don't weep over them-selves, don't go all tragic about how miserable they feel. They bear the pain, resolutely. Resolutely, dammit!

I've already said that, when I was a little boy, I saw a guy on a train burst into tears. I felt revulsion towards him for such a display. I found it disgusting. I couldn't stand such self-pity. That's my Achilles heel. We should bear our misfortune on our own, in solitude and with fortitude. Frankly, it's non-human to lament over your own fate, kind of messed up. I can't even describe it. I don't want to. I remember giving it really serious consideration, and then later on, even when I had tears in my eyes, I never wanted to show it. I'd be ashamed.

Jazz seems to me to be strong. That's why I love jazz so much. The misfortune of the heroin addicts, the addict's hunger, they manifest themselves differently in this music: in a lyrical, yet tough way. My style of playing is different again, and I have no hang-ups about my approach: I am the way that life has shaped me. But I am impressed by certain kinds of attitude to life, and I respect those more than I do others: that's why I like Burroughs so much. How the son-of-a-bitch endured those cravings, those hangovers. A tough cat. There's value in that. His heroin addiction would no doubt have had a certain kind of value, because he'll have learned how to endure all the related difficulties, and that would have toughened him up. As I understand it, Burroughs coped like nobody else: he lived a lovely life in his own way.

You mentioned the great Black tenor saxophonists. I'd be interested to know which trumpeters you hark back to these days?
Woody Shaw always knocked me off my feet. Clifford Brown, Booker Little, Fats Navarro, Don Cherry. I always enjoy listening to Miles. And I don't just mean his solos. He doesn't have any hang-ups about being a leader. For him the overriding value is pure music. I listen to lots of things, mainly old stuff. Bill Evans, Keith Jarrett, Coltrane, Mingus, Monk, Rollins.

You did play a Mingus programme at one time.
Hamburg Radio: Nord Deutsche Rundfunk organized a production with Mingus's music. We had Don Pullen, Danny Richmond, George Adams and me playing, plus the entire Hamburg big band. I think that Mingus's music has yet to be discovered. It has a strange irregularity. At one and the same time, it's conventional and strange. It has lots of blues in it, classical mainstream eight-bar blues, but with two or one added to it, and then suddenly we're in completely different territory. I keep wanting to go back to Mingus and study his incredible compositions, the strange way in which he elongated his phrases.

The same with Monk: the way he combines New Orleans music with a sudden strange bend . . . I'm sensitive to such differences. I've heard them in the bass lines of reggae guitarists, in Bob Marley. I mean, I didn't invent the dual voice that I use. That approach is more a consequence of my study of jazz.

You often mention Thelonious Monk.
Monk did not have a classical piano technique, but the bebop community had tremendous respect for him because he was Monk, pure and simple, a unique personality. Jazz allows for that kind of thing, which is refreshing. Maybe African-Americans have this awareness because of their ancestral lineage. That's what humanity's about – we strive for perfection, though what is our perfection compared to the structure of an atom, the perfection of nature?

Imperfection and the striving for perfection – art has to balance these two extremes. Art becomes stunted when perfection takes precedence over roots, dirt and intuition. I think that playing that balance is my strength. I'd like it to be. I'm now deliberately hiring musicians with a typically mainstream way of playing, and then I put in the dirt, which is fundamental to my technique. And that balance works. I believe that music that's balanced out like that is richer.

What about that dirt? Isn't that a harsh expression?
It's a dirty technique, an unconventional one that allows for a wide range of tone colour. Davis didn't have Gillespie's virtuosity: he simply had a different technique.

Did you use to listen to Gillespie?
Not so much. Out of the bop era, I preferred Clifford Brown, Kenny Dorham, Booker Little, Fats Navarro. Out of hard bop: Lee Morgan, Freddie Hubbard, Donald Byrd, Blue Mitchell, and then Charles Tolliver and Woody Shaw.

And what about that big dispute there used to be about who was the best trumpeter: Lester Bowie or Wynton Marsalis?
Wise people know that there is no dispute, because both those two extremes are important. I definitely prefer Bowie, but I also think highly of Marsalis because of his perfection. When Bowie played with the Art Ensemble, they consciously referred back to the New Orleans tradition, and they poured it all out. They went for what was natural; but with the kind of tone that Bowie had, you can't play the little gems that Marsalis plays.

We started with cool jazz, but we're ending with hot sounds. Did the bop legends make a big impression on you?
I was less influenced by the legend of bop. I began with Miles, Ornette Coleman and Coltrane. But I have recently heard a story about the origins of bop, which I found fascinating. Max Roach mentioned it in one of his last interviews. The whole thing was actually the unbelievably straightforward, basic effect of a tax imposed during the war on places that had dance music. Big-band jazz musicians had been hired for purely functional music, but when the tax was brought in, the bar and restaurant owners said, 'Well, you won't be dancing, then.' And they let the musicians play music for listening to. That's how bebop exploded onto the scene. That's the origin of those strange themes, jagged phrases. An art form took off. It's that kind of randomness that causes it to flourish. What human nature needs is an impetus. It might, on occasion, be a very superficial, mundane and commercial one.

The revolution was to free music from its functional dimension.
Improvisation took off. Charlie Parker's compositions are nothing other than improvised phrases. Improvisation and time, a swinging sense of time, which imposes some order on those phrases.

But if, by the 1960s, bop was no longer making such an impression on you, it would seem that the famous delirium of this music must have evaporated rather quickly.

Everything develops quickly these days. After all, Parker's music is a bit like the ravings of a heroin addict, and yet, these days, the conscientious student practises it at school. And that delirium is part of humanity, of our cultural way of comprehending the world. But then, what do we actually mean by the delirium of a genius? The form, the expression, the structure of these melodies is incredibly sophisticated.

We've now gone so deeply into the roots of jazz that I'd like to take it back as far as swing and ask you about your experience of Duke Ellington's music. In the late 1990s, you played solo in the *Ellingtonia* programme with Nord Deutsche Rundfunk's big band.

I don't remember it very well. I also played Ellington's compositions with Bobo Stenson. We got invited to a festival of his music in Brussels. I think it was after that concert that we got together as a duo. We played Ellington free, ad lib, in a very modern way, and we also used swing roots. It worked brilliantly because swing is close to free.

Free comes from Cecil, Ornette and Coltrane, though a whole group of musicians, starting with Ayler and Shepp, played a free that came straight out of swing, from the sound of the swing saxophonists, such as Coleman Hawkins or Don Byas. I've heard jam session recordings of Byas's that sounded like free. That lot were merciless: they weren't interested in pitch or scales, they went with the rhythm, with the time. Sometimes they played as if they were playing on drums. Once they'd really got going, things became so loose that it was easy for them to move over to atonal playing. The swing musicians didn't even play ballads with a nice sound: they played with a passionate sound.

22 A Bluish, Synthetic Man

The beginning of that new era in your life coincides with the stormy period of Polish transformation.
That's when finance minister Balcerowicz began his free-market reforms in 1989. I knew that the financial side of things was getting complicated. That watershed period was a very difficult one. Both because of my underground life and because of those changes. A dark time. I wasn't getting much work. In the early 1990s, I woke up and found myself in a terrible mental state and a lousy financial situation.

I realized just how far gone I was in my addictions. I was on the way back up. I was still living in the old way, but I did know that I had to do something about it. Everything in the marketplace had changed as well. I felt the youngsters were pushing: new bands, new people. It was all over for me with the high-value dollar. During the previous era, for years, my whole life had been set up by the fact that in Poland I'd been able to get a good exchange rate for the dollar. I'd depended on that. Just for a few concerts in the West, I'd been able to live here like an artist, to just pursue pure art. That was important to me.

But then that all came to an end, and I found myself at a crossroads. I didn't have any work. Some vague prospect of a visiting professorship in Linz. I played my first concerts with Christian Muthspiel at that time. Then there was Jazz Baltica. It went in leaps and bounds. I began to think about going clean once and for all. As Berendt once put it: 'to be reborn'. We spoke not long before he died. I mean, he could see what was happening to me: he said the best way out for me would be to be reborn. Those words have stuck in my mind.

When Freelectronic disbanded, you were left without a permanent band.
I was playing solo and in a duo with Janusz Skowron, but I didn't really know what to do. We still needed to get visas to go anywhere. Then I got an offer from Vienna, from a young musician, Christian Muthspiel. I didn't know him. He was the first person in that new era to offer me a professional engagement. I still have a soft spot for him. Muthspiel had an idea for a band of musicians from the East: Octet Ost. He didn't even know who I was exactly. It was only after we'd met that he found out that I'd worked for ECM. In the band we had

Anatoly Vapirov from Bulgaria, Vladimir Tarasov from Lithuania, although he's a Russian, and some Slovaks. We rehearsed, and then we went on tour. I have very fond memories of it.

That lifted me, my spirits, my physical form, but, most importantly, it lifted my spirits. During that long tour with Muthspiel, I gave up hashish. I started running. I followed a macrobiotic diet and I had shiatsu massage. I began crossing over to the other side, to the light. I also met a friend then, who was head of the jazz department at the University of Linz, and he offered me some work there. But I had to take an exam.

Did you want to teach?

I did think about becoming a professor at the conservatoire in Linz. I'd worked out that, if I lived in Austria, it would be easier for me to get a visa in Vienna than it would here among these crowds. I wanted to rent an apartment in Vienna and commute to Linz from there. The practical considerations were very important. But it got resolved of its own accord. I took an exam. They even paid for my flight, but then they took on somebody else, the American [*sic*] trumpeter Ingrid Jensen.* And, soon after that, I was actually very glad, because things had changed in Poland. Suddenly, it seemed, we didn't need visas anymore. We joined Europe quickly. The foreign jobs started, then ECM: a new period had begun. I really got going then, when Bobo Stenson and I got a band together. We travelled a lot with that band: France, Spain, Italy, Sweden. Good venues, festival gigs.

What did you have to do for the exam in Linz?

They wanted to see me teach: I had to teach a class. I tell you, it was needs-must that made me take that step, because I hate teaching. I don't know how to teach, and I don't feel comfortable in the role of teacher. I don't have it in me to be a teacher, which perhaps makes me a little less rounded.

Thanks to the Muthspiel engagement, you began playing a lot of concerts again, in Germany and in Austria.

At that time, in 1991, 1992, I played as a sideman. I recorded three albums with Octet Ost. We had tours in Austria and Italy. I remember the Bolzano Festival. I renewed my contacts. I also played with Sigi Finkel, a German musician who lived in Vienna. Then Nicolas Simion, a Romanian who I met through Muthspiel, offered me a few things. I recorded albums with them. I worked with young musicians. Vienna was a starting point for me at that time: they all lived there. That was actually what got things going for me again in my life. I still have a good rapport with Austria. I was the first winner of the European Jazz Prize in Vienna.

---

* *Translator's note:* Ingrid Jensen is a Canadian jazz trumpeter who studied at the Berklee College of Music in the US.

What's your recollection of Muthspiel?
A young musician, a trombonist, a composer. An interesting character. I liked
him a lot. He had a light way of playing, like Albert Mangelsdorff – modern
music, but melodic. His brother, Wolfgang, a guitarist who studied at Berklee,
was a well-known musician. Christian essentially wanted to be a composer.
He also wrote large-scale pieces for classical instruments, for symphony
orchestras. He wrote such a lot for Octet Ost. All the music was written down
– kind of suites.

**Octet Ost had a very carefully conceived line-up. A full range of musicians from
Eastern Europe.**
The idea was to have an Austro-Hungarian monarchy. I am from Galicia, after
all. Muthspiel did some shrewd manoeuvring: he managed to get some money
from somewhere or other. He once told me how you have to speak to officials
over there: 'You never gave Mozart a penny, and now look at how much money
you're making out of him.' And then they'd hand it over.

**Some really charismatic musicians from behind the Iron Curtain met
there. I mean, Vladimir Tarasov is a legend – a significant drummer on the
underground free music scene during the Soviet era.**
I knew him from way back. In Ost there was also a French horn player from
the Moscow Art Trio, Arkady Shilkloper.

**In Mark I of Octet Ost there was a famous singer from that scene, Sainkho
Namtchylak.**
There was indeed. A charismatic person from Siberia. She sang in that
characteristic Siberian way.*

**What's your recollection of recording your albums with Simion and Finkel?
There were quite a few of them.**
I don't think they're terribly important. I wouldn't put too much emphasis
on that period of my life. It was important in as much as it enabled me to get
myself back on my feet. I sobered up. I climbed out of the mire and slowly
began to look around me, to see what to do next.

**At that time you recorded the album *Suite Talk* for the German market. In
1993, in a trio with Manfred Bründl and Michael Riessler. It's been re-released
recently under the title *Too Pee*.**
And to me that seems such a long time ago . . . Now they've released that in
Germany under my name, for fuck's sake, but it's not mine. It was Bründl who
asked me to do the recording. I had work of some sort on all the time. The
young musicians used to hire me for their concerts, and the albums followed

---

* *Series Editor's note:* Sainkho Namtchylak (b. 1957) specializes in Tuvan 'throat singing',
  a style that creates vocal overtones and which, before her international success, had
  traditionally been the preserve of male singers.

1996.
Photograph
by Andrzej
Tyszko

on from the concerts. We recorded *Suite Talk* for radio in Frankfurt. We did a long tour of South America with that line-up. The Goethe Institute arranged it for us: the concerts were in their branches. We started in Venezuela, in Caracas. Then Bogota, Lima, La Paz, Guatemala, San José, a few concerts in Mexico. We finished in Cuba.

Your most important album from that period is definitely *Bluish*, recorded in 1991. You've actually said that a new era in your life began with that album. But, musically, that record gives the impression that you've put those rock, ethnic and electronic experiments from your previous decade in parentheses and recorded an album that is really a continuation of *Balladyna*. The melodic element has returned.

You could put it like that. I'll tell you what the situation was: I simply wanted to go back to ECM.

That's when the ratios changed. I began playing at the Jazz Baltica festivals. Anders Jormin kept trying to get me to do something with him. I still didn't know what I wanted to do. Krzysztof Popek set up a record label around then and wanted to produce an album. And I got this new band together. I'd known Arild Andersen for years. I'd played with him in bands with Edward, and I liked his sound. There was Jon Christensen too, and we recorded *Bluish* as a trio. It was actually just a session band: we went straight into the studio. It was meant to be a demo of some sort for Manfred Eicher. That was my understanding, anyway. But it never served its purpose as a demo, because it turns out that Manfred never listens to demos. He has a different approach. He doesn't make his decisions like that. But the recording ended up being superb, even though it didn't get picked up by ECM.* There wasn't any tour following on from its release.

The musicians you recorded *Bluish* with, Andersen and Christensen, were, essentially, a classic, tried-and-tested ECM rhythm section.
I knew the people who worked for ECM the best, and, what can I say, these are elite people. There are plenty of excellent musicians in Europe, but not many with individual flair like that. In southern Europe, they mainly play bebop, or very traditional, mainstream music. In France, they have a weakness for classical music, and they play something in between third stream and jazz. I'm closest to the aesthetic of the Scandinavian musicians, like Palle Danielsson, or like Bernt Rosengren going way back, or some of the Danes, like Palle Mikkelborg, or the Norwegians, starting with Jan Garbarek's trio with Arild and Jon. I also like the English: Tony Oxley and I ended up getting very close. The English are excellent. The Germans are too free and too much alike, at least to me. I still find Scandinavia the most interesting. That's why my new quintet has two Danes and two Finns in it.

What does your music have in common with Scandinavian jazz?
The aesthetic is close to my own. The ability to move around in a tradition that goes beyond bebop, pure jazz and a particular melodic approach to playing free.

You've played with Norwegians, Danes, Swedes and Finns. Does each of those Scandinavian nations have its own approach to jazz?
No. It's Scandinavia, pure and simple. Anyway, they're always mixing with each other, weaving their way through different bands.

Your Norwegian section on *Bluish* came from the original modern Scandinavian school of musicians who developed their playing in George Russell's big bands.
They started with George Russell. They also played free. I mean, Arild and Edward recorded *Triptykon* with Garbarek, didn't they?

---

* *Series Editor's note:* It did come out that same year on the Polish label Power Bros. (No 00113).

How did you prepare the programme for _Bluish_?
I wrote the music, as usual. There are also some old compositions, lots of old compositions, because I always put in some old ones.

In the titles there are quite a few hints of that diabolical period of your life: 'Pod wulkanem' ('Under the Volcano'), for instance.
That's an old composition. I'm not sure whether I wrote it for _Bluish_. But we also played it later with the quartet. Two new compositions that appeared at that time were 'Bossanetta' and 'Bluish'. I haven't played them since. I just haven't wanted to play that music anymore. There's also a composition on there that I like a lot: 'My W.S.B. Friend' – in other words, 'My White Small Ball Friend'. I wrote that a very long time ago, when I lived in Remont. I first played it with Zbigniew Wegehaupt; there was a bass line written down and a very strange melody. Very 'high'. A strange composition: to be honest, I still don't fully understand it. 'Daada' is also a very old composition, back from when Ania was born. I've also played it with Sławomir Kulpowicz.

What made you recall those particular compositions from the past, as opposed to any others?
There are certain things that live on. There are compositions that last: the better ones. Then I keep playing them. I'm always going back to 'Gama', which I wrote for the film _Pożegnanie z Marią_ (_A Farewell to Maria_), under a different title, but it's an older composition. I play 'Quintet Time' all the time. I recorded it on _From the Green Hill_, but the composition is from my time with the quintet. Certain compositions of mine don't age. 'White Ballad' and 'Green Sky' are two very old compositions, which I still absolutely love playing. I've been playing 'White Ballad' since 1975 and I can always play it, with every kind of line-up.

The album title itself is interesting: _Bluish_.
Bluish – that's how I translated it. Well, because it's a blue spot. There's a spot in the brain that is responsible for addictions. It's a really nice title: bluish.

Some people make an association between _Bluish_ and the blues, which is another reason why I kept that title. I even had my own company: Bluish Productions. I've still got it. It's still registered, but it's suspended its operations. It was my concert management company.

The _Bluish_ recording took place in Poland. It was organized by Krzysztof Popek.
Popek booked the studio. We played a gig first at Akwarium, and after that we drove over to Wisła to do the recording. We had to drive up a mountain. We recorded it pretty quickly, as usual. A day recording, a day editing, and goodbye. I have fond memories of that. There were lots of good things going on there. Arild with that beautiful sing-song tone of his on the bass.

He also plays electric bass on it.

I'm not so keen on that. Arild plays simply – powerfully and simply – but he has a beautiful tone, his own tone, his own colour, and that's his greatest strength.

What about Jon Christensen? Once again, you had one of the best European drummers in your band.

One of the greatest – a world-class drummer. Exceptional. He plays everything. He plays free too, and his timing's masterly.

What was Popek's role? He was a musician himself, involved with Pick Up Formation.

He didn't interfere in the recording.

It was a sign of changing times that a record label that released jazz was being run by a musician. It was called Power Bros. It released *The Complete Recordings of Krzysztof Komeda* and re-released *Music for K* and *TWET* on CD.

A sign of the times. He launched it like that, with re-releases, got it going, but the business folded eventually, because it's a difficult thing to pull off.

Those excellent early Polish records, such as *TWET* or *Music 81*, don't actually turn up in jazz record guides around the world; and yet Polish albums from the early 1990s – *Bluish* and *Bosonossa* – are everywhere and very highly rated.

The producers probably pushed them out into the world. *Bluish* is well known because the line-up was well known, although we didn't play any concerts after we'd released it. We recorded the album and went home.

The *Bluish* line-up fell apart because of a twist of fate: you weren't able to play any concerts because that's when you lost your teeth.

There was only one concert at Akwarium, before the recording.

On the other hand, your contact with the Jazz Baltica festival turned out to be fortuitous.

That festival meant a great deal to me. It was a huge festival. When I played there, it felt like I'd returned to the European stage.

You performed at the inaugural Jazz Baltica festival in 1991. How did you end up playing there?

I think the contacts came through Poland. One of the organizers was Christian Stormann – his wife was Polish, he was in touch with Poland. Zdzisław Gogulski and Marek Winiarski, who ran GOWI, knew Christian and set it up. Being fans and record collectors, they had lots of contacts in the West. I mean, that was the whole idea of the festival: Baltic jazz. And a big band was in fact put together based on musicians from the region. There were musicians from

Estonia, Lithuania, Russia, Poland, the whole of Scandinavia and Germany. Jazz Baltica, like it says. At first it was just me from Poland.

That festival was immediately accorded the status of a significant cultural event. The inaugural concert was a performance by Günter Grass, who recited his works in a duet with the jazz percussionist Günter Sommer.

Sommer is a well-known drummer from the former GDR. The festival director, Rainer Haarmann, had big ambitions right from the start. Jazz Baltica still takes place in the Salau Palace in Schleswig-Holstein.*

So then you played in the Jazz Baltica Ensemble big band. What kind of music was that?

The music was written by three percussionists: Vesala, Tarasov and Sommer. They were the big band's leaders.

That band also had trumpeter Manfred Schoof, whose early-'60s group, like your group Jazz Darings, were regarded as pioneers of European free music. You might be forgiven for thinking Schoof had been sidelined since the mid-1970s.

He hadn't been sidelined. He just wasn't doing anything concert-wise. He was into composing, writing music for films and ballets. Schoof was one of the most important European trumpeters. I didn't know about his quintet at first, the one he played in during the 1960s, but in some way it was a precursor of mine. When I heard them, it confirmed to me that I'd chosen the right path, although I was playing different music. Schoof's playing was inspirational, unbelievably modern for those times. A wonderful trumpeter with a distinctive technique and his own style.

There was also the group Blasser Quintet, a separate act coming out of the Jazz Baltica Ensemble: Bernd Konrad, John Tchicai, Conny Bauer, Nils Landgren and you.

Yes. I don't remember who wrote for that band. The music was very avant-garde for the time.

Then, in 1996, with the trombonist Nils Landgren, you recorded the album Gotland.

That was our duet with classical organ in a church in Stockholm. Music with an ECM-like character, written by Landgren, melodies with a hint of Scandinavian folk music and with our improvisations. A beautiful, acoustic timbre. Landgren recorded with the famous 'head': there was this method where you stuck microphones onto a dummy head. We chose the best acoustic places in the aisles of the church and we played there, walking around, to make the

---

* *Translator's note:* The location of the festival was changed in 2012. It now takes place in Timmendorfer Strand, Ostholstein, Schleswig-Holstein.

music walk, because that 'head' had a reputation for its multi-channel, vivid sound.

At Jazz Baltica 92, you appeared once again with the Jazz Baltica Ensemble which, this time, was led by David Murray.
Yes. That was after the famous disaster with my teeth. That new period of mine began in a very symbolic way: on the one hand I was partly a synthetic person, yet on the other hand I was a cleansed person. And at the same time, I went back to work. I had new ideas.

A synthetic person? Because of the dentures?
Yes. I was a pieced-together person. Please don't try to explain that. Just write: 'synthetic'.

How did the project with Murray go?
The idea of Jazz Baltica Ensemble is to invite different kinds of leaders, who can then impose their own style on the band. So we had Murray: a great artist, strong, who knows how to execute his own music. He arrived with a folder full of his own compositions with everything written down. But he's a free-jazz artist and he has a different kind of musical conception from the big-band arrangers. He had different systems for organizing the ensemble. Sometimes he had modern compositions which he'd written down graphically. Sometimes he had traditional, very jazzy ones. We went on a big tour with him afterwards. Copenhagen, Stockholm, Riga, Vilnius. The Jazz Baltica Tour.

Murray is very much part of the great African-American jazz tradition, yet at Jazz Baltica he had to work with a European big band.
Obviously there are great Black traditions within jazz – that's absolutely the case. And, obviously, the music of Zoot Sims, Gerry Mulligan, Lee Konitz is different from Coltrane's, Monk's and Miles's. The difference can be very great, especially in the spiritual nature of the music, and yet the technical elements of jazz, the swing, are common to both. They don't necessarily just belong to Black music. I think that the most important characteristic of Black music is its spirituality, its philosophy, its rhythmic nature; but a rendition of Black music by excellent European musicians can be surprisingly good – an interpretation with a fresh, interesting slant.

That band had a strong, charismatic Russian contingent playing in it, headed by the saxophonist Vladimir Chekasin from the Ganelin Trio.
Those Russians were very homogenous. Chekasin, as I recall, would only drink from this one particular metal prison mug, like from a gulag, which he took with him everywhere.

Free jazz remained underground in Russia, banned by the Soviet authorities. It had the same character as that mug. Underground music. They had their own style. Their music developed separately, under different conditions. They were even more restricted than we were in Poland. They had to create their own styles. I rate them highly.

Have you ever played any concerts in Russia?
I've only played in Moscow on one occasion.

In the 1990s, you appeared regularly at Jazz Baltica.
I played in the big bands with Vince Mendoza and Maria Schneider. I was forever going to Jazz Baltica. It was absolutely delightful. Sitting in the sun in the palace grounds, in that beautiful landscape. I did a lot of running there, lots of meditation. I was coming out of my addictions. I was in a very good place. We'd spend a few days there, two or three of which would be taken up with rehearsals. Sometimes, before the main festival, we'd play concerts in other cities. Then I got a bit bored with it. I stopped going. I had a few things on the go with ECM. I went back and played there recently. And I might play there again some time.

There's a record from Jazz Baltica 97, recorded during Bengt-Arne Wallin's concert within the *Rebirth of Swedish Folk Jazz* programme.
His original record, *Old Folklore in Swedish Modern*, from 1962, was one of the first jazz albums I ever had. I don't know where it came from: that was his album. Even before I was playing professionally, I'd got hold of that big-band album, a kind of Gil Evans done Swedish style, very delicate, with folk melodies. And he went back to that. At Jazz Baltica he redid material from the 1960s.

The CD album linked the recordings from that period with the contemporary versions. At that time in Scandinavia a whole series of records appeared with you on them: *The Birth and Rebirth of Swedish Folk Jazz*, *Gotland* and the *Amazing Orchestra* album with Thomas Jäderlund.
Yes, but I wouldn't connect them. I didn't play much on the Wallin album: I was a member of the big band. The Landgren album was more important. I toured with Thomas, and the album recording was part of that. Those were separate things. What they had in common was my appearances at Jazz Baltica, through which I got contacts, which led to tours in Sweden.

In the 1990s you had lots of gigs in Germany and Scandinavia. They needed you there, and yet you say that you don't like European jazz.
I don't know whether I don't like it, as there isn't any music that I dislike, providing it's good. It's just that I listen to certain things more than I do others. I'm less drawn to certain trends, particularly the intellectual ones. My aesthetic

is the opposite of those. It's a very lyrical aesthetic, which comes from the East, from the North-East, a coldly lyrical aesthetic.

Scandinavian jazz is closer to me than the work of some of the artists from Holland and England who I rate very highly. I value their music for its intellectual emotional neutrality, but then again, it's this measured approach that means it's much further away from me. Black lyricism is closer to me: harsh, masculine. It can be very modern, like Cecil Taylor, or traditional, too, like Coleman Hawkins. I'm deliberately mentioning such widely divergent examples, as I find both Hawkins's ballads and certain structures of Cecil's equally beautiful – deep things that have their origin in the blues, which symbolize pain. I'm less interested in intellectual digressions.

23 'Maldoror's War Song'

We've reached a very exciting time in your life. Just as the new era was
dawning, you were essentially teetering on the edge of a precipice, and yet a
few years later you had the best jazz band in Europe.

But then I was never really out of it. Regardless of what I was taking, I always
had an artistic awareness. It's just that my particular lifestyle slowed me down.
Artistically, throughout the whole of that period, I felt very good. And, who
knows, maybe it's because that particular lifestyle slowed me down that I can
continue to be creative. Because, let me tell you, with my new quintet I've had
a surge of strength. I'm having a great time composing fresh, slightly different
music. Obviously, it's still my music, but it's richer. Maybe it comes of laziness.
Because I'm quite a lazy person. I operate slowly, but I keep going.

Anyway, how did this unusual band come about: the one with which you
recorded *Bosonossa*, *Matka Joanna* and *Leosia* – the quartet with Bobo
Stenson, Anders Jormin and Tony Oxley?

I met Jormin at Jazz Baltica. We enjoyed playing together. Jormin kept trying
to persuade me, push me, into definitely doing something together for ECM.
We began talking about getting a band together. I said it would be good to get
Bobo in. So he said, 'Talk to him. He gets on well with Manfred, but it's going
to be difficult to persuade him.'

Did you know Stenson?

I'd known him for ages. From way back, when he was still in Jan Garbarek's
band. I was playing with Vesala at the time, and we used to meet while touring
in Scandinavia. He'd also been through difficult times, when Garbarek went
over to Jarrett, and he was sitting around with nothing to do. He had a band,
Rena Rama, with Palle Danielsson. We met up a lot while on the road. I used
to visit him with Vesala, but we never played together, although I often went
to Scandinavian workshops. But then, because Jormin was there, I started
thinking about a Scandinavian band. We were meant to have Jon Christensen
on drums. I spoke to Bobo: 'Sure man,' he says. So that was my session set up
in Poland. I wanted it to start like that.

What's Stenson like?
A fabulous cat. He's a really well-balanced human being. He likes women, wine, good food, he plays tennis, he's a sybarite. Charming. One of the loveliest people I know. Later, I also played with him as a duo.

So you started this project by setting up a recording session?
That's how I wanted it to start, to check out the band. I'd agreed the album release with GOWI. We were going to do a concert at Akwarium first, and then the session straight after that. That's when I rang Christensen. He couldn't come. I began wondering who I could have on percussion. It kept going around in my head, and I remembered Oxley. At the time, I didn't recall him having played free, because if I had, maybe I'd have thought twice about it, but I did remember him from a concert in Paris where he'd played with Enrico Rava and he'd played time – brilliantly! And I also remembered how in the 1960s he'd played time at a workshop with Andrzej Trzaskowski.

Oxley played with Trzaskowski!?
There was this workshop at the end of the 1960s, one of Trzaskowski's more interesting workshops. Gucio Dyląg and Oxley played in the rhythm section.

How was it talking to Oxley after so many years?
I rang him with my proposal and he said, 'Cool.' And it was only afterwards that I realized that he's a free drummer, a completely free drummer. He doesn't like playing time, but he did play it with me. Oxley felt good with Stenson, but he and Jormin hated each other. We once played a job with Arild Andersen and he really suited Tony. Tony liked Arild because Arild plays simply, and so Tony could play whatever he wanted to. But Jormin played complicated lines, which Oxley didn't like because it made it difficult for him to play free. Oxley has to have bass players who are subordinate to him. He hates bass players who play like soloists. And, likewise, Jormin didn't get on playing with Tony, because he couldn't go wild.

I soon realized that we had an unusual situation: 'Fuck me! I have a fabulous section. I'll have sparks flying behind me.' You know, when you have high-class musicians, they might not like one another, but they instinctively know the worth of what they're playing together. Oxley put the brakes on Jormin's solo inclinations, while Jormin in turn restricted Oxley a little, so he had to play more slowly, more securely. Rhythmically, Oxley hooked onto Bobo; he stuck to him artistically, while Anders played a little bit like a soloist. I had a very good band.

That band met for the first time in Poland in the spring of 1993, before the concert at Akwarium. How was it that first time, playing with that sparks-flying-in-conflict Oxley–Jormin rhythm section?
I saw straight away what was happening, but I take on good musicians so that's fine by me. I take a sudden curve, and my music goes off in that direction. On

Bosonossa Oxley didn't play rhythmically at all. At all. He did his noisy playing. I only had compositions with rhythmic playing later on (and they don't even appear on the albums). He liked playing with Bobo! Bobo kept the playing together with his left hand, and then Oxley liked to go really hard at it with the rhythm.

Well, exactly: that combination of Oxley's practically industrial sound (in terms of jazz) with Stenson's lyricism!
Bobo likes to play conventionally, but he does have a tendency and a desire to reach out to further regions, freer ones. I mean, he did play as a free pianist, and he has his own very particular timing. And then add Jormin to that: a great bassist – a virtuoso. An exceptionally wonderful combination. I had the flower of European musicians. To this day, when I think about it . . . That was some combination! You won't find combinations like Oxley and Stenson. I'm pleased with these musical combinations of mine, because I choose the right people . . .

So Oxley appeared in your quartet somewhat by chance, but surely his playing looks like the culmination of your penchant for percussionists who bypass the jazz templates. I mean, who else could you possibly have thought of after having played with an eccentric like Vesala? Only Oxley, European jazz's number one adventurous drummer. Someone who completely tore up the jazz drumming rule book.
Oxley simply built his sound through his drum kit. He had various instruments in it that went well together, especially the cymbals. He also built his own instruments. That's how he was able to play those sonic masses of his, those swooshing sounds. He always made such a racket.

He likes metallic sounds.
Noise. But Oxley played everything brilliantly for me. He immediately picked up the motif in 'Morning Heavy Song': *Tam-dam-tam, dee-doo-den, tee-too-tam*. He had various jazz tricks which free musicians don't play. He played everything because he was an old cat. Don't forget that Oxley had drummed at Ronnie Scott's; he'd played with Rollins. He'd started playing time, but at a certain point he moved over to free and ostentatiously stopped playing metrically, as if he had contempt for it. Oxley liked my compositions. He really liked playing 'Maldoror' and 'Bosanossa'. Manfred bought it because he was intrigued by the combinations that I had in the band.

What's Oxley like in person?
He's a curious cat. Funny. He travels by train: he doesn't like aeroplanes. He's different, like an artist – an eccentric. He paints as well. He's not your most civil guy. He has his moods. He's confident, demanding. He really takes care of his own interests.

The quartet, 1990s (from left): Bobo Stenson, Tomasz Stańko, Anders Jormin, Tony Oxley.
Photograph by Andrzej Tyszko

You mentioned that Jormin is the person who feels your music best.
Jormin knows the harmonic structure of my music like no one else. You know, I set up my chords very precisely and logically in a none-too-conventional way, supposedly very simple melodically, but with that bend of mine, that 'minor sixth'. I pay attention to such things. And Jormin, the fucker, knows it all, and he knows why. I work, in effect, through modes, not chords, and I try

to connect the modes through movement, which is determined by intuition or aesthetics. I like modes. The chords are determined by the melody. Jormin calls these modes by their Greek names and he understands how they're linked: he instantly picks up the logic. Because he has the knowledge.

I have a very strong amateur streak. I love amateurism in art, its folk nature, a certain kind of ignorance. I apply my knowledge, but I soon take a curve. Into magic, into I don't know what. And I don't worry about it in the least. I don't use my knowledge in the traditional way. I go a completely different way, I don't exactly know how. Sometimes, it's embarrassing, the things I don't know, and don't even want to know. I prefer to do things differently in my life. I know very well that a certain kind of ignorance adds some freshness. I don't fall into routine and cliché. Ignorance like that could make my life difficult, if I went the conventional way, but that's not what I do.

Jormin and Stenson played together with Christensen in Charles Lloyd's ECM quartet.
I know. About the same time as they played with me. I met Jormin at Jazz Baltica when he was playing with Lloyd, although I knew him from before then. I don't remember when we first met. I've been playing for so many years that I don't remember. I have a peculiar kind of memory, generally. Time for me becomes elongated, shortened, like in a haze of delirium.

You recorded *Bosonossa* in Warsaw, straight after the concert. What was that session like?
It was all very free.

What part did the Kraków-based record label GOWI play in the making of that album?
They produced it. They paid for the studio. They paid the musicians.

When we were talking about *Bluish*, you said that you'd thought of this material as a demo for ECM. Did Manfred also get *Bosonossa*? He did sign the band up very quickly for his label.
No. He doesn't listen to such things, does he? The thing is: he knew that things were moving. There's Stenson, Oxley, Jormin. An interesting band. Serious business. If someone knows about these things and sees those names, he'll immediately say: 'Shit! What? Oxley with Bobo Stenson? From such different backgrounds but playing together. That's really interesting.' I think it was that combination of musicians that swung it for Manfred. And, also, Bobo telling him how sensational the playing was.

Knowing Manfred, he'll have spoken to Bobo. I know the way he talks: he's supposedly asking about something, about something entirely different, and then he'll suddenly fire a question from out of the blue, about something that really matters to him. He operates a bit sideways-on, supra-rationally, in a practical, half-magical way, like the best musicians.

This is the way musicians get bands together. When I pick people for my band, I don't know straight away how each one of them plays, or how they're going to play together. I'm guided by a certain kind of intuition. I might not know exactly why I've chosen these particular musicians, but then I create the kind of music that develops the people in the band. I soon know who's best at what, what his strongest point is, and I write my music in a way that makes everyone feel as comfortable as possible. I don't write it that way for me to perform my own music. The element of chance that appears in this situation co-creates the structure: everything starts to come together.

Once you'd got the new band together, your return to ECM after a twenty-year break went very smoothly.
It happened pretty quickly after that. I rang Manfred: 'Manfred, how shall I go about getting a recording date finalized with you?' He says, 'What do you mean? Let's just set a date and we're done.' So we set a date, on the phone.

And a year after recording *Bosonossa*, in May 1994 you wrote the material for *Matka Joanna*, which was released in 1995. Did you watch Kawalerowicz's film many times?
That was a film that I'd watched mainly in my youth. I was a film buff in the 1960s. In *Matka Joanna* there was such a strange and beautiful atmosphere. It's lodged in my brain to such an extent that often, even now, when I'm going somewhere, doing something, something clicks in my brain, and it comes back and kind of soaks into me. My whole body practically trembles when I go into this state. Very strong impressions. It's one of the best Polish films. Every shot in that film is important, precise, measured. The acting, the theme, the atmosphere – it's all brilliant.

But why did you give your 1995 album the same title?
When I was recording the album, I didn't have a title, as usual. And, while we were recording, I was chatting with Manfred (who's a film buff). He started out as a film critic. Before his time at ECM, he promoted Jean-Luc Godard in Germany – he's still in touch with him. Manfred filmed something himself not that long ago, just for his own personal use. He was very knowledgeable about Polish cinema, and I mean really very knowledgeable. Manfred, with his penchant for curiosities, rated *Matka Joanna* very highly. It started with me being like the actor Mieczyslaw Voit, according to Manfred.

   We arrived in Oslo for the recordings, and the session went brilliantly. Tony and his different way of playing created contrast in the band, breaking conventions. Everything began to fall into place. On the second day of the recording, I was in a positively euphoric state of mind. Then I met Manfred in a little side room, just next to the main recording room, where you could smoke and relax. I remember him saying to me: 'Do you remember that film *Matka Joanna od Aniołów*?' 'Of course.' 'You are that guy!' I said, 'Oh no,

Manfred!' So we began talking about this film. And then *Matka Joanna* hung over the album. Obviously, music is abstract, and titles for me have a different kind of meaning, definitely not a programmatic one. They're a way of describing my personality, my spiritual state, the time in which I find myself. *Matka Joanna* appears here because the atmosphere from the film hovered over the recording, and, at the same time, it's an expression of my admiration for Kawalerowicz's art.

Those vivid filmic track titles on the album – 'Monastery in the Dark', 'Nuns' – they were chosen for music that had already been composed: they weren't themes for improvisation, were they?
We agreed the titles while putting it together. I like sorting out things like that with Manfred. He's a Renaissance man with a very open mind. We get on brilliantly with our joint improvisations, as you might call them. When I'm working with a chap like Eicher, I'd be a fool not to take advantage of it, not to swim along with him for a while. I've seen how he responds, how he operates: he aims high, this guy. There's no other producer quite like Manfred. He has all the attributes. He knows about the market, how business works, and at the same time he's a thoroughbred artist.

Producers have yet to become like him: he's a precursor. Producers used to be one-dimensional: they'd know either about business or music.

What other titles has Eicher thought up for your ECM recordings?
Lots. Most of them. He thought up *Soul of Things. Suspended Night*. He has a knack for it. He feels the atmosphere of the music. We feel good together.

Let me put it a different way. If I play a specific chord – *dam, dam* – well, if I give it to Marcin Wasilewski, I don't tell him how he should play it, because he's a pianist and he knows how to modify it, how to broaden it out, how to arrange it on the keyboard – in what configurations and inversions. It's the same with the albums. I record my mood, my music, but Manfred, who's produced thousands of records and has titles rattling around in his head, will find a better name for that music. I wholeheartedly agree with his artistic conception and his production process. I like the way in which he grasps the abstract within music. I'm delighted to be able to use him, as I do Marcin, to enrich my output.

It's my music, my creation. Everything is mine, but I'm an improvisor. I work with people, and, ultimately, they're the ones who pin that music down for me. A conscious and deliberate decision.

How did you choose the stills from Kawalerowicz's film that you used on the album cover?
I got the stills of the film and permission to publish, and Manfred chose the photos for the cover.

And on the back he placed a photo of a deranged Voit, wielding an axe. A very suggestive still.

Ah! Yes. Brand at the height of his madness.

But, just like Brand in that still, you also sometimes went around carrying sharp implements. Did you ever use them?

That's how it was when I was going through my difficult period, when Małgosia used to tremble in fear as I tied that headscarf around my head. I'd put my hat on, don some elegant clothes. I'd put some knives in my pocket, take a spear with me, which I'd have made out of a bamboo walking stick, and I'd go out on the town. The knives would be sticking out of my pocket. I had a couple of kitchen knives. I'd take the nice-looking ones. I didn't carry them with a view to using them. I wouldn't know how to, would I? That was my trip.

Wasn't Eicher's comparison between you and Voit in that diabolical role – he actually underlined the association with that particular still – some sort of comment on that diabolical period of your life?

I don't think so. Definitely not, because he didn't know that much about my life. It doesn't prove anything. At all. It was just an image. What mattered was that he loved that film and I loved that film. That gave the album some spirit. Manfred doesn't get involved in the musicians' private lives: he's not interested in that. He has a gift for knowing everything about people, but it doesn't influence his decisions – the only thing that counts is artistic merit.

Berendt once said to you that it was time you were reborn. I thought that Eicher's comment was not dissimilar.

Manfred's not like that. Berendt meant it as friendly advice, but let me tell you: I prefer Manfred's approach. He only works with great people, and each person knows what he or she has to do: they don't need advice. Do you think I took what Berendt said to heart? No way! Only my decision mattered. Not what my girlfriends or therapists said. We have to sort out all the matters in our lives ourselves. Of course, we do need help from other people – and those who do help are wonderful – but, essentially, we have to figure it out for ourselves.

Manfred is certainly a compassionate person. All the little things that I've noticed during our times together have led to my deep admiration for him as a person. He's a very important person in my life.

We've already talked about the influence that Lautréamont's poetry has had on you and about the wisdom of Isidore Ducasse, but I'd just like to ask you about a certain piece from this area of inspiration. 'Maldoror's War Song.' You recorded it both on *Bosanossa* and on *Matka Joanna*. Why 'Maldoror's War Song' in particular?

That's what I called it. I had a composition, 'War Song', and at some point I called it 'Maldoror's War Song', and it stuck. As you know, I have a very odd approach to titles; in fact, you might even call it careless. That initially came through negligence, through my stoned nonchalance. But Ducasse kept following me around. When I read about Maldoror, who sits there covered in moss and cruelty, it felt right. I associated that with 'War Song'. One day I put the two together.

I did wonder whether it might be a war song that you perform when you go to war with yourself?
Maybe. A little bit, yes. I came out of my addictions in a specific way. I'd have this moment of agitation during a hangover, when I'd be chemically unstable, especially after the first two days of giving up alcohol. I'd be overcome by a kind of aggression mixed with hypersensitivity, and this aggression would be bursting out of me. I thought I'd pass it onto my hatred of addictions, personify addictions in a poetic way, save an image in my brain and unleash the whole of my aggression onto that devil. I'd imagine that alcohol was the devil, and that I'm fucking ripping out his horns with my hands. I'd feel his bones crunching! And I'd walk around here, in the park in front of my house. And I'd imagine myself ripping out his tail. And the bones! And the flesh! I'm breaking his legs! His claws! As for marijuana: that was the moss, the slimy ropes that had entangled themselves around Maldoror's legs. And I'd rip that out as well. Wrench it out!

Well, I'm a fucked-up cat, no doubt about it. But I do think that those kinds of images, those personifications, really helped me through therapy. That was my idea. In this way, I made use of the knowledge that I had about myself, my vices, my states, my aggression, which is always there after alcohol. When you're coming out of an alcohol addiction, for the first two days, you're so pissed off, you'd tear everyone apart, kill them; so I'd tear my addictions apart. The brain remembers everything: those unusually powerful states, the hatred. Others suppress it, because they actually love whatever it is they're not supposed to have; but I did the opposite: I made myself hate it.

And then I'd throw the shit out. All those years! Right here; I'd throw the dope out the window. No dope addict throws dope away; but I did.

Was Matka Joanna the first session when you didn't smoke dope?
One of the first, elementary techniques I used when coming off dope was to stop smoking in situations in which I most liked to smoke – in other words, while playing. At one time, when Vesala and I arrived at a gig, the first thing we'd do was go and see what the joint was like, to find out whether we'd be able to light up just before going out on stage. And I did that for years.

Once I'd made the decision to come out of all of that, I decided to start with the hardest thing. I knew that dope didn't affect my work. I didn't believe that it increased my talent. At the ECM sessions I already had a routine going where there was no question of smoking. Those things were important to me, and I wanted to be completely sober.

And, in January 1996, you recorded yet another album for ECM with that line-up: *Leosia*.

According to both Manfred and me, that's the best album from that quartet. But it went unnoticed, although it did get very good reviews. It came out just before *Litania* and that overshadowed it.

In the British reference book *The Penguin Guide to Jazz on CD*, which has already run to seven editions and is the oracle for many jazz fans, *Leosia* has been given a crown, in other words the highest distinction, awarded to only a few dozen albums in the entire history of jazz, albums like *Kind of Blue*, *A Love Supreme* or *Astigmatic*. It is regarded as one of the most important jazz records of the 1990s.

Well, it is. It's a refined thing in terms of composition. There are excellent compositions on it: 'Morning Heavy Song', 'Die Weisheit' and 'Farewell' – a different thing altogether, as it's from a film. My Polish quartet, they're a fabulous band, but they're children, who got their wings with me. How they develop remains to be seen.

But working in *that* quartet, there were four mature, exceptional artists. Tony Oxley, a huge personality: painter, composer and charismatic drummer. Bobo Stenson, who, let's just say, underpins ECM: his trio was one of their first records. He co-created Garbarek's famous quartet. He has his own touch, unlike anyone else's in the world. Anders Jormin, who is regarded as one of the greatest double-bass players, because few have that combination of virtuosic technique and personal language. So, it's hardly surprising that, after many years of playing together, when we recorded another album, it turned out to be exceptional. It *is* exceptional.

Was that particular session exceptional as well?

To be honest, I don't remember that session. It was a routine one, professional. Not particularly exciting.

But you did dedicate the record to your mother, just after she died, didn't you?

We recorded it just after my mother died, but I keep these things separate: they don't have that much influence on my music. That death did affect me, because I was closest to my mother, but she was eighty-three; it was only natural. Obviously, I named the record after my mother, but it was essentially a stable, emotionally balanced recording.

People interpret the album in different ways. I was amused by one of the reviews on Amazon. It refers to a gloomy, Slavic style, which is, I quote: 'darker than the darkest Miles'.

I am dark! Let everyone listen in their own way. I'll give you one example from my own life. When Joaśka and I were splitting up, we got back together for a while and we listened to music: Stevie Wonder, let's say. Well, the way she heard him was incredibly joyful: for her he was synonymous with optimistic music. But I found his music unbelievably depressing; its beauty came from its sadness. Then I thought to myself: 'Isn't the abstractness of music wonderful, that each one of us perceives it differently.' Nothing's black and white! I nurture that awareness within me: to me it's a positive phenomenon. Some people might experience that music just as a buzzing sound, while others will be drawn in by its heavy feeling, and my depressive states will start to affect them.

A critic from the popular music website *All Music* suggests, in turn, that 'Morning Heavy Song', the opening track on *Leosia*, should be called 'Morning Suicide Song'.

It is heavy stuff. 'Heavy' – I did write that, after all. And yet Bobo, who is such a naturally cheery person with a joyful approach to music, to life, loves playing that piece. 'Morning Heavy Song' is his favourite composition. You see how it goes. To me that's terrific. That's a victory for me, the fact that my music can be experienced in such different ways, that I affect each person differently.

24 Thoughts on Simplicity

Let's just go back for a minute to the film *Mother Joan of the Angels*. You could say that it's a story about the power of suppressed passions, which fester and explode.

That might even be its main message. But I find the intensity of the characters' experiences more interesting than the passion that gave rise to them. The intensity and the kind of distortions that it caused interested me the most. Those nuances. Like the beetles in Lautréamont. It's just a meaningless episode in his life, after all. What's more important is his literature, his writing technique. But the beetles? And yet I was really taken with that. I like details like that. I learn a lot about the world, looking at things sideways on, observing the nuances.

And have you been driven by a passion of any kind throughout your life?
I haven't been driven by passion throughout my life. I've been driven by life throughout my life. The fact that I'm alive and that I want to live. That drives me. I like to look around me. I'm hugely fascinated by the richness of life. That's why I like New York so much. There are so many people there on the streets! All so different! It's wonderful that evolution has created such richness.

I'm reminded of a popular science film: one of the hypotheses about our ancestors, the first hairless monkey. In it there was a visualization of a pack of hominids. A terrifying wilderness, with the herd racing through at such fuckin' speed that we can see their superhuman strength and stamina. Despite appearances to the contrary, it's strength and stamina that have been our most important traits. We'd run our victim to exhaustion. And then we'd eat it. On a sign from the chief, the strongest one – *Arrrr!* – the pack would attack the victim and tear it apart. The bastards leaning in, after running such a long way after one animal. You could see it all on the chief's face as he gave the sign to the pack. That film had a terrible effect on me: that cruel, flat wilderness, and that predatory pack, our forefathers.

I'm reminded of that now when I see such a multitude of different people on the streets of New York. We've all come from that: all that diversity! Such richness! So many people, so many things! I'm really glad that I'm an improviser, because it's not logic that dictates to me what I should reach for, where I should turn, but improvisation.

We can take more in as a result of improvisation?

More, because then we operate by chance. And chance: that's me. It's me who decides. My personality has been formed right from the very beginning by assorted van Goghs and Cézannes. Another reason why New York is so important to me is that I can walk across Central Park and go to the Metropolitan Museum, to the Neue Galerie. I have to go somewhere like that to work seriously and systematically on a new programme. I'll stand in front of my beloved nude by Modigliani. I mean, Modigliani led the same kind of life as I did. And that contradiction, that he died just as his career was taking off. I'll stand in front of that nude. I'll soak it up. I'll say: 'Fuckin' give it to me!' I'll hum whatever I like to myself. The vibrations will come, and that strange unreal state of a waking dream.

Is this you talking about composing for the quintet's new album?

Yes. That's how I do it. That's how I live. There's a huge contradiction there. Because I'm a person who wears slippers, a realist, who very coldly, without passion, you might say, analyses certain things. And, at the same time, I'm a manic depressive. I know how to induce mania at will. I just go and stand in front of that picture and it's difficult for me *not* to induce mania. The endorphins come flooding over me. I'm high. Crude and simple. It's like putting the ingredients together to make salsa. The way you make food, that's how I form my own psyche.

You might say that you've learned how to harness your mania.

I harness my personality.

And I was just about to bring up this story, which makes an excellent conclusion to our theme of how art – music in particular – can form our psyches. It's something from the war diaries of Michał Choromański, a writer who had an exceptional ear and who, incidentally, was a mate of Witkacy. During the siege of Warsaw in 1939, he met a composer in the street who before the war had been a known avant-gardist, a man who was forever talking about 'Schönberg! Schönberg!' Choromański recalled seeing him take refuge in a doorway during an air raid, yelling, 'Mozart! Mozart!' I was wondering whether – when you renewed your association with ECM, after your 'diabolical' experiences – you might have had a similar moment in your life. Your music has become more nostalgic and subdued; since *Litania*, it's been more 'Mozart'.

I don't think so. My approach in general is to go with the conventions. My music remains homogenous in its melodiousness and its mood, but it changes according to who I'm playing with. For me it's a kind of creative technique: when I work with the ECM label, I play within its conventions, which appeal to me a lot. That's probably also a result of the fact that I have a wide range: I can transcend differences and view the music from above. If I hear something that has value, I can switch my attention within a fraction of a second and enter into that convention, pick up its value. To me it's a natural process. When I played with the Turkish flautist Kudsi Erguner, I immediately picked up on his particular quality and I blended in with it. He's a strange character, but I immediately felt the beauty of his playing.

Where did you play with Erguner?
In Lebanon, at a festival in Beirut. In the second half of the 1980s. At a workshop in Germany, I met a musician, a drummer from Hamburg who played with Erguner. They invited me to join them on a project where they had Turkish musicians and jazz musicians playing. There were a few French musicians, me and the drummer from Hamburg – I don't remember his name. The music was Turkish, composed by Erguner. Trance music, but Turkish musicians play Sufi trance in their own way. I found their stuff difficult to play: I remember going wrong. That's one thing, but I instantly recognized the value of their music. What the story was, what they were playing with, what kind of trip they were on. Beautiful music, totally different.

Going back to Choromański's anecdote, you might say then that ECM's particular aesthetic, which you picked up, has as much to do with your roots in hot free jazz playing as Mozart has to do with Schönberg.
I wouldn't categorize it so much. To me, Manfred's vision is about values that are far removed from just being cool. It contains thousands of diverse elements. Obviously, he has his own aesthetic, which has been formed through the prism of films, a sensitivity to detail and a refined approach. The fact that he's been holding his own for years, that he's able to sell artistic music, that too has value. A critic can play at judging such things, but I don't want to.

All the same, it does make you think when you read what a specialist and authority such as Berendt wrote about the ECM aesthetic. He referred to it in a text where he'd already gone in all guns blazing with the title 'Jazz and the New Fascism'. This was aimed, among other things, at the musical aesthetic of ECM stars Keith Jarrett and Chick Corea, who he snidely referred to as the 'new romantics'. Using them as an example, Berendt lamented the fact that the key word in 1970s jazz had become 'beauty'. He declared that he wasn't opposing beauty and harmony as such, but the fixation with them. He stated that it was a short step from aestheticism to fascism, and he referred to the message in the films of Visconti and Bertolucci.
Berendt and Eicher did not like each other. You see, that's life. Two strong, charismatic individuals start forming their opinions, I think, through a prism of competition.

A conflict of power over people's souls?
Yes. Competition between pack leaders. This affects their judgement. What does it prove? It proves that there is no objective opinion. They're all subjective. None of these things are certain and objective. But Berendt's statement is a

wise one: there's some truth in it. ECM does promote what's 'lovely'. That's Eicher, who has his own vision of pure beauty, a vision of the purity of art. That's his aesthetic and that's how he makes his choices.

As a counterpoint to the fixation with beauty, Berendt namechecked artists whom you hold dear: Schönberg, Stravinsky, Kandinsky, Picasso, Kafka, Joyce.
That's true. I'm not that keen on Picasso. Because of his coldness. I wouldn't stand in front of him to compose. I prefer Modigliani, who wrung his pictures out of his pain.

You've often stressed that the dirty and coarsely lyrical sound of African-American musicians makes a huge impression on you.
Black music is passionate. I like the incredible depth of the blues.

From the blues, you can naturally go into playing free, into atonality.
That's the miracle of consequences, of changes. One extreme can cross over to its opposite. Hot Black free playing led to Peter Brötzmann, who's a cold motherfucker, to the English, who play structures that they've drawn up in cold blood. It started with Coleman Hawkins, Don Byas, that kind of smoky, beautifully high stuff, and from there the music went to Coltrane and Ayler; and all European free jazz comes from them. Jazz from the Ruhr Valley is totally different, because the technical side of their playing appealed to the Europeans. A different set of values appeared.

The young Garbarek also started off in the Albert Ayler free vein, but later went into an aesthetic that was practically New Age.
That's his direction. Similar to mine. I like that too. There's something in me that makes me like photo frames, for instance. One of my girlfriends used to tease me about how I wanted to put everything in those frames. My home is pedantically organized, yet I'm a devil. A contradiction. But that's how I am.

Have you ever wondered where such a turnabout in aesthetics comes from?
No, I don't give it any thought. It's irrelevant. Krzysztof Penderecki also took that direction, from avant-garde to monumental compositions that are more communicative. Yet others develop in the opposite direction, like Wayne Shorter, or they do the same thing all the time, like Ornette or Cecil. It's often determined by chance. The aesthetic might be different, each to his own. What matters is consistency.

And what do you prefer listening to: Mozart or Schönberg?
I enjoy listening to both Mozart and Schönberg equally. I like Webern's cold, mathematical structures: he's more Schönberg than Schönberg. I love playing his music when I'm practising. It's the same with Ives. I put a piece on and I play along with the record.

It is striking, however, that, as your collaboration with ECM has developed, your music has become more relaxing.

Above all, it's become more communicative. These days, art has to take the audience's views into account, which isn't a bad thing at all. It's perfectly normal that an artist should be able to live off his work. To me, the ideal composition is one that speaks to everyone. The sophisticated listener will catch the nuances, while a different listener will come to my concerts because he likes my hat. That's the ideal of art. I don't want to force it. I want to know about it, and I want that knowledge to accumulate within me. During *Leosia*, Manfred said that it had gone well and that it would be worth recording Komeda's music. I said, 'Terrific!' My first thought was that this would give me an excuse to perform rhythmic music. So that was the outcome: first of all there were two records of free, then *Litania*, where there are some beautiful, lyrical versions of the simplest of waltzes, which were later recorded in quartet form. I'm moving forward. I'd like to go in a melodic, rhythmic and simple direction. This is my path to simplicity. It's what my return to ECM is all about.

Might one say that you willingly subjugated your conceptions to the rigour that comes of the ECM aesthetic?

It's not like that. I haven't applied any rigour. I've made the most of the greatness and the charisma of this record label. The idea of simplicity, of the communicative nature of music that kept going around in my head, was able to germinate in that ground, and it's now grown into a beautiful tree. I didn't want to force anything myself. If I act consciously, then I'm Tomasz Stańko, but, if not, then I'm evolution's final link: my brain has half a billion years' worth of evolution operating inside it. I'd prefer that to direct my life. As for consciousness . . . if it could just set that half a billion years of evolution on the right path, not through chaos. To synchronize those two elements and use both of them – that's what I want. It sounds serious, but it's no great theory. The same kind of knowledge as the one telling us we should drink out of a cup. All my philosophical thoughts are just little snippets of knowledge that I treat in a utilitarian way, so there's no pathos in them. Pathos can ruin such thoughts within a fraction of a second because they appear trivial, but if we use them they don't. Life verifies that knowledge.

Did Eicher float the idea of *Litania* while you were recording *Leosia*?

Yes, and I realized straight away that it was going to be interesting. I was going to be able to move closer to more conventional music, because of course Komeda's old ballads are rhythmical and beautiful with their Komeda-like melodiousness. Right away, I immediately picked up the essence of the project.

So Komeda's music created a bridge which enabled you to cross over to more traditional playing?

Yes. Definitely.

During those thirty years that separate your actually playing with Komeda from *Litania*, did you often go back to his music?

No. In fact, I didn't go back at all. I just played 'Kattorna'. We played it all the time in all sorts of combinations, all of us Polish musicians. In the quintet we played 'The Witch'. With Makowicz and Vesala, I didn't go back to Komeda. It was only because of Manfred's commission that I returned to the past.

Around the time you were playing with the musicians from Marcin Wasilewski's Simple Acoustic Trio (we're talking about 1995 here), they released their own album, *Komeda*, on which they played his music.

I didn't know about that. I only played Komeda with them after *Litania* had been released.

What did you start with when you were putting the record together?

With the choice of pieces. I basically knew that I wanted to play 'Svantetic' and 'Requiem' because those are Komeda's most mature compositions. There were those two big things. Oh, and I also had a few ballads: 'The Witch', 'Ballad for Bernt' and 'Moja ballada' ('My Ballad'). I was also thinking about 'Sophia's Tune' because he really loved that piece, but we didn't play it in the end.

After all those years, when you listened back to that music, did you notice anything new?

I didn't listen to the music. I had it written down. I got sheet music made up. Young Wojciech Majewski, the pianist, Henryk Majewski's son, wrote down the music. I remember something else . . . One time I was listening to some Komeda recordings with Marcin Wasilewski. Marcin was listening objectively, like a person from a different world; and he declared that Komeda's playing was the best. Komeda underestimated himself. After all those years, it turns out that his playing was the most pure. My playing was weird, but his playing, the bastard, was the purest, because he played sparsely. He was good. And yet he had hang-ups as a pianist.

You mentioned not long ago that, years later, Komeda reminded you of Andrew Hill.

Very much so. Because of the compositions. I think that Komeda, with his particular harmonic sense, was similar to Hill. Both of them suit our contemporary times. They were both able to write in interesting, unusual ways.

How did the septet line-up for *Litania* come about?

I wanted Bernt Rosengren, and Joakim Milder turned up at the same time. He was recording for ECM with Palle Danielsson. Manfred knew him and rated him. So I was happy to take Milder on. I also took Palle. Palle and Jon Christensen made up the rhythm section. There was also Terje Rypdal: his guitar sound suited the whole thing. A very good line-up.

Getting ready for the *Litania* concert in the TVP (Polish Television) studio in the Łęg district of Kraków, 1998. (On double bass: Palle Danielsson; on trumpet: Tomasz Stańko. To his right on drums: Jon Christensen; on saxophone: Joakim Milder.)

Photograph by Rafał Garszczyński

You specifically wanted Rosengren, as he was the eponymous hero of one of the pieces. He'd recorded 'Ballad for Bernt' with Komeda for *Knife in the Water* in 1961. On *Litania* he played the same theme thirty-five years later. He must have been a completely different person by then.

He didn't remember the recording with Komeda. For him that had been one of many jobs. He'd come over to Poland, played *Knife in the Water*, and left. For us that had been an event. We used to listen to that little record. To me that had been an exceptional record, and it was because of it that I'd remembered Rosengren's tone. He might not even have known that the record existed. He played brilliantly on *Litania*. He was in excellent form, because he'd been playing throughout all that time.

How did the actual session go?
Manfred didn't even touch the arrangement. He went with the unusual idea (during the actual recording session) of putting three versions of 'Rosemary's Baby' on the album. The improvisatory way in which Manfred works is interesting as well. Once we'd recorded the big pieces, and there was still time to spare, he let us play different combinations of the motif. I played it with Bobo first; the second version was with Rypdal; and the third one, the rhythmic one, made an excellent ending to the whole – it was a return to tradition.

During the time when he was working with me, Komeda actually rejected tradition. There was a radio session where we were recording 'Ballada', and he didn't want to play rhythmically anymore, just free, ad lib. Whereas me, I liked the older pieces, the beautiful ones. I liked the traditional in Komeda; that's why I often return to it.

We also played the *Litania* theme a few times. There were a few versions, and we chose one of them for the album. That came naturally. The idea was to set up a different solo each time – if Bernt's playing, I'm not. The final decisions were made during the editing and mixing. That's the time when you balance everything out. It's the final touch, establishing the endings. It was the nuances that decided on the running order. A very agreeable part of the recording process.

Anyway, the album ended up having a marked contrast between the large-scale, dramatic compositions and the ballads. And that contrast was mine, not Komeda's anymore. Something I like, and that I've always stressed – that *ta ra ra ra ra* – that little melody from *Rosemary's Baby* played as simply as possible. Komeda would never have played it as simply as that. And then, added to that, 'Svantetic', which is a heavy, tiring beast, based on one triad, three notes: *ta da ra, ta da ra dee dee dee doo da*.

Contrast, again. From what you say, it would appear that you regard *Litania* as very much your own record.
I regard it as my own, very personal record. During the last few years, I really have been like one organism with Komeda. I've identified incredibly closely

Litania in the TVP (Polish Television) studio in the Łęg district of Kraków. To the left, next to Tomasz Stańko, Bernt Rosengren; at the piano Bobo Stenson.
Photograph by Rafał Garszczyński

with him in an artistic sense. I don't put any restrictions on myself with regard to changing some of his things. I change what I want, just as I might change my own music, but I make the changes within his spirit, or within the spirit that we created together as a quintet.

I've always put the musical whole above myself. Jazz is a soloist's music, but, just as we had Coltrane, a great virtuoso, who mainly played solos but did have his own band, so we also had Miles, who invested in other people and, on occasion, played very little himself. And I think that was a great strength of Miles's and took him to such heights. We jazz musicians are composers, but at the same time we play. Maybe classical music is so powerful because there are two roles there: composer and performer. So the composer will write differently because the performer has a tendency to show off his virtuosic talents. I really liked those types of combinations in jazz. I once wrote a piece called 'Perła' ('Pearl'), just for drums. Michał Miśkiewicz played it solo.

For Eicher, *Litania* was a producer's jackpot.
A producer's jackpot, and it essentially turned out like that purely by chance. That's what this is all about.

That album was your first international bestseller.
We all knew, as soon as we'd finished playing. It just came out. You can't plan these things.

Do you think the context around Komeda's persona helped?
It's a strange business, because no one knew Komeda. They got to know him after I'd performed him, and it was only then that they got to appreciate him. Komeda died young and he dropped out of the jazz scene, a scene he'd never got very far in. We just didn't play that many concerts. Komeda was mainly a composer of film music. On ECM's and Manfred's recommendation, I presented a kind of small anthology of his wonderful music. The critics picked up on the fact that Komeda had been this exceptional person in Poland, someone hired by Polański, and someone whose Hollywood career had been interrupted by a tragically premature death. It's a very media-worthy story. All these factors added together was why the record was so successful.

Was that a breakthrough in your career?
Nothing dramatic happened. This is jazz, not pop. But there's no doubt that *Litania* propelled me forward.

Did you play many concerts with the septet?
There was an ECM-arranged tour – as a sextet: Rypdal didn't play with us – Germany, Switzerland, a festival in Nancy in France. A few nice, big bookings.

You also played the *Litania* programme with Billy Harper.
That was later. Harper joined the quartet in New York. The next wave of playing *Litania* was concerts with the Polish quartet and assorted saxophonists. In Vienna I played with Gianluigi Trovesi. In Poland I did a concert with Louis Sclavis, who also played bass clarinet. In the States Harper played tenor and soprano.

Completely different personalities: each of them representing different traditions.
They played differently. Harper was *fabulous*!

He's a saxophonist from the old Coltrane school.
And that school's close to Komeda. Harper suited it perfectly. A masterly choice. I'd initially thought of Joe Lovano. He wanted to play but he couldn't: he already had his own gigs lined up. Someone suggested Harper to me. I think it was Piotr Wojtasik's idea! It wouldn't have occurred to me.

Harper's an excellent saxophonist, but I think he's somewhat forgotten these days.
It's difficult to say whether he's been forgotten or not. Life moves at a fast pace. Sometimes we get tired. I'm envious of painters who can just set up

their easels and paint. I have to do battle all the time. You can't just stand up on stage and play. Belligerence gives you claws, which make the music more dramatic, stronger.

So was it Billy Harper in the end, with his classic Black sound, who turned out to be the best interpreter of Komeda, out of that whole galaxy of star saxophonists you played with?
I can't say that. I was very surprised at how strangely Trovesi played. Sclavis, with his French *esprit* was also remarkable. Harper's playing was masculine, tough: he wasn't worried about nuances. The way he played 'Knife in the Water'! I don't know how he approached it. To me he was wonderful. I've also played Komeda with Adam Pierończyk, an excellent, powerful musician.

After your success with *Litania*, did you have a free hand and an unlimited budget to choose the line-up for your next album? Because that's the impression you get with *From the Green Hill*, which came out in 1999.
I could do anything I wanted, but it's not quite as simple as that. You can buy the best musicians, but that's not enough. Because, if you buy some of the best, you might not have control over them. They'll come and play, but none of them will give their all. You have to be the best in an organizational sense – command respect. A good leader (that's what I think anyway) chooses musicians that he can always have control over. Like Komeda: he ruled without saying a word. It didn't matter who he played with, he didn't have to say anything. You have to have authority, otherwise it's not going to work: it's going to be hard-going. The John Surman and Dino Saluzzi line-up was an excellent one, but I can't have people like that all the time because you have to go on tour afterwards.

Was it difficult to control the band on *Green Hill*?
Difficult on the one hand but, on the other hand, it was session playing and so diverse that we flew together without any problems.

Weren't there any concerts with the band after the album had been released?
We did one tour.

In the case of *Green Hill*, it seems as if the idea for the album came from the actual band line-up.
Yes; Manfred and I decided jointly on the line-up. It started with a concert in Badenweiler. It's a health resort near Lake Constance, where the ECM Festival was being held in a picturesque old hotel. The owner was an interesting man who loved ECM and had given Manfred the run of the hotel. A strange concert hall – not built for opera or for theatre. The auditorium was below, and there were some balconies. We played on these balconies. I was on one, Surman was on another, Michelle Makarski, Dino, Palle and Jon were on some others. Each one of us played on a different level. We just played the one piece together, at the festival opening: 'Litania'. Manfred absolutely loved it. You could say that

he'd got his favourites together so that they'd play him that particular piece. And that's where that line-up came from. Manfred and I discussed it at the time.

The line-up was unusual, rustic, you might say – accordion, clarinet and violin. And that pastoral title as well.
We agreed on that line-up. As for the title, that was to do with *Anne of Green Gables*. An old composition back from when Ania was born. That's how it came together for me. The first time I recorded that piece was back with Vesala on *Almost Green*.

In the melodies on *From the Green Hill*, we can hear East European folk music. Why was it, then, that you had the idea to accentuate that theme in particular?
I don't do these things consciously. They come from within me, naturally. The sound was determined by the line-up.

The 'Stone Ridge' piece is actually a klezmer motif.
That's Surman's composition. He brought it to the studio. We had the time and the space to record it. He wrote it for this particular kind of line-up. He's a modest cat, but he's a good composer.

The folk element is also there in the Latin music. Dino Saluzzi's bandoneon plays a crucial role here.
A beautiful sound! Powerful, dynamic.

From bossa nova to tango, the Latin element keeps cropping up in your music. What thoughts lie behind this penchant for Latin music?
I like South America. I'm drawn to it for some reason. Fado. A particular kind of melancholy. Joy through the tears. Fate, some strange purpose. Like with Borges or Garcia Márquez.

Did Saluzzi, a charismatic Latin musician, make an impression on you?
He doesn't display Latin expressiveness. Rather, he presents himself as a composer. He's a naturally spiritual person. Take, for example, the words he said on that record. About life. With such depth. He has it in him.

The configuration of sounds on *Green Hill*: bandoneon, violin, clarinet – all of that added depth to the lyrical side of your music.
It did.

Since that time, you've never gone back to playing folk. Do you find the tone a bit plaintive?
My path sometimes deviates. I'm aware that these things often border on kitsch, and that you have to be very careful with the lyricism. If you overdo it just a teensy bit, then right away you'll have a tapestry with a rutting stag,

and everything will fall into an abyss of kitsch. Polish lyricism borders on the extreme. Those willows . . . I like the masculine approach of other cultures, Anglo-Saxon or Black, while we have a hysterical approach. Either weeping or fighting. We have that Somosierra* thing in us. Maybe it's because of our climate that we're like that, or our history. It's as well to be aware of it, to stop us from descending into kitsch.

You later occasionally played with the accordion group Motion Trio.
Yes, but that was due to something else altogether. It was the music to Michał Rosa's film *Cisza* ['Silence'], and the director suggested that some of it be done on accordion. Motion Trio are a very serious band. We played a few concerts together after that – their music, and I added my commentaries. They came out really well. They're good musicians.

How did your collaboration go with those leading Polish exponents of ancient music, Marcin Bornus-Szczyciński and Tadeusz Czechak?
I played with Czechak at a festival in Nowy Sącz. It was like music of the troubadours. And I performed with Szczyciński's vocal group in the cathedral in Toruń. They sang Gregorian chants with some added trumpet improvisation. I think the reason they asked me to do it was because of the success of Garbarek's *Officium*. I used to get offered those kinds of commissions. I'd take them on. We'd play. And now I'm about to go off to do a strange gig with some folk singers: lullabies. I like things like that. As an improvisor, I feel comfortable with that sort of thing, and I enjoy playing it.

Did you play with the chamber orchestra AUKSO on the same principle?
Yes. Those were all concert situations. We played some of my music as arranged by Wojciech Karolak. Milder arranged Komeda's pieces for AUKSO.

You've also recorded some of Wojciech Kilar's compositions.
That was a recording with Anna Maria Jopek. She asked me.

Have you ever considered doing another album with Dino Saluzzi?
I had considered the following line-up: Saluzzi, Anja Lechner, plus organ, so I could compose some classical pieces. But it blows over. These are passing ideas. The speculation alone develops me. It exercises my mind.

---

* *Translator's note:* A Polish symbol of patriotic struggle, desperate bravery and bravado. The Battle of Somosierra took place in 1808 during the Napoleonic Wars, when Polish cavalry fought on the side of the Napoleonic forces. It was allegedly due to their bravery that Napoleon's forces prevailed.

25 Theme for Trumpet

In the 1990s, at the same time as you were recording your ECM projects, you began composing quite a bit for film and theatre. How did this come about?
I don't have any control over that sort of thing. I don't seek these things out. The offers just arrive and, undoubtedly, they're linked to how active I am. When my market position is high, directors remember that I exist, and they'll periodically approach me with those kinds of offers.

When you're preparing to compose music for a film, do you have to see it first?
I have to know about it, to have at least heard the story, not necessarily seen it. Meeting the director is important. When a director tells me about his film, I intuitively know how strong it is. Sometimes, I actually prefer not to see the film. The director's conscious decision is important, as well as his expectations. They draw the music out of me, even subconsciously. That's how I wrote for *The Master and Margarita*: an animated film by Mariusz Wilczyński. I just pulled the motifs out of my hat. I was supposed to write two motifs: the day and the night of the devil. Mariusz wanted to have the music in advance, to help him with the drawing.

You've worked with Mariusz Wilczyński a lot. You've made a few films together.
We're still collaborating. We're in constant contact.

The first time you met Wilczyński was for a film called *From the Green Hill*.
That was a video he made me for my album. I wanted to have a video. Stanisław Soyka recommended him to me. I was popular among media people at the time. I was trying to break the stereotype I had acquired, but it didn't really come off. It was more of an artistic undertaking than a promotional one. In the end, they didn't even show it on TV. It was a rather unusual thing.

And then you took part in Wilczyński's film *Szop, Szop, Szop, Szopę* ['Chop, Chop, Chop, Chopin']. It was intended as an attempt to demythologize Chopin. His music was interpreted by you, Michał Urbaniak and Justyna Steczkowska.
I don't remember that. I probably played a solo or something.

Which director was the best storyteller?

They all told their stories well. I'll always remember Andrzej Domalik. I recorded the music for *Terminal 7* for him. You can still see the play at the Polish National Theatre, on the Small Stage.

Do you see a difference between the way you work on film music and music for theatre?

I treat them the same. I write motifs. My speciality is evoking a certain atmosphere, a mood through music, which plunges an individual deep into a particular state. That's how I see the role of music. It leads people into a certain state. Music of a high quality induces a state, which is difficult to define as either cheerful or sad, because what matters is the depth of the experience.

Your intensive film period began with recordings for *Damage* in 1993. Was recording for Louis Malle a breakthrough of some sort? Maybe that's when directors started remembering you?

I don't think so. The music was Zbigniew Preisner's. I just played the trumpet. My name wasn't even in the opening credits.

You then went and recorded a Hollywood soundtrack with Preisner: *When a Man Loves a Woman*.

Yes. We recorded it in Poland. His compositions.

While we're talking about film, you also collaborated with Jan Kanty Pawluśkiewicz. This was on Feliks Falk's 1984 film *Idol*.

Maybe I recorded something for Pawluśkiewicz. I might have done.

And which of these film sessions turned out to be the most important one for you?

For me the most important one was *Pożegnanie z Marią* ['A Farewell to Maria'], a recording for Filip Zylber. That was excellent music. I got an award for it at the festival in Gdynia. I'm still playing it. I recorded 'Love Theme' on *Green Hill*. That's an old piece from back in the 1970s. I wrote it during the time I was playing with Adam Makowicz. It used to be called 'Gama'. The music to Andrzej Domalik's film *Łóżko Wierszynina* ['Wierszynin's Bed'] was important as well. That's when I wrote the ballads that I later played with the quartet, over a long time and very well.

How did the work on *A Farewell to Maria* go?

I watched the film, and I made the music specifically fit the image. There were a couple of beautiful scenes in it. The scene in the church. Zylber is a very talented director. I also composed the music for his *Egzekutor* ['The Executor'].

What about writing for action films? I'm thinking about Władysław Pasikowski's *Reich*. He was famous at the time for being the hard man of Polish cinema.

He is a hard man, certainly, but we had an excellent collaboration. Pasikowski is a jazz fan. Originally it was meant to be Marcin Pospieszalski composing, but he backed out of it – as far as I can recall – for ethical reasons. He has a very definite outlook on life. He's clear about what he does. Incidentally, he's a brilliant bassist.

And do you remember the music for Bogdan Nowicki's 1981 film *Skazaniec* ['The Condemned Man']? I read about it on the film website filmpolski.pl. A short animated film. The synopsis caught my attention: a condemned man sits in an electric chair and all he can hope for is a power cut. That's an interesting subject for your trumpet.

You know, I can't remember. Maybe I played solo trumpet.

You made quite a few recordings for animated films. That started with some Mirosław Kijowicz films. He's now a legend of Polish animation.

An exceptional figure. I did collaborate with him a bit. I first recorded for him with Komeda; then I wrote my own music for him as a kind of replacement for Komeda. I did three or four films. For *Science Fiction* I even got an award of some sort in Kraków. Kijowicz cared about the music. And, as far as I can remember, I was a bit of a disappointment to him after Komeda. Too bad. He really liked working with Komeda, but I went more with the mood. My music was less illustrative. Komeda had an exceptional talent for writing film music. I'm not a film music composer. I don't put all my effort into it, all my inner passion. It was great working with Kijowicz, but at the time I was more interested in playing with the quintet: pure music.

You also began writing for Andrzej Kondratiuk as a substitute for Komeda on *Klub profesora Tutki* ['Professor Tutka's Club'], and then your music appeared in *Jak zdobyć pieniądze, kobietę i sławę* ['How to Get Money, Women and Fame'], in *Dziura w ziemi* ['Hole in the Ground'] and, years later, in Iga Cembrzyńska's short film *Pamiętnik filmowy Igi C* ['The Film Diary of Iga C'].

We got to know each other well during *Dziura w ziemi*. He's a very interesting character. Whereas I got to know Iga well later on. They made a lovely couple. Expressive people. Kondratiuk put passion into his films. He cared about the music. He'd intervene if he didn't like something.

There are also a few interesting musical films that you took part in. They were made by Andrzej Wasylewski. I had to dig them out of the filmpolski.pl database because, unfortunately, I've never seen them. *Jazz Yatra '78*, for example.

Jazz Yatra was that festival in Mumbai that I went to with Vesala, so that we could get into the Taj Mahal. But what was I actually doing in the film? I remember Wasylewski: he was with us. There was this whole big crew. But I don't remember where he filmed us.

In 1982 Wasylewski made *We'll Remember Train* – reportage from workshops organized by Berendt. Interpretations of Coltrane with his key drummer Rashied Ali taking part.

There was a gig like that. I played with Sławomir Kulpowicz and Leszek Żądło. I'd got back from London with Kulpowicz and we'd gone on to Baden-Baden. We had a great time playing with Rashied. An excellent drummer. He'd played completely free with Coltrane, but on that occasion he played a lot of time.

While we're on the subject of film, I have to ask you about your acting cameos, and what you actually appeared in.

Indeed. I appeared in the film *Poniedziałek* ['Monday']. It was a rare thing, but I did do it.

Whose idea was it?

The director, Witold Adamek, offered it to me. He was making a film with Bolec* at the time. My music's not in it. I'm playing the trumpet as an actor – just a few notes. I was playing myself – a trumpeter.

He was a trumpeter, but a dodgy businessman at the same time.

A dodgy businessman. Yes. I felt strange out there. Before that I'd also acted in one of Maciej Wojtyszko's productions, a Cervantes play, where I had no idea what I was supposed to be doing. I have absolutely no acting talent whatsoever. With that experience behind me, I didn't want to do it, but Adamek persuaded me. He made me too good an offer, I guess. So I did it. Bolec pulled me through it. He used that coarse, slang-like language of his, lots of swearwords, and then I got into it as well. I can remember spending quite an enjoyable day on set. But that was all down to Bolec and Adamek, who'd got it well organized.

Bolec died recently.

Yes. I don't know what happened. He'd had some problems recently with his mental health. He was a sensitive cat. He felt things deeply. You know, life's hard.

You also had a cameo in *Cisza* ['Silence'], a 2001 film by Michał Rosa, which we've already spoken about: a trumpet player in a club.

There is indeed a scene in there with me playing along to club music. I'm pleased with that clip. A cool young fellow, Kuba Ostapkiewicz, created some beats for me and I added the trumpet. I don't know what he's doing now. I absolutely loved those beats. In the film I played alongside a DJ. It was Maceo

---

* *Translator's note:* Grzegorz 'Bolec' Borek (1971–2009) was an actor and rapper and one of the pioneers of Polish hip-hop.

Wyro. Wyro and Envee have a collective – Niewinni Czarodzieje ('Innocent Sorcerers') – and I played some gigs with them for a while. They had their backing tracks, and I played solo. We often had a rhythm section playing with us.

So you stepped into club territory: funk, hip-hop. A set-up like Miles's *Doo-Bop*. Different music, obviously, but that kind of set-up.

Was the idea to record it?
No. It wasn't ready.

You mentioned your role in a Wojtyszko production. In 1989. The production in question was Cervantes's *Theatre of Miracles* at the Television Theatre. How did that debut come about?
Jan Janga-Tomaszewski was in it: an actor who sings and plays the guitar. He's a very interesting guitarist, plays in an unorthodox way. I've played with him on occasion. Anna Maria Jopek used to sing with him. He got me into the Wojtyszko production.

Were you tempted after that to appear in front of the camera?
Absolutely not. I'm not remotely interested in acting.

And can you remember *Nienasycenie* ['Insatiability'] at Warsaw's Wielki Theatre? You also appeared on stage then.
That was a Zofia Rudnicka ballet production. The script was based on Witkacy's *Nienasycenie*, but the music was from the *Peyotl* LP. I gave them a tape. I'd tweaked the recording slightly, especially for the production. At the start, I played solo on stage, setting the mood, and then the ballet production followed to taped music. We did lots of performances.

Do you think the *Peyotl* album was the inspiration for it, seeing as the premiere of the production took place just after its release in 1987?
I think so, but the idea was Rudnicka's. She did the choreography. Wiesław Olko did the stage design. That was an interesting production.

In the 1990s you began composing theatre music as well. That started in 1994 with Rudolf Zioło's *Balladyna* at the Ludowy Theatre in Nowa Huta.
And then I collaborated with Krzysztof Warlikowski for a while. He was looking for a composer at the time, although he didn't really find what he wanted with me, but I found my collaboration with him extremely creative. Warlikowski eventually found Paweł Mykietyn, who suits him perfectly. I do wonder whether he might be the most interesting Polish composer of the young generation.

I remember Warlikowski inviting me to a production at the Dramatyczny Theatre. Mykietyn was on stage playing his music on bass clarinet. I immediately thought, 'Warlikowski has finally found his composer.' Directors like that have a knack with people. When he came to see me, he immediately knew exactly what he wanted. I composed some good music for him for *Roberto Zucco*.

How did the Warlikowski collaboration go?
He came to see me and asked whether I'd like to work with him. He had a serious approach to the matter. He knew what he was after, because he knows a great deal about music, and he was particularly keen to have my dark mood. He told me about *Zucco*. He gave me the text. For this story about a cruel murderer, we agreed I'd write my dark, melancholy and lyrical music. It was a very appropriate choice, because the whole performance boiled down to strange, ephemeral things. It did well in Poznań.

About six months later, I did the music for Warlikowski for a production in Kraków on one of the stages at the Stary Theatre. It didn't go well that time. That Kraków atmosphere, those actors who wouldn't bring his ideas to life . . .

That was the play *Zatrudnimy starego klowna* ['Old Clown Wanted'].
The music was kind of circus-like. We did the recording session in the theatre. I recorded more music than we really needed. Warlikowski added the sound effects to it later. I think he may have had a hard time doing it. He needs a composer who'll sit with him all the time during rehearsals and participate in creating the production. I'm completely unsuited to that: I'll write something to highlight the scene and then disappear.

Where did the idea come from to include 'Blue Velvet' in the *Roberto Zucco* music – a retro hit made popular at the time because of David Lynch's film?
That was Warlikowski's idea.

The theme music was sung by Dorota Miśkiewicz. How come she ended up doing it? That must have been right at the start of her singing career.
I asked her. I knew the Miśkiewicz family. I knew they were brilliant. The whole family lived for music.

You said that your collaboration with Warlikowski was extremely creative.
Warlikowski is the sort of personality who radiates charisma. It's difficult to put into words. You know, when you talk to someone with a personality like that, even a short conversation will enrich you. We talked a lot when I was recording for him in Kraków, about all kinds of things. He had some unusually astute, concise observations about the arts and lots of other things. Good directors are the kind of people who know a lot about everything: they have to have a kind of multi-media-like knowledge. Warlikowski's like that.

You also wrote the music for Camus's *Caligula* at the Witkacy Theatre in Zakopane.

Ah! That's some very good music. I got the commission from Andrzej Dziuk, who I rate very highly. He's built up a real team and he leads them with an iron fist. I've been playing concerts in his theatre for years, with the quartet, with Włodzimierz Kiniorski.

I really enjoyed writing *Caligula*. I asked Dziuk to pick out some scenes for me to illustrate so that I could get down to creating some pure music. It was a professional production: Dziuk hired a studio in Warsaw and sat in at the recording – demanding but at the same time tolerant towards me as the composer. I had a motif in different versions, in different keys – major and minor. I created some space for myself on the trumpet, so I could play what I most enjoyed playing. Lakis (that's Apostolis Anthimos) played percussion instruments, Zbigniew Wegehaupt was on bass, and Marek Napiórkowski on guitar. Dorota Miśkiewicz sang and also played the violin. The music that you can hear on my website actually comes from *Caligula*. I don't play it live, but it's music that's very important to me. I've been meaning to release it on an album for ages.

Why is it so important?

Because it came out well. Minimalistic, very subtle. That's when I started writing trance-like pieces. The music from *Terminal 7* is essentially a continuation of *Caligula*. The difference being that I found playing those pieces tough-going on stage, whereas *Terminal 7* is great to play live.

Terminal 7 is your most recent theatrical production.

Yes. Andrzej Domalik's production. I'd worked with him earlier on *Łóżko Wierszynina*. We're thinking about *Peyotl*. We work really well together. He tells me everything, and he lays out his requirements simply and clearly. He describes the mood in an evocative way, and so I find it easy to work, because I know what he expects. When I was writing *Terminal 7*, I didn't expect to be performing that music at concerts, but now I'm playing two of the themes with the quintet. 'Terminal 7' and 'May Sun', both based on a monotone piano riff. My new bassist fits in with this mood brilliantly. I want to record those pieces on an album.

Do you have any particular approach to composing illustrative music?

No. I like working with motifs. I like to have one or two motifs, so they can take turns, create different moods. One motif's perfectly fine. I've recently taken on my own sound engineer, Sebastian Witkowski. He's even fast catching up with Rafał Paczkowski. He's been doing good trumpet recordings for me since we first started, and he's developing all the time. We'll record in the studio and then we'll edit at my house. I have Pro Tools, good playback equipment, a high-quality reverb unit with different parameters and modulations. I like working with Witkowski at home. Janusz Skowron occasionally comes over and puts something on top. That's how I recorded *Terminal 7* and *The Master and Margarita*.

Your motif work can clearly be heard on the album that GOWI released of the music for *Balladyna*. In fact, there's one motif there that keeps coming back in different versions.
That's right.

I'm now wondering whether you might have used the motif method when you recorded with your quartet. You can hear something along those lines on *Soul of Things* and *Suspended Night*.
It's always there in my music. My music is consistent, and so music written for one purpose will dovetail with and influence another: the music for stage and the illustrative music.

Your first recordings with the quartet musicians were the film sessions. Would you describe it as a kind of workshop for the band?
I took on the musicians. It was all a workshop, and they were great from the start. What's essential is having the skill to play sparsely. Only mature musicians know how to play like that, but by doing film music you can learn that skill. I said to Marcin Wasilewski, 'Don't play so many sounds – a quarter as much. This is film music, not jazz!' And so they did.

Looking at the bands that you made film music recordings with in the mid-1990s, you might conclude that you were on the hunt for a pianist in Poland. On *A Farewell to Maria* you have Leszek Możdżer playing and on *Roberto Zucco* you have Andrzej Jagodziński.
There wasn't any hunting. The decisions arose from the various requirements I had at the time. I had Skowron at the *Zucco* session, and Jagodziński also played a few bits. I needed a pianist with the kind of style that he represents – basically traditional, yet modern at the same time. For 'Blue Velvet', where Dorota Miśkiewicz is singing, I wanted Jagodziński.

And how did it go with Możdżer? He played with you in 1993. That was when he first came on the scene in a big way. He was playing with Miłość, and Jan 'Ptaszyn' Wróblewski and Zbigniew Namysłowski used to take him on.
I got to know him through Miłość because I played a concert with them in Gdynia, in some small club or other quite early on. We played their music.

Your first encounter with the yass wave?
You could say so.

How did that gig come about?

I can't remember. The club owner approached me about the concert. It went well. I liked them. Możdżer, Jacek Olter, Tymon Tymański. I think we played as a quartet.

How did you get on playing Tymański's compositions?

Out of everything Tymański does, I like the way he plays double bass the best. He had a staccato, Mingus-like attack and a particular strength: self-confidence. His technique was a bit artsy, which I really like. He didn't play in a virtuoso-like way: he just brought the bass back to its old function, when it was primarily a rhythm instrument and only a bit melodic. He didn't need harmonic knowledge because his compositions were kind of Monk/Mingus-like. I liked them a lot. I also remember hearing a trio that he was in, along with Maciej Sikała and Jacek Olter. An interesting band. Except Tymański later gave up playing the double bass.

What did you think of the yass scene in general?

I looked at it in two ways. I mean, when I was a youth, I was just like them. I rebelled against the old stuff and wanted to play new music. But, on the other hand, they gave the imposters too much space. It's easy to have imposters in set-ups like that, because you can get away with not having any technique and just playing with power, with expression – making up for it with your words: preaching manifestos. I had so little interest in it that I can't really say anything more about it. If you haven't played with someone, then you don't know anything about them. The yassers were a counterbalance to the Katowice-based mainstreamers, who were becoming increasingly fossilized. And that's why they were undoubtedly a very positive phenomenon. They renewed the music scene and refreshed it.

Did you play with Możdżer much after that?

We played together occasionally. In a quartet, as a duo. He played Komeda with me. We had little projects on the go the whole time. We still play together from time to time. He's a high-class musician. A virtuoso artist.

What did you make of Możdżer's success? He's had the kind of career that's unprecedented in Polish jazz: all at once he acquired pop-star-like status, was all over the media, had best-selling albums. Quite astonishing for someone from our scene.

That's his strength. Quite aside from his talent, what I also appreciate about him is that he's become a figure within popular culture. That's how an artist should be these days. To me that's a really significant, positive thing, and it's precisely because he's been able to strike out and go beyond the jazz niche that I really rate Leszek, and I mean *really* rate him. Because being niche, so it turns out, is just provincialism: confining yourself to your own inner circle makes the art, the higher things, wither away. That's how traditional jazz died out, although there are some people still playing it.

The universalism of jazz does, however, allow for two possible paths. One of these is represented by, say, your New York friend Craig Taborn, who knows how to play with hip-hop artists, who's open to avant-garde electronica, who plays roots music and mainstream. As brilliant and modern a jazz musician as they come. Whereas Możdżer, for me, is an example of the second path. The one where there's a danger that, by going further, jazz evolves to such an extent that it stops being jazz. I don't even mean that it necessarily becomes easier, but that its sound gets smoothed out into the mould of pop.
Możdżer has gone for virtuosity. He presents himself as a virtuoso who does what he wants with the piano. He's an unconventional character, that's for sure: he manages to thrive in all kinds of situations.

But what can you say about an album like *The Time*, which generated a lot of noise when it was released? Covers of hits, oriental touches, a mystical haze. That record sounded like New Age, not like jazz.
I can remember Tony Oxley laughing at Herbie Hancock and the rest of them. I don't want to judge music. The older I get, the less I want to hang on to fixed views. Yesterday, I found out from a doctor that she doesn't believe in the theory of evolution. And because she was an intelligent woman, I thought: 'Shit! I'm going to have to give this some thought, because it could just be that nothing in this life is certain.'
   I like musicians to be active. I will always have a soft spot for Leszek. I don't know his music well enough to be able to talk about it. Nor do I know Lars Danielsson's music, but I think very highly of what he does. People like that have my respect. The same goes for Jarosław Śmietana, who's an active sort of guy, who doesn't complain: he just gets on with his thing, one project after another. An excellent guitarist, as a matter of fact – he's very highly thought of. I'll always prefer musicians like that over those who complain and don't do anything.

Getting away from specific individuals, though, I'd just like to ask you about smooth jazz, which is in vogue nowadays. What do you think about that phenomenon?
I heard Chuck Mangione on the radio recently. I liked it. That clear tone, beautifully wrapped up in air. I've always liked pop. I've always enjoyed listening to George Michael. I used to like listening to those Black female groups like Destiny's Child – you could call it fast food. I still like Snoop Dogg and Pharrell Williams.

I've known from the beginning that the days of *Johnny the Musician** are over. You have to know how to make yourself visible, present yourself to people, otherwise no one's going to notice you. It's a huge world, and without that it's a no go.

But I'm just going to go back to smooth jazz. Because this is supposedly jazz, but a sterilized version, stripped of its dirty energy, its rich sound. That music is essentially a crime against jazz.

You're right. But it's a big old world, and there's a place for everything. The world is so rich that its most important feature ought simply to be consistency of action. In one sense, Jan Garbarek is smooth jazz as well, but of a high quality. I'm naturally tolerant of everything. I object to puritans who want every genre to stick to its pure form. I don't like them.

---

* *Translator's note: Johnny the Musician* is a short story by the Polish Nobel Prize-winning author Henryk Sieńkiewicz (1846–1916). In depicting the wasted life chances of peasant children, the author also shows how talent, however great, goes unnoticed by the world if not identified, supported and promoted.

26 The Children and the Vampire

You've been in a duo with Wisława Szymborska.* You performed at the launch of her volume of poetry, *Tutaj* ['Here'].

It was her author's evening. Except that Mrs Szymborska did actually say at one point, 'I don't know what's happening, because I've come to Mr Stańko's concert and they're telling me to read my poems.' She turned the situation around. It was in the large hall at the Kraków Opera: she read eleven poems from her *Tutaj* volume. She did an excellent reading. It was a big success, with a crowd of people. Adam Michnik was thrilled. They're going to make a little disc from it and put it in with the book.

You could say that you punctuated Szymborska's readings.

I did punctuate them. Let me tell you, it comes out really well for me. A long time ago, a friend of mine, Jerzy Illg, asked me to do some mini-concerts at a poetry convention. That's where I first did one of my trumpet commentaries on the poems that the authors read out. It was a fascinating discovery. I'm going to carry on developing that. I play brief solos, a kind of passing commentary. They have to be very brief: just a few notes, just like poetry that doesn't need many words. That's why they fit the poetry so well. Poets have their own special kind of voice.

Are you talking about conciseness of expression?

An incredibly concise sound. I get some lovely compositions out of it, though I can hardly call them compositions: they're more like commentaries, limericks almost. A synthesis of certain things. Unusual in music.

One of the poems in *Tutaj* is dedicated to Ella Fitzgerald. Does Szymborska listen to jazz?

She does. In spite of appearances, jazz is a serious contemporary phenomenon.

---

* *Translator's note:* Wisława Szymborska (1923–2012) was a Polish poet who explored philosophical, moral and ethical issues in her works; she was awarded the Nobel Prize for Literature in 1996.

Did you talk about music?

We didn't talk much to each other. We had dinner together. Mrs Szymborska is a wonderful woman, very authentic. She's over eighty, but she acts like a twenty-year-old: she's suspended time.

One of Szymborska's poems also makes an appearance on Komeda's *Meine süsse Europäische Heimat: Dichtung und Jazz aus Polen*, on the first track, 'The Trumpet Player Is Innocent'.

You know, I don't actually have that record, but that's possible. I wasn't aware of her poems at the time. We recorded the music separately: the readings were added later.

This time, when I played, I followed the melody of the poem exactly, and it felt really comfortable playing it that way. Szymborska's voice made a huge impression on me. It communicated the character of the poem to me, its depth. The content and character of the poem are not actually that important to me during the performance. What I find fascinating is that, when a poet reads out her poem, what we have contained within that reading, is the tons and tons of days during which she was actually writing it. Poets take a long time to write. All those reflections and all that depth mean that the words carry so much weight that no actor will ever be able to convey it. Never. Ever. Well, maybe some particularly weird actors with depth in their voices might, though that wouldn't be a thespian depth, but one that comes from the lives they've led: hard-living, edgy lives. Maybe Harvey Keitel could read things like that. He has gravitas. He's a motherfucker.

So, during the Szymborska concert, were you led by her voice?

Her voice. Her way of speaking, of presenting the text. Her phrasing. Her punctuation, which meant that, when she was finishing, the sounds would come out of my instrument of their own accord. I just had to be ready. I had to be in a trance.

Did you manage to get to the Metropolitan Museum, like you'd intended to, to get into a trance in front Modigliani's nude and think up a composition for the new album?

Yes, I did. I went there because I wanted to write something, and I did write something. There are so many things there. Museums have their own particular atmosphere, despite all the crowds of people. Especially those big museums, where the number of people gets spread out. You can linger awhile and stand there and focus on a particular picture.

So you've turned your visits to galleries and museums into a way of composing?

With difficulty recently, as I don't have much time. I want to write my new album like that.

Do you have any other ways of composing?

No, I don't. The best method is simply to be diligent. But it's difficult for me to force myself to do anything, and I make a point of not forcing myself to write over an extended period of time. It's easy to burn out. I know that I'm still developing, as far as composing goes. Personally, I think my compositions are becoming increasingly mature. But there are also ones like 'White Ballad' that I've been playing for years and which I still like. I'm now wondering whether to record *Astigmatic* with the quintet.

With your new band, you've already started playing a different Komeda piece altogether: 'Dirge for Europe', from the *Dichtung und Jazz* album that we mentioned a moment ago.

We play 'Dirge for Europe' and 'Ballet Etude 1' all the time. Alexi Tuomarila really likes playing it.

When we were talking about *Litania*, you made the point that recording Komeda's music had been the bridge that had led you to rhythmical, traditional music. You developed that music with your Polish quartet.

That's true. The quartet was the next stage in my return to more communicative music. It's been quite a long process for me, one that began with *Litania*.

I'd like to talk about that band. You refer to the musicians in your quartet – Marcin Wasilewski, Michał Miśkiewicz, Sławomir Kurkiewicz – as children.

Because they are children: there's a large age gap between us.

They really were children when you started playing together.

Michał was sixteen. Marcin and Sławomir were eighteen. They were really young. They were still at high school, and when they were playing with me, they were students in Katowice. And they were good right from the beginning.

What was it about them that particularly appealed to you?

Artistic maturity. And the fact that they were gifted. They immediately picked up whatever I wanted.

Were you a teacher to them, or a vampire?

It's hard to say. But I like that word: 'vampire'. A vampire – of course! I once read an interview with Miles, where the interviewer said that so many musicians had learned from Miles. And he replied, 'No. The other way round. I was doing the learning.' That's contrariness, saying it for effect, not entirely true.

Playing with me, they benefit from my confidence and my stage experience. That's invaluable. I can remember my first job with Komeda, how I absorbed his charisma. You absorb it in a flash. Now, when I think back to *Astigmatic*, I think, 'Hell, that got everything out of me; it fast-tracked and developed me.'

They've had the same. But I haven't given them any advice. If it had been about me advising them how to play, I wouldn't have hired them. We'd talk about certain things to do with tempo, about nuances to do with style, and about the way to improvise or interpret. Essentially, the trick with the music that I play isn't to do with playing the theme well, because obviously that has to be played well – that's basic. It's about the nuances. I give the musicians a certain chord, but they can do whatever they want with it. I'd give it to these children, and then I'd wait.

Marcin often changed things, if only accidentally. That's how we learned. He'd accidentally play major instead of minor, but I wouldn't interrupt him. I'd say, 'Keep it like that!' because I'd suddenly hear freshness. It's a certain kind of wisdom. He sees the effect of something random, how I can work with that, and how much I like it.

The way I compose is that sometimes a certain chord comes out randomly, and then that sound makes me wonder. That's our speciality. Taking advantage of something random is fundamental to improvised music, because these associations are made quickly, at lighting speed. The power of the mistake changes its value. Because what is an accident? It's a mutation. A mistake. Well, we are, after all, alive thanks to mistakes and mutations.

You mentioned that in Komeda's quintet you took the edge off the traditional sweetness of his music.
Yes. I made it avant-garde.

In the quartet, you might say that Marcin Wasilewski's piano added some traditional 'sweetness' to your music.
Wasilewski plays a communicative groove, but I wasn't presenting my music like that.

Wasilewski is the most romantic musician that you've worked with.
A conventional musician. You could say romantic, but it would be more accurate to say conventional.

I said that because he's from the Keith Jarrett school.
That tradition. But I also felt good with him because we rather quickly began playing free in his romantic, more harmonic style. Wasilewski's greatest strength is that he can play both traditional and free, in the way Bobo can, so casually. There are more and more musicians able to do that these days. I'm curious to see what it's going to be like playing with Dominik Wania, because he's also very traditional. He had his roots in classical music, but he plays very rhythmic music at the same time. He was guided by Danilo Perez, who taught him in Boston and thought highly of him. Except that, in contrast to Marcin, Wania's playing is anti-romantic. He plays cold, which I'm also starting to find

The 'Polish' quartet, circa 2001 (from left: Marcin Wasilewski, Michał Miśkiewicz, Sławomir Kurkiewicz, Tomasz Stańko).
Photograph by Andrzej Tyszko

exciting. I'm curious to see how our job in Vienna's going to turn out, because I've only played with him once before.

The quartet is a band that you've been playing with for practically the last fifteen years. Is that a result of your decision to focus on communicative music, which needs just this kind of line-up?
It was about the quality. I've never been a purist by nature. I liked the flexibility of art, because it gave me freedom. I had my roots in playing free and I loved playing free. My technique and instrumental predispositions took me in that direction. I'm talking about the expression that you can get through non-technical playing, through non-musical means. That expression was the most important thing for me, and still is. It's flawed because you can't always do it the way you want to, the way the brain would play it, but this free expression was closest to my heart.

And, at the same time, by using my tone, through the beauty of tone, I was able to play the ballads that I liked. In the quartet, I had more conventional musicians. They'd get me into a certain mood, which I liked and which I'd take further. I'd already played things like that with Makowicz who, at the end of the day, was a conventional musician. That's why, throughout the whole period of our collaboration, we played standards and ballads. I was always inclined to get together with those kinds of musicians. When I realized that I had access to a good band at home, I could hardly not take advantage of it. A stable bassist, an interesting percussionist and a charismatic, powerful pianist. What a line-up! It's such a joy. This isn't New York where musicians congregate from all over the world. And that's why we spent so many years playing together.

In the mid-1990s, you had two bands going in parallel: that famous European quartet with Tony Oxley, Bobo Stenson and Anders Jormin and, at the same time, the Polish quartet.
Yes. They dovetailed with each other.

So what were the circumstances that led to the Polish quartet – Wasilewski, Miśkiewicz, Kurkiewicz – becoming your priority band?
As usual, it was pure chance. When I had one-off jobs in Poland, where there was no question of bringing over a band with Oxley in it, I played with Polish line-ups, which I organized myself for one-off concerts. The backbone was Janusz Skowron, because he's an excellent pianist. What's absolutely essential to me is the quality of the music and who I play with. I give the musicians a lot of space, and I can't put myself in a position where someone might play the wrong chord. He can't go wrong and play a major sixth instead of a minor one. I can't have him play a wrong note, which is the mark of musicians of average talent and sensibility. I need high-level musicians, so that I don't have to say anything, or explain anything to them, and they'll play the notes I want. That's why I played with Skowron.

I had this terrible problem once. At the end of 1993, I had a job in Przemyśl, in a quartet with Skowron. We were meant to have Zbigniew Wegehaupt and Bernd Konrad in the rhythm section. Well, a few days before the job, Wege-haupt rings me: 'I can't come; I've got an important gig over here.' 'Well, you'll have to recommend someone, then,' I say. 'Play with young Miśkiewicz.' 'What Miśkiewicz?' 'Henryk Miśkiewicz's son: he plays drums – a lad, very young.' That really got my attention because I thought highly of Miśkiewicz's father. His strongest point is his so-called 'jazzy' playing: he plays like a jazz musi-cian – he can really swing it. I thought his son might have the same thing, which is important on the drums. I rang him, and he recommended Sławomir Kurkiewicz. They'd been playing together for a long time, and so obviously I was going to take both of them on.

How did the first concert go? Did you have any rehearsals beforehand?
We went straight to the job in Przemyśl. We drove straight to the venue, where we had half an hour to rehearse. Very little time for a first meeting. Well, as it turned out, within that half-hour we'd got through the whole programme. They had knowledge and learned quickly. There's no need to rehearse: this is improvised music. I was surprised to see how brilliantly they actually played. I was moved. And they soon persuaded me to give Marcin a try.

I remember, it was a concert in Łódź. We had a quick rehearsal and then we played. I tried him out and I really liked him. I'd got my entire line-up. They'd played a lot together; they were tight. And we very quickly started doing concerts. More and more of them. I took them to Germany. With Skowron I was just playing keyboard things by then. Anyway, I'm still playing with him, and I'll always play with him. There was this one point, I noticed to my surprise that, whenever I came back off tour with Oxley, Jormin and Stenson, I loved playing with those children and the freshness of the thing. It was different, of course, but I find that satisfying artistically. That took me by surprise, and that's how our collaboration began. Manfred Eicher found out about the band, and he approached me himself about making an album.

Recording the quartet for ECM was Eicher's idea?
Yes. I did want to record with them anyway, but Manfred suggested it independently. He said, 'Why don't you record the next album with the young band?' He has a nose for these things, evidently a result of his knowledge and experience.

I mean, it was Manfred who made me aware of Maciej Obara, because I didn't know him before. Now I listen to his records: he's just recorded a new one. I'm telling you: Obara's a dude! He has his own particular sound. I don't know whether he'll be able to make a career of it or not, because it's difficult. I'll take him on when I need to. Recently, though, I've not been playing with saxophone that much: I don't have a need for it.

Did Eicher hear the quartet play live before you recorded *Soul of Things*?
Sławomir and Michał performed well at the ECM festival in Ferrara, where I played the *Green Hill* programme with them. Dino Saluzzi, Michelle Makarski and John Surman were there – I suggested they take my rhythm section on. I can remember how anxious they were before that concert. I said to them, 'Gentlemen, it's all down to you whether Manfred takes you on or not.' And he liked them. Then we agreed a date for the first album.

And how did you disband the Jormin–Oxley–Stenson quartet?
That died of its own accord. We carried on playing for quite a while after *Litania*, but increasingly less so. I also had a few concerts as a duo with Bobo.

Did you play many concerts with that line-up?

We did, we did. We had jobs straight away. I remember New Morning in Paris. A concert in Kuwait. A festival in Lisbon. Tours of Germany and Scandinavia. At a festival in Sweden, instead of Oxley we had Jon Christensen playing with us – brilliant, sensational.

Out of all your bands, it is actually the Polish quartet that holds the record for the number of concerts with you.

Yes. I played with them the most. We did big tours. That's why we made so much progress. American jazz progressed as it did because, over there, they play non-stop. That's why some musicians work so hard to keep playing.

Straight after releasing *Soul of Things*, in 2002, you went on your first and very long tour of the States. You mentioned that they play completely differently over there compared to Europe.

All four American tours were very long ones. The first one lasted several weeks. Firstly, over there you play two shows a day, two concerts, which is purely a commercial operation, to make a few bucks. A club pays for one job, but people come for two concerts – a very practical solution. Two long sets with a longer break.

But we also played in the south; in San Diego and La Jolla we played four sets. They let the audiences in twice for two sets. For fuck's sake! Two concerts in one evening. And in the 1960s they used to play three sets. At Jazz Bakery in Los Angeles, we played two sets a day for five days in a row.

It's really hard keeping up that level of fitness. The American tours taught the whole quartet how to play. The children don't even realize that everything they know is down to that. Before then, our stamina would dip in the middle of a piece. That's a very Polish way of playing: start off strong and then play crap. They all play the other way around: they get going as they play. That's why I'm comfortable playing with the Americans: they know how to build tension, so a concert has its own dramatic structure.

Did you talk about music while on tour?

We did. About our fitness, about details: for example, how to end pieces. But I preferred to demonstrate, because that's longer-lasting knowledge and it's quicker to convey it. You could say: 'Gentlemen, let's make the ending long; we will hold this pause for a very long time.' That's all very well – not. It's just easier to demonstrate it through sound. When the time comes for the final note, to set it up solidly, do a good, long pause, do it confidently, so it's clear to them that this is the place where they have to hold it. Play it once like that and you don't need to say anything else.

And do you remember who it was that described you as a leader who: 'Says little and demands a lot'?

No.

It was Janusz Muniak, in an interview for *Tygodnik Powszechny* [Universal Weekly], when he was talking about the quintet.
I don't talk. Same as Komeda. What am I supposed to say? When you're playing with me, you're supposed to be playing.

Have there been instances where you haven't been able to play with musicians who've been recommended to you?
Many.

Have you ever removed anyone from the stage?
Not from the stage. I'm not such a bastard, but I do terminate a collaboration if I don't like something. I don't play.

Music apart, in your interactions with the quartet, were there any topics, any subjects that set sparks flying?
Music is very important: it connects me to people. I'm a loner, and basically I only interact with people in the band. Right now, for example, I feel affection for Tuomarila. We barely know each other. He may not feel it, but I feel more affection for him than I do for others, because sometimes on stage I absolutely adore his playing, to the point that I'd give him everything, just because he's playing like that for me.

You're talking now about the pianist in your new quintet?
Yes. Alexi Tuomarila. He's my little pet in the band. I loved Marcin or Sławomir in the same way when they were playing. They were brothers to me then. I'd have given them everything.

Maybe that's a kind of fatherly instinct?
It's more like the love you feel for a woman than fatherly love. Passion. Because they're playing beautifully, because the bastard's giving it his fuckin' all, because the whole thing has such power, and the ending's so beautiful.

Socializing with the musicians in the quartet couldn't have been easy with such an age difference.
We didn't socialize. We interacted while on tour. We always had a common language. We felt great. I always feel great on tour. We addressed each other as 'Pan'* for years, but then that became a kind of inverted-commas 'Pan'.

Don't young musicians like that cause trouble for a leader? They could have gone crazy while on tour.
So they went crazy. I didn't take part in those drinking sessions. But it says a lot about them that, in the dozen or so years we played together, they only let

---

* *Translator's note:* 'Pan' literally means 'Mr' or 'Sir'. (The female equivalent is 'Pani'.) It is a formal way of addressing someone, the equivalent of the French formal 'vous' form of address.

me down two or three times, by which I mean they didn't play so well during a concert, because they were hung-over. Two or three times. Being ill can actually fuck things up a lot more. Strong people.

Did you have any incidents like the one that you mentioned with Freelectronic, when you were on tour and you lost Skowron?
Not with them.

It's a different generation, isn't it?
Different. They were more aware. They never drank themselves under the table, ever. They value work.

Maybe we're not really aware of it, but communism was an unbelievably weird system. Life under communism was incredibly demoralizing. When the new conditions came in, we had to change. Well, you can't afford to screw up. There's no choice. There's no support.

In those new times, you started earning a lot of money. *Litania* was a worldwide jazz bestseller. We were going to have to talk about money eventually.
My earnings went up. Strong line-ups. Bigger festivals. I started getting good jobs straight after the first ECM albums. But what a band that was! *Litania* sold in the tens of thousands. It did best out of all those albums. The Polish quartet albums sold very well.

When the big money appeared, you began to invest.
I took care of my future. I invested some money in real estate. But mainly I like throwing it around. I have a closet full of handmade suits from Jerzy Turbas's atelier in Kraków. He said to me, 'You'll have to build yourself a wardrobe, Mr Stańko.' He also makes coats for me.

Have you had bespoke shoes made as well?
I used to, but my shoemaker, Kamiński, died. And Kielman doesn't suit me. I have a few handmade pairs from Vienna and Budapest. I do buy shoes as well. There's plenty of choice now.

You also have an impressive real estate portfolio.
I like real estate, probably because I've spent my whole life knocking around. I never had my own apartment. I mean, there was a period when I was sleeping at Remont, wasn't there? That was a breaking point. I was living in a dark room which had a painted window. It had been painted on the wall. It was a very nice window with a beautiful view.

Did you paint it for yourself?
No. They painted it for me, so that I could go up to the window. Whatever scenery I imagined, that's the scene I had outside the window. Nice. But I did have to walk up two flights to go to the bog.

27 From Afar

The albums that you recorded for ECM from the mid-1990s onwards were essentially the next stage in your huge success on the international jazz scene.
It's a very condensed kind of success. I've always had the respect of musicians and the jazz community. For one thing, my quintet was a mesmerizing band, highly regarded. The groups I had with Makowicz, with Vesala, Freelectronic – they were known all over the world.

The first album that you recorded with the quartet in 2001, *Soul of Things*, was in fact a significant breakthrough. It brought your music and sound to the American market. For a European jazz musician, that kind of success must be particularly meaningful.
Of course. That's when we did our first American tour. The Australian market opened up for me as well. Stuart Nicholson wrote some brilliant things about that album: thanks to his reviews of *Soul of Things* and *Suspended Night*, they won awards in Australia for best international jazz album of the year. Manfred particularly liked that album. Sarah's told me that, during that time in the ECM office, they only talked about me.

Did you become Eicher's pet?
Yes, kind of. He thought very highly of all of the quartet's albums, because they combined my free playing with a conventional thing. A very jazzy combination.
I was at a Sun Ra Arkestra concert yesterday: you can hear the same thing in their playing. Sun Ra started out back in the 1940s. He was a swing musician – he played swing pieces plus free. Because free has always been there in jazz. There have always been musicians who've not worried about technique, but have played with power, pushed for expression and drama, gone with the dirt. In the quartet, along with my free-jazz dirt, I followed my affinity for lovely music, and on top of that, we played free, subtly and very musically. I think it was an interesting band.

There was also the prestigious European Jazz Prize, which you were awarded in Vienna.
I got that award not long after *Soul of Things*. That established my position.

And in 2004 you were awarded the Commander's Cross of the Order of Polonia Restituta.

President Kwaśniewski gave me the cross. I stood next to Korzeniowski.* I remember us feeling pretty good standing there in that line. There were masses of people there. It was a kind of state ennoblement, which rather amused me, seeing as I was the kind of person who hung out on the margins.

In your *Playboy* interview, you mentioned that, among that crowd of distinguished people, it was only you and Korzeniowski who had nice shoes.

Yes. I pay attention to shoes – although not everyone does.

That period of 'condensed success' coincided with your clean period.

One of my best compositions, 'Morning Heavy Song', was the first composition I wrote while straight. I was straight, and yet it's incredibly high – you could say it's my most high composition. That really helped me, because I was a bit worried about creative inspiration. When American writers stopped drinking, they stopped writing. But it was different for them: Faulkner, for example, who used to get up early in the morning, drink a glass of vodka – and he was off! And he'd write. That's how I imagine it. It's difficult to get yourself out of that. You could easily stop writing. I didn't compose for a long time. I recorded a lot of old compositions, both on *Matka Joanna* and on *Leosia*. I tinkered around.

The main effect that being straight had on me was to make me start pursuing my interests, and it gave me a single-minded strength. I feel good. I'm very pleased that in this regard my life has taken the course it has, rather than any other. When I did need an anaesthetic to survive, I used to anaesthetize myself.

Dope can help you keep going, to withstand the blows that life gives you, the lack of success or lack of money, nerves, stress, attacks by the press. And, in my case, when I had that trouble with my teeth, I wouldn't have got through it . . .

Let's just say that for many years I didn't have a home, didn't have a future. Hell, if I'd thought at the time, 'What's going to become of me? What future have I got?' – sober, I'd never have made it through. No prospects. Well, how could I have predicted that my career would really take off in the 1990s and I'd make some money?

I've seen other musicians. It's a nightmare of a life. A wonderful life, but you have to be plastered the whole time so as not to feel the nightmare. I remember us smoking hashish when the quintet was on the road. Nine hundred kilometres in a cold car, with the wind blowing fucking gales through the gaps, because it was an old car. We're driving from Basel to Göttingen.

---

* *Translator's note:* Robert Korzeniowski (b. 1968) is a Polish racewalker, former world record-holder and winner of four Olympic gold medals and three gold medals at World Championships. At the 2000 Olympic Games in Sydney, he became the first man to win both racewalking events (20 km and 50 km).

All day long. A nightmare. We arrive at the club, totally washed out after the journey. And right away the barman says, 'Wine?' And we all go, 'Yes!!!' So he pours us each a small glass of very good white wine. And then I ask him, 'Have you got anything to smoke?' 'Of course!' We light a joint. Instant euphoria. The concert went brilliantly. That's what that's for. We'd have played fine without a joint, but highs like that get the very best out of you. And then you remember those things when you play: they become stabilized, they stay in your brain.

I'd never go back to not being sober. Touch wood! I was very far gone. Many people cave in: they have some problems, and they go back to it. Because it's hard. You have to be really single-minded. I know that I have one motivation, the most important one: artistically, I feel fantastic when I'm sober. My life is a little less rich, but my art's going better than ever. I'm particularly pleased that I have a strange kind of intuition in my life, which makes me do what's right for me at a given moment in time.

Six months before the disaster with my teeth, I gave up alcohol. If I hadn't done it by then, I might not have won this mighty battle. I mean, I had to battle both with myself and with my own body's physical resistance. There's a bit of the Neanderthal in me. They had a genetically inherited programme in their brains. They knew what they needed to do: they didn't know why. And that's the way I go – through instinct.

When that clean period began, did you devise routines for your healthy new life?
They're kind of like daily ablutions. You get up early; you go for a run. Macrobiotics. Special diets. Teas. I remember that's when I started getting high on tea. I went around looking for good-quality teas. That was the only stimulant I had left. Good tea. Good coffee. Thank God that during my alcohol period I never got into the wine-drinking culture. I had no temptations because you couldn't get good-quality wine under communism. People drank vodka, and when I was drinking heavily, I didn't care what I drank. The wine-drinking culture that you have nowadays, that vibe, knowing about the different types of wine, what year it is, that really appeals to me. It would have been difficult for me to get myself out of that.

What kind of tea did you like drinking?
I drank strong teas, good-quality ones. Green, white. They're very strong: they have up to six per cent of pure theine in them. Sometimes they work like cocaine, yet at the same time you're drinking rose petals, an incredibly delicate drink. I also like black teas, Indian ones: Assam or Darjeeling. All kinds of teas.

Did you follow any tea rituals?
I didn't perform an actual ritual. I do drink the ritual Japanese matcha tea, though, which you prepare with a whisk, and you whisk up the foam like with

an espresso. I have the utensils. I knew how to make it, and I do like this tea, but I never did it as part of a ritual – just for the taste and the theine effect, which in this particular tea acts as both a stimulant and a sedative at the same time.

What about your diet, macrobiotic food? You must have had to pay a lot more attention to your nutrition.
It was a kind of activity. One of the dopeheads, one of those young drug dealers, once said to me, 'Mate, you want to get yourself into something else. I've started taking evening primrose.' I even went out and bought some evening primrose, a herb with tranquillizing effects. He says, 'You need to change your habits.' He wasn't making a particular big deal about it, but I picked up on it all the same. 'Ah!' I thought, 'The clever thing to do is to live differently, eat different food, take an interest in something different, change my daily rituals. Turn everything the other way around!'

I started having compression massages. Massage, diet, macrobiotics and running: it all worked together. I forgot about it later on, but, to begin with, I took it so seriously that, when I was doing gigs with Christian Muthspiel, my cooking machine came with me all the way to Vienna. So that I'd be able to prepare everything in my hotel – buckwheat groats, you know. That was my diet: vegetables, buckwheat groats. I still eat those, though I eat everything now, including meat. However, I still don't put seasoning on my food. I like it like that. I like freshly made, steamed vegetables with groats. I didn't find that yin–yang equilibrium, which is so important in macrobiotics. I never even wanted to find it. My approach was that other things were more important, like not eating much. What's important overall is changing your habits. Just the actual trip. Going to shops where they have groats, beans, chickpeas, different types of lentils.

Did you compose for the quartet under these new circumstances, with all your daily ablutions?
Absolutely. I composed rather a lot, in fact. I also had a lot of film music to do: 'Olga', 'Masza', 'Irina', 'Cruel', 'Utrata ładu' ['Loss of Order']. I played all of those with the quartet, lots of ballads. It's writing ballads that I enjoy the most, and they're what I most enjoy playing.

Do you remember your first ECM recording session with the quartet that gave us *Soul of Things*?
The recording was in Oslo. I like it there. I also recorded *Satu* there with Edward Vesala. Gary Peacock and I did a session there: *Matka Joanna*; *Leosia*. I also did a session with Jon Balke, but that album didn't get released.

I know Oslo well. I always stay in the same charming little hotel. It's gone a bit downhill recently, but it used to be very good, chic, though small. Right in the centre, just by the Royal Park. When I was recording *Matka Joanna*, I went running there every morning. I ran regularly for a long time. To be honest, I've stopped now because of my joints. Running isn't the best thing for the knees, but I was always running then. For a good ten years.

The conditions in Oslo were fantastic. I'd get up early. I'd run for an hour and then practise yoga. After all that, I'd practise for a bit, and then I'd go for breakfast with Manfred and all the musicians, who'd already be there. We'd drive out to spend the whole day at the recording session. In the evening, we'd have dinner together, a big winding-down. And it went really well. Every session. The third day was just brilliant, just putting the album together, which is essentially Manfred's job. I don't have to get involved at that stage: I just enjoy listening. The editing stage is actually the one time that I really listen to my own albums all the way through. *Litania* is the only one I listened to a little bit after it had been released.

You're recalling the cosiness of your recording sessions at ECM, but when you did *Soul of Things*, that's when your young band made its appearance. Was there any tension because of that?
There's always some tension, but Manfred was up for the idea right from the start, and he set the whole thing up. When the young band went into the studio, he made it clear to everyone that he approved of them. Sławomir and Michał had met him at their concert in Ferrara, and he'd liked it. Marcin plays like a master in the studio because he's very musical and he has a natural inclination for playing free stuff beautifully. Manfred took to him, and Marcin was able to develop.

You know, not everyone can manage that: the weaker ones are always scared. Manfred takes control of everything, not in a calculated way, but intuitively. That's why I feel so great with him when I'm recording. I don't get stressed: there's no bad atmosphere as far as I'm concerned. I have my poker face on, and inside, within, I feel at peace. I don't care about anything else. Things that a lot people might get freaked out about, they just wash over me. I just do my thing. Sometimes someone asks, 'Well, how was that, Manfred, the recording?' and he's sitting there with his head down, not saying anything, not a word. You don't know what to do – whether to wait or go. That's unnerving. I reckon a lot of European musicians would have been scared shitless.

Does Eicher try different approaches for the same track, different jazzy takes?
A few, certainly. Sometimes, when we're mixing, we'll edit some takes together.

Did the quartet have a smooth entry into the ECM recording process?
Exceptionally smooth.

On the quartet's first two albums, *Soul of Things* and *Suspended Night*, there are no titles, just numbers for consecutive variations.
It just came out like that somehow. The number idea is a good one, isn't it, because it's unconventional.

Soul of Things is a good title for your music. It suggests the concrete made spiritual, the drawing-out of nuances, and it has an inherent contradiction.

Yes, yes. The same for *Suspended Night*. Titles with many meanings. *Lontano* is even better: 'From afar'. Everything from afar, life from afar. A certain kind of outline. That's an excellent title.

The fact that there are no titles for individual parts, and with those variations coalescing into a larger whole – is that not an echo of your use of motifs, which you were talking about in the context of your film music?

Yes, it's the use of motifs. Essentially, I've been playing one thing all my life. I have my favourite chords, those minor sixths, minor thirds, and I use them all the time.

What led Eicher to make an association with Godard's films, meaning that stills from them turned up on the covers of *Soul of Things* and *Suspended Night*?

That was just chance, I think. Manfred is a fan of Godard, and he was on friendly terms with him back then. I've met Godard: he was very nice. *Green Hill* was awarded a German music critics' prize, and we met when we were picking up our awards. Godard's album – a huge one: *Histoire(s) du cinéma*, which Manfred had produced – also won an award.

What's also striking about those quartet records is that they're long. I'm wondering whether, when you've got such a breadth of material, it becomes difficult to build a dramatic structure?

I don't know. It's difficult to say for sure. Those records are long ones because that's how much we recorded. I think that Manfred works on the assumption that if an album can accommodate eighty minutes, why not have seventy-five minutes' worth of music, if we have that much material and it all works as a whole.

That must be a big change for someone who used to listen to jazz on vinyl, where a side might have only lasted fifteen minutes. That kind of listening engages our attention in a different way.

I know. It's a different thing. I wasn't really thinking about that. I just recorded the music.

But it must have meant that, when you were preparing your subsequent albums, you'd assemble more material.

Yes. I always have a lot of material. That kind of situation gets me composing, but that's neither here nor there. Because I've been playing open form all my life.

On *Soul of Things*, you returned to the 'Maldoror's War Song' motif again. We mentioned it when we were discussing *Matka Joanna*, and you spoke about declaring war on addiction. And here we have yet another breakthrough album and yet another war song.

You're interpreting it in a literary way.

But it is a kind of leitmotif of yours, isn't it? You've recorded it on three landmark albums.

You could say that. I often played that piece. The reason why was because both quartets loved playing it. But I don't want to so much anymore. I'm planning to take it to New York to play at Merkin Hall, but I don't know if I will. These are the only real reasons for me – purely musical ones.

Have you thought about how this piece has changed over the years?

I haven't particularly thought about it. The first version was for solo trumpet. I practised it years ago with Zbigniew Wegehaupt, when I was living in Remont. When I was playing solo concerts, I had to have a few new compositions. I produced whole cycles of weird things. There was 'Almost Black', fragments of which appear on *Taj Mahal*, but that's a long, fuckin' crazy, more theoretical composition. One part of it was 'Maldoror'. Later on, when I played it with piano, naturally chords got added. Bobo added them first. And then I added some different ones for the Polish quartet. We sometimes played according to chord patterns, but often free.

That version of 'Maldoror's War Song' on *Soul of Things* is played by the quartet in the most flowing manner, lightly.

They played it rhythmically.

On *Soul of Things* you can also hear themes that you recorded for film in the 1990s.

I use film music all the time. In fact, I've always played film compositions.

What's the deciding factor in which film motifs take on a new life at concerts?

The ones I like. Because I don't write film music as such; I write my own music. Komeda sometimes did the same thing. 'Astigmatic' came out of 'Start'. When something has quality, you want to play it.

When *Soul of Things* appeared, the Polish critics enthusiastically picked up on the echoes of Kraków's *hejnał* [trumpet call].*

There was one composition on it that was based on the *hejnał*. When Piotr Skrzynecki** died, I was asked to play the *hejnał* here, in Warsaw. I was supposed to play Kraków's *hejnał* for Piotr from the Palace of Culture. As I

---

* *Translator's note:* The *hejnał* (St Mary's Trumpet Call) has been played in Kraków's Main Square on the hour, every hour, every day since the fourteenth century. It is based on five notes from the scale of F major.

** *Translator's note:* Piotr Skrzynecki was one of the founders of Piwnica pod Baranami, an iconic cabaret bar in Kraków.

was on my way in my taxi, I thought, 'I'll play the *hejnał* in a minor key. I'll change the trip.' What came out was a beautiful, completely different piece, but a trumpet call all the same. I wrote a second part to it, and we played it with the quartet. It was a substantive piece, a substantive composition, which is called 'Piotrada'.

You've recently been playing another trumpet call, which you've composed for Podkowa Leśna.*
That's another matter altogether. They commissioned it, and it was my duty to write it. I did it for the town. A trumpet call's a trumpet call. As a trumpeter, obviously I come into contact with trumpet calls. I presented them with the sheet music, and I recorded the motif in the studio.

Have you appeared in any other unusual official roles?
I can't remember.

You recorded the music for the Rising Museum in Warsaw.
I recorded it for a specific commission. You can hear the music in the museum, in the background. Sometimes more, sometimes less.

Were you shocked to receive a proposal like that from the museum?
Very, but I think they took a very direct route. They wanted to have a name. The status of the name reflects the status of the museum. A simple solution and the best solution. But the idea of having jazz in the background in a museum like that, that's an interesting thing. I really got into it. I got Wojciech Karolak to write string arrangements for large ensemble for three of the pieces, and I did three electronic pieces with solo trumpet, as music for film. I like the way that music sounds in the museum, so subtle, in the background.

Let's go back to the quartet. The second album, *Suspended Night*, has a transfixing kind of calmness about it: it actually feels meditative. And, essentially, it's similar to *Soul of Things*. *Lontano*, that's a different story. As far as I'm concerned, that's the band's best album.
Suspended Night is a very relaxed album: we recorded it after lots of engagements and long American tours. *Lontano* is different, because it's very free. That stage was coming to a close. I was writing less. I did actually have some compositions for *Lontano*, but for some reason they didn't make it onto the album. Free made it instead.

Did you originally have a different concept for it?
There was no concept, as per usual. I just had music that I'd played a lot, new compositions.

---

* *Translator's note:* Podkowa Leśna is a town near Warsaw, surrounded on three sides by forest, and home to a number of interwar villas. Tomasz Stańko owned a property there.

Did you record any other compositions that didn't make it onto *Lontano*?
We did, and a lot of them at that. Manfred has them. He also has material for a live album, a concert in Munich.

When the musicians in the quartet started playing with you, they were people from music school. When did they actually start playing free with you?
I asked them straight away, 'Gentlemen, do you play free?' We got playing it pretty quickly. Even before we'd started recording for ECM.

Did these musicians change very much during the time they played with you?
On the one hand, yes I think they did, but on the other hand I know that musicians don't change that much. The way a musician is to begin with, that's how he's going to be.

On *Soul of Things* Wasilewski is a romantic, but on *Lontano* he sometimes plays practically Cubist pieces.
Well, yes. That's what the record was like.

You did a remarkable recording at that time: a very interesting version of Komeda's 'Kattorna'. Its pulsating sound reminds me of Steve Reich. An interpretation of Komeda completely different from the one on *Litania*. Modernist.
Absolutely.

Do you think that long period playing with the quartet changed your frame of mind, your mood?
Yes and no. Manfred supposedly hammered us into his ECM mould, but that suited me fine. ECM has always suited me. And I always compose for a specific line-up.

It's a music that finds us from afar and remains hazy.
Yes, yes. Lontano.

The quartet's albums have now become a trilogy. Because you've already closed that chapter.
That's how it's turned out. We'd played together for over ten years, a long time. Everything comes to an end. I didn't want to have a permanent band like Jan Garbarek, who's still playing with the same people and likes it that way. I don't want to do that. I really enjoy it when I get to play with Marcin, Michał and Sławomir again, but we've played what we wanted to play. I've exhausted these people: now I want some different ones. Now I love playing with Alexi Tuomarila. I like Dominik Wania. They inspire me. It seems that as a quartet we were meant to play just as much as we did. It faded away of its own accord.

Since *Lontano* had been improvised music, I wasn't going to go back to composition. Improvisation, in other words, pure idea: you can't do that twice.

After that album, I decided the time had come to finish with the quartet. I didn't want to write any more compositions. They were recording their own album for ECM. We still play together regularly. We've just been to New Zealand: I really enjoyed playing with them. We'll soon be going on a tour of Holland. That's a project that I have in my hand, ready and absolutely solid, but I knew for sure that those three albums were ending a certain period of my life: the Polish quartet period.

New Zealand? That's some expedition.
We were invited to a festival, a big international festival, full house. The flight took nearly forty-eight hours. First to London, from London to Bangkok, a break there for the crew, and then another dozen or so hours to Sydney, and from there to Wellington, also quite a way – a three-and-a-half-hour flight.

If you were to add it all up, how many hours a month do you spend on a plane?
Loads of time. The trip to New York now just feels like I'm going to Podkowa Leśna. And yet it's fourteen hours from the time I leave home here to setting foot in my home over there. Well, one travels. You can't avoid jet lag. It affects some people badly, others not so much. On the whole, it doesn't affect me too badly. You do need to rest and get some sleep. I sleep well on the plane.

Do you sleep through flights? I was just wondering what you do then.
I sleep. Mostly, I sleep. That's why I don't have a big problem with jet lag. I'm going to have some trouble now, because I'm going to New York just for a short time, to play a concert at Merkin Hall, and the next day I'm flying to Vienna for three gigs at the Porgy and Bess Club. One concert with the quintet, one with the quartet with Dominik Wania, and the third concert with a Viennese band, where we'll be playing Komeda.

At the moment, what is it that determines whether you play with the quartet or with the new Scandinavian quintet?
It depends on what I've been invited to do. I guess I'm more interested in playing with the quintet, because it's fresh and we're working on an album.

How did you end up playing on Manu Katché's album *Neighbourhood*?
That was Manfred's idea. He got a whole band together for him. Garbarek, me. The names mattered, and the combination of musicians. And it turned out to be a good combo. We were colourful. Manu wrote his music in an interesting way.

That music of his is very smooth.
It is essentially smooth jazz, though in a completely different form: an ECM version.

Katché is a drummer with mainstream rock experience. As a leader, how did he cope with meeting all these jazz personalities?

Well, he'd played with the best people, hadn't he. With Peter Gabriel. He'd been playing with Sting for years. To some people, he's a huge name. When Rafał Paczkowski found out that I was going to be recording with Manu Katché, he had to sit down. We played a few gigs together, but it was difficult to get that line-up together for concerts: we were often busy with our own projects.

At that time, you also played on the *Levitation* album. An interesting trio with Billy Hart and the Irish guitarist Mark O'Leary. O'Leary manages to release three albums a year, and each time he has a different band, always a quality one.

He's worked with everyone, including Bobo and Jack DeJohnette. He wants big names, and he knows how to get hold of the money for the session. And if he's got the big names, the record label takes the material. O'Leary organized everything. He hired a studio in the Irish countryside. I remember all those very low houses. We recorded over the course of one afternoon. Totally improvised music. We also did two concerts.

Levitation has three big names on it, yet in Poland the album was reviewed as being one of your works.

It's his album, but you see what a clever cat he is. That's what they do. That's why I no longer take on those kinds of jobs. It's a similar situation with *Too Pee*. It's not actually my album, but the re-release has come out under my name. The record label took me for a ride.

28 A Certain Kind of Vitality

In his autobiography, which he dictated in his early sixties, Miles Davis said that great jazz musicians are like great boxers in that they know about self-defence. What do you think about that?

Miles was a boxer. 'They know about self-defence.' You know, you could have a lot to say on that subject. Essentially, it means that, these days, an artist has to know how to survive in an increasingly complex world. At one time, a painter was a painter. Nowadays it's a complex business. Talent's nothing. It would appear that there are very many people with talent. Not that long ago, when Paganini was playing his stuff, people thought that it was the devil's work, that he wouldn't have been able to do that on his own. But these days, every pupil can play it. Everything's moving forward. Talent alone, ability: that's not enough. The art of self-defence is a matter of survival.

When he was talking about that, Miles had his own things on his mind. Those new bands that he kept putting together. First of all, he had *Birth of the Cool.* Then there was his famous band – the famous one! – with Coltrane and Adderley. And then he went looking for new drummers with whom playing was different, harder. He had to fight! Fight with those young musicians to maintain control over them. In a sense, he was defending himself all the time.

He stresses the self-defence, rather than the combat.

I don't know much about combat. I know nothing whatsoever about boxing. But knowing how to defend yourself is essential, because then your opponent misses. Mindless fighting; that's nothing. Defending yourself: that's also combat.

During our initial meetings, you used the term 'predatory beasts' in relation to musicians.

People in the world of art are beasts. They have to be incredibly sensitive, but also resilient to blows, because there's competition, isn't there? Getting through a concert is a difficult business for a musician. I still get the jitters, even now. I did a concert in New York. Now I'm recording an album. I still have a kind of stage fright. Constant stress. It's not that I'm scared. I'm in a brilliant position, established. I have excellent musicians. But there is a kind of stress, which you have to put up with in order to achieve something, not just do a perfunctory job. That's something that would be beneath us.

Every concert that I play is meaningful to me. That New York concert, regardless of all the other concerts going on there, was important to me. There wasn't much time: the rehearsals were short, two little short ones – nothing, really; and then we were up on stage. Craig Taborn, Thomas Morgan, Jim Black. They played brilliantly because these are high-class professionals. But I was anxious all the time – well, kind of excited, really. Then Vienna. Again, I could have said: 'It's only the Porgy and Bess Club: I've played here so many times before.' But no. These were three different, demanding gigs that I had on consecutive days.

So I can understand Miles. I think that, to every concert he played, even the one where he just stood there and played one note, Miles attached a colossal amount of importance. I think that's a sign of strength. Maybe that's what everyone does. But I don't really believe that those joyful artists, ones like Lee Konitz, wonder whether a gig's going well or not. Konitz is a soloist, a virtuoso – he plays other things; but Miles had a band. He attached a huge amount of importance to each of his bands. He selected the musicians. In fact, he attached a hell of a lot of importance to it.

What makes you say that talent is nothing?
Talent's an obvious thing. Rubinstein had talent in his actual hand: a long fifth finger and a hand like a shovel. He only had to stretch his fingers out to have what others practise day and night to achieve. There is an extraordinary number of talented people in this world. But it's difficult to break through. In a moment of weakness we say, 'Oh, fuck it! I can't do this anymore.' But noooo! Grit your teeth, cut off your ear like van Gogh did, but don't give up. Keep going, dammit! Because that's what's hardest. To carry it through, you need a certain kind of vitality. Because there's talent everywhere you look. Outside the window, if you frame the window well, you'll see a bit of beauty. It's not art itself that has absolute value, but its vitality.

What is this vitality?
That's what I call it. Vitality. I think of it as a divine spark, charisma. A kind of consistency and persistence that makes us not give up on what we want to do, and even a kind of inability to realize oneself in any other way.

Like Modigliani, who was told that he was going to die in a few months' time; and then he went to Paris, and that was when he really became Modigliani, when he was meant to be dying. I like talking about painters, because I'm interested in their lives, in their persistence.

Nowadays persistence is important, also because it's easy to make a living doing other things. You can easily move over to something else, get something set up, teach in some school or other, tinker around. But it's difficult to keep it going on stage. On a real stage where ruthless laws apply. Where there's no mercy. On stage, everyone is governed by the same rules, whether you're twenty years old or seventy-five. You have to play! Play! And play the truth at that. It's a kind of self-realization. A stressing of the 'I'.

I can compare it to what I saw in Podkowa Leśna recently. There was this lovely little dog, wandering around on its own. He saw me, just as I was on my way out. He came up to the fence, wagged his tail. And then he calmly wandered a little way off and, just by my gate, he lifted his leg up high and peed all over it. Just to show it was fuckin' his. He was asserting himself. This is me. Self-realization.

You could say that by cultivating self-realization we shape the art of living. An old friend of mine recently wrote tongue-in-cheek about your talent for being yourself: 'I admire how, without ceasing to be himself even for a second, he has transformed himself from freak to bourgeois in his tailor-made suit, with a collection of rugs and an apartment in Manhattan. The power of his music comes precisely from his talent for being himself.'
Who wrote that!?

Marek Karewicz, who recently published an album of his photographs of jazz musicians. And he added a commentary to each portrait.
Aha! A bourgeois! He's right. I do use that, the fact that I have that latent trait within me. I have my music in hand. I've had that from the beginning. At the very beginning, when I started writing compositions, they came out of a certain kind of instrumental impairment of mine, out of certain deficiencies.

I remember having an exceptional dislike of my own tone. People compared it to Don Ellis's, which I didn't like. And I was furious about it. I can't say that I've worked on my tone. I was just quite sad and angry about it. But, in the end, it became my calling card. I've just bought myself a new trumpet, so that I can have an even more beautiful tone. I emphasize the tone rather than the technique. Tone is my strength; it gives me all my soul. My compositions gain power only when I play them with my own tone. I lead with it entirely, everything, casually, easily. It means I give myself some slack. Especially as there are very many things that I like.

I'm increasingly catching myself listening to music that shouldn't really appeal to me on account of my artistic notions. And yet I like it. Simple rubbish. I like it because it's melodious and formulaic. I didn't show that to begin with, but then I thought, 'What the hell! Why shouldn't I do what I want?' And so, whatever I touch is mine. I still have my melancholy tone and my melodiousness. No matter what I do, I'm not going to lose that. And that's why I can play any music I like, because either way, my tone, which is me, Tomasz Stańko, is still there, holding it all together.

Hence my admiration for Miles: he had the same thing. He just added a touch to his final album *Doo-Bop* right at the end. At home! He played three notes! And that's his own album. Do you see? And that's why he put his personal stamp on Hermeto Pascoal's track 'Nem Um Talvez' on the album *Live-Evil*, which begins: *taa tee ra raa taa tee ra raa ra da ra*. Hermeto might have written it, but Miles knew that he'd done it. Because it was Miles playing it!

I don't know what this composition as played by Hermeto sounds like, but I bet the original version is different. Miles gave it all its power. With his tone. With his timing. With his narration.

I make use of my tone in a similar way. And I don't give a shit what anyone else thinks about it. My tone has changed. It was Don Ellis to begin with. For a very brief moment. The older the artist, the better the tone. That doesn't age. A person can have no strength left whatsoever, just play one note, but with an increasingly beautiful tone. I think that's what happens if you play, if you're on stage the whole time. Because my tone, that's me.

Does your tone come from your vitality?
Obviously. That's life! You can't get that by practising. I play long tones all the time, breathing exercises with sound. And I try to play those long notes beautifully. But the tone comes of its own accord.

It's closely connected to your life. If your life is shallow, you have a shallow tone. It's *totally* connected to your life. Why did Coltrane have such a beautiful tone? Or Coleman Hawkins, Wayne Shorter, Roy Eldridge?

The old African-American jazz musicians used to say, 'Miles has the sound', 'Monk has the timing'. That makes it sound as if they had some kind of *mana*, a supernatural power, something to do with the world of magic.
There is magic in it. But it's not a magical world. It's a very professional way of defining the essence of our music. We're improvisors. We're supposed to have our own sound. Opera singers as well: they have their own individual characteristics, tones. It's the same in classical music: Horowitz attacked the piano keys differently from Rubinstein. In jazz we have a great variety of sounds.

There are certain defined types, such as the 'Brownian' tone, which Clifford Brown had, and then Kenny Dorham, Woody Shaw, and more recently Wynton Marsalis in particular. That's a classic, jazzy tone. But even Lee Morgan had his own very characteristic tone. All the swing musicians had a very characteristic sound. Coleman Hawkins, Johnny Hodges, Lester Young. And that was a source of pride.

'Monk has the timing.' Monk did indeed have the timing because he didn't play like a virtuoso; he had something of his own, something strange. Timing is a good word, which describes everything and nothing. But it's very important to us because timing is essential in our music. There are all sorts of timings: everyone plays differently. Whether it's light or heavy. We either delay a note or hurry it up. Do you know what's magic? That these terms are so broad that they are actually poetic terms. But, between us, we know what we mean. That 'timing' describes Monk's greatness, because having timing: that is great art.

You often use the word 'magic'. For instance, in relation to intuition in art, to trance, to rhythm.

Magic is in the same domain as art. It exists in the mind and externalizes itself, interacts with the outside world. When you're listening to Beethoven, it's not just the music that counts, but your emotions as well. The tears of a woman listening to Piotr Szczepanik are worth just as much. Because something's happening; atoms are migrating. The product of a composer's mind, in conjunction with the emotions of the listener, form a higher state of organized matter. That sound, those emotions that it gives rise to, are a form of matter, because everything is matter.

I think that we exist (this is my belief, my own cosmology) in order to continuously complicate matter. And art is our brain's most complicated product. After all, everything stems from one thing, from the fact that an electron stuck itself to a nucleus to produce a helium atom; then another one attached itself to produce hydrogen, and so on and so forth till we get to Mahler's 'Adagio'. That's why I'm not religious, because for me this is as rich as the greatest god.

Magic is also a certain technique.

The kind of technique where there is no technique. Suprarational. Using intuition. What I find most interesting about magic is that it's richer than rationality. I kind of feel my way through life. All my actions are slightly irrational, including the practical ones. I've started feeling like I'm in my element here. I'm convinced that we can harness magic. I know how I do it. I need some music, and I get myself into a particular mood. I go the whole hog, whether it's by starving myself, or by concentrating, so as not to think about anything else. And, basically, it works like a charm.

In the last few months, you've been playing very intensively, taking part in all kinds of different projects. You're playing with the quartet and the new quintet; and you're also playing gigs in a quartet with Dominik Wania; and concerts with Smolik on the *Peyotl* project. And there's also been a mini-festival in Vienna, a concert in New York with an American line-up. You've performed a Komeda programme with symphony orchestra and played a concert with folk singers. So much has happened in the first half of 2009. Where has this explosion of activity come from? I began with a question about self-defence because I'd been wondering whether this increased activity might not be some sort of new tactic of yours for being on the scene.

It's the opposite of what I did before. I'd spend years playing with one band. Convenience had a large part to play in that: I had excellent musicians and I didn't want to change anything. You don't need to rehearse. Then at some point the quartet stopped moving forward. Now, the more rehearsals I have, the more creative I am. I'm receptive. I've got going. Whereas before, I didn't want to do it, now it's the opposite. I play differently with Wania, differently with the quintet. I'm enriching myself. I'm moving through a diversified world of sound.

The Tomasz Stańko Quintet at the Porgy and Bess Club, Vienna, 2009.
(From left: Alexi Tuomarila, Tomasz Stańko, Anders Christensen, Jakob Bro.)
Photograph by Wojciech Kornet

Now I'm focusing on an album with the quintet. Never in my life would I have thought that this new band would have turned out the way it has. That bass player! A strange cat. No one plays the electric bass like Anders Christensen. He plays some mysterious sounds; he mutters things. I have two guitars in the band: two Danes, like a kind of gigantic guitar coming out of my hallucinatory dreams, piano, drums and trumpet. The guitarist, Jakob Bro, has already recorded for ECM with Paul Motian.

When you said goodbye to your quartet after *Lontano*, did you already have the quintet in mind, or just a new band? Was it still a blank sheet of paper?
A totally blank sheet of paper. I began tinkering around with musicians. I took Tuomarila on first. I played a bit with Jormin, but Tuomarila was there all the way through.

How did you discover Tuomarila? He's a pianist from Finland.
I heard him in Norway, in Oslo. I was doing a concert in a duo with Bobo, and his trio played just before us. I thought, 'He's fuckin' giving it some, that pianist. He's young, but he plays brilliantly.' I didn't even take his contact details. I asked Ania to track him down afterwards. I couldn't remember his name: we looked for it in the programme. And so I read about him in the programme. The fact that Stuart Nicholson was full of praise for him meant a lot. I don't usually take journalists' opinions on board. But occasionally I do. It also depends on intuition. Thousands of factors influence my decisions.

I got Tuomarila over for a gig in Poland, and at the rehearsal I thought, 'What have I done? He's not playing my kind of music.' Later on, when we were playing with Jormin, something in him opened up, and it went brilliantly. Tuomarila began playing with me as a core band member. I was thinking about guitar. I wanted to play in unison with a guitar. I was moving intuitively. What? A saxophone? I didn't want a saxophone. I was writing music that a guitar could play, kind of riffs, a bit like a harp. I took on Bro, and he recommended Christensen. I thought to myself, 'What a model!' I was most surprised at the way he played free on electric bass. He plays groove in his own way as well. I tell you – no one plays like that. He plays individual, monotonous notes – *trrr duu duu duu dam daam daam daam dam* – and he doesn't get bored doing it.

Does Christensen only play on electric bass?
Just electric.

What's Tuomarila like compared to other pianists you've played with?
A strong personality. He has a phenomenal technique, a classical technique. He's rhythmically very precise, yet lyrical at the same time. He plays lovely lines, very much his own, very mainstream. A prize musician. High class.

Having got your core piano and guitar band members, you've spent the last two years trying out a lot of rhythm-section musicians.
I've searched and searched. Emotionally, Christensen is the one who has appealed to me the most. I took Jim Black on drums with me to Brazil. He's brilliant, but I see he's busy all the time. The same with Joey Baron. I played with him in Bielsko-Biała. He'd be the best. In my opinion, Baron is actually one of the best drummers alive, as is Brian Blade from Wayne Shorter's band. They both have a similar way of playing, with lines: they play lines, the bastards, but they don't half swing. It's just that Baron has lots of engagements, so it was difficult to get our schedules to fit in with each other. I do have to have someone from Europe. Tuomarila had his own trio. I tried out his percussionist. I liked him. He's stayed on and he plays very well: he swings. A Finn: Olavi Louhivuori. I'm absolutely delighted with this line-up. We've worked out a certain style of playing. We play a lot in unison: piano, trumpet, guitar. The bass also plays in unison now and again. Sometimes we play duets. We're primarily creating a sound. A band sound where there are different solos. Tuomarila plays classy jazz solos. Bro plays similarly to Jim Hall. Nicely, simply. The free bits are played mainly by the bass player and me.

Hall! He's old-school – back from before the Pat Metheny and John McLaughlin jazz-rock era.
Old-school. And it's coming back. Bro plays simply and sparsely. He knows how to play sparingly, subtly. He goes with the melody. Jim Hall! Beautiful music. I'd like to play with Jim Hall.

He must be well past seventy. I mean, he came to fame back in the 1950s.
He still plays brilliantly. I've heard him a few times. Who knows . . . ? That's why I'm pleased I have a New York apartment.

It struck me that Bro was educated at the most famous American jazz academy of them all – Berklee – and that Tuomarila is a graduate of the Royal Conservatoire in Brussels. Is the fact that you chose them proof that the era of brilliant jazz amateurs is now over?
It's hard for the amateurs. To play nowadays, you do need to have a technique.

Yet Christensen plays in a popular Danish rock band, the Raveonettes.
The way Christensen is – when I was talking to Bro about Christensen, 'I don't think he ever practises anything, does he?' Bro smiled: 'No. Well, no.' He doesn't practise at all. He doesn't need to. That's how he is. But he's brilliant at reading music, fast – my difficult notation, my broken phrases. He might make one mistake, but he can play straight off. He naturally finds it easy. The band has a good mix. I think that in jazz it's always important to choose musicians with different profiles: the virtuosos along with the real ones. That's why I'm so happy to have Christensen: he brings in a different way of thinking, the kind that school takes away.

In your new quintet, you're in the role of vampire once again.
I like playing with the young ones. They have a breadth of approach, a freshness.

You said that with your new band you'd like to go in a melodic, rhythmical, easy direction. Are those the kinds of compositions that you've written with this band in mind?
In a way, yes.

The album that you're going to be recording at the beginning of May with the quintet – has it taken you a long time to get the material together for it?
Nearly two years. I began thinking about it when Bro appeared. Sławomir was playing with us on bass. That was in November 2007. The first I time had Bro playing was at a concert in Gdańsk. That's when I wrote my composition 'Nice One', and that's how the quintet started. At that time I also wrote 'Terminal 7', which I play with the quintet. It takes me a long time to write. My writing only really got going in New York.

Did much of the material for the new album get written in New York?
'Dark Eyes of Martha Hirsch', 'Amsterdam Avenue', 'Grand Central' and 'Samba Nova'. Four compositions. But there are going to be seven new ones. I wrote 'Nice One' earlier. 'Terminal 7' and 'May Sun' are theatre pieces. Out of Komeda's pieces I'd like to record 'Ballet Étude Number 3' and 'Dirge for Europe'. And from my older stuff possibly something from *Balladyna*: 'First Song', 'Last Song' or 'Balladyna'. There's also a piece from the film *Cisza*, which I've already played with the quintet: 'Oni'. We might record that as well.

Does the title 'Dark Eyes of Martha Hirsch' refer to a painting?
Kokoschka. That painting hangs in Ronald Lauder's Neue Galerie. I wanted to finally bring my New York inspirations to fruition. It's a small gallery with Austrian art, Secession, Decadence, Klimt, beautiful furniture. I used to visit it, and Kokoschka definitely had his effect on me. I began to write. It took me a very long time to write that composition. I kept changing it. It's three ballads, and a fourth at the end, a fast section: 'Dark', 'Eyes', 'Martha', 'Hirsch'. I'm going to be able to play that for a long time. A rich composition. Enjoyable to play.

As we discussed, you also sought inspiration in the Metropolitan Museum of Art.
I used to go there as well. 'Amsterdam Avenue' is partially a result of that. To tell the truth, it doesn't really work. What works is my wanting it to work, the fact that I talk about it. It's guaranteed stimulation. The road through Central Park. I'm walking along. Something's happening. I'm working. In the end, it's work, and work alone. It's just that some people are strong: they can work all fucking day and night, but I can't, because I get tired. It's different for me.

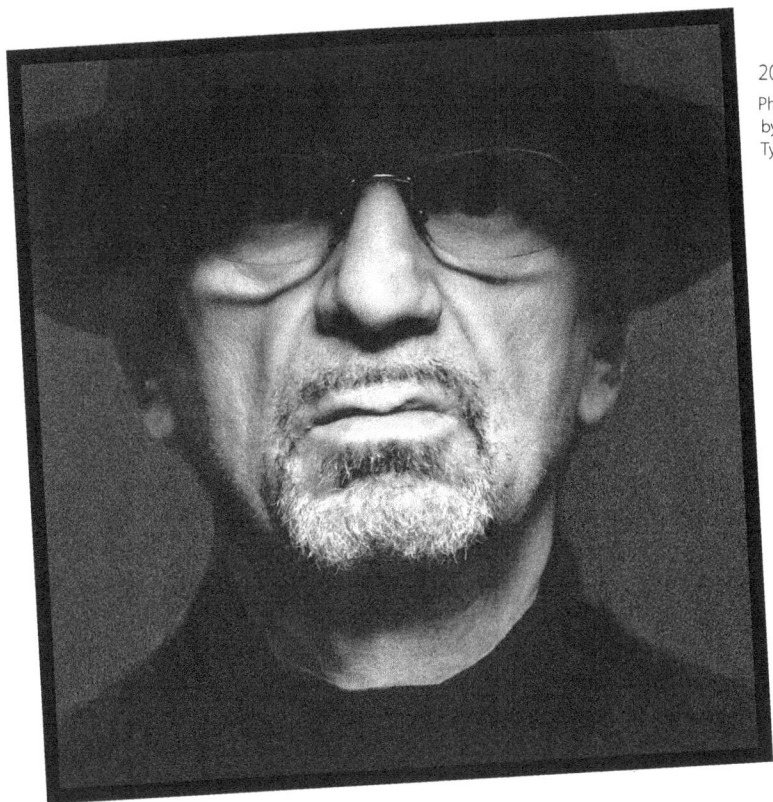

2004.
Photograph by Andrzej Tyszko

Do you have to manufacture your inspiration?
Manufacture my inspiration. There are different ways, but there are no rules.

In two weeks' time, you'll be going into the studio with the quintet.
I'm under pressure. Because this is an important thing. I don't want to record the kind of albums that old people do, the *pa pa pa pa* kind. I don't want to do that. I want every album to be meaningful. I don't know how it's all going to sound. There's not much time left. We're rehearsing now, two concerts, three days of rehearsals.

Is it a question of perfecting your compositions?
Compositions. Little things. Giving it shape, phrasing. I want to check what we're doing with Komeda, what we're going to play. Share out the solos, decide who's playing what. To make sure that everyone has the bits that they're most comfortable with.

Do you have a preliminary idea of what kind of material it's going to be?
I do, although all that might change in the studio. It's going to be an album ranging from free ballads to trance-like rhythms. Trance-like rhythms with a very monotonous bass. Trance-like playing on one note.

Well, I have another quote up my sleeve from Michał Choromański, concerning rhythm. A fabulous extract from *Biali bracia* ['White Brothers'], his first novel: 'There's an underlying rhythm on this earth, to which we are subject, and it's only by feeling this rhythm that we can be assured of good fortune in our lives. To be able to experience happiness, we indisputably need to be musical. A so-called wasted life calls to mind a person dancing out of time.'
Beautifully written. Being musical isn't enough: we need to feel the rhythm of life. I've been wondering why the hell things work out for me. Why have things gone well for me right from the start, but not for my sister or my father? Maybe they didn't find their own rhythm. They might have been frightened of taking the dangerous route, which I wasn't frightened of, as I'd numbed myself with all those toxic substances.

Do you think that your sense of rhythm is such that, even after so many different turnings, you can feel fulfilled in life?
In a certain sense, yes. I could say that. Things have worked out for me. When I was going through bumpy terrain, I had to desensitize myself, but, when the road became normal, I cleaned up my system, because clarity is the best thing. The people who are successful in this business are people who are sober, because they want to make the most of their position and their money. To be conscious without being desensitized, however – that is the most perfect state. I managed to find my own rhythm, to find myself and to synchronize the two. I was unusual, so I made an unusual choice. Jazz was the one thing that could draw me in.

Do you feel like a successful person?
I can't say that because I don't think in those terms. Obviously, I'm happy (and increasingly so these days) to have achieved certain things and to have had some successes. When I think back to when I was young: I didn't think that things would have worked out as they have. I'm pleased with my achievements and my playing, but I still believe, and I can feel it, that I'm moving forward, and that I'm going to keep moving forward. There's an empty space ahead of me. As ever.

Like those Portuguese sailors in Lisbon, who stood looking out at the ocean, knowing that 'There's something out there!' But they didn't know what. They just hoped that, by sailing out there, they'd see something different, something mysterious. And indeed they did. I still have that sense of mystery, that, musically, something strange is going to happen to me, that I'll be moving into areas as yet unknown to me. And that's where I'll be hanging around.

Tomasz Stańko's Life and Works: A Chronology

1942
- 11 July: Tomasz Stańko is born in Rzeszów, son of Józef Stańko (a lawyer) and Eleonora, née Jakubiec (a teacher).

1949–1957
- Attends junior music school in Kraków: violin class.

1957–1964
- Attends Kraków's Liceum im. Kochanowskiego (high school), then from 1959 the Liceum im. Sobieskiego (high school) in conjunction with the Intermediate School of Music, in the trumpet class.

1958
- First jazz concert: Dave Brubeck at the Rotunda in Kraków – just as an audience member.
- Starts learning to play the trumpet.
- Public debut as a trumpeter at a party.

1959
- First professional engagement: a performance at a New Year's Eve party at the Kraków club U Plastyków as part of Stanisław 'Drążek' Kalwinski's band.

1960–1961
- Takes part in jazz jam sessions in clubs in Kraków.

1962

- Forms his first band, Jazz Darings, with the line-up: Tomasz Stańko (trumpet); Jacek Ostaszewski (double bass); Adam Matyszkowicz (later Makowicz) (piano); Wiktor Perelmuter (drums).

1963

- The Great Contest of Southern Poland's Amateur Jazz Musicians. First prize in the soloist category, and first prize for the band Jazz Darings.
- First concert tour in Silesia with Michał Urbaniak's quintet.
- Debut in Krzysztof Komeda's new quintet at Jazz Jamboree. Begins a close collaboration with Komeda, which lasts until Komeda's departure for the US in December 1967.
- Recording of the album *What's Up Mr Basie* with Krzysztof Komeda at Jazz Jamboree in October. These are his earliest recordings to appear on record.

1964–1969

- Student at the Higher School of Music in Kraków, in the instrumental section, studying trumpet under Professor Ludwik Lutak.

1964

- Second line-up of Jazz Darings: Stańko, Ostaszewski, Perelmuter and Janusz Muniak (saxophone).
- First concerts abroad: with Andrzej Trzaskowski's quintet at a jazz festival in Antwerp; with Komeda's quintet at jazz festivals in Kongsberg (Norway), Bled (in the former Yugoslavia) and Prague (former Czechoslovakia). During the last of these, Stańko records music which appears on the compilation album *Jazz Greetings from the East*.

1965

- January: album recording session – *The Andrzej Trzaskowski Quintet* for the 'Polish Jazz' series – and records Komeda's music for the Polish stage version of *Breakfast at Tiffany's*.
- January–February: a several-week-long tour of Scandinavia with Komeda's quintet; concerts at the Montmartre club in Copenhagen and at the Gyllene Cirkeln (Golden Circle) club in Stockholm.
- Performs at Jazz Jamboree with Komeda's quintet: the premiere of the *Astigmatic* programme.
- December: records the Komeda Quintet's album *Astigmatic* for the 'Polish Jazz' series.

1966

- Takes part in an International Jazz Contest in Vienna.
- Records Komeda's music to Jerzy Skolimowski's film *Barrier*.

1967

- Performs the first cycle of his composition *Jazz Mass* in the Dominican Church in Kraków.
- Records the music to Skolimowski's film *Ręce do góry* (*Hands Up!*).
- Goes to Hamburg with Andrzej Trzaskowski's band for Die Jazz-Werkstatt (workshop).
- Records the album *Meine süsse Europäische Heimat: Dichtung und Jazz aus Polen* with Komeda's quintet in Baden-Baden for Electrola/Columbia.
- Performs 'Nighttime, Daytime Requiem' with Komeda's quintet during Jazz Jamboree. The concert is preceded by a radio session, during which this piece is recorded.

1968

- Forms the Tomasz Stańko Quintet with the line-up: Tomasz Stańko (trumpet); Zbigniew Seifert (violin; alto saxophone); Janusz Muniak (soprano saxophone; tenor saxophone; flute; percussion); Bronisław Suchanek (double bass); Janusz Stefański (drums).
- Moves to Warsaw.
- Goes to Hamburg again with Trzaskowski for Die Jazz-Werkstatt.
- Concert at Jazz Jamboree with the quartet: Tomasz Stańko (trumpet); Jan 'Ptaszyn' Wróblewski (saxophone); Jacek Bednarek (double bass); Grzegorz Gierłowski (drums).

1969

- Defends his thesis on *The Role of the Trumpet as a Solo Instrument in Modern Jazz* at the Higher School of Music in Kraków.
- Performs with the quintet at Jazz Jamboree and wins first prize for *Music for K* in a composition competition.

1970

- January: records his first album under his own name: *Music for K*, in the 'Polish Jazz' series.
- PWN publishes Stańko's score, *10 Studies of Jazz for Trumpet*.
- A breakthrough performance for the quintet on the international scene at Berliner Jazztage, alongside such big names as Oliver Nelson, Charles Mingus and George Russell.

- First performances in Germany with the international free-jazz big band Globe Unity Orchestra, led by Alexander von Schlippenbach.

1971–1973
- Plays concerts with the quintet in Germany, including at the most prestigious festivals; joins the ranks of elite European jazz musicians.
- Intensive collaboration with Jan 'Ptaszyn' Wróblewski's big band as part of the Studio Jazzowe Polskiego Radio (Polish Radio Jazz Studio) project.

1971
- Performs at the Donaueschinger Musiktage in Germany with the European Free Jazz Orchestra big band, playing Don Cherry's music and Krzysztof Penderecki's composition 'Actions for Free Jazz Orchestra'.
- The quintet performs at Jazz Jamboree with Diana Black's ballet troupe, just before Ornette Coleman's concert.
- Winner of the Polish Jazz Association's prize for his music to Mirosław Kijowicz's animated film *Science Fiction* at the National Festival of Short Films in Kraków.

1972
- The quintet's live album *Jazzmessage from Poland* is released in Germany.
- Records the album *We'll Remember Komeda* with Michał Urbaniak in Germany.

1973
- Records the album *Purple Sun* with the quintet in Germany.
- Records the album *Fish Face* for the PSJ Record Club with the experimental line-up of Stu Martin (synthesizer, drums) and Janusz Stefański (drums).
- The quintet's last appearance at Jazz Jamboree alongside Don Cherry's Organic Music Theatre. A recording of this concert was released in 1983 on the A side of the LP *W Pałacu Prymasowskim* ['In the Primate's Palace'].
- Formation of the band 'Unit', with the following line-up: Tomasz Stańko (trumpet); Adam Makowicz (Fender Rhodes; electric bass); Czesław Bartkowski (drums).

1974
- Concerts with the rock supergroup SBB.

- Starts a collaboration with the percussionist Edward Vesala, who becomes Stańko's closest collaborator and friend up until the early 1980s. Their musical collaborations are expressed in every possible configuration, from duets to Stańko's appearances in Vesala's big bands. They tour extensively all over Europe.
- The new quartet records the album *TWET* for the 'Polish Jazz' series with the line-up: Tomasz Stańko (trumpet); Edward Vesala (percussion); Tomasz Szukalski (saxophone); Peter Warren (bass).

1975
- European release of the album *Tomasz Stańko & Adam Makowicz Unit*, recorded in Germany.
- Records *Balladyna*, his first album for ECM with the line-up: Tomasz Stańko (trumpet); Edward Vesala (percussion); Tomasz Szukalski (saxophone); Dave Holland (bass).

1976
- Takes part in the recording of Edward Vesala's albums *Rodina* and *Satu*.
- Records the Stańko–Vesala Quartet's live album *Live at Remont*.

1978
- Records *Almost Green* in Finland with the quartet, on Vesala's record label Leo.
- First concerts on solo trumpet.
- Marries Joanna Renke.
- A daughter is born – Anna Stańko.

1979
- A solo performance at Jazz Jamboree.
- A solo concert precedes a performance by the Art Ensemble of Chicago at All Souls' Jazz in Kraków.
- Takes part in the recording of Vesala's album *Neitsytmatka* ['Maiden Voyage'].

1980
- Travels to India with Vesala. Solo recordings for the album *Music from Taj Mahal and Karla Caves*, released that same year on Vesala's record label Leo.

- Stays with Vesala in New York. Records material for Vesala's album *Heavy Life*, alongside big names like Reggie Workman and James Spaulding.
- European concerts for the trio of Tomasz Stańko, Edward Vesala and Reggie Workman, including a performance at Jazz Jamboree. A performance at this same Jazz Jamboree with Vesala's 'Heavy Life' project.

1981

- Extensive concerts for the Stańko–Vesala–Workman trio.
- Stays in Stockholm. Records with the Swedish Radio Big Band.
- Records in Oslo with Gary Peacock – an album for ECM: *Voice from the Past: Paradigm.*
- Sets up a new band, a quartet with the line-up: Tomasz Stańko (trumpet); Sławomir Kulpowicz (piano); Witold Szczurek (later Vitold Rek) (double bass); Czesław Bartkowski (drums).

1982

- Records two albums with the quartet: *Music 81* (April) for the 'Polish Jazz' series and *A i J* (July).

1983

- Collaborates with the Graham Collier Orchestra; tours in Germany and performs at the Bracknell Festival in the UK.
- Records the album *Korozje* ['Corrosion'] as a duo with Andrzej Kurylewicz.
- The live album, *W Pałacu Prymasowskim* ['In the Primate's Palace'] is released.
- Sets up the band C.O.C.X.; records the album *C.O.C.X.* with the line-up: Tomasz Stańko (trumpet); Apostolis Anthimos (Lakis) (guitar; electric bass; percussion); Vitold Rek (double bass, gong); José Antonio Torres (congas; percussion).
- Performs with C.O.C.X. at the Róbrege New Wave festival in Warsaw.
- Records the album *Good Luck, Bad Luck* with Vesala and the Finnish big band UMO.

1984

- Records the album *Lady Go* with the line-up: Tomasz Stańko (trumpet); Apostolis Anthimos (Lakis) (guitar; percussion); Vitold Rek (double bass; electric bass); Tomasz Hołuj (percussion).

- Plays with Cecil Taylor's big band 'Music from Two Continents'. European tour and recording of the album *Winged Serpent* (*Sliding Quadrants*) for the Italian label Soul Note.
- Performs at Le Mans Festival in France.
- Performs at Jazz Jamboree in a trio with Rufus Reid and Jack DeJohnette.
- Stańko and Szukalski start their live collaborations as a duo.
- Starts work on the *Witkacy Peyotl* project.

1985

- The Freelectronic formation is set up with the line-up: Tomasz Stańko (trumpet); Vitold Rek (double bass; electric bass); Janusz Skowron (synthesizer); Tadeusz Sudnik (synthesizer).
- Freelectronic performs alongside top Italian jazz musicians at the Rumori Mediterranei festival in Italy.

1987

- The *Witkacy Peyotl/Freelectronic* album is released.
- The premiere of *Nienasycenie* ['Insatiability'], a ballet performance by Zofia Rudnicka with music by Stańko at Warsaw's Wielki Theatre.
- Freelectronic concerts with Sonny Sharrock and a performance at punk-funk-jazz 3. Ruhr Jazzfestival in Bochum, Germany, alongside the Rova Saxophone Quartet, Material, Ronald Shannon Jackson, Blurt and Toshinori Kondo.
- A Freelectronic concert at the Montreux Jazz Festival, released the following year on the album *Switzerland*.

1988

- Freelectronic plays at the Le Mans Festival in France.
- Performs with Cecil Taylor's European Orchestra during a Berlin festival dedicated to his work. The concert is documented and released in Germany in the form of an eleven-album box, which includes the album *Alms/Tiergarten (Spree)*, on which Stańko performs.

1989

- Records the album *Chameleon* for Utopia Records in Greece.

1990

- Begins a collaboration with Christian Muthspiel. Between 1990 and 1995, Stańko is involved in Muthspiel's East European project Octet

Ost, playing concerts and recording two albums: *Octet Ost* and *Octet Ost II.*

1991

- First edition of the Jazz Baltica festival. Plays in two versions of the Jazz Baltica Ensemble.
- Records the album *Tales for a Girl, 12* with Janusz Skowron.
- Records the album *Bluish,* in a trio with Arild Andersen (bass) and Jon Christensen (drums).

1992

- Plays with the Jazz Baltica Ensemble again with David Murray as leader.
- Records the trumpet parts for Zbigniew Preisner's composition for Louis Malle's film *Damage.*

1993

- A South American tour with the trio: Tomasz Stańko, Manfred Bründl, Michael Riessler; that same year, they release the album *Suite Talk* in Germany.
- Forms a quartet with the following line-up: Tomasz Stańko (trumpet); Bobo Stenson (piano); Anders Jormin (bass); Tony Oxley (drums).
- The quartet records the album *Bosonossa and Other Ballads.*
- Records his own music for Filip Zylber's film *A Farewell to Maria.* Wins first prize for his film music at the FPFF Polish Film Festival in Gdynia.
- Begins a collaboration with Marcin Wasilewski, Sławomir Kurkiewicz and Michał Miśkiewicz.

1994

- Records his own music for the play *Balladyna,* in Rudolf Zioło's production at the Ludowy Theatre in Nowa Huta.
- Records the album *Matka Joanna* with the quartet, which marks Tomasz Stańko's return to the ECM label.

1995

- Records his own music for Krzysztof Warlikowski's play *Roberto Zucco* at the Nowy Theatre in Poznań.

1996

- Records the album *Leosia* with the quartet.

1997

- Records *Litania*, an album of Komeda's music.

1998

- Records the album *From the Green Hill*.
- A solo performance with the German NDR Bigband on the *Ellingtonia* project.
- Appears in Witold Adamek's film *Poniedziałek* ['Monday'].

1999

- Nominated for a Polish Film Award for his music for Andrzej Domalik's film *Łóżko Wierszynina* ['Wierszynin's Bed'].

2000

- Nominated for a Philip Award and a Polish Film Award for his music to Filip Zylber's film *Egzekutor* ['The Executor'].
- Awarded the prestigious Schallplattenpreis German Film Critics' Award for the album *From the Green Hill*: best jazz record of the year.

2001

- Records the album *Soul of Things*, which is released the following year, drawing critical attention to the Polish quartet: Tomasz Stańko (trumpet); Marcin Wasilewski (piano); Sławomir Kurkiewicz (double bass); Michał Miśkiewicz (drums).

2002

- The quartet's first tour of the US.
- Winner of the inaugural European Jazz Prize, awarded in Vienna.
- Nominated for a Polish Film Award for his music for Michał Rosa's film *Cisza* ['Silence'].

2003

- Records the album *Suspended Night* with the quartet.
- Performs solo with the UMO Jazz Orchestra at the Helsinki Jazz Festival in Finland with a classical Miles Davis programme and Miles's and Gil Evans's *Sketches of Spain*.

2004

- The *Billboard* magazine chart lists *Suspended Night* as one of the best-selling European jazz albums on the American market.
- A record year for the quartet in terms of performances: concerts in Europe, tours of the UK and the US.

- Polish President Aleksander Komorowski awards Stańko the Commander's Cross of the Order of Polonia Restituta for his outstanding contribution to musical culture and his artistic achievement.
- Artistic director of two international festivals in Poland: 'Sygnowano Stańko' in Warsaw's Fabryka Trzciny (Textile Factory) and 'Jazz Autumn' in Bielsko-Biała. The annual Jazz Autumn festival continues to this day.

2005

- The quartet's third tour of the US.
- Records music for the Rising Museum in Warsaw. Stańko's recordings provide background music for the exhibition.
- The quartet's first tour of Asia and Australia: concerts in Japan, Australia and South Korea.
- Records *Lontano*, which turns out to be the quartet's farewell album.
- Concerts with the trio: Tomasz Stańko (trumpet); John Abercrombie (guitar); Marc Johnson (double bass).

2006

- Fourth tour of the US.

2007

- Presents the programme *New Balladyna*, with Tim Berne (saxophone) and Anders Jormin and Stefan Pasborg (rhythm section) at the Aarhus International Jazz Festival and the Copenhagen Jazz Festival in Denmark. Stańko plays this programme in Poland with the New Balladyna Quartet in the line-up: Tomasz Stańko (trumpet); Maciej Obara (saxophone); Maciej Grabowski (bass); Krzysztof Gradziuk (drums).
- This year's 'Chopin and his Europe Festival' carries the strapline 'From Mozart to Tomasz Stańko'; Stańko performs with pianist Makoto Ozone.
- Showcases a band that is the nucleus of his new quintet during the Jazz Autumn festival in Bielsko-Biała. Stańko is joined by Alexi Tuomarila (piano); Sławomir Kurkiewicz and Anders Jormin (double bass); Jakob Bro (guitar); Maciej Obara (saxophone); Joey Baron (drums).

2008

- Buys an apartment in Manhattan.

- Concert of Komeda's music in the Museum of Modern Art in New York with the quartet and the saxophonist Billy Harper.
- Launch of the *Peyotl* project at Jazz Autumn in Bielsko-Biała, presenting a new version of the *Witkacy Peyotl* material with Andrzej Smolik taking part.

2009
- January: records the album *Tutaj* at the Kraków Opera with Wisława Szymborska.
- First concert at the Merkin Hall in New York with local musicians: Craig Taborn (piano); Thomas Morgan (double bass); Jim Black (drums).
- Records the album *Dark Eyes* with the new quintet in the following line-up: Tomasz Stańko (trumpet); Alexi Tuomarila (piano); Jakob Bro (guitar); Anders Christensen (electric bass); Olavi Louhivuori (drums).

2010
- A concert tour of the US promoting the album *Dark Eyes*.

2014
- January: Tomasz Stańko is awarded the Polytika Passport for his cultural work, and the same day receives the Prix du Musicien Européen in Paris.
- Records and releases the album *Polin* (music for the POLIN Museum of the History of Polish Jews) with Tomasz Stańko (trumpet); Ravi Coltrane (saxophones); David Virelles (piano); Dezron Douglas (bass); Kush Abadey (drums).

2016
- Records his final studio album for ECM, *December Avenue* (released in 2017) with Tomasz Stańko (trumpet); David Virelles (piano); Reuben Rogers (bass); Gerald Cleaver (drums).

2018
- Tomasz Stańko dies of lung cancer in Warsaw on 29 July.

Discography

I. Albums as leader

Tomasz Stańko, *Music for K*
Polish Jazz Series, 22
LP, Polskie Nagrania Muza, 1970; CD, Power Bros, 1995; CD, Polskie Nagrania Muza, 2004; CD, Metal Mind Productions, 2009
Tomasz Stańko, t; Zbigniew Seifert, as; Janusz Muniak, ts; Bronisław Suchanek, b; Janusz Stefański, d.
Recorded January 1970, National Philharmonic, Warsaw.

    Czatownik (The Ambusher) / Nieskończenie mały (Infinitely Small) / Cry / Music for K / Temat/Czatownik (Theme/The Ambusher)

Tomasz Stańko Quintet, *Jazzmessage from Poland*
LP, JG-Records, 1972
Tomasz Stańko, t; Zbigniew Seifert, vn, as; Janusz Muniak, ss, ts, fl, perc; Bronisław Suchanek, b; Janusz Stefański, d, perc.
Recorded live 28 May 1972, Parktheater, Iserlohn, Germany.

    Aeoioe/Heban / Piece for Diana

Tomasz Stańko Quintet, *Purple Sun*
LP, Calig, 1973; CD, Selles, 1999; CD, Milo Records, 2006
Tomasz Stańko, t; Zbigniew Seifert, vn, as; Janusz Muniak, ss, ts, fl, perc; Hans Hartmann, b; Janusz Stefański, d, perc.
Recorded 9 March 1973, Musikhochschule, Munich, Germany.

    Boratka and Flute Ballad / My Night, My Day / Flair / Purple Sun

Tomasz Stańko, *Fish Face*
Biały Kruk Czarnego Krążka Series, PSJ Record Club
LP, PolJazz, 1974
Tomasz Stańko, t; Stu Martin, d, synth; Janusz Stefański, d.
Recorded August 1973, Polish Radio Studio, Warsaw.

    Fish Face / Fat Belly Ellie / Mike Spike

Tomasz Stańko, *TWET*
Polish Jazz Series, 39
LP, Polskie Nagrania Muza, 1975; CD, Power Bros, 1999; CD, Polskie Nagrania Muza, 2004; CD, Metal Mind Productions, 2009
Tomasz Stańko, t; Tomasz Szukalski, ts, ss; bcl; Edward Vesala, perc; Peter Warren, b.
Recorded 2 April 1974, PWSM Hall, Warsaw.

  Dark Awakening / TWET / Mintuu Maria / Man from North / Night Peace

Tomasz Stańko & Adam Makowicz Unit, *Tomasz Stańko & Adam Makowicz Unit*
LP, JG-Records, 1975
Tomasz Stańko, t; Adam Makowicz, elec p; Czesław Bartkowski, perc.
Recorded 1975, Germany.

  Countdown / Unit / Matce / Solar / Ballad for Randi Hultin / Pony Lungz / Zaduma

Tomasz Stańko & Adam Makowicz, *Unit*
Biały Kruk Czarnego Krążka Series, 13, PSJ Record Club
LP, Pronit, 1976
Tomasz Stańko, t; Adam Makowicz, p, elec p, elec b; Paweł Jarzębski, b; Czesław Bartkowski, d.
Recorded 7 October 1975, Warsaw.

  What Is This Thing Called Love / Blues Dla Ireny ['Blues for Irene'] / Over the Rainbow
  / Reminiscencje Moskiewskie ['Moscow Reminiscences'] / If I Were a Bell / Fiolety
  ['Purples'] / Shadows / Końcówka ['Ending']

Tomasz Stańko, *Balladyna*
LP, ECM, 1976; CD, ECM, 1994, 2008 (Touchstones Series)
Tomasz Stańko, t; Tomasz Szukalski, ts, ss; Dave Holland, b; Edward Vesala, perc.
Recorded December 1975, Tonstudio Bauer, Ludwigsburg, Germany.

  First Song / Tale / Num / Duet / Balladyna / Last Song / Nenaliina

Tomasz Stańko/Edward Vesala Quartet, *Live at Remont*
LP, Helicon, 1978
Tomasz Stańko, t; Tomasz Szukalski, ts, ss; Antti Hytti, b; Edward Vesala, perc.
Recorded 24 October 1976, Remont club, Warsaw.

  Komba / First Song / Little, Beautiful Dancing Girl / Sowa ['Owl']

Tomasz Stańko, *Almost Green*
LP, Leo Records, 1979
Tomasz Stańko, t; Tomasz Szukalski, ts, ss; Palle Danielsson, b; Edward Vesala, perc.
Recorded, 1978, Love Studio, Helsinki, Finland.

  New Song / From Greenhills / Slowly By / When on Earth / Almost Green / Megaira

Tomasz Stańko, *Music from Taj Mahal and Karla Caves*
LP, Leo Records, 1980
Tomasz Stańko, t.
Recorded late February/early March 1980, Temple of Taj Mahal and Karla Caves, India.

  Sbigi / Shadow of the Midnight Moon / Daada / Almost Black / For You / Night Flight
  / Almost Black / Small Rooms' Magic / Daada / Mountain Bird / Slambura Road / And
  the Ancient Ones Smiled / Nightly Whisper

Tomasz Stańko, *A i J*
LP, PolJazz, 1985; CD, Polonia Records, 1997

Tomasz Stańko, t; Sławomir Kulpowicz, p; Vitold Rek, b; Czesław Bartkowski, d.
Recorded July 1982, Akwarium club, Warsaw.

 Natka / A i J / Stambura Road / Monday

Tomasz Stańko, *Music 81*
Polish Jazz Series, 69
LP, Polskie Nagrania Muza, 1984; CD, Polskie Nagrania Muza, 2004; CD, Metal Mind Productions, 2009

Tomasz Stańko, t; Sławomir Kulpowicz, p; Vitold Rek, b; Czesław Bartkowski, d.
Recorded April/May 1982, Studio 12, Polskie Nagrania, Warsaw.

 Alusta / Daada / Bushka / Third Heavy Ballad / Ahuha

Tomasz Stańko, *W Pałacu Prymasowskim* ['At the Primate's Palace']
LP, PolJazz, 1983

Tomasz Stańko, t; Zbigniew Seifert, vn, as; Janusz Muniak, ts, ss, fl, perc; Bronisław Suchanek, b; Janusz Stefański, d.
Recorded 28 October 1973, Jazz Jamboree Festival, Congress Hall, Warsaw.

 Flair – Piece for Diana

Tomasz Stańko, t.
Recorded April 1982, Primate's Palace, Warsaw.

 W Pałacu Prymasowskim

Tomasz Stańko, Andrzej Kurylewicz, *Korozje* ['Corrosion']
LP, PolJazz, 1986; CD Polonia Records, 1997

Tomasz Stańko, t; Andrzej Kurylewicz, p.
Recorded February 1983, Polish Radio Studio, Warsaw.

 Korozja Pierwsza ['First Corrosion'] / Korozja szósta ['Sixth Corrosion'] / Korozja trzecia ['Third Corrosion'] / Korozja druga ['Second Corrosion'] / Korozja czwarta ['Fourth Corrosion']

Tomasz Stańko, *C.O.C.X.*
LP, Pronit, 1985; CD, Polonia Records, 1997

Tomasz Stańko, t; Apostolis Anthimos, g, elec b, d, perc; Vitold Rek, b, gong; José Antonio Torres, cnga, perc.
Recorded May 1983, studio of the STU Theatre, Kraków.

 Mademoiselle 'Ka' / Babylon Samba / Gama / Mr DD / C.O.C.X. / Jose i Lak / Kameleon / Song for Pula / Fioletowy Liquor

Tomasz Stańko, *Lady Go*
LP, Polskie Nagrania Muza, 1986; CD, Metal Mind Productions, 2009

Tomasz Stańko, t; Apostolis Anthimos, g, d; Vitold Rek, b, elec b; Tomasz Hołuj, perc.
Recorded June 1984, Warsaw.

 Modi Modi / The First / Mr Paul at Marta's Place / Lady Go / Last Song / Lakis & Basia / Violet Liquor / Les Papillons Gris / Modi Modi

Tomasz Stańko, *Witkacy Peyotl/Freelectronic*
LP, PolJazz, 1988; CD, Polonia Records, 1996

I. *Witkacy Peyotl*: Tomasz Stańko, t; Marek Walczewski, v; Tadeusz Sudnik, AKS synth; Janusz Skowron, Yamaha DX7 synth; Vitold Rek, b, elec b; Andrzej Przybielski, t; Apostolis Anthimos, g, d, perc; Zbigniew Brysiak, perc.
Recorded Warsaw, April 1984–November 1986.

My W.S.B. Friend / Witkacy, Wizje Cz. I (Belzebub/Cudownej Piękności Morze/ Skuropatiwe Nie Jastrzębia/Brzeg Jeziora) / Witkacy, Wizje Cz. II (Hades/Wieże Znikające/Wyciory Cylindry/Olbrzymia Czaszka/Potworny Negr/Cudownie Piękna Blondynka) / Hej!

II. *Freelectronic*: Tomasz Stańko, t; Tadeusz Sudnik, AKS synth; Janusz Skowron, Yamaha DX7 synth; Vitold Rek, b, elec b.
Recorded April, June 1986, Remont club, Warsaw.

Too Pee / Kwa, kwa / Sunia / Ha, ha, ha / Gama / Euforila / Freelectronic / Dwaj / Shaky Chicka / Asmodeus

Tomasz Stańko Freelectronic, *Switzerland: Live at Montreux Jazz Festival 1987*
LP, Polskie Nagrania Muza, 1988; CD, Metal Mind Productions, 2009; CD, Polonia Records, 2000 (as *Freelectronic: Live at Montreux Jazz Festival 1987*)

Tomasz Stańko, t; Tadeusz Sudnik, AKS synth, electronica; Janusz Skowron, Yamaha DX7 synth, p; Vitold Rek, b, elec b.
Recorded 14 July 1987, Montreux Jazz Festival, Switzerland.

Lady Go / Asmodeus / Sunia / Too Pee / Switzerland / Ha, ha, ha

Tomasz Stańko, *Chameleon*
LP, Utopia Records, 1989; CD, Metal Mind Productions, 2006

Tomasz Stańko, t; Janusz Skowron, p, synth; Apostolis Anthimos, g, elec b, synth, d, perc.
Recorded 1989, Spectrum Recording Studio, Athens, Greece.

Mademoiselle Ka / Euforila / Hej! / Balladella / Whistle Walk / Green Song / Chameleon / Gray Flower / Babylon Samba / Violet Liquor / Illusion

Tomasz Stańko, *Bluish*
CD, Power Bros, 1991

Tomasz Stańko, t; Jon Christensen, d; Arild Andersen, b, elec b.
Recorded October 1991, Christian Music Studio, Wisła.

Dialogue / Daada / Under the Volcano / Bluish / If You Look Enough Part II / Bosanetta / Third Heavy Ballad / My W.S.B. Friend / If You Look Enough Part I

Tomasz Stańko, *Tales for a Girl, 12*
CD, JAM, 1991; CD, Polonia Records, 1995

Tomasz Stańko, t; Janusz Skowron, synth.
Recorded April, October 1991, S-4 Studio, Warsaw.

Tales for a Girl, 12 (The Two First, the Third and a Few Others/Fourth and Seventh/8, 9 and 11/Moon Tale/Mystery Tale/Weird Tale/Seventeenth and Eighteenth/Second Tale/5 & 5/Crazy Tale/Perverse Tale/Final Tale) / Shaky Chica

Tomasz Stańko, *Bosonossa and Other Ballads*
CD, GOWI, 1993

Tomasz Stańko, t; Bobo Stenson, p; Anders Jormin, b; Tony Oxley, d.
Recorded 29–30 March, 1 April 1993, S-4 Studio, Warsaw.

Sunia / White Ballad / Maldoror's War Song / Morning Heavy Song / Bosonossa / Die Weisheit von Isidore Ducasse

Tomasz Stańko, *A Farewell to Maria/Pożegnanie z Marią*
CD, GOWI, 1994

Music from the Filip Zylber film of the same name.
Tomasz Stańko, t; Tomasz Szukalski, ts, ss, bcl; Maciej Strzelczyk, vn; Janusz Skowron, keyb; Leszek Możdżer, p; Andrzej Cudzich, b; Adam Cegielski, b; Cezary Konrad, perc; Piotr 'Jackson' Wolski, perc, string section; Anna Staniak, 1st vn; Patrycja Barwińska, 2nd vn; Bogusława Brajczewska, viola; Wojciech Nowacki, cello.
Recorded June 1993, Studio S-4, Warsaw.

Leitmotif / Love Motive / Ave Maria (Bach) / Love Motive in a Church / Wedding Waltz / Love – Main Scene / Wedding Tango / Love Theme – Farewell / Wedding Party / Love Theme / The Slower Waltz from Wedding Party / Wedding Party – 'Orgy' / Conclusion

Tomasz Stańko, *Balladyna: Theater Play Compositions*
CD, GOWI, 1994

Music for the play *Balladyna* by Juliusz Słowacki, directed by Rudolf Zioło, Ludowy Theatre, Nowa Huta.
Tomasz Stańko, t; Tomasz Szukalski, ts, ss, bcl; Ewa Wanat, v; Marcin Wasilewski, p; Sławomir Kurkiewicz, b; Michał Miśkiewicz, d; Piotr Wolski, perc; Zbigniew Brysiak, perc.
Recorded 16–20 April 1994, Studio S-4, Warsaw.

A / B / C / D / E / F / G / H / I / J / K / L / M / N / O / P / Q / R / S / T / U / V / W

Tomasz Stańko Quartet, *Matka Joanna*
CD, ECM, 1995

Tomasz Stańko, t; Bobo Stenson, p; Anders Jormin, b; Tony Oxley, d.
Recorded May 1994, Rainbow Studio, Oslo, Norway.

Monastery in the Dark / Greek Sky / Maldoror's War Song / Tales for a Girl, 12 / Matka Joanna from the Angels / Cain's Brand / Nun's Mood / Celina / Two Preludes for Tales / Klostergeist

Tomasz Stańko, *Roberto Zucco*
CD, Polonia Records, 1996

Music from Bernard-Marie Koltès's play *Roberto Zucco*, produced by Krzysztof Warlikowski, Nowy Theatre, Poznań.
Tomasz Stańko, t; Janusz Skowron, synth; Sławomir Kurkiewicz, b; Zbigniew Brysiak, perc; Michał Miśkiewicz, d; Andrzej Jagodziński, p (on 'Blue Velvet'); Dorota Miśkiewicz, v (on 'Blue Velvet').
Recorded August 1995, Sonus Studio, Warsaw.

Roberto Zucco version 1 / Blue Velvet version 1 / Roberto Zucco version 2 / Roberto Zucco version 3 / Roberto Zucco version 4 / Roberto Zucco version 5 / Roberto Zucco solo version 1 / Roberto Zucco version 6 / Roberto Zucco version 7 / Blue Velvet version 4 / Roberto Zucco version 8 / Roberto Zucco version 9 / Roberto Zucco solo version 2 / Roberto Zucco version 10 / Roberto Zucco solo version 3 / Blue Velvet version 3

Tomasz Stańko, *Leosia*
CD, ECM, 1997

Tomasz Stańko, t; Bobo Stenson, p; Anders Jormin, b; Tony Oxley, d.
Recorded January 1996, Rainbow Studio, Oslo, Norway.

> Morning Heavy Song / Die Weisheit von Le Comte Lautréamont / A Farewell to Maria / Brace / Trinity / Forlorn Walk / Hungry Howl / No Bass Trio / Euforila / Leosia

Tomasz Stańko Septet, *Litania: Music of Krzysztof Komeda*
CD, ECM, 1997

Tomasz Stańko, t; Bernt Rosengren, ts; Joakim Milder, ts, as; Bobo Stenson, p; Palle Danielsson, b; Jon Christensen, d; Terje Rypdal, g.
Recorded February 1997, Rainbow Studio, Oslo, Norway.

> Svantetic / Sleep Safe and Warm (version 1) / Nighttime, Daytime Requiem / Ballada / Litania / Sleep Safe and Warm (version 2) / Repetition / Ballad for Bernt / The Witch / Sleep Safe and Warm (version 3)

Tomasz Stańko, *From the Green Hill*
CD, ECM, 1999

Tomasz Stańko, t; John Surman, bars, bcl; Dino Saluzzi, bandoneon; Michelle Makarski, vn; Anders Jormin, b; Jon Christensen, d.
Recorded August 1998, Rainbow Studio, Oslo, Norway.

> Domino / Litania (Part One) / Stone Ridge / . . . y después de todo / Litania (Part Two) / Quintet's Time / Pantronic / The Lark in the Dark / Love Theme from Farewell to Maria / . . . from the Green Hill / Buschka / Roberto Zucco / Domino's Intro / Argentyna

Tomasz Stańko, *Egzekutor* ['The Executor']
CD, Universal, 2001

Music from the film *Egzekutor*, directed by Filip Zylber.
Tomasz Stańko, t; Justyna Steczkowska, v; Janusz Skowron, synth; Sławomir Kurkiewicz, b; Michał Miśkiewicz, d; Zbigniew Brysiak, perc.
Recorded 1999, S-4 Studio, Warsaw.

> Komentarz pierwszy ['First Commentary'] / Śmierć, motyw na trąbke solo ['Death, Motif for Solo Trumpet'] / Egzequsya, wersja w duecie ['Execution, Duet Version'] / Egzequsya ['Execution'] / Komentarz liryczny ['Lyrical Commentary'] / Śmierć, motyw brata ['Death, Brother's Motif'] / Komentarz przetworzony ['Recreated Commentary'] / Egzequsya, wersja uproszczona ['Execution, Simplified Version'] / Szepty, motyw z Justyną ['Whispers, Motif with Justyna'] / Komentarz skrócony ['Shortened Commentary'] / Egzequsya, wersja potrójna ['Execution, Tripled Version'] / Komentarz dialogowy ['Dialogue Commentary'] / Śmierć, starsza pani ['Death, Older Woman'] / Komentarz skromny ['Modest Commentary'] / Szepty, Oficer ['Whispers, Officer'] / Komentarz krótki ['Short Commentary'] / Egzequsya, wersja z trąbką ['Execution, Version with Trumpet'] / Komentarz spokojny ['Calm Commentary'] / Szepty, żona mecenasa ['Whispers, Lawyer's Wife'] / Komentarz dziewiąty ['Ninth Commentary'] / Egzequsya, wersja na trąbkę z fortepianem ['Execution, Version for Trumpet with Piano'] / Egzequsya, wersja końcowa ['Execution, End Version'] / Komentarz kończący ['Concluding Commentary']

Tomasz Stańko, *Muzyka z Filmu Reich* ['Music from the film *Reich*']
CD, Universal, 2001
Music from the film *Reich*, directed by Władysław Pasikowski.
The album contains twelve of Stańko's instrumental pieces with songs from the film recorded by Tomasz Lipiński & Tilt, KarmaComa, Kangaroz and Millennium.
Tomasz Stańko, t; Piotr Baron, saxophone; Sławomir Kurkiewicz, b; Marcin Wasilewski, p; Michał Miśkiewicz, d; Janusz Skowron, keyb; Sinfonia Varsovia conducted by Tadeusz Wicherek.
Recorded, 2000, Studio S-4, Warsaw.

> Intro / Egzekucja ['Execution'] / Alex i Klein / Alex i Ola / Wyznania, Seszele i gwiazdy ['Confessions, the Seychelles and the Stars'] / Andre i Iwona / Droga ['The Way'] / Kokaina i dziewczyna ['Cocaine and the Girl'] / Masakra ['Massacre'] / Zasadzka, zabójcy ['Ambush, Assassins'] / Andre i Iwona, rozstanie ['Andre and Iwona, Separation'] / Grand finale, ostateczna rozgrywka ['Endgame']

Tomasz Stańko Quartet, *Soul of Things*
CD, ECM, 2002
Tomasz Stańko, t; Marcin Wasilewski, p; Sławomir Kurkiewicz, b; Michał Miśkiewicz, d.
Recorded August 2002, Rainbow Studio, Oslo, Norway.

> Soul of Things, Variations I–XIII

Tomasz Stańko Quartet, *Suspended Night*
CD, ECM, 2004
Tomasz Stańko, t; Marcin Wasilewski, p; Sławomir Kurkiewicz, b; Michał Miśkiewicz, d.
Recorded July 2003, Rainbow Studio, Oslo, Norway.

> Song for Sarah / Suspended, Variations I–X

Tomasz Stańko, *Selected Recordings*
CD, ECM, 2004
Tomasz Stańko, t; Juhani Aaltonen, alto fl ('Together'); Jon Christensen, d ('Pantronic', 'Quintet's Time', 'Litania '); Palle Danielsson, b ('Litania', 'Together'); Jack DeJohnette, d ('Moor'); Jan Garbarek, ss ('Moor'); Dave Holland, b ('Tale', 'Balladyna'); Anders Jormin, b ('Tales for a Girl, 12', 'Pantronic', 'Cain's Brand', 'Die Weisheit von Le Comte Lautréamont', 'Morning Heavy Song', 'Quintet's Time'); Michelle Makarski, vn ('Pantronic'); Joakim Milder, ts ('Litania'); Tony Oxley, d ('Tales for a Girl, 12', 'Die Weisheit von Le Comte Lautréamont', 'Morning Heavy Song'); Gary Peacock, b ('Moor'); Bernt Rosengren, ts ('Litania'); Dino Saluzzi, bandoneon ('Quintet's Time'); Bobo Stenson, p ('Tales for a Girl, 12', 'Cain's Brand', 'Die Weisheit von Le Comte Lautréamont', 'Morning Heavy Song', 'Sleep Safe and Warm', 'Litania'); John Surman, bcl ('Quintet's Time'); Tomasz Szukalski, ts ('Balladyna'); Edward Vesala, perc ('Tale', 'Together', 'Balladyna').

> Tales for a Girl, 12 / Pantronic / Cain's Brand / Tale / Moor / Die Weisheit von Le Comte Lautréamont / Morning Heavy Song / Quintet's Time / Sleep Safe and Warm / Litania / Together / Balladyna

Tomasz Stańko, *Wolność w sierpniu (Freedom in August)*
CD, FIRe, 2005
Music composed for the Rising Museum in Warsaw.
Tomasz Stańko, t; Marcin Wasilewski, p; Janusz Skowron, synth; Sławomir Kurkiewicz, b; Michał Miśkiewicz, d; Apostolis Anthimos, perc; Tomasz Szukalski, ts; Wojciech Karolak, arrangements.
String section of the Polish Radio Orchestra, directed by Mariusz Nałęcz-Niesiołowski.
Recorded 12–14 September 2005, Studios S-2 and S-4, Warsaw.

> Wolność w sierpniu (Freedom in August) / Pieśń nadziei (Hope Song) / Ballada powstańcza (Rising Ballad) / Pieśń ruin (Crash Song) / Dee / Pieśń kanałów (Song of the Sewers)

Tomasz Stańko Quartet, *Lontano*
CD, ECM 2006
Tomasz Stańko, t; Marcin Wasilewski, p; Sławomir Kurkiewicz, b; Michał Miśkiewicz, d.
Recorded November 2005, Studios la Buissonne, Pernes-les-Fontaines, France.

> Lontano / Cyrhla / Song for Ania / Kattorna / Lontano II / Sweet Thing / Trista / Lontano III / Tale

Tomasz Stańko, *1970–1975–1984–1986–1988*
CD, Metal Mind Productions, 2008
Five-CD box set, gathering together all of Stańko's albums that he recorded for Polskie Nagrania Muza (Polish Recordings): *Music for K, TWET, Music 81, Lady Go* and *Switzerland*.

Tomasz Stańko Quintet, *Dark Eyes*
CD, ECM, 2009
Tomasz Stańko, t; Alexi Tuomarila, p; Jakob Bro, g; Anders Christensen, elec b; Olavi Louhivuori, d.
Recorded April 2009, Studios La Buissonne, Pernes-les-Fontaines, France.

> So Nice / Terminal / The Dark Eyes of Martha Hirsch / Grand Central / Amsterdam Avenue / Samba Nova / Dirge for Europe / May Sun / Last Song / Etiuda Baletowa no. 3 ['Ballet Etude no. 3']

Tomasz Stańko/Wisława Szymborska, *Tutaj/Here*
CD, Not On Label
Tomasz Stańko, t; Wisława Szymborska, v.
Recorded 2012.

> Powitanie / Myśli Nawiedzajace Mnie Na Ruchliwych Ulicach / Mikrokosmos / Nieczytanie / Zamachowcy / Identyfikacja / Kilkunastoletnia / Portret Z Pamięci / W Dyliżansie / Ella w Niebe / Tutaj / Metafizyka

Tomasz Stańko New York Quartet, *Wisława*
CD, ECM, 2013
Tomasz Stańko, t; David Virelles, p; Thomas Morgan, b; Gerald Cleaver, d.
Recorded June 2012.

> Wisława / Assassins / Metafizyka / Dernier Cri / Mikrokosmos / Song for H / Oni / April Story / Tutaj – Here / Faces / A Shaggy Vandal / Wisława (variation)

Tomasz Stańko, *Polin*
CD, Polin, 2014

Muzyka Dla Muzeum Historii Zydów Polskich Polin (Music for Polin Museum of the History of Polish Jews).
Tomasz Stańko, t; Ravi Coltrane, ts; David Virelles, p; Dezron Douglas, b; Kush Abadey, d. Recorded 2014.

   Gela / Yankiel's Lid / Margolit L. / Polin / The Street of Crocodiles

Tomasz Stańko New York Quartet, *December Avenue*
CD, ECM, 2017

Tomasz Stańko, t; David Virelles, p; Reuben Rogers, b; Gerald Cleaver, d.
Recorded June 2016.

   Cloud / Conclusion / Blue Cloud / Bright Moon / Burning Hot / David and Ruben / Ballad for Bruno Schulz / Sound Space / December Avenue / The Street of Crocodiles / Yankiel's Lid / Young Girl in Flower

II. Recordings with Krzysztof Komeda

Krzysztof Komeda, *What's Up Mr Basie*
CD, Power Bros, 1998

Tomasz Stańko, t; Michał Urbaniak, ts; Krzysztof Komeda, p; Maciej Suzin, b; Czesław Bartkowski, d.
Jazz Jamboree, Warsaw, October 1963.

   What's Up Mr Basie / Knife in the Water / Roman Two

Krzysztof Komeda, *Live in Copenhagen*
2 × CD, Polonia, 1993

Tomasz Stańko, t; Michał Urbaniak, ts; Krzysztof Komeda, p; Bo Stief, b; Simon Koppel, d.
Jazzhus Montmartre, Copenhagen, 1965.

   Repetition / Svantetic / Sophia's Tune / Kattorna / Crazy Girl / Dwójka rzymska

Krzysztof Komeda, *Astigmatic in Concert*
CD, Polonia Records, 1995; CD, Power Bros, 1998

Tomasz Stańko, t; Krzysztof Komeda, p; Janusz Kozłowski, b; Rune Carlsson, d. Jazz Jamboree, Warsaw, 1965.

   Astigmatic /Kattorna

Tomasz Stańko, t; Michał Urbaniak, ts; Krzysztof Komeda, p; Bo Stief, b; Simon Koppel, d. Jazzhus Montmartre, Copenhagen, 1965.

   Svantetic

Krzysztof Komeda, *Astigmatic*
LP, Polskie Nagrania Muza, 1967; CD, Polskie Nagrania Muza, 2007, 2016

Tomasz Stańko, t; Zbigniew Namysłowski, as; Krzysztof Komeda, p; Günter Lenz, b; Rune Carlsson, d.
Warsaw, December 1965.

   Astigmatic / Kattorna / Svantetic

Krzysztof Komeda, *Meine süsse Europäische Heimat: Dichtung und Jazz aus Polen*
LP, Columbia (Germany), 1967; CD Polonia Records, 1998 (as *Love and Poetry*); CD, Wydawnictwo
Anex, 2012 (expanded edition)
Tomasz Stańko, t; Zbigniew Namysłowski, as; Krzysztof Komeda, p; Roman Dyląg, b; Rune
Carlsson, d; Helmuth Lohner, poet.
Cologne, 7–10 October 1967.

> The Trumpet Player is Innocent / Dirge for Europe / Miserere / Choral / Hameln is
> Everywhere / Prayer and Question / Canzone for Warschau / No Lovesong At All /
> Theme for One and Variations for Another World / Free Witch and No-bra Queen /
> Poet in Circus / Sketches for Don Quichotte / Waltzing Beyond

Krzysztof Komeda, *Nightime* [sic]*, Daytime Requiem*
CD, Power Bros, 1998
Tomasz Stańko, t; Zbigniew Namysłowski, as; Krzysztof Komeda, p; Roman Dyląg, b; Rune
Carlsson, d.
November 1967.

> Nightime, Daytime Requiem / Don Quixote / The Witch / Ballad for Bernt

III. Selected albums featuring Tomasz Stańko

The Andrzej Trzaskowski Quintet
Polish Jazz Series, 4
LP, Polskie Nagrania Muza, 1965; CD Polskie Radio, 2005

Jazz Studio Orchestra of Polish Radio
Polish Jazz Series, 19
LP, Polskie Nagrania Muza, 1970

Krzysztof Penderecki/Don Cherry & The New Rhythm Orchestra, *Actions*
LP, Philips, 1971; LP, Wergo Spectrum, 1977; LP, Everest, 1980; CD, Transparency, 1998; CD, Intuition,
2001
Recorded live at the Donaueschingen Music Festival, 17 October 1971.

Michał Urbaniak/Tomasz Stańko/Attila Zoller/Urszula Dudziak, *We'll Remember*
Komeda
LP, MPS/BASF, 1973; CD, Polonia Records, 1998
Also released as Michał Urbaniak & Urszula Dudziak, *Tribute to Komeda* (LP, MPS [USA],
1976).

Studio Jazzowe PR Orchestra, *Koncert Podwójny na Pięciu Solistów i Orkiestrę* ['Double
Concerto for Five Soloists and Orchestra']
Biały Kruk Czarnego Krążka Series, PSJ Record Club, 6
LP, PolJazz, 1973, 1974; CD, Cracovia Music Agency, 2000

Studio Jazzowe PR/Jan 'Ptaszyn' Wróblewski, *Sprzedawcy Glonów* ['Seaweed
Peddlers']
LP, Polskie Nagrania Muza, 1973; CD, Polskie Nagrania Muza, 2006 (credited to Jan 'Ptaszyn'
Wróblewski/Studio Jazzowe PR)

Edward Vesala, *Rodina*
LP, Love Records 1977; CD, Love Records, 2000

Edward Vesala, *Satu*
LP, ECM, 1977; CD, ECM 2000

Czesław Bartkowski, *Drums Dream*
Polish Jazz Series, 50
LP, Polskie Nagrania Muza, 1977, 2017; CD, Polskie Nagrania Muza, 2006

Ossian, *Ossian*
Biały Kruk Czarnego Krążka Series, PSJ Record Club
LP, Polskie Nagrania Muza, 1975; CD, Pomaton EMI, 1999; CD, Milo Records, 2006

Edward Vesala, *Neitsytmatka* ['Maiden Voyage']
LP Polarvox, 1982

Edward Vesala, *Heavy Life*
LP, Leo Records, 1980

Gary Peacock, *Voice from The Past – PARADIGM*
LP, ECM, 1982; CD, ECM

Edward Vesala, *Bad Luck, Good Luck*
LP, Leo Records, 1985

Cecil Taylor Segments II (Orchestra of Two Continents), *Winged Serpent (Sliding Quadrants)*
LP, Soul Note, 1985; CD, Soul Note

Cecil Taylor European Orchestra, *Alms/Tiergarten (Spree)*
CD, FMP, 1989
First released as part of the eleven-album box set *Cecil Taylor in Berlin '88* (FMP, 1989).

Young Power, *Man of Tra*
CD, Power Bros, 1991

Tomasz Stańko/Sigi Finkel/Ed Schuller/Billy Elgart, *Caoma*
CD, Konnex Records, 1993

Christian Muthspiel, *Octet Ost*
CD, Amadeo, 1992

Jazz Baltica Ensemble & David Murray, *Jazzbaltica '92 Live at the Kiel Opera*
CD, GOWI, 1993

Tomasz Stańko/Manfred Bründl/Michael Riessler, *Suite Talk*
CD, ITM Pacific, 1993
Later release credited to Tomasz Stańko under the title *Too Pee* (CD, New Edition, 2005; CD, Megaus, 2007).

Christian Muthspiel, *Octet Ost II*
CD, Amadeo, 1994

Nils Landgren, *Gotland*
ACT World Jazz Series
CD, ACT, 1996

Yá-sou/Tomasz Stańko/Osjan, *Tribute to Don Cherry*
CD, GOWI Records, 1996

NDR Bigband, *Ellingtonia: The Homage to Duke Ellington*
CD, ACT, 1999

Alexander von Schlippenbach's Global Unity Orchestra, *Globe Unity 67 & 70*
Unheard Music Series
CD, Atavistic, 2002

Stanisław Soyka, *Polskie Pieśni Wielkopostne* ['Polish Songs for Lent']
CD, Pomaton EMI, 2001

Manu Katché, *Neighbourhood*
CD, ECM, 2005

Mark O'Leary/Tomasz Stańko/Billy Hart, *Levitation*
CD, Leo Records, 2005
Recordings from 2000.

SBB, *Sikorki*
CD, Metal Mind Productions, 2006
An anthology of recordings from 1974–2004.

Graham Collier, *Hoarded Dreams: Recorded Live at The Bracknell Jazz Festival 1983*
CD, Cuneiform, 2007

Index of Names*

---

* The index does not include names that appear in the chronology, the discography or the
  list of illustrations.

www.ingramcontent.com/pod-product-compliance
Lightning Source LLC
Chambersburg PA
CBHW071916160426
42812CB00098B/1250